DATE DUE

AR 12 '98		
6/8/98		
OC 7 '98		

DEMCO 38-296

Nationalism and the Genealogical Imagination

Comparative Studies on Muslim Societies

General Editor, BARBARA D. METCALF

Nationalism and the Genealogical Imagination

Oral History and Textual Authority in Tribal Jordan

ANDREW SHRYOCK

University of California Press

BERKELEY   LOS ANGELES   LONDON

University of California Press
Berkeley and Los Angeles, California
University of California Press, Ltd.
London, England

Parts of this book were published in earlier versions in:
"Tribes and the Print Trade: Notes from the Margins of Literate Culture
in Jordan," *American Anthropologist* 98 (1996): 26–40.
"Tribaliser la nation, nationaliser la tribu: Politique de l'histoire chez
les bédouins de la Balqa, en Jordanie," *Monde Arabe, Maghreb-
Machrek*, no. 147 (Jan.–Mar. 1995): 120–30.
Writing Oral History in Tribal Jordan: Developments on the Margins
of Literate Culture," *Anthropology Today* 11 (1995): 3–5.
"Popular Genealogical Nationalism: History Writing and Identity
among the Balqa Tribes of Jordan," *Comparative Studies in Society
and History* 37 (1995): 325–57.

Library of Congress Cataloging-in-Publication Data

Shryock, Andrew.
    Nationalism and the genealogical imagination : oral history and
textual authority in tribal Jordan / Andrew Shryock.
        p.   cm. — (Comparative studies on Muslim societies ; 23)
    Includes bibliographical references (p.   ) and index.
    ISBN 0-520-20100-0 (alk. paper)—ISBN 0-520-20101-9 (pbk.: alk.
paper)
        1. Bedouins—Jordan.   2. Jordan—Genealogy.   3. Bedouins—
Jordan—Historiography   4. Oral tradition—Jordan.   I. Title.   II. Series.
DS153.55.B43S57   1997
956.95'004927—dc20   95-39809
                                                                              CIP

Contents

Illustrations

Plates

Figures

Map

Acknowledgments

My research in Jordan was supported by a Fulbright-Hays Fellowship and a grant from the National Science Foundation; it was sponsored by the Institute for Archaeology and Anthropology at Yarmouk University; and it was shaped, at every turn, by the patronage of Dr. Ahmad 'Uwaydi al-'Abbadi, a Jordanian anthropologist who introduced me to tribal life in the Balga and invited me to settle in his home village of Swaysa. None of these persons, institutions, or agencies would necessarily endorse the arguments I make in this book, and none is responsible for errors found in the text. It is customary to protect funding sources and sponsors by offering a disclaimer of this sort. I am equally concerned, however, to establish a protective distance between my own analysis and the man who, by sheer force of personality, dominates much of this book.

Dr. Ahmad 'Uwaydi al-'Abbadi has been known, at various points in his career, as a screenwriter, public security officer, media pundit, and folklorist. In 1989, shortly after my fieldwork began, he was elected to Parliament. Dr. Ahmad was, for me, an inexhaustible source of information. My conversations with him were always intriguing, if sometimes a bit perplexing as well, and his willingness to speak frankly on matters of tribal and national politics gave my knowledge of Jordan a dimension it would not otherwise have had. Dr. Ahmad insisted that I cast him as a leading character in this book. Given his current notoriety among the Jordanian tribes, I believe he fully deserves the attention. Dr. Ahmad is a public figure, admired by thousands and despised by thousands more. He does not agree with all the things I say about him in this study, but my decision to interpret his career critically was part of an ethnographic bargain he eagerly struck. The portrait of Ahmad that emerges here will disturb his friends and enemies alike; even I am unsettled by it. Dr. Ahmad is not an ordinary man. His involvement in my work made a conventional ethnography impossible to write, and for this I am especially grateful to him.

My stay in Swaysa, Dr. Ahmad's home village, was among the most enjoyable and challenging experiences of my life. I give my heartfelt thanks to the Rashidat lineage, especially the family of 'Ali Khlayf al-'Uwaydi, who educated me and my wife, Sally, with true affection. They taught us how to speak the Balgawi dialect of Arabic; they coached and corrected us in the elaborate, taken-for-granted rituals of daily life, and they never subjected us to embarrassment when we failed. Our "becoming ʿAbbadi" was the accomplishment of ʿAli Khlayf and his family, and the ethnography I have written is as much a product of their intellectual labor as it is my own.

The ʿAdwan tribe received us with an equal measure of kindness. Dr. Yasser Mannaʿ al-ʿAdwan graciously arranged our stay in his home village of Salihi. I am especially indebted to Yasser's brothers, Abu Firas and Fayiz, who accepted us into their own families, and to the rest of the ʿAmamsha clan, who never tired of feeding us, involving us in their personal affairs, and telling us stories of the ʿAdwani past and present. My one-month stay among the ʿAdwan of the Jordan Valley was, thanks to the energetic efforts of Muhammad Hamdan al-ʿAdwan, the most productive period of my research. Muhammad shared his immense store of ʿAdwani history with me, introduced me to the elders from whom he had collected it, and read to me aloud from the preparatory notes to his unpublished manuscript, *The History of the ʿAdwan*. My collaboration with Muhammad was collegial and exciting. He understood what I was trying to accomplish, and he did everything in his power to help. Even with the completion of this book, which he has anxiously awaited, my debt to Muhammad remains largely unpaid. I also owe thanks to Faris Salih al-Nimr, who was a true friend in the valley and a companion in research as valuable to me as his ancestor, the great Shaykh Goblan al-Nimr, was to the European scholars who explored ʿAdwani territory over a century ago.

Several people gave large amounts of time to the onerous task of transcribing and translating the oral testimony I gathered from tribal elders. Husayn al-ʿUwaydi al-ʿAbbadi wrote down hours of talk, and his commitment to accuracy was strong even when the narratives in question were spoken against his own tribe. Mishrif ʿIsa al-Shurrab, also of ʿAbbad, put his subtle knowledge of English and Arabic to the difficult task of translating Bedouin poems: all of them marked by archaic phrasing and arcane vocabulary; most of them recited by old men without a full set of teeth. My deepest appreciation, however, goes to Bahiyya ʿAli Khlayf and Shahiyya ʿAli Khlayf, who dedicated the free time between their homework and household chores to the transcription of my tape-recordings. This meant writing down page after page of testimony they considered bombastic, scandalous, repetitive, silly, or excruciatingly dull. Despite my pleadings, they would not accept financial remuneration—"Does one take money for helping her own brother?"—and the acknowledgment I offer them here is meager compensation for the immense respect they gave to all aspects of my work.

I would like to thank Ray Kelly, Nick Dirks, Paul Dresch, and Sherry Ortner for their helpful readings of the dissertation that gradually became this book. Paul Dresch, who coaxed each chapter through all its stages of development, deserves special mention. His critiques of the ethnography strengthened it immeasurably, and his ability to draw neglected insights from my material was a constant source of encouragement (and amazement) to me. I could not have wished for a more discerning critic than Dresch, and I thank him for the careful attention he lavished on my work. I should also thank Walter Armbrust, Dale Eickelman, Richard Antoun, Barbara Walker, Aaron Shryock, Steve Caton, Lucine Taminian, Benjamin Orlove, Michael Fahy, and Brinkley Messick, each of whom read and made useful comments on early drafts of the manuscript.

To Sally Howell, my wife and companion in fieldwork, I owe the deepest gratitude. She brought to her many readings of the manuscript a perspective rooted in our shared experience, but her contributions have always been more than intellectual. Her knowledge of Arabic, her openness to Bedouin sensibilities, her eagerness to learn almost anything—how to embroider, spin wool, weave, milk, churn, harvest wheat, string tobacco, and sing wedding songs—made her beloved among tribespeople, and insofar as ethnography is susceptible to moods, my work benefited greatly from the good feeling Sally generated. I thank her also for making the separation of male and female worlds less extreme for me than it would have been had I gone to Jordan alone. An unmarried male ethnographer cannot experience Bedouin culture in all its richness. By rendering me less of a sexual threat to our hosts, Sally allowed me to cross the gender divide with relative ease, and my ability to develop friendships on either side of that boundary enhanced the quality of information I collected.

It is not without embarrassment, then, that I realize now how absent from the text are the women I knew through Sally's intervention. Such is the price of topical ethnography. The shift from oral to written history on which this study focuses is undertaken and dominated by men. The relentless masculinity of the historical universe I explore is not in the least bit imaginary. It does, however, obscure other dimensions of social reality. It is meant to do so. History making, after all, is a way of censoring and shaping the past, and Bedouin women, who are themselves heavily invested in the proud androcentrism of tribal history, would hardly expect me to pretend otherwise on their behalf. In the tribal Balga, as in all human societies, there are hegemonic structures that gratitude and affection, no matter how keenly felt, can never overcome.

Ethnography as a Shared Labor of Objectification

A meaning only reveals its depths once it has encountered and come into contact with another, foreign meaning: they engage in a kind of dialogue, which surmounts the closedness and one-sidedness of these particular meanings, these cultures. We raise new questions for a foreign culture, ones that it did not raise itself; we seek answers to our own questions in it; and the foreign culture responds to us by revealing its new aspects and new semantic depths. Without *one's own* questions one cannot creatively understand anything other or foreign (but, of course, the questions must be serious and sincere). Such a dialogic encounter of two cultures does not result in merging or mixing. Each retains its own unity and *open* totality, but they are mutually enriched.

Bakhtin, *Speech Genres and Other Essays*

This book is a study of history making in oral and written forms. It is based on fieldwork done among the Balga tribes of central Jordan in 1989–90. During that time, I took part in local attempts (all of them made by Bedouin tribesmen) to write down and publish a body of historical traditions that, until very recently, existed only in speech. These first efforts at historiography, which began in the 1970s, have proved difficult from the start. The publication of tribal histories demands that a parochial and highly antagonistic discourse— one composed of contested genealogies, tales of warfare, and heroic poetry— be adapted to a modern print culture that is public, nationalistic, and committed to themes of Arab unity. My involvement in this process brought me face to face with issues that are now of great interest to scholars working in the subaltern quarters of complex societies. These include (1) the interplay of oral and textual accounts of the past, (2) the political consequences of mass literacy, (3) the reconfiguration (or loss) of spoken authority in modern print cultures, and (4) the relationship between nationalist ideologies and the precolonial structures of historicity and identity they now encapsulate.

In Jordan, these issues are working themselves out in fascinating and controversial ways. As the reader will soon discover, publishing the "talk of the elders" (*sawalif al-kubar*) is an act of commemoration that, although seemingly innocuous and folkloric, comes fraught with political sensitivities. The appropriateness of recording tribal histories—especially in a modern nation-state where tribalism often stands for "backwardness"—has been called into question by tribal and nontribal Jordanians alike, and the outcome of current textualizing projects is by no means certain.

My own analysis, not surprisingly, partakes in the same mood of boundary testing and reconstruction. Like Bedouin historiographers, who describe their work as a struggle against "old mentalities," I have found myself writing against (or around) well-established habits of thought and have framed much of this study in opposition to analytical styles that are overly dependent on documentary evidence and textual analogies. I have not, for example, manufactured a conventional ethnohistory of the Balga tribes, nor have I subjected Bedouin verbal arts to the latest devices of literary criticism. The Bedouin already have their own highly nuanced ways of talking and writing about the past; indeed, a careful examination of these indigenous hermeneutic and historiographical practices lays bare many of the cultural assumptions that shape (and constrain) the methodology of ethnohistory. It also forces literary theory out of its self-referential salon and into a world where its terminologies and tropes can, at times, seem hopelessly impertinent.

The reader should not assume, however, that I intend merely to pick apart analytical styles that are currently in vogue. The materials I examine in this study, of their very nature, actually *further* the ends of historical anthropology and critical theory. They do so by making the "constructedness" of historical knowledge explicit in unusual ways. It is now widely assumed, for instance, that identity, representation, and power are issues that manifest themselves in the very form of anthropological writing itself and can, therefore, be problematized by means of literary experiment and the deconstruction of familiar ethnographic genres. This reflexive stance, for all its potential merits, has been plagued from the start by a debilitating tendency. Instead of producing better ethnography, it leads all too easily to theoretical introversion, to writing about writing about culture, to a reluctance to engage in representations of "the Other" that are not, at the same time, subordinated to representations of the ethnographer as self-conscious author of the text. In the Balga of Jordan, this tendency toward analytical implosion is held in check by a fortunate turn of events. In the Balga, it is tribespeople themselves who are experimenting with writing; it is *they* who are casting the authority of their own traditions in doubt; it is *they* who must come to terms with their own "positionality" in relation to the identities they create in print. The postmodernist, who wages war on received forms, and the new historicist, who seeks to represent the past in novel ways, have in every sense been beaten to the punch.

The fact that I shared an agenda with tribal historiographers, all the while pursuing representational goals they found disagreeable, endows the study at hand with the same feeling of complicity and aloofness Georg Simmel attributed to the peculiar "objectivity" of the stranger.

> Because he is not bound by roots to the particular constituents and partisan dispositions of the group, he confronts all of these with a distinctly 'objective' attitude, an attitude that does not signify mere detachment and nonparticipation, but is a distinct structure composed of remoteness and nearness, indifference and involvement. . . . Objectivity can also be defined as freedom. The objective man is not bound by ties that could prejudice his perception, his understanding, and his assessment of data . . . he is the freer man, practically and theoretically; he examines conditions with less prejudice; he assesses them against standards that are more general and more objective; and his actions are not confined by custom, piety, or precedent (1971,145).

Simmel's observations, which first appeared in 1908, will strike many readers as theoretically retrograde, even arrogant. It is more common nowadays to dismiss objectivity as an illusion and to display one's own subjectivity as proof of analytical savvy or, in an ironic turning of tables, as a new source of ethnographic authority. When writing about the Other, many scholars now find it advantageous to *be* the Other. Even the Bedouin, whom Ibn Khaldun described as the most remote of all peoples, have not escaped the reach of cosmopolitan ethnographers who are willing to claim kinship with them. Smadar Lavie invokes this imagery of "collapsed otherness" when she reflects on the paradox of Jewish-Arab identity that colored her ethnographic experience among the Mzeina Bedouin of the southern Sinai.

> Part of my identity is that of a Western-trained professional anthropologist. Moreover, my father was a Northern European. From my mother I have my Arab culture, color, and temperament. In spite of the fact that ethnic identity is determined by the Israeli government according to the father's origin, . . . it is my Arab half that counts socially. Since I am of dark complexion, Israelis always assume that I am a full Yemenite and treat me accordingly. Unlike my European descent, my Arab heritage qualifies me (at least in Israel) as a genuine, semicivilized Other. During my graduate studies, as I went back to classifying and analyzing my fieldnotes, I noticed that a theme of two exotic and voiceless Others emerged: my life experience in Israel was somehow mirrored in the life experience of the Mzeinis—and theirs in mine (1990, 307).

Subjective identifications of the sort Lavie describes are no less constructed, revealing, deluded, or potentially blinding than those modeled on more "objective" presentations of self. They are, in fact, self-objectifications carried out in a personalized, confessional idiom, and they lend ample support to the conclusion that the ethnographer is always an anomalous figure; they suggest that what passes for ethnographic understanding inevitably turns on the fact that ethnographers are strange to, or at least bring unusual concerns to, the worlds they depict in writing.

When stated plainly, these observations teeter on the edge of banality, but it is worth stating them plainly all the same, since reflections on the "positionality" of the ethnographer can cause us to push simple truths aside. Lila Abu-Lughod has even suggested that the ethnographer's status as an "outsider" is itself a faulty construction. After weighing the peculiar effects her status as a "Palestinian American woman" had on her ethnography of Egyptian Bedouin, she concludes that

> the outsider self never simply stands outside; he or she always stands in a definite relation with the "other" of the study, not just as a Westerner or even halfie, but as a Frenchman in Algeria during the war of independence, an American in Morocco during the 1967 Arab-Israeli War, or an English-woman in postcolonial India. What we call the outside, or even the partial outside, is always a position within a larger political-historical complex (1993, 40).

The point is certainly correct, but the entire ethnographic enterprise turns on a converse truth: what we imagine to be the *inside*, even the partial inside, is always a position *external to* a local political-historical complex. "In order to understand," Bakhtin reminds us, "it is immensely important for the person who understands to be *located outside* the object of his or her creative understanding—in time, in space, in culture" (1986, 7).

This sense of being on the periphery was real for me in obvious ways. I am neither a Palestinian American, nor an Arab Israeli Jew, nor a Muslim, nor even a "halfie" of any advantageous sort. When I arrived in Jordan, I had no "natural" ties to the tribal community I intended to study, only "political" ones—American, guest, client, financial resource, Orientalist, future patron, potential spy—and my hosts sought vigorously, and with genuine concern, to "naturalize" me. I was taught to speak the Balgawi dialect of Arabic; I was schooled in Bedouin manners and customs; I was even grafted, always a bit playfully, onto 'Abbadi and 'Adwani lineages. No one, however, mistook me for part of the local world. I was constantly slipping in and out of that world, and it was precisely this slippage, which increased alongside all efforts to incorporate me, that made me interesting, problematic, appealing, troublesome, and forever in need of instruction.

So, like all such liminal artifacts, the ethnography I have produced is an oblique commentary on the already formed notions of history, nationality, kinship, and religion I brought with me to the field. It is also an intellectual argument steeped in the odd and utterly personal experience of "objectivity" that my marginal position in tribal society made possible. As I struggled to understand Bedouin history-making in Jordan, it was important that I not shy away from the implications of this objectivity, since the tribesmen who are writing their oral traditions down for the first time are engaged in a labor of objectification that provokes a range of similar, yet systematically different, analytical concerns. In chapters 4 and 5, I explore how my externality to the clan system allowed me to move about the tribal landscape and accumulate historical knowledge in ways local tribesmen could not. Because I lacked "natural" ties to any local personage or group, I was often assumed to be a disinterested (and ideally suggestible) collector of oral traditions. Despite all my protests to the contrary, tribespeople were quick to believe that my point of view, insofar as it was free of clannish loyalties, was also free of historical bias. This belief, which is based on indigenous notions of impartiality and fairness, is itself the groundwork for the kind of intellectual authority tribal historiographers, who must work *within* the local clan system, are now striving to create for themselves. They aspire, with all the moral intensity of revivalists and prophets, to possess the freedom of Simmel's stranger, "whose actions are not confined by custom, piety, and precedent."

The intellectual authority tribal historiographers hope to claim for themselves is constructed of very old cultural materials. It turns on a popular link between "externality," "textuality," and "truth." As I suggest in chapters 6 and 7, this link is an enduring feature not only of Bedouin social thought, but of the "epistemology of revelation" that has shaped political, religious, and philosophical discourse in Arab-Muslim societies for centuries. The forms of oral and written history-making I encountered in the tribal Balga belong to an intellectual tradition of immense antiquity. It certainly predates Islam, and its basic principles, I suggest briefly in chapter 8, were woven into the early structures of Muslim polity and historiography. They still inform popular images of community in the Middle East today. Because this historical tradition is based ultimately on genealogical models of society, Western observers easily equate it with tribalism. The role genealogical thought plays in the political culture of contemporary Middle Eastern states is then ignored or accentuated (depending on the analyst's agenda), since tribalism, the emblem of all that is primitive, is supposed to have little to do with the operations of rational, bureaucratic governments.

The tendency to speak of genealogical thought and tribalism in the same analytical breath is based on gross misconceptions. In the Middle East, as I argue in chapter 8, the two concepts are clearly distinguishable. Among Arabs there is widespread acceptance for the idea that authentic forms of human community, and certainly the most reliable forms of human knowledge, are reproduced genealogically, whether in biological pedigrees or intellectual chains of transmission. Arab identity itself is often defined, like family or clan affiliation, in an idiom of descent; most Arab states are ruled by family cliques or hereditary dynasties; even Islamic learning, which transcends the world of biological ties, has traditionally been depicted as an inheritance whose authenticity is safeguarded by the accurate, lineal, face-to-face transmission of sacred Arabic utterances and authoritative texts: in other words, by legitimate "genealogical" succession. At the same time, however, the idea that tribes are (and should be) peripheral to the concerns of the high culture—to Law, Religion, and Government—has been the moral bias of urban intellectuals in the Middle East since ancient times. To the metropolitan elites of Baghdad, Damascus, and Cairo, the tribesman has loomed for centuries as a reminder of pre-Islamic ignorance: he is ungovernable; irreligious; a menace to all refinement.

Such views are easily kept up-to-date. In the postcolonial era, when "modernity" and "authenticity" have become the twin fixations of political thought in the Middle East, it is quite ordinary for the culture-making classes to drape new identities in the legitimacy of older, genealogical traditions, and vice versa: absolute monarchies array themselves in the cloth of modern nation-states (Morocco); modern nation-states pose as big families (Libya); big families pose as state governments (Kuwait); state governments assume the shape of Islamic theocracies ruled by descendants of the Prophet (Iran). Amid all this ideological anachronism, it is still quite common for tribespeople to be portrayed (and to portray themselves) as remnants of another age, wholly atypical in their traditionalism and marginal to the national cultures in which they live.

This is certainly *not* the case in Jordan, where tribal groups of both Bedouin and peasant origin account for 40–50 percent of a general population that is rapidly approaching four million. Men of Bedouin descent control the upper ranks of the Jordanian military; tribal law was officially recognized and administered in much of the countryside until a uniform civil law code was adopted in 1976; tribesmen sit in parliament; they hold title to their own lands; they live in both urban and rural settings; and, like members of Jordan's Palestinian majority, they participate in all fields of public endeavor. Despite the fact that tribes are seemingly everywhere in Jordan (or perhaps *because* tribes seem to be everywhere), "tribalism" ('asha'iriyya) remains a source of political friction and, to the self-consciously sophisticated, a cause for embarrassment. In 1984, when anti-tribal sentiment flared during parliamentary elections and editorials criticizing tribal custom began to appear in the national press, King Husayn defended the tribal way of life in terms that were bound to rattle modernist sensibilities.

> Most recently, I have noticed that some articles have been directed against the tribal life, its norms and traditions. This is most regrettable because it harms a dear sector of our society. I would like to repeat to you what I have told a meeting of tribal heads recently that "I am al-Hussein from Hashem and Quraish, the noblest Arab tribe of Mecca, which was honored by God and into which was born the Arab Prophet Mohammad." Therefore, whatever harms our tribes is considered harmful to us, and this has been the case all along, and it will continue so forever (*The Jordan Times,* January 28, 1985).

The Hashemite regime is heavily invested in its "tribal sector." The local Bedouin tribes were effectively pacified by the 1930s, and state-sanctioned tribalism, in its politically domesticated forms, is flourishing under the king's watchful eye. In a recent essay on cultural representation in Jordan, Linda Layne (1989) explores the images of tribal life the state finds ideologically useful in its attempts to construct a national identity that is appealing both at home and abroad. These include the diacritica of tent life, coffee-making paraphernalia, elements of Bedouin wardrobe and cuisine, and other material residues of a nomadic camel culture that is now a thing of the past. This heritage is marketable, wearable, consumable, detachable from its original contexts, and thus ideally suited to touristic exploitation and political revaluation. Layne rightly points out, however, that:

> In response to the denigration of tribal culture by its critics and the appropriation of tribal culture by the State as the keystone of Jordan's national heritage, the tribes of Jordan are reconceiving and reevaluating their culture. In so doing, they are utilizing some of the same discursive practices as those employed by the State and the Jordanian intelligentsia in constructing tribal representations of Jordan's past. However, these practices do not mean the same thing for local actors as they do for the bearers of the dominant discourse. Rather, they provide frameworks that tribesmen and women will fill with local content and interpret in terms of indigenous cultural constructions such as *asl*, (noble origins), honor, and gift exchange (1989, 25).

This dialogic encounter between tribe and state transpires not only in the realm of material culture and its meanings, but also (and more controversially) in the new historical and ethnographic literature Jordanian tribesmen are now producing. As educated Bedouin attempt to nationalize their tribal identities by writing about them, a model that envisions a nationalist framework being filled up by tribal content begins to unravel in interesting ways. The conceptual boundaries that set tribes apart from the nation are often indistinguishable in practice—the Balga tribespeople I knew never seriously doubted that they, along with other "indigenous" Bedouin, were the *true* Jordanians—and the tribal content of this national identity, because it is answerable to its own hegemonic structures, is sometimes capable of reconfiguring the dominant, nationalist discourse to which it reacts.

To understand this ideological encounter, one must appreciate notions of historicity, spoken authority, and genealogical community that, despite their salience in tribal life, have never been adequately examined by ethnographers. In chapter 1, I map out the intellectual prejudices, most of them rooted in the demands of textual history-making, which have kept anthropologists from engaging fully with nonliterate ways of making the past. In chapters 2 and 3, I place the Balga tribes and their oral traditions in a context that is informed both by nationalist and pre-nationalist images of community. In chapters 4 and 5, I study the character of the oral tradition in closer detail: its form and content, its modes of transmission, and the methods by which authoritative historical speech is created and preserved. In chapters 6 and 7, I analyze the careers of two Bedouin historians: Muhammad Hamdan al-'Adwan and Dr. Ahmad 'Uwaydi al-'Abbadi. The successes and failures of these authors serve as a lens through which popular conceptions of national identity, power, and historical knowledge in Hashemite Jordan can be clearly seen. I end the book by arguing in chapter 8 that genealogical and nationalist images of community are merging to form new modes of identity that, among Jordan's tribal and Palestinian population alike, give the modern nation-state a familiar, patriarchal shape. At the same time, these new forms of identity encourage tribespeople to ask, who are the true sons of this country? Insofar as the answer to this question does not include the Palestinian majority or the Hashemite elite, both of whom come originally from outside Jordan, this striving after essential identities threatens to undermine the ideology of national unity that inspires it.

The latter conclusion, though commonly drawn in Jordan, is politically subversive, and its full implications cannot be publicly discussed there. Indeed, much of the local material contained in this study, whether it deals with grave national issues or ephemeral clan gossip, will be politically offensive (in one way or another) to the Jordanians who eventually read it. This is because the collective identities I examine—Bedouin, peasant, Jordanian, Palestinian, 'Abbadi, 'Adwani, and numerous others—are all contested from multiple points of view. Contest is part of what defines them.

Early on, I realized that this ethnography could not be sympathetic in the way so many of the best ethnographies appear to be. Had I decided to respect the sensitivities of everyone involved (a relativistic stance that merely accomplishes a subtler form of insult), this book could not possibly have been written.

Once again, I found these representational challenges hard to avoid, since they confront tribal historiographers as well. In chapters 6 and 7, I examine local attempts to resolve these problems, or avoid them altogether, in print. My own solution to the problem of "partisan multivocality" was to engage actively in the historical disputes that define tribal identities and, when writing about this practice, to keep the terms of my engagement (which were not entirely local) as visible to the reader as they were to the tribespeople who sought to influence what I wrote. To attain this end, I have given special attention both to the content of the oral traditions I recorded and to the situations in which my ability to understand and evaluate these traditions gradually took shape. Conversations are reconstructed; transcripts of interviews and oral testimony are set in context; analytical distinctions between speaking and writing, between the archives and the field, between the medium of historical presentation and the message, are all repeatedly collapsed and built up again.

By showing my work in this way, I am trying to reproduce in writing the sense of intellectual migration I experienced during fieldwork. My analysis moves, as I did, from an understanding of history based on textuality to one based on orality and the authority of received speech. It moves from an outsider's suspicion that tribal history is a logjam of variant and equally irreconcilable traditions to an insider's certainty that some accounts of the tribal past are more accurate than others. The tribal historiographers with whom I worked were traveling the same road, but they were headed in opposite directions. We could tell one another what lay ahead, but our initial premises, our reasons for going on, and our methods of intellectual movement were sometimes radically at odds. This arena of shared interests and divergent preconceptions is the space in which I worked. As the reader will discover in chapter 1, it is a space in which implicit notions of community and history distinguish themselves with unusual clarity, and a peculiar kind of ethnography, one in which informants and analysts are caught writing up the same data in different ways, can be mined for all its insights.

ONE

Writing Oral Histories

One must face the fact that when it comes to apprehending the historical record, there are no grounds to be found in the historical record itself for preferring one way of construing its meaning over another. Nor can such grounds be found in any putative science of man, society, or culture, because such sciences are compelled simply to presuppose some conception of historical reality in order to get on with their program of constituting themselves as sciences. Far from providing us with the grounds for choosing among different conceptions of history, the human and social sciences merely beg the question of history's meaning, which, in one sense, they were created to resolve. . . . The human and social sciences, insofar as they are based on or presuppose a specific conception of historical reality, are as blind to the sublimity of the historical process and to the visionary politics it authorizes as is the disciplinized historical consciousness that informs their investigative procedures.

Hayden White, *The Politics of Historical Interpretation*

A History of Secrets and Slanderous Talk

When I began my work among the Balga tribes of central Jordan, I had no intention of studying their histories. I wanted to examine the rise and fall of shaykhly families within two particular tribes: the ʿAbbad and ʿAdwan. This problem was historical—it addressed change over time—but I had failed to anticipate how tightly the tribal past and present were woven together, and I little understood the principles that created this mesh of time. My early conversations with Balga tribesmen made clear, however, that any claim to shaykhly authority was also a comment on "origins" (*usul*); it had to arise, literally or figuratively, from a genealogical past.

> [Shaykh Khalaf Salama Dahish is sitting next to me in his hospitality suite, an old goat-hair tent he pitches in front of his cement-block house during the hot summer months. Khalaf, the ranking shaykh of the Slayhat clan of the ʿAbbad tribe, is eating a fresh bowl of strained yogurt and olive oil. I, meanwhile, am changing the batteries of my tape recorder. Shaykh Khalaf has been a garrulous informant; one of my two cassettes is already full. I've had trouble, though, eliciting the kind of information I need. I'd hoped Khalaf

would talk about his own career as a tribal leader, but when I began our interview by asking how he became a shaykh, he obviously thought the question was premature.

"No," he said. "We must bring it all from the beginning. Step by step. In an organized way."

He then recited an extensive genealogy of the Slayhat clan and followed it with an account of how the clan's "first ancestor," Abu Silah, arrived in the Balga.

I snap the battery compartment shut and turn on the recorder. Shaykh Khalaf, eager to resume, nods his consent.]

SHAYKH KHALAF: Fine. What do you want me to talk about now?

ANDREW: I want to return to this generation. I want to know about your life as a shaykh.

SHAYKH KHALAF: About me? About my life?

ANDREW: Yes.

[Khalaf thinks for a moment, then launches, again, into the distant past.]

SHAYKH KHALAF: Yes. At first there was [the tribe of] 'Abbad. The shaykh of 'Abbad back then was Kayid Ibn Khatlan. Shaykh of the shaykhs of 'Abbad. He was the shaykh. Kayid Ibn Khatlan. And who was his *'alim* (his learned advisor)?

ANDREW: Who?

SHAYKH KHALAF: The *'alim* of 'Abbad was Abu Mahayr, of the Mahayrat clan. The first shaykh was Ibn Khatlan. Abu Mahayr . . . he was, you might say, shaykh of the Afgaha, our tribe. He had knowledge. He said, "You, O Ibn Khatlan, are shaykh, and I am the one who knows knowledge."

ANDREW: The *'alim*, what does he do?

SHAYKH KHALAF: The *'alim*, you might say, he's the *'alim* who judges between the people and instructs the people in the ways that are right. He knows our customs (*'awayidna*). The shaykh, when people come to him, he sends them to the *'alim*, to Abu Mahayr. That is what we know from our customs and ancestors. Yes indeed. The shaykh of the Afgaha was Fandi Abu Mahayr. And who stood before Fandi Abu Mahayr, the horseman and shaykh? Who stood before him?

ANDREW: Who?

SHAYKH KHALAF: Before him stood 'Ali al-'Awad, from the Slayhat. From us. The tribe I already told you about. Filah al-Shidad

Abu Mahayr, in his era, became shaykh of the entire Afgaha tribe. The shaykhdom belonged to the Mahayrat. Hilayil al-Dakhil (my ancestor) rose up against Filah al-Shidad in Turkish times. The Turks were in Jerusalem and Syria. He took the shaykhdom from the Mahayrat. Who? Hilayil, my grandfather. He took [control of] the Slayhat, the Mahamid, and the Sikarna [clans of the Afgaha tribe]. He became their shaykh: Hilayil al-Dakhil.

[My head is swimming in names. I can no longer keep them straight, yet I nod approvingly, as if I am well acquainted with these illustrious men. As I grasp for points of orientation, Khalaf adds steadily to the flood of detail.]

SHAYKH KHALAF: After Hilayil became shaykh, Sa'id al-'Aswid became shaykh: Sa'id Basha al-Slayhat. In Turkish times. After Sa'id Basha, the shaykh was Mahmud al-Hilayil, my father's uncle. After them, my father took the shaykhdom: Salama al-Dahish, well known in all the land. On the West Bank and the East, he was renowned. Salama al-Dahish took the shaykhdom. After his era, the shaykhdom ended. There are no shaykhs today.

[Silence. Khalaf wipes the bowl of yogurt clean with a sliver of bread, pops it in his mouth, and watches me intently as he chews. He has evaded my question once again. His closing statement— "there are no shaykhs today"—is partly a show of modesty. It is also a terse commentary on the declining fortunes of 'Abbadi shaykhs, who, since the establishment of the Jordanian state in 1921, have experienced a steady loss of political power. To conclude, however, that Khalaf is not himself a shaykh would seem, in light of the prestige he still enjoys among his clan, preposterous. It is not even consistent with his earlier testimony. When I remarked, just a few minutes ago, on the vastness of his genealogical memory, he responded: "A shaykh must know his tribe." I decide not to let the matter drop so easily.]

ANDREW: The people call you shaykh. You solve disputes. You know tribal law. What do they mean when they call you shaykh?

SHAYKH KHALAF: I'm a good man, you might say. I don't bring evil to the people. I'm a man who informs the people. I settle disputes between the people and solve problems. I'm not despised among the people, and I don't despise them. They admire me. I'm not a troublemaker, and if a problem has a solution, I'll solve it, even if it's from my own pocket. I don't divide the people, and I don't sow chaos among the people; I reconcile them. The people admire me. And they say, "Khalaf is a shaykh. Khalaf understands things." I received this from my father, and he received it from his father, and his father received it from his grandfather. And I received it from them: a chain from one to the other.

The belief that an age had ended, that "there are no shaykhs today," went hand in hand with attempts to link oneself to the shaykhly era, to its values and luminary figures. Ancestral ties to men of renown, or the lack thereof, were offered as proof of a tribesman's social standing. When local histories could not support a man's claims to preeminence; when he could not produce a chain linking himself to a glorious past, then local histories had to be subtly, or brazenly, reinterpreted. Tribesmen were forever laying discrepant claims to the past, and I, cast in the role of "learned outsider," was asked to assess these claims, to defend or denounce them. Historical arguments were going on all around me, and my neutral pose suggested only that I was ignorant of everything at stake.

During the first weeks of fieldwork, I gathered information on Irwayij al-Dwaykat, an 'Abbadi leader who died in the time of Ottoman rule, around 1912. He had been the last paramount shaykh of the Zyud clan, and his name was still mentioned whenever shaykhs were discussed. I wanted to fashion a biography of Irwayij, but the materials I had collected—some heroic incidents, a few idealized character traits, a short poem—did not amount to a life history. Sensing my predicament, a Zyudi man named Musa agreed to let me tape what he called, simply, "The Story of Irwayij" (see chapter 4). Musa talked for about half an hour, mostly on the origins of his own lineage, the Jabur, one of several unrelated lineages that, along with Irwayij's group, the Dwaykat, comprise the Zyud. His story began some two hundred years ago, when the Jabur were "lords of the Jordan Valley." Irwayij's ancestor appeared as a fugitive under Jaburi protection about halfway through the narrative. From that time to the present, Musa's aim was to show that the renown of Irwayij al-Dwaykat and his lineage was based on property crimes against the Jabur, who were the true, original shaykhs of the Zyud.

Musa's account was told *against* the Dwaykat. Yet there was no real animus in his voice. As far as Musa was concerned, he had faithfully recounted "The Story of Irwayij." I remember thinking the story was not about Irwayij at all. What I had accomplished in approaching the problem as I did was to set our views of the past in sharp contrast: I wanted information about a notable person who could be linked to other notables by use of simple chronology; Musa could discuss such persons only in relation to lineages, and the identities of lineages and persons merged in the telling. I wanted a story about Irwayij, who was not a member of Musa's lineage; Musa could tell the story—he *knew* the story—only as it pertained to his own people, the Jabur, and their conflicts over many generations with the Dwaykat, to whom Irwayij belonged. Enduring opposition was, in fact, what organized the narrative. The very act of relating such stories, Musa warned me, was political and highly offensive: "Don't let anyone listen to your tapes."

If relating such stories was offensive, then collecting them was equally provocative. An old 'Adwani shaykh asked me about the nature of my research in terms which, during my time among 'Abbadis, I had come to expect:

SHAYKH: What is it that you want to know, my brother?

ANDREW: I want to know about the shaykhs of 'Adwan. You know, who were the famous shaykhs, what were the relations among them like? That kind of thing. The people say you know many stories about the shaykhs.

SHAYKH: What do you want with such talk? Do you want to sow discord among us?

ANDREW: No. I don't want problems, I just want history.

SHAYKH: Our history is all about problems. Do you want to write it down?

ANDREW: Yes, but not as a troublemaker. I'm writing a dissertation on the history of the tribes, so I can become a professor.

SHAYKH: This is knowledge? God help you. Empty talk brings problems. Everyone recollects the way he wants. Everyone makes his ancestor big; people lie and exaggerate, and the others get upset. By God, there is no benefit.

ANDREW: Empty talk is no good. I just want the events. The well-known things.

SHAYKH: Are you recording on tape?

ANDREW: Yes. If you permit it. I just want what you know is right; what is reliable; what you heard from your father and grandfather.

SHAYKH: Do you want the truth? I'll give it to you, as my father recollected it. Look here. When 'Adwan was shaykh, he wanted to divide the land among his sons . . . .

Most tribesmen were less obliging. The fear of "discord" (*fitna*) was an effective censor. But some shaykhs were always willing to talk, and the fact that prominent men had spoken to me was enough to impel others to do the same. This was not a matter of gaining entrée. I was told stories not as the mark of my acceptance, but as a rebuttal to whatever shaykhs X and Y might have said. The historical talk of other tribes and clans was assumed to be insulting to one's own group. It was also taken, of necessity, to be false. My attempts to gather information from different clans thus met with disapproval and cautionary tales about "lying" (*kidhib*): "Why talk to them? They are all liars (*kidhdhabin*)! They won't tell you the truth." The urge to malign other groups, and the fear of being maligned, were great: "You must write in your book that those people are descended from gypsies and slaves." Or: "What did they say about us? All lies, by God. Don't believe a single word of it!" The fear of discord was well founded; *fitna* and historical discourse were never far apart. Often, they were the same thing.[1]

I was dealing, amid secrets and slanderous talk, with a different kind of history, with other conceptions of narrative and time, and my habit of recording oral traditions made them even more scandalous than they usually were. I soon found myself immersed in a field situation very like the one encountered by Favret-Saada during her study of witchcraft in the Bocage of France.

> So long as I claimed the usual status of an ethnographer, saying I wanted to know for the sake of knowing, my interlocutors were less willing to communicate their own knowledge than to test mine, to try to guess the . . . use I intended to put it to, and to develop their force to the detriment of my own. I had to accept the logic of this totally combative situation and admit that it was absurd to continue to posit a neutral position which was neither admissible nor even credible to anyone else. When total war is being waged with words, one must make up one's mind to engage in another kind of ethnography (1980, 12).

If I wanted to discuss the rise of shaykhly families and, at the same time, avoid discord, I had to appreciate a unique language of historical claims. The language, and the logic behind it, were a fascination in themselves. Both were segmentary. Both expressed a profound sense of "honor" (*sharaf*). But honor and segmentation did not capture the richness of tribal history; in fact, these ideal concepts, as ethnographers ordinarily employ them, take the *absence* of history for granted. Still, my attempts to reconstruct local history along *non-segmentary* lines—by piecing together narratives taken from different lineages—led to an impasse. Not only was the technique offensive to tribesmen, who see no logic in mixing their story with someone else's, it also ignored the process of relentless disagreement by which 'Abbadi and 'Adwani histo-

---

1. To understand the cultural assumptions that shape the language of *kidhib*, the study by Gilsenan (1976) is still the best (and virtually the only) place to start. The topic can be easily politicized, and most ethnographers choose to ignore it.

ries are made. Moreover, the tribesmen who have actually published clan histories make little use of sustained narrative; they focus instead on genealogies, clan origins, and poetry (al-'Abbadi 1984, 1986; al-'Uzayzi 1984; Abu Khusa 1989). Most oral history, which is long on contentious storytelling, never sees print, and the reasons for its absence are obvious to all concerned.

> Hamud listened carefully to the tapes I'd recorded from his uncles. His response hovered somewhere between fascination and dread. He was pleased by all the scholarly attention I was giving to his clan history, but he was also concerned as to how the material would be received in print: "It can be used to divide the tribes, to turn Jordanians against each other." Hamud was reacting to the antagonistic tone of his uncles' talk. It was clearly authentic historical talk, the kind he'd heard all his life, but it wasn't without consequences should it be published. The tapes reflected a confrontational attitude that must be suppressed if tribal history is to be displayed publicly in Jordan. But without the attitude, what remains of the history (field notes)?

The problem that confronted me, and Bedouin too, was how to write down (or even write about) a history that, until very recently, existed only in oral and inherently oppositional forms. The spoken traditions were already organized in a particular way—Musa's "Story of Irwayij" turned out to be the norm—and my insistence on a history composed of shaykhly biographies, with genealogies off to one side, proved unworkable. Other ventures in tribal historiography, these by 'Adwani and 'Abbadi authors, have met with similar fates: they are stalled in production, or they have alienated much of the tribal audience for which they were intended.

The Balga tribes are caught, for now, between speaking history one way and writing it, if it is to be written at all, in others. The misfit between speech and print is a challenge for tribesmen, who feel compelled to close the gap (or widen it) by producing novel forms of historical discourse, or by engaging in older forms more rigorously. This contested area is also fertile ground for cultural analysis. It makes an ethnography of history writing possible while, at the same time, it renders tribal ethnography historical in ways that have not quite been possible before.

The Stories of Toothless Old Men: A Spoken History Yet to be Heard

In the Middle East, tribal histories have seldom inspired ethnographic interest. There are obvious reasons why this should be so. The Islamic world possesses a literate, metropolitan culture of great antiquity and richness. It has also, for centuries, been an object of study for Western specialists, the Orientalists, whose philological and historical approaches have produced their own highly exclusive universe of expertise. Tribalism lay at the margins of that universe. Among Bedouin and peasants, illiteracy drew Orientalist scholarship away from the privileged terrain of classical texts and forced it to embrace less learned genres: namely, scholarly travelogue and folkloric monographs of the "manners and customs" variety.[2] In the tribal zone, textual analysis (with its orthodox measures) was seldom possible; adventurism and intellectual eccentricity flourished in its place.

The boundary between lettered and unlettered domains was not always so starkly drawn. During the early centuries of the Islamic era, a sound knowledge of Arab genealogy, poetics, and popular accounts of tribal "battle days" (*ayyam*) was essential to the writing of good history. In the classical works of al-Tabari (d. 923 A.D.) and al-Baladhuri (d. 892 A.D.), the oral testimony of tribal *akhbariyyun*, or "storytellers," was displayed side by side with evidence taken from documentary sources. By the nineteenth century, when European scholars began to study Muslim society in earnest, this easy juxtaposition of high and low traditions was no longer taking place. The local Muslim intellectual classes, the jurists, *littérateurs*, and religious scholars who defined the limits of proper knowledge, had made their own retreat from the "illiterate margins" long before European scholars ever arrived there. What Said (1978) rightly discerns as the hegemonic textuality of Orientalism—its "citationary nature"—stems, in ways he fails to recognize, from the interregional (and unequal) collusion of learned elites heavily invested in their own textual authority.

Thus, when Lt. C.R. Conder, acting on behalf of the Palestine Exploration Fund, conducted the first topographical survey of the Balga in 1881, the tribal landscape he encountered was utterly remote from the concerns of both Arab-Muslim and Orientalist erudition. Instead of Islamic learning, Conder found

> the survival of the original Paganism of the Jahilin, or "Ignorant," before Islam was preached—stone-worship, the veneration of ancestors, of

---

2. This literature, which fills the gaps between classical Orientalism and modern ethnography, is large and quite useful. For the Arabian Peninsula alone, the genre of "scholarly travelogue" includes such indispensable works as Doughty's *Travels in Arabia Deserta* (1888) and Niebuhr's *Travels in Arabia* (1792), along with more controversial pieces, like Burton's *Pilgrimage to al-Medinah and Meccah* (1855). The "folkloric monograph," a rarer undertaking, is represented by Burckhardt's *Notes on the Bedouins and Wahabys* (1831), Musil's *Manners and Customs of the Rwala Bedouins* (1928), and Dickinson's *Arab of the Desert* (1949), among others. For a good introduction to this literature, see Freeth and Winston (1978).

Plate 1. Decoration on the gravestone of an 'Adwani shaykh. From left to right: a stirring rod and roasting pan (for coffee beans), a pot, a mortar and pestle, two cups, a cooling tray, and a sword. Emblems of hospitality and bravery.

> streams and springs, like that which Herodotus or Porphyry describes, or which is the religion of Dravidians in India. The Bedawin, as we knew them, were a prayerless people, without mosque, Imam, or even Derwish, superstitiously afraid of the desert demons, and adoring the graves of the dead and the relics of former prophets. They possess also a mythology of most interesting character, and their only approach to Moslem custom is in those points where Islam is founded on ancient Arab Paganism (1883, 329).

Instead of historical documents and epigraphic inscriptions—the groundwork of Orientalist scholarship in Conder's day (and our own)—he found a textual tradition consisting almost solely of cattle brands and mortuary pictographs (see plate 1).

> It is interesting . . . to mark, among a people entirely unable to write, the way in which the virtues of the dead are recorded, and we found that on the tombs of great chiefs were modeled in plaster the horseman, with his sword and bow, on one side, and on another the coffee-cups, pestle and mortar, jug, and spoon for roasting, the paraphernalia, in short, of Arab hospitality. In this rude manner the prowess and liberality of the dead man were set forth by descendants who could only mark the tribe to which he belonged [by means of a *wasm*, or "tribal brand"], and were obliged to commit his name to the pious memory of his children (1883, 313–314).

This paucity of documents was a challenge to scholars trained in bookish methodologies. The attention Musil gives to the transcription of oral poetry in his classic, *Manners and Customs of the Rwala Bedouins* (1928), is consistent with the desire, still common among Orientalists, to attain understanding *via* the exegesis of "exemplary texts." For social anthropologists, however, many of whom were (and still are) functionally illiterate in classical Arabic, the tribal hinterland offered a refuge against textuality and textual historicism. It was, in a sense, the only niche Orientalism had left uncolonized and the only space that an infant anthropology, modeled on the textless and seemingly timeless worlds of Black Africa, Amerindia, and Australasia, would be intent to fill.

Throughout its career in the Middle East, professional anthropology has kept remarkably close to the intellectual margins.[3] The bulk of ethnographic research (and certainly the most influential research) is still done among tribes, townsfolk, and peasants. The manner in which these traditional social types are portrayed, however, is changing. The lives of townspeople have, in recent years, been delicately historicized by ethnographers (Brown 1976; Eickelman 1976; Munson 1984), and the study of indigenous constructions of history among peasant communities, especially in Palestine, is now commonplace (Swedenburg 1990). In the tribal literature, discussions of social change have grown into a distinct genre as well (Lancaster 1981; Chatty 1986), and the notion that tribespeople belong to a primitive milieu—to a cultural world marked, as Conder believed, by "ancient pagan survivals"— is nowadays dismissed as quaint romanticism.

As an object of analytical scrutiny, however, tribalism continues to be portrayed as a social form that is basic rather than complex; structural rather than historical; rural rather than urban; parochial rather than cosmopolitan. It stands for all that is essentially premodern, and the exploration of a specifically tribal *historicity* is, for that reason, a task few researchers find compelling. The tribespeople of current ethnography are remarkable, instead, for their poetic sensibilities (Caton 1990), their taste for allegory (Lavie 1990), their unique notions of honor, sexuality, and self (Abu-Lughod

3. In the nineteenth century, before anthropology was "disciplinized," the finest ethnography of the Arab world was urban: namely, Lane's *Manners and Customs of the Modern Egyptians* (1836) and Hurgronje's *Mekka in the Latter Part of the Nineteenth Century* (1931). Yet by the 1960s, when the anthropology of the region finally took off, the city had become an alien space. As Gilsenan observes, "To arrive in Cairo International Airport in 1964 with *The Nuer* metaphorically under my arm was to give a new meaning to the new phrase 'culture shock': a city, a capital city, a metropolis at the heart of an independent state with an ancient history. . . . I was uncertain of what fieldwork in such a context ought practically to mean" (1990, 227). Writing in 1993, I faced the opposite problem. Many of the people I lived with in Jordan reside in or on the outskirts of Amman. The reader, however, upon seeing the words "tribal" and "Bedouin," will automatically push the Balga tribes into conceptual spaces that are utterly marginal. I encourage the reader to unthink this mental reflex in chapter 2.

1986), and their enduring resistance to the centralized power of the state (Davis 1987; Dresch 1989). Tribespeople are often said to possess a sense of history as well, but tribal knowledge of the past, which lacks chronology and derives largely from oral sources, has not come across as *realistically historical* to most nontribal observers. It registers, instead, as a myth of ancestry or, more technically, as "segmentary genealogy." The latter commodity has long been treated, in the spirit of Evans-Pritchard's *The Nuer* (1940), as "a projection into the past of actual relations between groups of persons. It is less a means of co-ordinating events than of co-ordinating relationships, and is therefore mainly a looking backwards, since relationships must be explained in terms of the past" (1940, 108).

Evans-Pritchard's model of lineage structure has left an indelible mark on the tribal ethnography of the Arab world. Since *The Nuer* first appeared, "segmentary genealogy" has stood for numerous things in the Middle East:

1.   A form of tribal political organization in which a balance of power is maintained by the fission and fusion of groups (Gellner 1990).

2.   A folk model of tribal politics that is systematically contradicted by "empirically observable" political behavior (Peters 1967).

3.   A "structure of meaning" that gives shape to notions of honor, which in turn give significance to political events (Meeker 1976; Dresch 1986).

4.   A practical idiom in which social identities and the responsibilities of kinship are continually renegotiated (Eickelman 1989; Rosen 1979).

5.   A territorial system rooted in competition for rights in land and water (Marx 1977; Benhke 1980; Wilkinson 1987).

These various approaches, so often pitted against each other, are united by a common tendency. In each, a genealogical system, which tribesmen use to represent and explain their *past*, is analytically detached from the local histories it informs and is then identified with timeless social relations, with practical interests of the moment, with static images, changeless values, and backward projections.

As one might suspect, the segmentary models that result are hopelessly at odds with the passage of time. In his classic essay, "Meaning and Society in the Near East" (1976), Meeker suggests that genealogical thought is rooted in a "sacred historiography" that "never recognizes any fundamental change in the affairs of the world" (1976, 257). Just as the theological traditions of Islam represent a divine truth that is unalterable in time and space, so too does the "idiom of descent" convey a sense of *sharaf* ("social honor") that stands apart from temporal process and the conventions of modern historiography. Because the *sharaf* that attaches to ancestral names can accumulate (or dissipate) against the flow of calendrical time, Meeker advises us not to mistake pedigrees for ordinary historical facts. Genealogies, he rightly notes, are not "a tradition which draws men together because of accidental copulations and births, they are very much alive. They are alive because they represent the display of the Truth of the sacred historiography" (1976, 259).

Meeker's approach holds open the possibility of extending analysis beyond the ethnographic present by reconnecting local notions of genealogy and history, by historicizing *genealogically* rather than *processually*, thereby creating historiographical forms as lively as the genealogical imagination itself. Meeker does not, however, pursue an analysis of this sort. His conclusion—that "genealogies are not a record of the past" (1976, 259) because they are still "very much alive"—simply reaffirms an old anthropological orthodoxy: namely, that historical approaches to tribal society are basically out of place, since tribal history is only an elaborate commentary on the tribal structure we see before us.

Some ethnographers go even further in the same direction. Peters (1977), in his account of history making among the Bedouin of Cyrenaica, suggests that tribal history, as tribesmen themselves construct it, "has nothing to do with the past, and it would be seriously erroneous to assume that the processes [of group formation] . . . about which the Bedouin reflect, actually occur. The Bedouin know nothing of this past: they cannot know anything about it" (Peters 1977, 77). All the Bedouin *can* know, he argues, is that certain people live in certain places, and when asked to do so by ethnographers, they can produce stories that explain how this spatial arrangement came to be. Once again, the oral tradition—which might not be a tradition at all—is too lively to be used as evidence of a past which is truly *behind* us.

After only a few months in the Balga of Jordan, I began to wonder how this view ever attained the general acceptance it now enjoys. 'Abbadis and 'Adwanis argued convincingly that their genealogical knowledge was not simply a model of social topography; it was a way of articulating past and present, a way of transmitting and talking about history. This talk, which contained poetic and narrative genres as well as calculations of descent, was commonly described to me as *tarikh*, a term which means, in much the Western sense, a "chronicle of actual events" as opposed to "myth," "legend," or "fable."[4] The *tarikh* I recorded from Balga tribespeople (over 40 hours on cassette tape) was neither fabulous nor, as some ethnographers seem to suggest, was it concocted on a moment's reflection. While doing archival

---

4. The use of the classical Arabic word *ta'rikh* may be recent. It is certainly more common among the young and educated. Among the older generation, the term

work in Amman and London, I found that many of the stories tribesmen told me in 1989–90 had been told by their ancestors, in roughly the same form, to Burckhardt in 1812, Finn in 1854, and Conder in 1881. Some high points of local history—the incursions of the Bani Sakhr, the expulsion of the ʿAdwan from the Balga, the Turkish invasion of Salt, the capture of Shaykh Dhiyab al-ʿAdwan—had been witnessed by English travelers or noted in diplomatic correspondence. The long genealogies of ʿAdwani shaykhs, which I was prepared to dismiss as fiction, could be traced, using textual and epigraphic evidence, well into the eighteenth century. Even the poems of Nimr Ibn ʿAdwan, which old men recited to me from memory in 1990, had been taken down by H.H. Spoer in 1904, when Nimr had already been dead for eighty-one years.

It was hardly possible, then, to pretend that the history I recorded from ʿAbbadis and ʿAdwanis had "nothing to do with the past." The evidence (both oral and textual) pointed to the opposite conclusion: tribal history was a *received* tradition, a rich canon of memorized stories and poems, most of them demonstrably old. The travelers of the nineteenth century, who did not labor under the heavy weight of anthropological ahistoricism, arrived rather easily at the same conclusion. In 1868, when the Rev. F.A. Klein toured the Balga as a representative of the Church Missionary Society, he was amazed by the historical sensibility of the Bedouin.

> Our guide described to us in glowing language the fights he had engaged in against the Adwan, the Beni Sachr, the Anazeh and a number of less famous tribes. He knew by heart many poems commemorating those fights and singing the praises of valiant men who had fought and fallen on the field of battle. I was very much struck to see how faithfully & correctly these people transmit to their children by means of such poems the remembrance of the deeds of their fathers (F.A. Klein 1868).

Lt. Conder, during his 1881 survey of the Balga, recorded a summary (and slightly garbled) version of ʿAdwani history from his escort, Shaykh Goblan al-Nimr. The shaykh's testimony, which spanned "about three centuries . . . or nine generations, all known by name" (1883, 309), impressed Conder, who later wrote: "The ease with which Goblan recounted these pedigrees gives a good example of the way in which such knowledge is orally preserved among a people entirely illiterate" (1883, 310).

---

sawalif is more often heard. This word, the plural of *salifa*, has several meanings—talk, reportage, gossip, reminiscence—but all carry the sense of speech about past events that are thought actually to have occurred.

The Balga Bedouin, it would seem, have been talking about history for quite some time now. Ethnographers, for their part, are still not likely to understand what is being said, and a principled ahistoricism is no longer (in the Balga at least) the most obvious source of failed comprehension. In her study of the reproduction of Bedouin identity among 'Abbadis in the Jordan Valley, Layne (1986) is reluctant to assume that the tribal past is an invented tradition. She draws heavily, in fact, on Western travel literature in order to fashion a suitable ethnohistory of the Balga. At the same time, however, Layne frankly resigns herself to the inaccessibility of 'Abbadi *oral* traditions. Her attempts to record the words of tribal elders "were thwarted by my inability to make out what they were saying. This was due in no small measure to their toothlessness, as well as their use of many words particular to their Bedouin dialect but no longer used to describe events of everyday life in the 1980s" (1986, 21).

The incomprehensibility of spoken discourse, as Layne describes it, is oddly metaphorical. The archaic vocabulary, the toothless old storytellers, the quaint anachronism—all extreme images—combine to render 'Abbadi oral history an antiquarian interest. What was once dismissed as too "lively" to be historical is here portrayed as too "geriatric" to be effectively sociological. The reader is apt to conclude that tribal histories are told *only* by old men, that they belong to the realm of folklore and, like the arcana of camel raiding or the rules of mounted combat, are remote from everyday constructions of Bedouin identity in contemporary Jordan. These assumptions conform nicely to anthropological prejudice, which grants the urgency of "working in the present" (Fox 1991), but it is important to stress that none of these assumptions is true.

The stories of toothless old men played a conspicuous role in Jordan's 1989 parliamentary elections (see chapters 6 and 7). In the fifth district of Amman, for instance, ten 'Abbadi candidates from the Afgaha, Zyud, and Manasir clans vied for seats. The victor, Dr. Ahmad al-'Uwaydi al-'Abbadi, was from the Sikarna, an Afgaha clan who, because they have produced no dominant shaykhly families, have traditionally been considered weak. Much campaign rhetoric was committed to discounting or accentuating this interpretation of historical fact. Indeed, Dr. Ahmad, a well-known writer and historian, has spent much of his career repairing the Sikarna's image, arguing in print that they come originally from the Hijaz and are *ashraf*, descendants of the Prophet Muhammad. The oral tradition, which traces the Sikarna to the Ta'amira, a Palestinian tribe from the West Bank, has been deliberately obscured in the process.

Ahmad's campaign oratory was strongly anti-shaykh. Most of his 'Abbadi opponents hailed from shaykhly lineages, and their proud histories had to be deflated. Ahmad's rejection of the shaykhly past did not, however, entail a rejection of the principles that shape tribal historicity. These he avidly embraced. His attack on the shaykhs was delivered in a powerful language of genealogical identities coupled, often in the same breath, with tirades against the backwardness of old-style tribal politics. While driving me home from one of his campaign speeches, Ahmad proclaimed, in his exuberantly arrogant style, the reason why he would win the race.

> I know how to influence the tribal mentality. I know the exact words to use. If you know their history, as I do, you can divide them and bring them together, like sheep. This is the lesson the sons of shaykhs have forgotten. They consider themselves great, like their dead ancestors, but they are less than shepherds. They cannot lead men as I do (personal communication).

The "tribal mentality" Ahmad speaks of is intrinsically historical. It predates and makes necessary much of Hashemite Jordan's political culture. By no means, however, is it antique. Among 'Abbadis, talk of the past is always linked to present-day concerns—why else would people bother to remember such talk now?—and historical discourse is thought to be the object of manipulation, even though it is always the other clan that manipulates it deceitfully. The toothless old men, who look with suspicion on the revisionist projects of Dr. Ahmad and others like him, know this best of all.

Overwriting Oral Histories: The Practice of "Historiographical Imperialism"

The development of more innovative ways of writing about the past would have implications far beyond the confines of Middle Eastern ethnography. Since the late 1970s, anthropologists everywhere have given increasing attention to history in the analysis of social change.[5] This historic turn comes at a time when nationalist ideologies and postcolonial states are tightening their hold on the marginal populations among whom anthropologists have typically done their work. The boundaries of political and intellectual sovereignty are being radically redrawn, and ethnography (no less than cartography) is caught up in the tumult. Ohnuki-Tierney is not alone in concluding that "shifting geopolitics and shifting paradigms are part and parcel of a phenomenon that has affected both disciplines [history and ethnology].

---

5. For an incisive, unorthodox account of anthropology's long-term relationship with history, see Faubion (1993).

In hindsight, anthropologists' previous failure to tackle history seriously was due primarily to their colonial *mentalité*" (1990, 2).

Paradigms are indeed shifting, but the colonial mentality is entirely adaptable to new circumstances. Western modes of historiography, the very methods anthropology now enlists in its attack on old hegemonies, are themselves utterly hegemonic: they envelop foreign conceptions of history as readily as colonial powers once amassed foreign soil. This fact has been received inconsistently across the ethnographic spectrum. A surprising number of authors seem not to find it troublesome at all; others see it as a matter of routine bias that, given adequate care for method, can be kept safely in check. Few authors address the deeper problem of how *writing* history affects our conceptualization of it, and the category "history," as the *analyst* comprehends and deploys it, is rarely subject to critical scrutiny. The use of historical methods can be justified by ethnographers in countless ways—the payoff, we are often told, is a higher level of political awareness and theoretical sophistication—but historical methods themselves call for no justification whatsoever.

This absence of reflexive critique is altogether odd. In recent years, anthropologists have acquired a high tolerance for the deconstruction of ethnography as a culturally-informed practice (Clifford and Marcus 1986). Thus, Siegel's dictum—"Ethnology being a discipline cast in Western terms, it is necessary, though not fully possible, to try to find a way around it when describing non-Western thought" (1979, ix)—falls pleasantly on the ear. But once the term "ethnology" is replaced by "history," or better yet "historiography," the dictum becomes something very difficult to achieve in practice. As Parmentier astutely observes: "It is unfortunate that, in contrast to other forms such as ethnoastronomy and ethnobotany, the term ethnohistory does not normally indicate indigenous forms of knowledge, discourse, or social practice. In fact, the term is widely taken to mean exactly the opposite of an 'emic' category" (1987, 5).

Political economists (e.g., Mintz 1985; Fox 1985) should find little in this criticism that convicts them. The "people without history," to use Wolf's (1982) phrase, are exactly those people who fall outside Western historiography, much as the barbarians, in an earlier age, were those who did not speak Greek. The impulse to examine the diverse ways in which non-Western societies perceive history cannot be great when "the global processes set in motion by European expansion form the context of *their* history as well" (Wolf 1982, 385). The contact situation, in this confidently European view, is not merely a distinct historical moment: it is the point at which *their* past is made real by becoming part of the narrative apparatus—the interlocking tales of capital accumulation, industrial revolution, empire building, and popular resistance to these forces—that gives metropolitan history its familiar shape.[6]

For the ethnographer who seeks to understand the durability and persistent novelty of cultural forms that develop on the edges of, or in the gaps between, world systems (e.g., Sahlins 1981; Comaroff 1985; Bloch 1986; Ortner 1989), easy recourse to Western historiography is a serious analytical blockage, since history, in any place or time, is informed by parochial dynamics of change as well as the external, global processes to which those dynamics respond. The past is a cultural construct made of both foreign and domestic materials, yet like politics, it is always tenaciously local. "Even history which claims to be universal," Lévi-Strauss observes, "is still only a juxtaposition of a few local histories within which (and between which) very much more is left out than is put in" (1966, 257). This partial quality is intrinsic to history making; it cannot be avoided, and attempts to "globalize" our accounts of the past will result only in historical genres that are more *exclusive* than ever.

> Insofar as history aspires to meaning, it is doomed to select regions, periods, groups of men and individuals in these groups and to make them stand out, as discontinuous figures, against a continuity barely good enough to be used as a backdrop. A truly total history would cancel itself out—its product would be nought. What makes history possible is that a sub-set of events is found, for a given period, to have approximately the same significance for a contingent of individuals who have not necessarily experienced the events and may even consider them at an interval of several centuries. *History is therefore never history, but history-for* (Lévi-Strauss 1966, 257; emphasis added).

To understand the role locally constructed histories play in social transformation, one should avoid contextualizing them by means of historiograph-

---

6. This is the working assumption of most Western historians, even those who subject their discipline to trenchant criticism. Consider Hayden White's claim:

> [the] "history" of the "historical" cultures is by its very nature, as a panorama of domination and expansion, at the same time the documentation of the "history" of those supposedly nonhistorical cultures and peoples who are the victims of this process. Thus . . . the records that make possible the writing of a history of historical cultures are the very records that make possible the writing of a history of the so-called nonhistorical cultures (1987, 56).

This argument does not explain why "nonhistorical" peoples," when they finally write their histories, often do so in ways Western historians find unacceptable; nor does it tell us why so much of spoken tradition cannot be written down at all. These are questions the anthropology of history needs urgently to address.

ical conventions that immediately render them obscure. Yet even among ethnohistorians attuned to local knowledge, these alien conventions—which
seem little more than necessary protocols for writing history—become powerful tools for the conceptual subordination of other histories to hegemon-
ically Western ones.

The models of historical reality ethnographers take with them to the field
are rarely taught to them outright. These models belong, instead, to the com-
monsense epistemology of the modern intellectual classes; as such, they are
more rigorously "disciplinized," more reliably uniform, than any of the self-
conscious axioms that define ethnographic theory and practice. To the extent
that anthropologists do history without reflexive insight into the limits of
this historiographical discourse, they will always be struggling to reconstruct
(or, in some cases, to deconstruct) an image of history that demands:

1.   The analysis of textual-documentary remains.
["No history without archives" *per* Goody (1977, 92)]
2.   The alignment of texts within a uniform chronology.
["No history without dates" *per* Lévi-Strauss (1966, 258)]
3.   The creation of a plot that weaves distinct strands of textual evidence
into a single story.
["No history without narrative" *per* Rosaldo (1980, 21)]

We use this template to construct the past *even before we analyze it,* and
the ethnohistorical realities the template authorizes belong to a narrowly
conceived type. They exist in chronological time—even when the local histories we study do not—and the events that occur within these calendrical
frameworks become "certain" through the corroboration of outside, usually European, sources. The most reliable sources are written, but they should
be original as well, unchanged, and certifiably of the past. Oral history, because it exists only in living speech, is rendered "speculative." It enters analysis as a code to be broken, a body of narrative fragments to be meticulously
stitched together using linear chronology as a key. The work most frequently
cited as the catalyst for anthropology's historic turn, *Ilongot Headhunting
1883–1974: A Study in Society and History* (Rosaldo 1980), represents, in
method if not in spirit, a point by point application of these principles.

Rosaldo's struggle to piece together the recent history of a small Luzon
hill tribe—a struggle provoked (and eventually won) by his reliance on
chronologies, maps, and other textualizations of time and space—is by now
a familiar ethnohistorical motif. I resort to it myself throughout this study,
and never simply for rhetorical effect. When the past must be analyzed without the aid of texts, dates, or interconnectable narratives, the methodologi-

cal anxiety that results is perfectly *real*. In *High Religion* (1989), for instance, Ortner analyzes the establishment of the first Buddhist monasteries among Sherpas in Nepal. To reconstruct these distant events, she makes heavy use of oral testimony, and the shortage of more "reliable" sources provokes an exasperated response.

> I simply found it difficult to assemble the narrative account of what happened in the foundings of the monasteries. I had bits and pieces of stories, and different versions of the bits and pieces, and different dates (or no dates) attached to the different versions. It took me about two months to construct a narrative account of the foundings of the first two monasteries. My anthropological training simply hadn't prepared me to put together stories of this sort, and I found it all quite frustrating (Ortner 1989, 10–11).

The difficulty Ortner encounters is not based on her unfamiliarity with narrative history. Any Western academic, versed in the social sciences and humanities, would *think* in that genre. Rather, it results from applying to speech a textual methodology that is radically at odds with the conventions of oral history-making. Testimony is taken out of ephemeral, spoken contexts and is made permanent by writing it down. Its consistency is then established by juxtaposing it to, or combining it with, separate utterances that normally would either resist comparison or be flexibly determined by changes in the speaker's audience. Situations are turned into manipulable texts, and the historical "evidence" that results is (to the eyes of Sherpas or Ilongots) exogenous and entirely new.

This reconstructive exercise requires that the *practice* of oral history be overwritten; consequently, the *structures* that distribute historical knowledge in "bits and pieces" are not examined, or they are examined only as synchronic forms—as genealogies, folktales, epics, origin myths, narrative motifs, plotlines—each divorced from the temporal sensibility inherent to it. In this way, oral traditions can be removed from the spoken present, where they lack "historical authenticity," and located in frameworks more appropriately reserved for the interpretation of texts. Once tape-recorded and carefully transcribed, old stories and chants acquire the erudite luster of palm-leaf manuscripts written in ancient languages, and they can suddenly be put to similar uses. "Although historians have been exhorted to look for evidence in [oral performances]," Tonkin notes,

> that advice simply repeats the methodological expectations of historians versus literary critics, who study, supposedly, style and form. Each side looks for its own material to appropriate and this means a division of labour which in no way fits oral performances since these lack an oral

apparatus of critical specialism and the social, political and economic institutionalisation which underpins professionalised literate commentary (1992, 15).

Whether it treats oral tradition as a source of evidence (i.e., "ethnohistorically") or as a kind of talking literature (i.e., "ethnopoetically"), modern scholarship fixates on the *documentary* and *documentable* aspects of the spoken past. This unshakable commitment to the analysis of exemplary texts brings to mind Bakhtin's critical portrait of Indo-European philology, a field of study that "matured over concern with the cadavers of written languages; almost all its basic categories, its basic approaches and techniques were worked out in the process of reviving these cadavers" (Volosinov 1973, 71). Textual manipulations of oral history are peculiar, however, in that they apply the philologist's bookish methodology in reverse. The "written monuments" ethnohistorians create by way of transcription were originally acts of speech; they were unlettered *and very much alive* when analysis began.

Problematizing Textual Authority: A First Step Toward Reflexive Historiography

As media of historical representation, orality and textuality seldom confront each other on equal terms. This is especially so in the Middle East, where tribal societies flourish on the margins of complex states, and all attempts to examine oral history must be made in the shadow of written records that are immediately recognizable as "historical data." When compared to the fissiparous tales told by Bedouin, these records—most of them generated by nontribal (often anti-tribal) elites—promise secure access to the past, and it is not surprising that ethnographers repeatedly base their accounts of tribal history on the legible observations of Islamic jurists, Ottoman administrators, and European travelers. In criticizing this tendency, Dresch argues that dominant images of historicity, both Western and Islamic, have made the overwriting of tribal oral tradition unavoidable, even necessary.

> The tribes in any case have no unified story to tell, only the indefinitely fragmented body of heroic tradition. The time line that might inform our own theories of cycles, evolution, and so forth is not independent of our data but is intrinsic to the material and always to the statelike part of that material. We are engaged, inevitably, with a partial view that has already been abstracted from a reality that may well be more complex; and what counts as tribal is what learned histories leave as their residue (1990, 258).

The alternative, however, is equally possible: we could engage a partial view that is tribal, indefinitely fragmented, and lacking a unified story to tell. The learned tradition, from this point of view, would exist only as the negation of certain tribal principles of history making. The whole enterprise of *writing* history would be called into question, and the past would have to be interpreted apart from the documentary residue literate culture has left behind. Engaging history on these terms would demand an act of complicity with tribespeople; it would demand that the first principles of literate history-making be opened up for criticism.

For many scholars, privileging oral tradition in this way would also entail a sacrifice of truth and, more urgently, a forfeiture of the ability to stipulate a priori what the content of "real history worth knowing" can be. It is exactly this relinquishment of intellectual authority that Leach seeks to avoid when he dictates the terms on which anthropologists should engage with the spoken past.

> I use *history* to mean written history, a fixed text that explicitly claims to record what happened in the past in potentially datable sequence. For me the concept of "oral history" is misnamed. If an oral tradition happens to be concerned with events that we know (on other grounds) to be historical, this concern does not convert the tradition into history. . . . I will not pursue this matter; I simply wish to insist that when any of us who are anthropologists are presented with stories that purport to be history, we should be skeptical. We always need to ask: In whose interest is it that the past should be presented to us in this way? (1990, 229)

One might easily turn the tables and ask, whose interests are served by this official skepticism? The answer would not be hard to discern: knowledge is power, and the textual historicity Leach espouses is a means by which social worlds are created and given shape. In his reflections on the origins of nationalism, Benedict Anderson singles out the agenda of "real history" as a shaping strategy: it is to insert a "harsh wedge between cosmology and history" and to manufacture, within this newly opened space, "a new way of linking fraternity, power and time meaningfully together" (1991, 36). Indeed, the current stylishness of historical ethnography is itself a by-product of the relentless spread of nationalism and the modern state, sociopolitical forms that describe themselves, and all peoples under their sway, in ways that engage the historical imagination of Western observers.

Today, even the "people without history"—those who entered the modern age on terms diminished by their lack of ready-made textual cultures— are prepared to confront (or appropriate) the shaping power of metropolitan historiography in the only way possible: by developing their own brands of written history. Anthropology seldom plays a leading role in this transition;

more often than not, ethnographers "discover" history only after the *indigènes* have already done so. Ortner's *High Religion* (1989) came at the heels of Sangye Tenzing's *The Unprecedented Holy Sceptre: A Religious History of the Sherpa People* (1971). Cunnison's pioneering study, *History on the Luapula* (1951), was published after elders of the Lunda tribe (working under "missionary influence") had produced their own "70-page typescript history" of the Kazembe chiefdom. Parmentier's historical ethnography of the Pacific island of Belau, *The Sacred Remains* (1987), appeared some seventeen years after the Belauan government began transcribing the oral traditions of its citizens. We, the "external others of the 20th century" (Dirks 1987), are no longer the only ones making ethnohistorical interventions.

If the movement from "mere talk" to textuality presents a challenge to ethnography, it is doubly problematic for the keepers of oral tradition. It brings an erosion of spoken authority, a relinquishment of sovereignty over speech, and, very often, a test of new identities. The Balga tribes now find themselves face-to-face with these challenges. Their spoken traditions were first compiled and published in Arabic in 1935 by Frederick Peake Basha, first British commander of Transjordan's Arab Legion. Peake's *History of Transjordan and Its Tribes*, dedicated to the Amir ʿAbdullah, remained for many years the only authoritative written history of tribal Jordan. Before literacy became widespread in the 1970s, few tribespeople were able to read it. It was not until the 1980s that tribal histories authored by local Bedouin began to accumulate in Jordan's bookstores. Their reception among local readers has been, at best, mixed.

History, to paraphrase Dumont, is the means by which a community reveals itself for what it is. The tribal community of the Balga is segmentary; it reveals itself only and always in momentary contexts. Until recent decades, it was politically marginal as well, and proudly opposed to central government. Yet today Bedouin historiographers fix spoken traditions in permanent forms; they assert a special relationship between local tribes and the Jordanian state; and they force themselves and their fellow Bedouin into novel relationships with political identities that remain, in many respects, premodern, fragmentary, and "state-renouncing" (Davis 1987). As a representative of literate culture, I soon found myself conducting historiographical experiments of a similar kind, and my results were of great interest to ʿAbbadi and ʿAdwani authors. By engaging in tribal projects of textualization, counter-textualization, and anti-textualization—activities that often proved "refractory to the understandings of any and all concerned" (Sahlins 1981, 68)—I attained a level of *complicity* in Bedouin history-making that, almost against my will, made the tribal past "real history worth knowing."

When Orality and Textuality Collide

I stress "complicity" because (1) I was not alone in my work—I was taken under the wing of two local historiographers, Dr. Ahmad ʿUwaydi al-ʿAbbadi and Muhammad Hamdan al-ʿAdwan—and because (2) I was always compelled to write *for* and *against* specific tribesmen and their clans. History, for ʿAbbadis and ʿAdwanis, is a polemical endeavor, overtly contentious, apologetic and offensive by turns. I was expected to take sides—though, in this segmentary community, the sides were always changing—and elaborate strategies of co-optation and exclusion were deployed against me. From the vantage point of any single tribesman or clan, I was forever straying into the malign influence of other groups. The tribal landscape was replete with "external others," all of them (with the exception of me) entirely local.

In this confrontational setting, certain principles of history making were apparent and accessible to analysis, while others—the shared assumptions that made historical disputes intelligible—were less salient to tribesmen themselves. These assumptions became problematic only when they came into contrast with ideas organized along different lines. Such contrasts occurred whenever I was drawn into Bedouin historical disputes. The materials and arguments I used to evaluate historical claims were often markedly different from those used by tribesmen. The sticking points in our various interpretations turned out, almost always, to be points at which a translation from one discourse to another could most effectively begin; indeed, I often heard my own arguments, accurately translated, being used against other tribal groups in what was otherwise an ordinary exchange. We were all, in a sense, doing ethnohistory.

And yet our dialogue was never abstruse. Tribesmen find it difficult, and somewhat strange, to discuss forms of oral history apart from the specific contexts of their use. History making is, for them, a consummately practical activity. Its critical potential unfolds spontaneously as familiar notions of history confront a world that undermines, accentuates, or negates them. The tribal past, in the absence of standard texts, is continually reconstructed in speech. The reconstruction is quite accurate, but it is flexible as well. The changes, conflicts, and shifts of power now happening in the Balga are bound, therefore, to become deeply (and contestably) historical, since the historical associations they bring to mind are extremely responsive to context. After a certain feud was settled, ʿAdwanis told me "the Salih and Mindil clans have been brothers for ages," and the past could be made to support this claim, though just last week the two were sworn enemies, and always had been. After Dr. Ahmad won a seat in parliament, some ʿAbbadis argued that "the Sikarna have been shaykhs from the beginning," and certain stories could make them so, though old men told me during the campaign (and after) that the Sikarna once were weak, and still are.

This mode of history making is not only textless, it is avowedly *antitextual* as well. My attempts to tape-record spoken recollections were often vigorously resisted. The efforts of Bedouin to write down oral histories, likewise, have generated an indignant backlash from within their own ranks. The challenge of textuality is evident in the cries of libel, the empty death threats, and the feelings of insult that often follow the publication of tribal histories; it can also be seen in the way local Bedouin, apart from writing books, try to bring literary and photographic materials into their past. Some 'Abbadis and 'Adwanis have Arabic translations of books written by the British tourists, missionaries, and archaeologists who visited the Balga in the nineteenth century. The uses to which they put these materials range from the grandiose (e.g., politicized reconstructions of clan history) to the mundane (e.g., the aesthetic, but no less political task of decorating a public guest room). In each case, experiments with textuality have been strongly criticized (see chapter 7). It would seem that tribal history, in its spoken forms, simply refuses to become historiography. It cannot be made textual and, at the same time, retain its peculiar genius: its malleability, its capacity to include and exclude with a word—its deft ability, if need be, to disappear entirely.

Resisting the Lure of "Ethnohistory"

Tribesmen are not alone in their rejection of textuality; others are quite willing to reject it for them. When I told Palestinians, most of whom are not tribal, that I was studying Bedouin history, their first question was often, "What are your sources?" To which I replied, "The stories and poems of old men." This answer never inspired confidence: "History cannot be based on such things. The Bedouin don't have a real history. If its history you want, Palestinians have more of it, and in well-documented forms." When I mentioned that tribesmen are writing down their own histories nowadays, hardly anyone was impressed: "They publish the talk of old men and call it history? That's not proper history at all."

Many educated tribespeople would agree. The authority of "proper history" is based on the demonstrable antiquity—or, in the case of Muhammad's sayings (*hadith*), on the fixity and reliable *oral* transmission—of textual remains. This remoteness from the present, which talking alone cannot recreate, enables a temporal "distancing of self" (*per* Braudel 1980) that, although often taken as a sign of modernity in the West, has been a quality of historiography in the Islamic world for many centuries. The opposition of present-day structures to those of the past, a special effect that only the distancing of self can produce, is as much a feature of Ibn Khaldun's *Muqaddimah* (ca. 1377 A.D.) as it is of Braudel's *On History* (1980).

> The (writing of history) requires numerous sources and much varied knowledge. It also requires a good speculative mind and thoroughness. . . . If [the historian] trusts historical information in its plain transmitted form and has no clear knowledge of the principles resulting from custom, the fundamental facts of politics, the nature of civilization, or the conditions governing human social organization, and if, furthermore, he does not evaluate remote or ancient material through comparison with near or contemporary material, he often cannot avoid . . . deviating from the truth (Ibn Khaldun 1967, 11).

Such considerations carry little weight in tribal history-making. Although the Balga Bedouin distinguish the modern era from the "age of shaykhs" that preceded it, they do not (explicitly) set structures of the present against their own knowledge of "historical information in its plain transmitted form." In the years since the "age of government" began in 1921, life in the Balga has changed in countless ways. Still, the otherness of the past, the sense of discontinuity that renders the Dark Ages distinct from the Renaissance, that sets the Age of Ignorance apart from the Age of Islam—imaginative watersheds of this type are not ones tribespeople apply to their own world. The continuity of Bedouin history is visible in the branches of tribal genealogies, and these genealogical structures connect tribespeople to an "age of shaykhs" that, despite its passing away, cannot yet seem alien to them.

In other words, 'Abbad and 'Adwan are social configurations which reproduce themselves *across and apart from* historical periods, and the personal and collective identities that membership in these groups conveys are equally resistant to temporal periodization and the analytical problems it creates. Hence, the fixations of praxis-based ethnography—its craving for "double dialectics" (Comaroff 1985) and "structures of conjunctures" (Sahlins 1981)—can be set aside in the study of tribal histories. The merging of diachrony and synchrony that practice theorists seek to attain is already taken for granted by Bedouin themselves, whose genealogies are both a structure and a history. It would be wrong to conclude from this fact (as so many ethnographers do) that tribal history is not really about the past; more to the point, the past, for tribespeople, is obviously inseparable from the present. History is *now* as it happened *then*.

The temptation is to bifurcate this simultaneity once again, thereby creating a history more amenable to textual modes of analysis. This can be done, but only at an exorbitant cost to insight. The travel literature of the nineteenth and early twentieth centuries, written mostly by aficionados of Biblical archaeology, devotes its energy to the description of antiquities and Balga topography. The names of tribes and notable shaykhs form, along with ancient ruins, the lay of the land. The "peculiar ways of Bedouin" are subjected, on occasion, to close scrutiny and moral critique (see Conder 1883 and Merrill 1881), but the reconstruction of a tribal past, as opposed to a specifically Biblical one, was never of paramount concern. I will draw freely from this literature: not, be it said, to determine "what really happened" in the past, but instead (1) to show what distinguishes it from a more indigenous view, and (2) to examine how some of these external texts are now being appropriated and put to use by tribesmen.

Readers in search of a conventional ethnohistory of the Balga are apt to be disappointed by the chapters that follow. I have tried, whenever possible, to keep this familiar genre at bay, since it accomplishes an end that, in the Balga, has not yet been accomplished on the ground: namely, the subordination of Bedouin history to that of the literate tradition. The colonial encounter, whether Ottoman or British, proved singularly incapable of subverting 'Abbadi and 'Adwani history to its forms. Although the Ottomans administered the Balga from 1867 to 1918, the tribes outside Salt remained effectively autonomous. As the old men say, "The Turks didn't care about tribal affairs. They just wanted taxes." Even the British, who finally gained direct control of the Balga after World War I, remained oddly peripheral to the making of Bedouin history. They soon became central, however, to the *rate* at which it was made. With the establishment of the British-backed Emirate of Transjordan in 1921, and the failed 'Adwani Revolt of 1923, tribal history in the Balga becomes, as it were, "event poor."[7] After the death in 1946 of Majid ibn 'Adwan, the last paramount shaykh of the Balga, tribal history ceases to accumulate at all.

As told today, 'Abbadi and 'Adwani histories have little to do with the last forty years. That period is seen through other lenses: Hashemite dynasticism, Pan-Arabism, Islamic revivalism, socialism, and nationalist ideologies, both Jordanian and Palestinian. And yet tribal history seems no less relevant to Bedouin; in fact, its weight in Jordanian politics and popular culture

---

7. According to Ardener (1989), "event richness" is a feature of "remote areas," which he defines as places "not properly linked to the dominant zone" (1989, 223). The shift from oral to written history in the Balga is an on-going attempt to build proper links to (and effective protections against) the dominant zone created by the Jordanian state.

is growing (Layne 1994). As tribal historicity confronts itself in terms borrowed from other ideologies, it is the borrowed terms that change most profoundly. This is especially so in regard to on-going attempts to construct a uniquely Jordanian national identity, an ideological project that provides the context (indeed, the impetus) for the creation of new forms of history writing among the tribes.

What the Bedouin sense of history cannot appropriate, it simply ignores or evades. Thus it has survived alongside much stronger ideologies for centuries. Perhaps for that reason alone the tribal spirit seems always to be fading away.

> Whereas but a few years ago the tribesmen and villagers would during the warm summer evenings gather round to listen to the poems and legends of the wars, deeds and loves of their tribal heroes, now the younger generation have other occupations; newspapers have come among them, politics must be discussed, travellers often from Haifa, Jerusalem, or even Cairo must be listened to. . . . There is no time, no desire to listen to the song of the old minstrel with his rababa , nor to the old story teller who relates but the deeds of long dead tribal heroes. . . . Thus it is that the history of the tribes of Transjordan is rapidly being forgotten; much has already gone beyond recall, and such as now remains will depart from among the people with the death of the few old men who happily can still recall some of the poems, folklore and legends of their ancestors (Peake 1958, 141).

When Frederick Peake wrote down the oral histories of the Balga tribes, he did so in a style surprisingly consonant with Bedouin ways of recounting the past. He found little alternative. The "disappearing" world of genealogy, poetry, and narrative he recorded, because it existed only in spoken forms, resisted colonial domination (and the modes of historiography that accompany it) much more effectively than did the Bedouin themselves. This forever disappearing world still resists its own expression in writing. As the tribes redefine their histories in opposition to textuality, a complex universe of thought, interests, and action comes fully into view.

TWO

A City of Shadowy Outlines

As works of imagination, the historian's work and the novelist's do not differ. Where they do differ is that the historian's picture is meant to be true . . . [and it] must be localized in space and time. The artist's need not; essentially, the things that he imagines are imagined as happening at no place and no date. . . . Secondly, all history must be consistent with itself. Purely imaginary worlds cannot clash and need not agree; each is a world to itself. But there is only one historical world, and everything in it must stand in some relation to everything else, even if that relation is only topographical and chronological.

R. C. Collingwood, *The Idea of History*

Gertrude Bell toured the Balga in 1905, photographing antiquities, sampling the austere pleasures of Bedouin tent life, and observing, with political interest, the slow decline of the Ottoman Empire. Her account of the trip, *The Desert and the Sown*, is now a classic of English travel literature. In one of the book's more graceful passages, Bell, speaking with the voice of Orientalist authority, recites pre-Islamic poetry to her escort and protector, Gablan al-Hamud, Shaykh of the Da'aja tribe. Amid the exchange, Bell is struck by the antiquity of the Bedouin world she has entered.

> As I sat listening to the talk round me and looking out into the starlit night, my mind went back to the train of thought that had been the groundwork of the whole day, the theme that Gablan had started when he stopped and pointed out the traces of his former encampment, and I said: . . . "[The great Arab poet] Lebid spoke best of all when he said: 'And what is man but a tent and the folk thereof? one day they depart and the place is left desolate.'"
>
> Gablan made a gesture of assent.
>
> "By God!" said he, "the plain is covered with places wherein I rested."
>
> He had struck the note. I looked out beyond him into the night and saw the desert with his eyes, no longer empty but set thicker with human associations than any city. Every line of it took on significance, every stone was like the ghost of a hearth in which the warmth of Arab life was hardly cold, though the fire might have been extinguished this hundred years. It was a city of shadowy outlines visible one under the other, fleeting and changing, combining into new shapes elements that are as old as Time, the new indistinguishable from the old and the old from the new (1907, 59–60).

Since the establishment of the Jordanian state in 1921, the Balga's tribal character has become increasingly difficult to discern. The Bedouin remain on the land, but without their tents and herds they are invisible to those who think of them only as nomads, and their "city of shadowy outlines" can seem, to those passing through it, even more obscure now than it did in 1905. Indeed, the people who live in the Balga today are mostly Palestinians of nontribal descent. It is their world, not that of the Bedouin tribes, which now greets the traveler's eye, and Amman, a city Palestinians confidently call their own, is not timeless and metaphoric, but modern and entirely real.

For local Bedouin, however, the Balga remains a distinctive space, and the dramatic transformations that have occurred in the "age of government" receive little explicit treatment in the oral histories they tell. The ideal categories that define the tribal Balga are meant to express continuity, not change, and most historical discourse seeks to perpetuate a conceptual landscape that exists today only in memory. Yet the memories exist only in the present. They are recounted *against* the "age of government" in which tribespeople now live, and they convey a sense of time and place that, as Gertrude Bell realized, has not yet gone cold.

A Bedouin Proverb: "The Likes of the Balga You Cannot Find" (mithil al-balga ma talga)

Consider the following sketch:

> The Balga is the area of central Jordan lying between the Zarga River to the north and Wadi Mujib to the south. Its southern limit is sometimes set at Wadi Zarga Ma'in , whence it becomes, in local parlance, "the land between the Zargas." The Balga Bedouin were, until recent decades, migratory farmers and keepers of sheep and goats. Today, they are mainly wage earners and sedentary agriculturalists, but they still distinguish themselves from the "peasants" (*fillahin*) who live north of the Zarga River. The people living south of Wadi Mujib are mostly tribespeople of Bedouin descent, but their affairs center on the town of Kerak; they have little contact with the Balga tribes, who frequent the markets and workplaces of Salt and Greater Amman. To the west, beyond the Jordan River and the Dead Sea, lies Palestine, a region which, in the minds of Balga Bedouin, joins all the attributes of a nontribal world: peasantry, a dense array of villages, towns, and cities, and long ages of government rule. To the east, the Balga fades into the Syrian Desert, land of the camel Bedouin (most notable among them, the Bani Sakhr) who, like the Balga tribes, are now settled in permanent villages.

Most Balga tribesmen would recognize this description. It is based on their own characterizations of the area. Few of them, however, would ever define the Balga in this way. The language is too general, too attached to an external point of view. When local Bedouin describe the "land between the Zargas," they begin by filling it with tribal names, and these names are said, always, to be old. According to ʿAbd al-Latif al-Shilash al-ʿAdwan,

> The Balga is the central region, between the Zarga and the Zarga, land of numerous tribes:
>
> the ʿAdwan,
> the Bani Hasan,
> the ʿAbbad,
> Bani Hamida,
> the Daʿaja,
> the ʿAjarma,
> the Ghanaymat,
> the Saltiyya,
> the Balgawiyya.
>
> You can't count them all because each tribe (*ʿashira*) is divided into many branches, and they are all called tribes (*ʿashayir*). They say the Balga is "the land of a thousand tribes." This is exaggeration, of course, but the main tribes are, as I told you, . . . [ʿAbd al-Latif repeats the list, adding some names, leaving others out]. Numerous and ancient tribes. Such is the Balga.

Each tribe has its own territory (its *bilad* or *dira*), its own history, and its own set of genealogies that link it both to the past and to the physical space it now occupies. I deal in this book with only two of these myriad tribes: the ʿAbbad and the ʿAdwan (see figures 1 and 2). Like most Balga tribes, ʿAbbad is a confederation of unrelated clans. Its exact size is unknown, but most ʿAbbadis say it is 80,000–100,000–members strong. Its territory stretches from Wadi al-Shitta in the south to the Zarga River in the north, from the Jordan Valley in the east to Amman in the west. Together, ʿAbbadi clans hold more land in the Balga than any other tribe, but throughout its history, ʿAbbad has been internally fragmented and politically weak. ʿAbbadis often describe themselves as *ahl al-hosha wa-l-ghosha* (the family of fracas and commotion): "We've never known agreement or unity." This lack of consensus is commonly attributed to the diverse genealogical origins of ʿAbbadi clans. Fawzi al-Khatalin, descendant of the first great ʿAbbadi shaykh, Ibn Khatlan, tells how his ancestor gathered the people of the Balga together in one giant tribe.

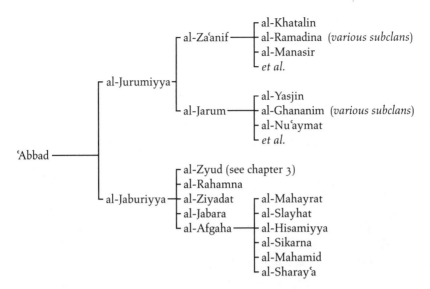

Figure 1. An abbreviated display of 'Abbadi clans. For more inclusive trees, see al-'Abbadi (1986) and Peake (1958).

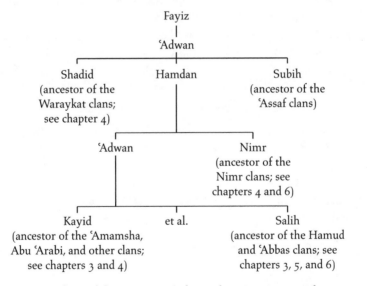

Figure 2. Genealogy of the prominent 'Adwani clans. For a more inclusive treatment, refer to Peake (1958).

ANDREW: Some people say 'Abbad was already a tribe when Ibn Khatlan came to the Balga. Others say Ibn Khatlan created the tribe himself.

FAWZI: Exactly. The latter talk is true. You heard it from the people. If I were not from the Khatalin, I would speak freely, but it is not fitting that a man boast about his own ancestors.

ANDREW: I just want to hear your view.

FAWZI: Yes. In our view, the word 'Abbad did not exist before Ibn Khatlan. The 'Abbad were individual families living separately. The Khatalin are among the ancient people who were present at the time of the creation of 'Abbad. Before the Khatalin, there was no name "'Abbad."

ANDREW: Only families and clans.

FAWZI: And tribes. Ancient and excellent tribes, with high origins. But they had other names. Not 'Abbad. When Ibn Khatlan came to the Balga, he was no better than anyone else. They were all equal. But he was the one who tried to gather them together. He gathered their words; he stood between them in times of dispute; he solved problems; he led them in times of war. The people he brought together became 'Abbad because, as we say, "they adored one another" (*'ibdu ba'd-hum*). And they were called 'Abbad because of this, and Ibn Khatlan was shaykh of their shaykhs. But before Ibn Khatlan came to the Balga and made them all one big tribe, the name 'Abbad did not exist.

The 'Adwan, by contrast, are a small tribe—probably one-tenth the size of 'Abbad—but they have always held power far beyond their numbers. The paramount shaykhs of the Balga, from the mid-1700s to the mid-1900s, were all 'Adwani, a fact the 'Adwan assert liberally and with great pride. As one old man put it, in a smattering of heroic verse: "We are the 'Adwan, shaykhs of the Balga for ages, pillars of the land, and a lantern in the midst of the country." The 'Adwan came to the Balga some twelve generations ago, which makes them one of the younger tribes in the region. Unlike most other Balga tribes, they boast a unified genealogy, and their legacy of power, which their noble pedigree enshrines, was built up at the expense of other tribes. According to Shaykh 'Abdullah Miflah Sa'id al-Sagr al-'Adwan,

> The 'Adwan are exceptional men. This country: we were the ones who ruled it. The 'Adwan came to this land from the east, from the Hijaz. Two brothers: Fayiz and Fawzan. One of them died. The other remained, and he seized the land and all the best wells, and springs,

and wadis from the tribes already living in the Balga. [The 'Adwan] took the shaykhdom . . . and ruled the land. From Zarga to Zarga.

That's the beginning.

As for the Arabs we found on the land—the 'Ajarma, 'Abbad, the Ghanamat, the Balgawiyya, the Mihadia, the so-and-so and so-and-so—these people became followers of the 'Adwan. Their shaykh was Ibn 'Adwan, from that day to this day.

The area the 'Abbad and 'Adwan inhabit (alongside dozens of other tribes) is small, about 1,000 square miles (see map 1), but across its entire length, scores of deeply cut wadis snake westward toward the Dead Sea basin, 1,290 feet below sea level, the lowest point on the earth's surface. The Balga is situated on the jagged edge of the Jordan Valley, which is known in Arabic as the *ghor*. The crest of that valley is called the *shifa*. At some points, the distance between *ghor* and *shifa* is less than 10 miles, but the difference in elevation can be more than 3,000 feet. This contrast produces dramatic shifts in temperature. The *ghor* is usually 5–7 degrees (centigrade) warmer than the highlands, and the Balga, as a result, enjoys a rare diversity of climates.

In the *shifa*, which receives 350–500 mm of rain each year, the landscape is Mediterranean. Evergreen oak forests cover much of the uplands; grassy meadows lie interspersed among the hills; and the wadi beds are overgrown with oleander shrubs, poplars, and willow trees. Nearer the lowlands, the rolling terrain is boulder—strewn and barren. This area, called *al-humra* ("the red earth"), gets less rain (200–350 mm per year), but for a few weeks in spring it turns a brilliant green, wildflowers shoot up everywhere, and the look of desert is momentarily forgotten. In the *ghor*, the broken hills end in a rich alluvial plain. Rainfall here is lower still (100–200 mm per year), but natural springs support wide stretches of palm trees and *sidr* bushes. The *ghor* is hellish in the summer months, when temperatures hover around 40 degrees centigrade. In winter, the weather turns mildly tropical, and heavy rains in the *shifa* flood the valley floor with runoff.[1]

The Balga is fertile ground for livestock and cultivation, and the local Bedouin tribes have traditionally mixed farming with transhumant pastoralism. Until the 1950s, most 'Adwani and 'Abbadi clans wintered in the *ghor*, where they grazed large flocks of sheep and goats. In spring and early summer, they moved their herds back to the *shifa* to escape the intense heat,

---

1. An excellent discussion of the ecology of central Jordan in the nineteenth and early twentieth century can be found in Raouf Abu Jaber's *Pioneers over Jordan: The Frontier of Settlement in Transjordan, 1850–1914* (1989).

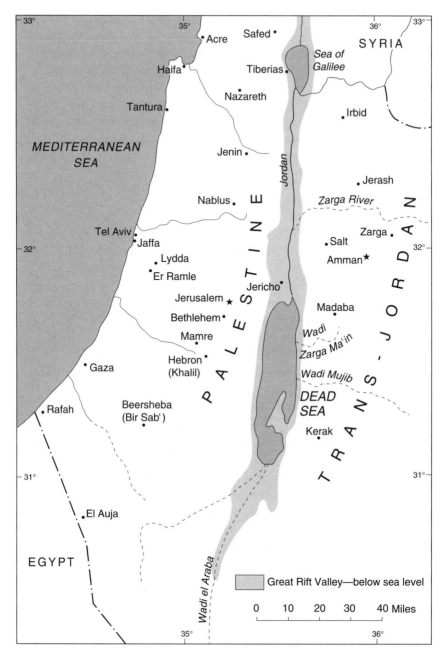

The Balga, "Land of 1,000 Tribes," in the early days of the Transjordanian Amirate, circa 1923.

biting insects, and malaria that beset them in the valley. They also harvested the cereal crops they had planted upland at the onset of the winter rains. The migration from *ghor* to *shifa* is recalled in a famous poem composed in the early 1800s by Abu Mismara, the slave-poet of Shaykh Hamud Salih al-ʿAdwan:

> I climbed Garʿ Najda at break of day,
> A mountain high atop other peaks ascending.
> O my country, mother of empty spaces and rugged terrain,
> And streams pouring forth in each wadi,
> [Where] waters flow and gather, trickling in their path.
> When the east wind blows and winter begins,
> We come to you, O *ghor* of plenty, at a gentle pace.
> And when (our) companions divide after gathering,
> Each goes in search of a cool summer place.
> Our summer place is Migtha, and Tab, and Kawm,
> And yonder is Yajuz, the light of my land.
> We will settle on our ground, pitch tents in a row,
> Amid the smell of herbs and peppergrass blending.[2]

The "cool summer places" are now permanent villages, and the "*ghor* of plenty" is filled with bustling farm towns. In Swaysa, a highland ʿAbbadi village located on the western fringe of Amman, members of the Sikarna clan opted, beginning in the late 1960s, for a sedentary way of life. As one man put it: "We all started building houses near the schools, so the children could stay here and learn to read." The old goat-hair tents were sold off in the 1970s, or they were rigged up beside newly built houses for shade. A few Sikarna families still keep tents in *al-humra*, the extensive grazing area between the *ghor* and *shifa*, but they also own houses uphill in Swaysa, where the rest of the family lives.

My first visit to Swaysa, billed by my eager host as "a trip into the heart of tribal Jordan," came replete with unexpected images. I was, to be honest, somewhat dismayed by the domestication of the landscape, by the neatly manicured flower beds and grape arbors that flanked the houses, and I caught myself wondering whether the people of Swaysa were truly Bedouin at all. My early field notes describe a Bedouin camp-turned-village that resembles dozens of others in the Balga uplands.

---

2. English transliterations of all poetry displayed in the body of the text are provided, along with additional commentary and translation, in Appendix A.

Swaysa has no discernible borders or center. It's marked only by a sign on a lamppost. Houses are close to the road, with clumps of three to five homes here and there. These are invariably groups of close, patrilineal kin (brothers and their wives and children). Swaysa itself is said to belong to one lineage: the 'Uwaydi, a section of the Sikarna clan of the 'Abbad tribe. All together, about five hundred people live here, though no one knows for sure.

Swaysa is about 20 kilometers up from the Dead Sea, which you can make out very clearly on most days. At night you can see the lights of Jerusalem on the horizon. The area is very hilly, and the earth has a deep, reddish-brown tint. Olive orchards are common, along with grapes, tobacco, figs, plums, and anything else that grows in a Mediterranean climate. The soil is very rocky, with stones too large to move by hand. The cost of clearing land for cultivation and breaking boulders into stones for fences and terracing is, by local accounts, tremendous. Most people tend a few goats and sheep in addition to their crops.

Few houses in Swaysa are over twenty years old. In the 1950s, people were still living in tents—the proverbial "houses of hair" (*byut sha'r*)— and, during the winter, they moved into caves dug out from the rock. In the 1960s, the first stone houses were built. All homes are now made of cement and cinder block, with nothing more than two stories tall in Swaysa. The architecture is unadorned and blockish. Attention is given to interiors; exteriors, it would seem, are designed to make as little statement as possible. New houses are painted white or lighter shades of brown. Pale blues and greens (colors that deflect envy) were popular in the 1970s.

In the Jordan Valley, which has undergone an agricultural revolution of its own, I found 'Adwani Bedouin living in what, to me, were equally unlikely surroundings. The opening of the East Ghor Canal in 1966 transformed the valley floor, which was already a natural greenhouse, into a rich industrial park of gardens. Modern systems of drip irrigation, supported by a lace of spillways, reservoirs, irrigation pumps, and miles of plastic tubing, funnel water into fruit plantations and vast, chemically fertilized vegetable fields. As in the *shifa*, local Bedouin have settled down in houses (this time, amid banana and lemon groves), sold off most of their livestock, and entered the competitive world of agro-business. The shaykhs of the 'Adwan, who still deem themselves "lords of the *ghor*," are now its landlords, a local gentry surrounded by farm labor in its various, impoverished forms: Egyptian and Pakistani guest workers, Sikhs, Palestinians, former 'Adwani slaves, and *ghawarna* , the "Afro-Arabs" of the Jordan Valley.

In the midst of this rapid change, the Balga tribes consider themselves fully Bedouin. Their involvement in farming has not led to an identity crisis; in fact, the 'Abbadis and 'Adwanis I knew were keen to point out that, unlike the desert Bedouin, the Balga tribes had always engaged in cultivation.

"We did not live in the wasteland with nothing but camels," an ʿAbbadi man told me. "We had the good land, and the best land is ours to this day. We have been farming it for ages."

Even the agro-managerial status of the ʿAdwan is nothing new. In 1855, James Finn, British consul in Jerusalem, toured the Balga under ʿAdwani escort. He made the following remark in his diary.

> Our ride [up from the Jordan Valley] was a gradual ascent; and after some time we were met by young ʿAli, the favourite son of the principal Shaikh Deab, (Wolf,) with a small but chosen escort, sent by his father to welcome us. We saw a good deal of corn land, and people reaping their harvest. This belongs to two or three scattered villages about there, under the immediate protection of the Deab ʿAdwan. The Arabs [i.e., Bedouin], however, in this part of the world, do condescend to countenance and even to profit by agriculture, for they buy slaves to sow and reap for them (1868, 9).

When Bedouin discuss change, they seldom treat the expansion of agriculture as a novelty in itself. More often, they dwell nostalgically on the abandonment of tent life and the dwindling of their goat and sheep herds. Both are linked to the demise of a distinctly Bedouin "generosity" (*karam*).

[I have just returned to Swaysa from a wedding in a neighboring village. The traditional feast dish, *mansaf*, was served—piles of rice heaped on sheets of unleavened bread, drenched in fatty broth and topped off with boiled lamb and almonds. With amazement, I tell ʿAli about the vast quantities of mutton that must have been consumed. He smiles indulgently, then tells me how things used to be.]

ʿALI: Ya Andrew, when my uncle Khalaf was shaykh, he had a large tent with four center poles, and people from all around would come to visit him wherever he pitched it.

[ʿAli calls out greetings to an audience of imaginary guests.]

"Welcome!
God grant you life!
Welcome to all!
Be at ease!
Drink tea!
Eat supper with us!
Spend the evening!"

Yes indeed. In a month of thirty days, he would slaughter 32 sheep for his guests. There are no men like that today. They are gone. God have mercy on all of them. The generous man is beloved of God.

Plate 2.   Men gather to eat *mansaf* at an 'Abbadi wedding. A tented affair.

ANDREW: But aren't people generous anymore?

'ALI: Today? Today, everyone sits at home. No one visits and no one is welcome unless it's an obligation or a formal occasion where gifts are given. Nowadays we just watch TV. That's not a good life. No. The generous man is beloved of God.

Plate 3. 'Adwanis convene for a ceremony of reconciliation; traditional attire and a fine goat-hair tent lend gravity to the event.

Such rhetoric makes sense only because Bedouin are supposed to be generous by nature, and tent life is thought, along with stock keeping, to be quintessentially Bedouin. Tents are still pitched on formal occasions: at weddings, funerals, dispute resolutions, and the official visits of government dignitaries, although the tent itself is often borrowed or rented (plates 2 and 3). And sheep are slaughtered whenever hospitality must be dispensed in grand style. Indeed, when Bedouin compare their hospitality to that offered by other social types—by Palestinians or peasants, for instance—they speak of themselves as if they were still living in tents.

> [I have been asking Haj Salih about the shaykhs of the last generation. What had they been like? How had they become powerful? His answers always return, sooner or later, to the subject of generosity. This, for the Haj, is the defining attribute of the great shaykhs of the past.]
>
> ANDREW: Ya Haj, it is known that the shaykhs were generous. But weren't all Bedouin generous?
>
> SALIH: The Bedouin is generous. Yes indeed.
>
> ANDREW: Why?
>
> SALIH: His hand is open.

[The Haj shows me his open palm.]

SALIH: But the peasant (*fillah*) is stingy. His hand is closed.

[The Haj turns his open palm into a fist.]

SALIH: The Bedouin lives in a house of hair [a tent]. Without doors. Without windows. The peasant lives in a house of stone. His doors are locked and his windows are closed. He hides from strangers and fears them.

These words were exchanged in the receiving room of Haj Salih's house, which is made not of goat hair, but of cinder block and poured cement. The windows and doors were wide open, and strangers, who came seeking the advice of Haj Salih's influential son, a member of parliament, were graciously received.

Warriors, Learned Men, and "Barnyard Hens"

Although talk of farms and tents, Bedouin and peasants, is common there, the Balga is by no means a remote area. It is heavily urbanized. Over 1.9 million people live between the Zarga and Wadi Mujib, more than half the population of Jordan. Most Balga Bedouin are, in fact, suburbanites in the sprawling conurbation of Amman, Zarga, Madaba, and Salt. Incorporation of their tribal lands in cities has brought with it paved roads, piped-in water, and electricity. The smallest Balga villages usually have their own primary schools, convenience stores, a mosque, and bus service that links them, ultimately, to downtown Amman. Even in the far countryside, the *rif*, the landscape is dotted with refugee camps, military installations, and the palatial weekend residences of wealthy urbanites who, behind their walls and fences, lead what—in the imaginations of local Bedouin—must certainly be sumptuous and immoral lives. Signs of the world system are ubiquitous, and the Balga Bedouin (no strangers to accusations of primitiveness) have little tolerance for a romanticism, anthropological or otherwise, that would make them seem backward or simple.

Even to portray them as farmers is to consign the tribes to an overly rural existence, with all its implications of folkishness and tradition. Consider the 'Amamsha, a Kayid branch of the 'Adwan, who live in the highland village of Salihi. They are a landed clan, and their houses are surrounded by the local signs of farm life: terraces, irrigation systems, olive and lemon groves, and large hen houses. The 'Amamsha do not, however, live off the fruits of their own agricultural labor. Of the clan's sixty or so adult males, fewer than ten are full-time farmers, and they, without exception, are older men and military pensioners with not much else to do. The rest of the ʿAmamsha work in the government and service sectors of Jordan's economy. They are military officers and policemen, cab drivers, truckers, accountants, a university professor, an engineer, civil servants, a customs agent, several graduate students, a real estate developer, clerks, secretaries, and schoolteachers. The handful of ʿAmamsha women who work outside the home are bank tellers, postal clerks, teachers, and seamstresses.

This diversity of careers is rooted in public education and literacy. Younger ʿAmamsha describe themselves, with serious pride, as a learned, progressive generation. Of their own volition, they have left the "age of ignorance" (*zaman al-jahiliyya*) behind, and a commitment to agriculture signifies, to them, a lack of more lucrative options. Farming is left to the weekends and late afternoons, to the women, old men, and children; the great bulk of it is done by hired hands, none of them ʿAmamsha, who are willing to work for shares. Since the 1920s, the ʿAmamsha have sold off nearly 8,000 acres of their land in the *ghor* and *shifa*; at least 4,000 acres remain. Selling off parcels of land to Palestinians is one way the ʿAmamsha have financed the college educations of their sons and daughters. Their shrinking patrimony is amply offset by the status of men like Dr. Yasser Mannaʿ, who returned from the University of Southern California with a Ph.D. in Public Administration and a faculty position at Yarmouk University; or the engineer Ahmad ʿArif, who received his B.S. at Wayne State University in Michigan and now works on government housing projects.

Saʿud Maniʿ, a man in his early sixties, is de facto shaykh of the ʿAmamsha. He concluded his oral history of the ʿAdwan—a sprawling account that dealt with old tribal conflicts and the martial prowess of ʿAdwani warriors—by commenting on the proud stature of the present generation. For all its attention to shaykhly ancestry and the begetting of sons, the image of worldly success Shaykh Saʿud projects is based on two rather familiar elements: higher education and a professional career.

> SAʿUD: And that is our history, as it was told to us by the elders. Kayid became shaykh. He slew fourteen Amirs and seized the Balga. His son, Shibli, became shaykh, and the son of Shibli, Slayman, became shaykh. And the ʿAdwan are still shaykhs of the land.
>
> We who live here in Salihi are the sons of Slayman. And those alive today are from the sons of Abu l-ʿAmash:
>
> Sayf Abu l-ʿAmash. He has sons.
>
> There's Zayd Abu l-ʿAmash, and he has sons.

Siran Abu l-ʿAmash. He has sons.
There's Mannaʿ Abu l-ʿAmash, and he has sons.
There's Maniʿ Abu l-ʿAmash, and he has sons.
And there's ʿArif Abu l-ʿAmash, and he has sons. All of them educated men, engineers and doctors and officers. Praise be to God. And we who are sitting here in front of you, we are the sons of:

Kayid, father of
Shibli, father of
Slayman, father of
Abu l-ʿAmash, who was father of
Sayf,
Siran,
Zayd,
Maniʿ,
Mannaʿ,
and ʿArif.

We are their sons, as you see us. Doctors, engineers, educated men, and military officers. Praise be to God, and may He keep you. Those are the lineage of Kayid al-ʿAdwan. Those are the generations of Kayid.

Kayid al-ʿAdwan, who slew fourteen Amirs and seized the land, and Dr. Yasser Mannaʿ, who lectures at Yarmouk University, are part of an unbroken, patrilineal chain of honor (*sharaf*) and reputation (*sit*). For Shaykh Saʿud, the gulf between the eighteenth-century warrior and the twentieth-century academic is not great: each man has distinguished himself, and his lineage, in the eyes of others.

Shaykh Saʿud has bridged the same genealogical distance, which threatens always to dilute the heroic aura it transmits, in his own flamboyant style. He is a traditional man in many ways: he maintains three wives and a capacious, three-storied apartment building to accommodate them; he wears the ankle-length gown (*thob*) and the red-checkered head scarf (*kufiyya*) that younger ʿAmamsha have abandoned in favor of "city" (*madani*) dress: shirts, jackets, and pants. He proudly accepts the title Shaykh, though few men aspire to—or can successfully step into—that position anymore. At the same time, he has obviously done well for himself in the modern economy. He is ostentatiously wealthy, and this inspires admiration and envy in equal degrees. Even his close kin believe his riches were amassed by sinful means: via real estate swindles, embezzlement of religious donations, and

Plate 4. The house of Shaykh Saʿud. His diwan, which is not connected to the family quarters, can be seen in the foreground.

smuggling, for which he was arrested and imprisoned in the 1970s. All these misdeeds, actual and imagined, serve only to enhance Shaykh Saʿud's image as a man who can accomplish things.

In front of Shaykh Saʿud's three-storied home is a long *diwan* (receiving hall) in which he entertains his many guests and petitioners (plate 4). The hall is lavishly appointed, and its interior design, which was overseen by Shaykh Saʿud himself, is an objectification of Saʿud's mastery over past and present. The diwan is divided into two sections. In one, the furnishings are "Bedouin authentic" (*badawi asli*). Stuffed-wool mattresses line the walls and camel saddles, intended as props for Saʿud's reclining guests, are placed every four feet. Handwoven Bedouin carpets cover the floor. In the middle of the room are short-legged coffee tables on which are displayed showy brass tea services, and in the far corner stands a giant ceremonial coffee pot and a charcoal brazier on which coffee beans can be roasted. Antique rifles and swords hang on the walls, along with pictures of Saʿud in traditional garb, King Husayn in flowing Hijazi robes, and Saʿud's father, Maniʿ, similarly attired (plate 5).

The other half of the diwan is equipped with modern furnishings. In place of mattresses are overstuffed armchairs; the rugs are still oriental, but of the classier Persian variety. There are no articles of Bedouin coffee kitsch;

Plate 5. The Bedouin half: a modern study in traditional decor.

no weapons on the walls. Everything is neat and elegantly arrayed (plate 6). In each corner of the back wall hangs a picture of Shaykh Saʿud, who has traded his Bedouin costume for a business suit. King Husayn, whose portrait hangs once again in the center, is wearing modern dress as well. The statement Shaykh Saʿud intends to make is almost audible as one enters this dichotomized space: "I am Saʿud Maniʿ Abu l-ʿAmash. Inheritor of two worlds, master of each."

For other ʿAmamsha—those who felt at ease in only one half of Saʿud's diwan—the continuity between past and present was much harder to discern. Haj ʿArif Abu l-ʿAmash, the octogenarian patriarch of the ʿAmamsha (plate 7), often complained to me that his legion of sons, grandsons, and nephews were growing up like "barnyard hens" (*jajat mazraʿa*), well fed but domesticated and ripe for the slaughter.

"The age of the sword and lance (*zaman as-sayf wa-l-rumih*) has passed away," he would exclaim within earshot of his citified offspring, "and now the Bedouin hide like peasants behind walls and doors."

> [The Haj's comment brings to mind the stone houses that lie abandoned and slowly collapsing on the hill above Salihi. The ʿAmamsha built them in the 1920s, and they have been living in houses ever since. Walls and doors are vices Haj ʿArif and his

Plate 6. The contemporary half: a traditional study in modern decor.

brothers introduced to Salihi; the current generation did not invent them. The real difference between now and then, the Haj suggests in his next statement, has little to do with architecture.]

HAJ ʿARIF: There are no shaykhs in the land today. Now we have government.

[These words are meant to conclude our session of historical talk. We are leaving the realm of nostalgia and heroic ancestors and entering what, for the Haj, is a more prosaic reality. I miss the cue. Instead of changing the topic, I treat the Haj's conclusion as if it were simply a statement of fact.]

ANDREW: But it's a known thing that the ʿAmamsha are shaykhs. Aren't you shaykhs?

HAJ: Yes. Shaykhs over our women.

[The Haj's wife and daughter-in-law, who sit with us, laugh into their hands. I have forced the Haj to justify a narrative cliché— "there are no shaykhs today"—and he rises gamely to the task.]

HAJ: The shaykh is one who slays whomever he desires to slay. *That* is a shaykh. He can lop off heads and the government will not interfere. *That* is a shaykh. But if I call myself shaykh and I fight with you and the government comes and puts me in prison: *that* is not a shaykhdom. The shaykh must be fierce and strong and free. The ʿAdwan had these attributes in the time of my father, Abu l-ʿAmash. But today they are all barnyard hens.

Plate 7.   Haj ʿArif stands in front of his old house, now abandoned on the hill above Salihi.

ANDREW: Except for you, ya Haj. You are the last "country rooster" (*dik baladi*).

[The Haj and his wife laugh in approval. The "country rooster," as the Haj told me earlier, is intelligent. It keeps its distance from humans. It forages for its own food. It runs when it sees the knife.]

HAJ: And you, O brother of mine, are a prince.

I was just as likely to hear this rhetoric in reverse: old shaykhs would praise education and the rule of law, while young men would speak nostalgically of a freer, more heroic age. The tribal past has many different meanings, yet Bedouin identity, bred in the bone, is not thought to be archaic or incompatible with modernity. In the early stages of my research, when I asked Balga Bedouin "who they were," their answers came back in an easy blend of old and new identities: "We are the people of the land (*ahl al-balad*). The tribes. The original Jordanians (*al-urduniyyin al-asaliyyin*). We have lived in Jordan for ages, and the land is ours to this day."

A Community of Disagreement

These proud assertions, made to an outsider who was still a stranger, belie a more complex state of affairs. Throughout the modern era (1918–present), the relationship between tribal space and the physical landscape in central Jordan has grown increasingly problematic. Large areas of the Balga, especially in Amman and its suburbs, are owned now by Palestinians, most of whom came to the East Bank as refugees of the 1948 and 1967 Arab-Israeli wars. Since the 1920s, the Jordanian military, the Hashemite royal family, and various government ministries have also amassed sizable holdings in the Balga. Tribespeople know quite well that they do not always control, or even own, the lands they claim; nonetheless, tribal space is described today in an idiom that, despite the relentless buying and selling of tribal lands, seldom acknowledges change.

[I drove to Amman today with Rashid, who was delivering a revised draft of his master's thesis to his adviser at Jordan University. As we entered the Baqaʿa plain, he began an impromptu lecture on tribal geography and past events.]

RASHID: This region is all ʿAdwani territory; it has been ours for ten generations. Part of it belongs to the Waraykat, who are my maternal uncles, and the rest belongs to the Abu ʿArabi, who are descendants of Kayid, like us. Over there is the place where my grandfather killed a Bani Sakhr shaykh. Have you heard the story?

ANDREW: Yes, I recorded it from Haj D.

RASHID: No! No! Record it from my uncle, Haj B. He's more reliable. Over there is 'Ayn al-Basha, the place where Dablan Shilash, a famous 'Adwani shaykh, cut off the head of a Turkish general. Did Haj B. tell you about it?

ANDREW: Yes, he did.

[And so on down the road. The travelogue was detailed and colorful. I had heard it several times before, spoken by other 'Adwanis, and the narrated geography was marked, as always, by the same gaping hole.

The Baqa'a plain is the site of the Baqa'a refugee camp, a congested city-unto-itself, home to one hundred thousand Palestinians. Even as Rashid filled the plain with 'Adwani personages, clan names and events, the camp stretched out to our left, filling the same space with jumbled rows of cinder block and corrugated tin. The Baqa'a camp was built on land acquired from the Waraykat (or, as the Waraykat say, on land taken from them) by the Jordanian government in 1967. It stands in the heart of 'Adwani territory. Local Bedouin shop in its booming market, pick up their mail at its post office, send their children to its public schools, and recruit cheap labor from its streets. But for Rashid, the camp did not belong on the 'Adwani landscape; it was not part of the world he wanted me to see, nor were the scores of Palestinian homesteads built outside the camp on land Rashid's kin have sold, and continue to sell, to refugee families.

When I told Rashid that I'd recently met a man in the camp whose grandfather supposedly knew 'Adwani poetry and had old books on the Balga tribes, he was visibly upset.]

RASHID: Don't believe him. He's a liar. What does he know about Bedouin? Nothing. He's a Palestinian, not even from the tribes. He just wants you to visit his house so he can ask you for a visa. Don't linger in the camp. It's dirty and the people are worthless.

[Rashid, like so many other tribesmen, used historical and genealogical identities to create a world in which refugee camps were invisible, and Palestinians, by definition, had nothing to say. I was surprised, several miles later, to discover the title of Rashid's thesis: "The European Powers and the Question of Palestine."]

Rashid's travelogue was an act of self-assertion. It was delivered *in spite of*

the Palestinians, and its polemic—Palestinians would perceive it as such—
was built on notions of descent, the arrangement of clans in space, the remembrance of illustrious ancestors and their deeds, and claims to precedence
in the land. To the extent that Palestinians lack a connection to the world
Rashid describes, they also lack a "significance" (a social value, or *gima*)
among tribesmen. In fact, tribesmen commonly refer to Palestinians as "Bel-
gians" (*baljikiyyin*), a term meant to accentuate both their foreignness and
the incongruity of their presence in the Balga. By suggesting to Rashid that
a Palestinian might aid in the compilation of 'Adwani history (or that he
might be trusted as a source), I was rejecting the very conjuncture of name,
place, and descent that made 'Adwani history, and tribal identity, possible. I
was opting for an historical account that, in Rashid's view, was insignificant
and inauthentic.

Problems of authenticity and significance are not confined to the arena
in which Palestinians and Bedouin negotiate their identities. The polemic
Rashid used to exclude Palestinians from tribal space is in fact the same
polemic Bedouin use to define the tribal system from within. Rashid saw
no point, for instance, in my taking testimony from 'Abbadis.

"They have no important history," he warned, "and they will only mis-
lead you and waste your time."

This was familiar talk. The Balga tribes are connected to each other, and
to the physical landscape, by a tradition of dispute. They form a "community of disagreement," and the points of contention among them—the remembrance of tribal wars, conflicting claims to the shaykhdom, genealogical controversies, and quarrels over land—are the points at which their
respective identities are most fully elaborated. Except for a list of tribal names
that belong to the region, there are very few historical representations internal to the Balga that local Bedouin *share*. In a community defined by
polemic, dissensus must be preserved (important contradictions must be kept
salient) if tribal names are to retain their significance.

I did not fully understand this link between identity and dissensus until I tried to construct my own tribal map of the Balga. The task should have
been simple. The current distribution of tribal villages is well known to most
Bedouin, and transcribing it onto a 1:50,000–scale map was not a complicated exercise. And yet the final product, a large (2.5'x4.5') tricolor map of
'Abbadi, Salti, and 'Adwani territories, inspired an oddly critical response.

> The map continues to cause trouble. The tribal borders I've drawn
> on it are current; they are based on my village survey and the
> verbal maps tribesmen themselves have given me. I've put 'Abbadi

territory in yellow, Salti in red, and 'Adwani in green. When I
showed the map to X, who is 'Adwani, he told me it was all wrong.

"The 'Abbadis and Saltis were given their land by the 'Adwan,"
he said.

The map should, technically, be all green.

"The other tribes don't have any land except what we granted
them as a gift."

He then repeated the story of Abu 'Arabi, the great 'Adwani
shaykh who "gave" the Balga tribes their lands, casually drawing
green lines around areas we both knew had not belonged to 'Adwan
for many generations. He also extended 'Adwani territory deep into
what is now Bani Sakhr land.

"All this area was given to the Skhur. It was a gift to Sattam ibn
Fayiz when he married 'Alia, daughter of Dhiyab al-'Adwan. It is
originally 'Adwani territory."

And so on.

Ironically, when I showed the map to Y, an 'Abbadi, he claimed
that a large section of the Jordan Valley, which belongs to the
'Adwan, was rightfully 'Abbadi land, since the 'Adwan had taken
it from 'Abbad by treachery.

"This should all be yellow," he said.

He then tried to rub out the green area with an eraser and nearly
ripped the map apart. Several other 'Abbadis suggested changes.
Each change had a familiar story attached to it, and the borders got
messy in parts. Z and Q thought some land should be taken from
the Salti tribes. The Saltis held land outside their city, Q said, only
because 'Abbad allowed them to.

"The Saltiyya bought land from 'Abbad as a purchase; it's not
originally theirs."

The red spaces were marked over in yellow. I told them they
were behaving like 'Adwanis, who claim the whole Balga. Z took
the challenge.

"In reality, the Balga was mostly 'Abbadi land in the past. We were
lords of the Jordan Valley before the 'Adwan even came here, and
we've defeated them and expelled them from the Balga many times."

He reached for a yellow pencil and, despite my protests, set about
illustrating his point.

The map slips easily out of time and space. No one objects to the
current borders I've drawn on it; these seem not to interest people
much: "everything is fixed and divided." The urge is to throw

the map back in time, to fit an unseen history onto it, and always at some other tribe's expense. The map is not allowed to stand still. The past, as 'Adwanis or 'Abbadis perceive it, must be colored in, and no point of comparison, temporal or spatial, is acceptable to both sides. People insist on the right to oppose the other tribe's image, as if it were a provocation that must be answered.

In redrawing the map, tribesmen not only denied one another's claims to space, they also destroyed the map as a text. It ceased to be a cross-section of abstract time and space and became, instead, a colorful residue of stories and arguments. The tribal identities in question could not be inscribed on a single map—at least not in terms acceptable to members of all three groups—since time and space figured only as variables in a polemical exchange that defined three tribal names: 'Abbad, Salt, and 'Adwan.[3] *The polemic, in fact, was the only constant.*

Thus, it is not surprising that Dr. Ahmad 'Uwaydi al-'Abbadi's formidable work, *The Jordanian Tribes: Land, People, History* (1986), attains the length of 834 pages without the benefit of a single map. Indeed, the kind of historiography the tribal perspective makes possible is quite unlike the one endorsed by R.C. Collingwood at the head of this chapter. It cannot, for instance, be easily localized on calendars and Mercator grids. It seems designed to clash and to be inconsistent. It is bereft even of the minimal chronological and topographical *agreement* that Collingwood posed as a starting point. Agreement, after all, is the point at which tribal history comes to an end. It is the logic of taking sides, played out in contestable time and space, that gives the tribal Balga its peculiar shape.

---

3. A table showing the distribution of Balga villages among the area's three principal tribes (the 'Abbad, 'Adwan, and Saltiyya) appears in Abu Jaber (1989, 71). It is interesting to note that Abu Jaber belongs to a Saltiyya clan, and his land division errs by at least 20,000 hectares in favor of Salt. Two villages he lists as belonging to the Saltiyya (Um al-Dinanir and Salihi) actually belong to 'Adwanis. Abu Jaber derived his information, not surprisingly, from Salti sources. It probably did not occur to him to consult with 'Adwanis or 'Abbadis. Had he done so, his table might well have met the same fate as my tricolor map.

This cartographic land-grabbing has almost no foundation in *actual, on-going* territorial disputes. In the 1930s, the Jordanian government broke up the traditional system of collective land-holding (the *musha'*). Since then, tribal lands in the Balga have been registered in the names of individuals, and this was the case for agricultural holdings even in Turkish times. Today, property law is administered by the state, and territorial disputes between tribes, I was often told, no longer occur: "We don't fight over borders now; everything is fixed and divided." As units of land tenure and collective ownership, tribes have been legislated out of existence.

Periodizing Tribal Things

The willingness to take sides is rooted, tribesmen say, in *'asabiyya*, a term often translated as "group feeling" and "solidarity," but also as "clannishness" and "factionalism." *'Asabiyya* attaches to tribes and their sections; it is not, however, a quality inherent to any one of them in isolation. *'Asabiyya* can be expressed only in opposition to some other, equivalent group. It is classically segmentary, and most tribesmen would agree that *'asabiyya*, as Ibn Khaldun proposed centuries ago, "produces the ability to defend oneself, to offer opposition, to protect oneself, and to press one's claims. Whoever loses it is too weak to do any of these things" (1967, 111). A sense of waning *'asabiyya*—and an attendant loss of social order—is evident in Shaykh Salih al-'Abd al-Tawahia's description of the 'Abbad tribe.

'Abbad is divided into two sections: the Ijburiyya and the Ijrumiyya. We here are the Ijburiyya:

the Ziyadat,
the Rahamna,
the Bagur,

and when you cross south of Wadi Shu'ayb,

the Ijbara,
the Zyud,
and the Afgaha.

They say: "These are the Ijburiyya."
As for the Manasir and the people of 'Arda, who include

the Khatalin,
the Nu'aymat,
the Ghananim,
the Yasjin,
and all those people,

we call them the Ijrumiyya.

And 'Abbad . . . if there were a clash among us 'Abbadis, those Ijrumiyya would definitely unite as one faction against us, and we Ijburiyya would definitely unite as one faction against them. The ancestors were organized in these things; they had more structure than we do today. The young men don't know these names anymore.

[Shaykh Salih points an accusing finger at his sons, several of whom are listening to the interview. They laugh nervously. They have heard this complaint many times. One of the older sons offers his view.]

SON: This division . . . Ijrumiyya and Ijburiyya . . . this is something ancient. Does one say, in this day and age, "I am from the Ijburiyya?" No. We don't concern ourselves with such things. We say, "I am from the Afgaha or the Ziyadat, or I am an 'Abbadi." That's all. Only the old men know all the names.

SHAYKH SALIH: See how it is? To them, it's something ancient. But we are [still] the Ijburiyya, and 'Abbad is [still] two divisions: Ijburiyya and Ijrumiyya. If a clash were to happen, we would turn against each other.

If Shaykh Salih's discourse seemed outdated to his sons, it is because the local configuration of *'asabiyya* has obviously changed. The old alliances no longer fall mechanically into place. "The ancestors," Shaykh Salih reminds us, "had more structure than we do today." Nonetheless, the idea of opposition—the sense that tribesmen stand for and against one another in certain, almost inevitable ways—colors every aspect of the histories Shaykh Salih told me. There was no other idiom in which these histories, or the identities they defined, could be expressed. The Shaykh's sons may have forgotten ancient tribal names, but the tribal names they remembered were organized along segmentary lines the ancestors would immediately recognize.

The longevity of this political language is a source of embarrassment for educated Jordanians, who are taught that the world of tribal alliances belongs to a shrinking, archaic, and stigmatized political space. Everywhere, *'asabiyya* is denounced as simpleminded and corrosive, and my Bedouin friends urged me not to dwell on it in my book. As a political theory, they found *'asabiyya* inadequate to explain what it means to be tribal in Jordan; nor, I was told, could *'asabiyya* make sense of recent changes in Bedouin society. These are sound conclusions. When Balga tribesmen discuss tribal matters today, they speak and write in a political universe which is only partly of tribal devising. The larger discursive realm in which they construct their identities is dominated by the Hashemite state and its nationalist ideology. Dr. Ahmad 'Uwaydi al-'Abbadi's tribal history, it should be remembered, is called *The Jordanian Tribes*, a title that would have been impossible to conceive in 1920 but seemed only commonsensical in 1986.

Segmentary *'asabiyya* still plays an important role in tribal life, especially during elections, but this fact is often loudly denied before outsiders. When

I noted the obvious impact "clannishness" was having on the tactics of a certain candidate in Jordan's 1989 parliamentary campaigns, an 'Adwani friend sought to refine my view.

"You cannot call this strategy tribalism," he said. "It is tribalism *plus*. Tribalism *plus* Islam. Tribalism *plus* Democracy. Tribalism *plus* Government Reform. The candidate who builds his campaign on tribalism alone and nothing else with it: he is sure to be defeated on election day."

The mechanics by which these diverse ideologies—Islam, democracy, reform, and tribalism—might be combined were never spelled out explicitly. The men who believed in these ideological combinations were fascinated, however, by visions of *'asabiyya* that transcended genealogy and did not, for that reason, seem distinctly tribal to them. Young Bedouin, when they spoke to me as Jordanians, were careful to distance themselves from any metaphor (segmentary or otherwise) that portrayed tribespeople as *uniquely* divisive and a menace to the body politic. The following statement, made by an 'Adwani graduate student in political science, was meant to temper the combative rhetoric of old men and, more importantly, my own interest in it.

[When the Haj finished his account of the rivalry between the Kayid and Salih shaykhs, I asked him what had started it all. Abu Firas, who was impressed neither by my line of questioning nor by the Haj's answers, quickly intervened.]

ABU FIRAS: As for rivalry, before an external danger, internal rivalry ends. All the 'Adwan are brothers, but when one takes the shaykhdom from another, misunderstandings can occur. But when there's an external attack or danger to the family, then nothing stands between them; they are all one hand. You could explain it in terms of political parties, like those present in America or Britain. The Conservative and Labour parties have permanent differences between them; each one tries to control the government. In every nation in the world there are parties, and inside each party there are differences; everyone wants to lead the party. This love of power has been present since the time of tribes. It was passed on from tribes to parties, then it went from parties to states. Every state wants to lead the world order. There are conflicts among them just as there are conflicts among tribes. Wars, *'asabiyya*, rivalry, feuding: these are not just tribal things.

Whatever the merits of this evolutionary model, Abu Firas' attempt to normalize the talk of the elders serves only to accentuate what Abu Firas, in fact, believes: namely, that a realm of distinctly "tribal things" *does* exist, and it exists apart from (or beneath) the structures of party and state that have grown up around it. These distinctly tribal things—which should not be aired casually in front of foreign researchers—are transmitted to tribesmen through particular genealogical links. They include land, histories, reputations, and most important of all: names. To be a tribesman; to gain access to tribal things, one must be able to produce a local genealogy. And the point of origin to which Balga tribespeople seek vigorously to connect themselves is not simply an "apical ancestor," but, in a more general sense, *the political community in which the ancestors lived.*

This community is located in both past and present. It exists in speech and memory, *now* and *then*, and the place one's ancestors occupied in it can still determine where one lives, whom one marries, how one votes and why. Local Bedouin call this community by various names: the "age of shaykhs" (*zaman ash-shyukh*), the "age of wars" (*zaman al-harayib*), or the "age of the sword and lance" (*zaman as-sayf wa-l-rumih*). It is spread temporally between two great political upheavals: (1) the collapse of the Mihadia shaykhdom, which occurred shortly after the 'Adwan arrived in the Balga (perhaps in the late seventeenth century or the early eighteenth); and (2) the establishment of the Amirate of Transjordan in 1921. The vast body of poems, genealogies, and stories that make up 'Abbadi and 'Adwani history is confined largely to this period. Events that occurred before the "age of shaykhs" are seldom remembered; periods of tranquillity within the "age of shaykhs," when power was uncontested, tend not to have generated memorable events; and the arrival of the Hashemites made possible new forms of community and power (monarchic, Islamic, pan-Arab, colonial, anticolonial, and nationalist) that rendered tribal history insignificant, even subversive. Indeed, as a political system, the Jordanian state was committed to the elimination of the kinds of events on which tribal history is based: feuds, raiding, warfare, and tactical migration.

The "age of shaykhs" has gradually taken shape in opposition to the "age of government" (*zaman al-hakuma*) in which the Balga tribes now live. "There are," to repeat the storyteller's formula, "no shaykhs today." The world in which shaykhs prevailed belongs to the years before 1921. The separation of tribal and state domains was, in those days, a *spatial* reality. It survives today as a *temporal* distinction activated by historical speech. The following account, told by Haj Dayfullah Sayf Abu l-'Amash, an 'Adwani elder, shows just such a rhetorical activation at work. It also reveals, by extreme contrast, the incompatible principles (both moral and jural) on which tribe and state are founded.

The Story of Hola Basha

[Hola Basha was an Ottoman military governor stationed in Nablus, on the West Bank, during the 1850s and 1860s. He led occasional punitive expeditions against the Balga tribes. Once, he invited the shaykhs of the 'Adwan to a feast in Nablus, where he showered them with gifts and titles. Later that evening, he broke his pledge of security, arrested the shaykhs, and imprisoned them all. Hola Basha's audacity gained him a permanent place in local oral traditions. Now all Turkish Bashas of the period are dubbed, in storytelling contexts, Hola.]

Hola Basha heard that the 'Adwan were making war on the tribes around them; they were all slaughtering one another.

Hola Basha said: "I want to go reconcile them to each other. They are Muslims, and it is a sin for Muslims to slay one another."

He came and camped at Basha's Spring. He had one thousand cavalry with him. He came and gathered the tribes together. He sent invitations to the shaykhs, and they came.

He said: "I want you to make peace and be done with the Devil. It is Satan himself who has stirred you up and caused you to kill each other."

They all made pledges and pacts. Only 'Abbad and 'Adwan remained [in disagreement].

Hola Basha said: "Come, ya 'Adwan, and swear an oath, you and 'Abbad!"

They said: "We won't swear. 'Abbad slew one of our shaykhs. One named Fari'."

The Basha said: "And how many men did you slay in revenge?"

They said: "We slew 14 men, but that will not suffice for Fari'."

The Basha said: "How many will suffice?"

They said: "One hundred. One hundred will suffice for Fari'."

Hola Basha stood up in front of all the clans who had come from every direction: the Bani Sakhr, the Bani Hasan, the Saltiyya.

He said: "Bless the Prophet! Does not the blood of a Muslim suffice for the blood of a Muslim?"

The people were silent.

Then a man of the Bani Hasan tribe stood up and said: "Bless the Prophet! The blood of a Muslim does not suffice. How could it ever?"

The Basha said: "What? Wasn't the slain man a Muslim, and the slayer a Muslim?"

The Hasani said: "No. The 'Adwani was renowned from Zarga to Zarga. One hundred people ate off his platter. The 'Abbadi was known only to his wife. He stood guard over other men's gardens. Except for his wife, no one knew him. How can his death suffice as revenge?"

Hola Basha said: "Hang him! Hang that man!"

The man had a son, about twelve or thirteen years old. He saw them apprehend his father and put chains around his neck. They were getting ready to hang him. The boy started to cry.

Someone said to him: "Go! Go to Dablan!"

[The man just named is Dablan 'Ali Kayid al-Salih, a great 'Adwani warrior of the mid-nineteenth century.]

He went. He saw Dablan sleeping in his tent. Dablan had a long mustache which he tied into his braids. When the boy saw his likeness, he was afraid.

He said: "That's no human being. I don't know what that is."

He began to weep. Dablan heard his weeping. It woke him. His slave was standing next to him.

He said to the slave: "See who that crying child is."

The slave went out and saw a boy standing beside the tent, crying.

He came back and said: "By God, O Master, it's a boy. I don't know what he wants."

Dablan said: "Bring him here."

The slave brought him, and Dablan said to the boy: "What's with you?"

The boy said: "O my uncle, they want to hang my father."

Dablan said: "Why?"

The boy said: "Because he said this, that, and the other."

Dablan said: "Your father, what is his name?"

The boy said: "His name is Ishhada. Ishhada of the Bani Hasan."

[This man, I was later told, belonged to a Bani Hasan clan loyal to Dablan. Dablan was bound by honor to protect them.]

Dablan called out to the 'Adwan: "Rally round! Mount your horses and ride!"

The 'Adwan came riding down on the Turkish camp, and Dablan unsheathed his sword. Hola Basha was sitting in the shade of a sun screen erected in front of his tent. The 'Adwani horsemen knocked the sun screen down. It fell on the Basha's head. He was wearing a tarboosh. Dablan ran his sword through the tarboosh, just above his head.

He said: "Hey Piss Basha! Why is Ishhada in chains?"

The Basha said: "Pardon, O Dablan Basha. Forgive . . . ."

And before the words were out of his mouth, his head was rolling on the ground.

The 'Adwan fell upon them, and of the thousand Turkish troops, not one soldier remained. Slayman, father of my grandfather, rode after one of the officers who escaped to the north.

He said: "By God, if he's a Turk, I'll take the horse he's riding for myself."

Near the town of Suf, sure enough, he overtook the Turk, slew him, and took his horse.

My ancestor, Slayman, was present at that battle.

The tribesmen Haj Dayfullah describes in this story are ignorant of Islam and its legal conventions; or, what is worse, they willfully reject them. They do not admit the existence of abstract equality: one 'Adwani life is worth the blood of one hundred 'Abbadis. Their society, which lies outside government jurisdiction, is structured by the relations of alliance and enmity that prevail among specific tribes; and power is accorded, within that society, to men of renown who protect their clients, accomplish heroic deeds, and allow other people to live off their platters. And, most significant of all, *these heroic men are Haj Dayfullah's own ancestors.* Slayman, father of Abu l-'Amash, father of Sayf, father of Dayfullah, is the Haj's genealogical link to the events the story relates. This link turns mere narrative into a source of identity. It makes the story of Hola Basha part of all that tribal genealogy conveys: part of name, honor, and place. Haj Dayfullah's testimony belongs to a community—the descendants of Slayman al-'Adwan—that, because its genealogical structures grow forward and backward in time, continually reconstructs itself using historical materials rooted in an "age of shaykhs" from which Haj Dayfullah cannot, and does not wish to, disengage.

A Tribal Area in Flux

Bedouin are quick to admit, however, that the modern Balga is no longer a thoroughly tribal place. In 1990, the Balga had spent nearly seven decades under Hashemite rule. The "age of shaykhs" was an era only a handful of very old people had seen, and the associations it conjured up in the popular imagination bore all the markings of a more nationalistic age. In the following portrait of the shaykhly era, spoken by 'Abd al-Qadir al-'Assaf, an

'Adwani shaykh born and raised in the "age of government," the ideology of the Arab-Muslim state pervades every phrase.

> This country, Jordan, was ruled by the Ottoman Turks who rose up against Islam and took the Caliphate from the Arabs. The Turks destroyed this country. There was not a single mosque, not a single school in the land. The Balga was a haven for the bandit, for the man who slew his paternal cousin; he could flee here and be safe [from vengeance]. There were no people here; there was no state, nor was there a government in Jordan. There was no law, no order, only tribes and shaykhdoms. The Turks oppressed us. Even though the Turks were Muslims, they despised Islam. They despised the Arabs. Whoever was not a Turk, whose language was not Turkish, they considered him no better than a gypsy. Life was hard. Life was hard in the Arab country. The tribes slew each other, and the strong devoured the weak.

This description, which 'Abd al-Qadir (approximately sixty-five years old) offered with no sense of stigma, is simply an inverse image of the society in which he lives. Today, Jordan is ruled by descendants of the Arab caliphs. It is filled with mosques and schools in which the best Arabic is spoken. Law and order have been established throughout the land, Turkish oppression has ceased, and the once empty spaces are covered with villages and cities. Life is much easier in the Arab country, and the local tribes and shaykhdoms, as they existed in the Turkish period, have been radically transformed.

The land between the Zargas is divided now among three administrative units, the Amman, Zarga, and Balga governates, none of which is based on the old tribal alliances or traditional clan boundaries. Since the establishment of the Jordanian state in 1921, the Balga tribes have not, in any official sense, been considered Bedouin at all. The term "Bedouin" was a legal designation reserved by the British for certain camel-herding tribes of the eastern and southern deserts. These "official Bedouin" were administered under the Bedouin Control Laws, which were set up in 1936 and enforced by Gen. John Bagot Glubb's Arab Patrol. The Balga tribes, in contrast, were placed under civil law. The distinction persisted until 1976, when the special legal status of the Bedouin tribes was officially dissolved. The rationale for this legal separation had ostensibly been one of enlightened rule. In the words of Glubb Basha:

> nomadic tribes were not controlled by the government in Ottoman times or ever before them. The tribes had consequently made their own laws

which were administered by their own judges. For example, a man who killed a man of his own tribe was obliged to go into exile and live with another tribe (*jila*). He could not return to his tribe unless he paid compensation (*diya*). When a man killed another, all his relatives for five generations (*khamsa*) were involved. The *khamsa* also shared in the *diya*. In the ordinary criminal law amongst non-bedouins, the murderer only was responsible and could be imprisoned or executed, but his relatives to the fifth generation were not involved. Among nomadic tribes, if the murderer were imprisoned by the government, the family of the murdered man were not satisfied. They still tried to murder a relative of the murderer as revenge (*thar*). . . . To prevent further murders, the government therefore arranged for "diya" to be collected and paid to the family of the murdered man. The government tried gradually to bring the tribes to understand and obey the ordinary criminal law, but this usually took many years (al-ʿAbbadi 1986, 807–810).

The Balga Bedouin recognized the same laws with respect to murder and revenge; they applied them in exactly the same manner. But because they tilled the soil, Glubb categorized them as *fillahin*, "peasants." They were, Glubb writes, "all cultivators. Some lived in tents but they owned and cultivated land. They did not move into the desert. . . . I should not call [them] bedouins. They were Balgawiya and fellaheen [peasants], not nomadic" (al-ʿAbbadi 1986, 804, 812–813).

Caught up in the colonial romance that flourished between British officers and desert Bedouin, Glubb ignored the fact that the Balga tribes were migratory; he dismissed the weight of tribal law among them; and in calling them peasants, he badly misread the local geography of identity. The affront did not correspond to the lived reality of ʿAbbadis and ʿAdwanis, who continued to solve their disputes, informally at least, by legal means traditionally available to them. Tribal law has since worked its way firmly into civil jurisprudence, and most government judges in the Balga will decide a case involving tribesmen only after the dispute has been settled by customary means: for example, by calling a truce, appointing guarantors, assessing fines, and hosting a formal reconciliation. A security officer in the Jordan Valley, himself a member of the Bani Sakhr tribe, told me that "tribal laws are not official, but they are necessary to keep the peace, so we respect them."

Just as tribal law in the Balga has proven resilient, so too has tribal identity: that is, pride in being of Bedouin descent and, more important, an awareness of one's place in a specific tribe and lineage. Like tribal law, tribal identity has no official status in the Balga, and tribalism, with its potential for divisiveness, is actively discouraged in political life. The effects have been far-reaching. Tribes are not treated as official political bodies, and political organization along tribal lines is strongly discouraged. The old system in which a lineage headman (*mukhtar*) acted as local agent of the government has been all but replaced, in the Balga at least, by direct relations between individuals and their local municipality or district office. Tribal areas do not appear on government maps, and census figures on the Balga tribes, if they exist at all, are not available to the public. Official representations of the Balga's geography, its administration, and its population have been almost completely detribalized.[4]

In view of current Balga demography, this transformation is understandable. Most of the people who live in the Amman, Balga, and Zarga governates today, perhaps as many as 70 percent, are Palestinian. The Balga is not a tribal space for them, and "tribalism" ('asha'iriyya), to the extent they value it at all, stands for backwardness, poverty, and anti-Palestinian sentiment. My research among tribespeople was often criticized by Palestinians who saw little merit in the study of Bedouin society, and it was commonly believed by these critics that my only intention in undertaking such study was to make Jordan look primitive. Indeed, the rhetoric Palestinians deploy against tribespeople bears an uncanny resemblance to the Zionist rhetoric that, just a few miles to the west, has been effectively deployed against Palestinians themselves.

"How can you live with those people?" I was asked by an influential Palestinian businessman who, when I began my fieldwork, was building a posh country house—complete with swimming pool, landscaped gardens, and

---

4. The maps of Amman, Kerak, and Ma'an printed in 1949 by the Department of Lands and Surveys of Jordan bore dozens of tribal names, as if to suggest that tribes, like rivers, mountains, and cities, were objects on the natural landscape. The likelihood of tribal names appearing on such maps today is close to nil. Indeed, the removal of tribes from abstract space goes hand in hand with their removal from electoral politics. In the Balga, specific tribes are not recognized as electoral districts —how could they be if they are unmappable?—although tribal groups do sometimes hold informal caucuses to select candidates who will represent them in general elections.

Alongside the tribes' shadowy existence in political space, one finds gift shops in Amman filled with Bedouin kitsch: daggers, long-stemmed pipes, coffee-making paraphernalia, handwoven and embroidered textiles. Moreover, Bedouin soap operas appear regularly on Jordanian television. This blend of commercialization and political invisibility, Layne argues, "has been facilitated by the Jordanian government's policy over the last several decades to unify and integrate individual tribal identities into one broad tribal identity, that is, to promote Bedouinism in a general way rather than encouraging each tribe to maintain and develop its own individual identity" (1989, 35). This policy is the context in which tribal histories are now being written.

squash courts—on land he had recently purchased from 'Abbadis. A good deal of architectural investment was going toward the construction of high stone walls and a security system designed to keep his Bedouin neighbors at a safe distance from his miniature Eden. He was a stranger in 'Abbadi territory, a man resented and suspected for his wealth, and his inquiries into my presence there (a presence that seemed even stranger than his own) were rich in the usual overtones: curiosity, incredulity, disapproval, and concern for my safety.

"They are not important people, these Bedouin," he told me. "*We* are the ones who built this country. When we came here, there was no civilization. Only desert. The Bedouin had nothing. They were living like Red Indians. You should keep a close eye on them; they are still very close to savages."

The idea that tribespeople belong to a primitive era is sometimes understood more literally. When I talked about Bedouin village life with scholars at the American Institute for Oriental Research—most of whom were archaeologists—a Palestinian staff member interrupted, deeply offended, and said, "People do not live like that anymore." In 1990, it was entirely possible for this upper-class Palestinian, who had spent her entire life in Amman, to know little or nothing about the way ordinary Bedouin live.

Tribespeople returned this prejudice in full measure. I was often subjected to harangues against the ill-gotten wealth of Palestinians, their nefarious influence in government, their tight grip on the media and the professions, and, most important, their will to power, which revealed itself in Jordan's 1970–71 civil war: "They tried to kill our King. They wanted to rule over us, but we slaughtered them. Praise be to God." One man, a professor at a major Jordanian university, gave me a private lecture, complete with hand-drawn maps and time charts, demonstrating how the Palestinians, "since the days of Bani Israel," had been ruled by outsiders. An independent nation-state, he argued, was historically impossible for them. Besides, they had proven repeatedly "by their destructive actions" that they do not deserve a state of their own.

Despite the extremity of such rhetoric, local Bedouin could not pretend, nor did they ever claim, that Palestinians were a figment of my imagination. In 1990, there was too much evidence to the contrary. The 1967 Arab-Israeli War forced about 310,000 Palestinians refugees onto the East Bank, where they joined the 100,000 or more who had already settled there since Israel's creation in 1948. The low-grade antagonism that prevails between "native Jordanians" and "Palestinians" (many of whom were born and raised in Jordan) is often explained as a direct reaction to these massive human displacements. The level of tension between the two communities has always been responsive to the condition of Jordan's economy as well, and to external political factors, such as Israel's policies toward the Palestinians who live under its rule.

The ill will I observed in 1989–90 was certainly related to sluggish international oil markets that, over the course of the 1980s, had brought about (1) a decrease in the remittances sent home by the approximately 350,000 Jordanian citizens working in the Gulf and (2) a drop-off in the amount of financial aid offered to Jordan by the Gulf states (Satloff 1986). As the economy of the Hashemite Kingdom withered, competition for employment intensified, and old social resentments flourished. During the same period, Israel's Likud government embarked on a propaganda campaign that served only to heighten the distinction between East and West Bankers. As Layne reports:

> In the early 1980s Israeli Minister of Defense, Ariel Sharon, proposed that Jordan, with its Palestinian majority, was de facto a Palestinian state and the slogan "Jordan is Palestine" began to receive a good deal of attention in the Israeli and international press. Implicit in this argument was the assertion that Jordan was a country without a people or a history of its own. . . .
> The dramatic steps that King Hussein took in the summer of 1988 to sever Jordan's administrative links to the West Bank can be interpreted as an effort to solidify a clearly defined and easily recognizable Jordanian nation. In his televised speech of 31 July 1988 to explain his decision, King Hussein made explicit his assertion that, "Jordan is not Palestine." More recently, Marwan al-Kasim, chief of the royal court is quoted as saying, "From now on Jordan is Jordan and Palestine is Palestine" (*The New York Times*, 18 October 1988) (1989, 27–28).

The Bedouin I knew were well acquainted with these political and economic trends. Very few of them, however, thought their attitudes toward Palestinians had anything to do with the price of oil or the pronouncements of Ariel Sharon. Even the issue of demographic imbalance was not as salient as one might expect. Tribespeople realize that Palestinians outnumber them, but to what numerical degree they have only the vaguest conception. The quantitative dimensions of their own tribes, their own villages, oftentimes their own families, are simply unknown to them, and counting the membership of any group is thought to be an inherently political act. The resulting knowledge, I was told whenever I tried to obtain it, can be used to divide, stratify, tax, and control. These attitudes are by no means limited to Bedouin. The drawing of statistical distinctions between Jordanians and Palestinians—or between one Balga tribe and another—is also discouraged by the government, which insists that its citizens be indistinguishable in their loyalty to the Hashemite regime. "We are all," the official rhetoric goes, "Jordanians."

In the local dialogue between Palestinians and Bedouin, it is *qualitative* differences that rise to the surface, and these are handled in essentialist terms. Thus, local tribespeople are apt to cultivate a forthright disdain for the Palestinian "nature," which derives, it is said, from their mixed genealogical origins and peasant blood. The Palestinians, I was instructed over and again, are not true Arabs; they are not sons of the great Bedouin tribes of Arabia. They are peasants. Proof of this can be seen—once again, from a tribal vantage—in their stinginess, their ignorance of genealogical pedigrees, their political weakness, and the immodesty of their women. When necessary, more ingenious proofs can be fabricated. An ʿAbbadi tribesman who studied medicine in Yugoslavia told me, with unshakable conviction, that Palestinians are actually a European race. He based his conclusion on the similarities in Palestinian and Slavic folk costume, both of which feature colorful, intricately embroidered dresses. For most tribespeople, however, the assumption that Palestinians are of peasant stock explains virtually everything about them. When I pointed out the obvious—that most Palestinians are no longer peasants—I received the obvious in return: "Yes. But they are peasants by origin."[5]

The predominance of erstwhile "peasants" in the Balga is a demographic anomaly that most tribespeople find threatening. It signals the breakdown of a geographic pattern—and the political morality associated with it—that has kept remarkably stable for centuries: namely, that peasants reside in the areas north and west of the Balga, where the government is strong and the people are weak. The Bedouin, meanwhile, belong to the Balga and the areas south and east of it, where the government is weak and the people are strong. The historical disparity in power between Bedouin and peasants, which showed itself most completely in the absence of state control, is summed up nicely by the Rev. John Zeller, head of the Church Missionary Society in Jerusalem, who traveled extensively on the West Bank in the 1860s. "Bedawins," he writes,

> are by every peasant considered to be the greatest curse of the land. There is a proverb: "If a Bedawin is your guest, hide your clothes." All attempts on the part of the increasing agricultural population in Palestine to redeem

5. The importance Bedouin give to "blood" (*damm*) and "origins" (*asl*) in dealing with matters of identity, both individual and group, is discussed with unusual clarity in Abu-Lughod (1986, 39–49).

parts of the waste ground by extending their field from the hilly country into the plains, have hitherto been unsuccessful because it is easy for the Bedawins to destroy the crops of several villages in a few hours. Their ravages are not less fatal than those of the locusts, and the villages bordering on the plains which are allowed to gather in their harvest have invariably to submit to the visits of the Bedawins who never cease to claim the hospitality of the peasant til his whole harvest has been eaten up, is carried off, or is sold to his noble guest at a price fixed by him (Zeller 1866).

The dominance of the Balga tribes over their peasant neighbors, which is remembered today as a feature of the "age of shaykhs," is part of every Bedouin's genealogical heritage. Yet the bringing of tribal space under government jurisdiction—a process that has transpired within living memory and, in many ways, is not yet complete—has brought this dominance to an end. In so doing, it has opened to question much of what once stood for tribal identity. By the 1930s, it was already possible for Glubb Basha to propose, with all the might of government behind him, that the Balga tribes were not really Bedouin. By 1990, it was possible for Palestinian urbanites to claim that the people I lived and worked with were relics of another age or, more ominous still, that they no longer existed at all.

Among the Balga tribes, the sense that their own reality is slipping away provokes a vigorous reassertion, in the form of historical speech, of the world as it used to be. Speakers valorize this world; they criticize it as well. It was warlike, chaotic, unjust, and irreligious. Still, the very act of affirming one's genealogical connection to the past is an attempt to retain possession of it, prolong its reality, and impose it again on others.

THREE

Remembering
the Sword and Lance

And covenants without the sword are but words, and of no strength to secure a man at all. Therefore, . . . when he can do it safely, if there be no power erected, or not great enough for our security; every man will, and may lawfully rely on his own strength and art, for protection against all other men. And in all places where men have lived by small families, to rob and spoil one another has been a trade, and so far from being reputed against the law of nature that the greater spoils they gained, the greater was their honor, and men observed no other laws therein but the laws of honor; that is, to abstain from cruelty, leaving to men their lives and instruments of livelihood. And as small families did then, so now do cities and kingdoms.

Thomas Hobbes, *Leviathan*

If the Balga tribes are to keep hold of their history, prolong it, and impose it again on others, they must do so in competition (or collusion) with the state, a political institution that makes its own claims on the past. Tribespeople and nontribal observers describe this contest in markedly different terms, and the political language of the state, whether Ottoman, British, or Hashemite, has always been more widely understood. What follows is a brief account of power and resistance in the Balga, circa 1812–1923. It intermingles 'Abbadi, 'Adwani, and English sources in ways that illuminate the political language spoken by tribespeople. It is not a new history; nor is it a corrective to histories already written. It is a commentary on enduring images of government and community: *conflicting* images that, now more than ever, shape the way tribespeople speak and write about the past.

The Rights of Brotherhood:
Power and Protection in the Age of Shaykhs

Shaykh Sa'ud Abu l-'Amash gave me the following account of his great grandfather's political career:

> When Slayman al-Shibli was leader of the 'Adwan, he expanded
> their lands, the lands they ruled. In the area of Jabal 'Ajlun and

the mountains before you, [Shaykh Saʿud points northward] there is a mountain called Najda's Peak. The name used to be Jabal Agraʿ; they changed the name. In history and even in land deeds the name Najda's Peak is written. Slayman's slave woman was called Najda [and the mountain was named after her]. This slave woman made the rounds of that area; she went to the shaykhs and the headmen.

She said: "Bring the taxes you owe, and I will send them to my master, Slayman."

Slayman extended ʿAdwani rule and pacified widespread lands, even the Hauran was paying *khawa* ("brotherhood") to the ʿAdwan. What we call *khawa* is like a tax. The *khawa* is the right of brotherhood between the people who become brothers. I give you the *khawa* because you protect me, or so you won't attack me. The two: protection from another tribe or other people who want to raid you; and the second aspect, that you don't attack the one who pays the tax. They call this *khawa*. Like taxes. Shaykh Slayman took *khawa* all the way to Syria for the ʿAdwan.

In the days of Shaykh Slayman al-ʿAdwan (ca. 1850), the people of ʿAjlun were sedentary farmers, as many of them still are today, and the *khawa* they gave the ʿAdwan consisted of a cash payment, a percentage of their staples, or both.[1] The exact mode of payment is seldom discussed nowadays—most people do not remember it—but this tendency to overlook tributary protocol is easily explained. The ʿAdwan have not taken *khawa* from ʿAjlun in well over a century. The Ottomans forbade the custom when Rashid Basha, Wali of Damascus, conquered the Balga in 1867, effectively bringing the era of ʿAdwani regional dominance to an end.

When the Rev. F.A. Klein toured the Balga a year after the Turkish invasion, Dhiyab al-ʿAdwan, paramount shaykh of the Balga tribes, was being held prisoner in Nablus, and his son, ʿAli Dhiyab, had sought refuge in the camp of Fandi al-Fayiz, paramount shaykh of the Bani Sakhr, inveterate enemies of the ʿAdwan. Klein spent several days as a guest in the same Bani Sakhr encampment, during which time he broke bread with tribesmen and women who, even in defeat, were regarded as "giants in the earth."

> In the course of the afternoon, I had several visitors to my tent, among them one of whose courage & remarkable skill in fighting I heard so much

---

1. The substance of *khawa* payments is often summed up nowadays in the following expression: *"ath-thiniyya wa-l-ʿakka al-mamliyya"* (the two-year-old goat and the ʿakka coin). The ʿakka, known in the West as the "asper," was a silver coin traded in Ottoman domains (Abu Jaber 1989, 25).

& whose acquaintance I was very anxious to make *viz*: 'Ali the son of Diab who had lately fought the government troops like a lion. He is now staying here under the protection of Fendi; the government is very anxious to get him into its hands but according to the Bedouin laws of hospitality Scheich Fendi would rather deliver up his own son than a guest to whom he has promised his protection. . . . [The following day] I went to pay a visit to *Ali Diab* who received me very kindly in his large tent where breakfast, consisting of boiled milk with sugar, butter and bread was served. His mother, Schaka, an old courageous looking woman also made her appearance with a long pipe in her mouth, and sat down conversing with the men who all treated her with great respect. This woman is quite famous and I was told many nice stories relating to her courage and chivalrous spirit. She used f.i. to go after the men in time of war with a long stick and a sponge at its end which was dipped in black colour and applied to the cloak of any men who turned back. By this sign she knew them afterwards when they assembled in the Scheich's tent and put them to shame and sent them away without giving them the customary cup of coffee till they repented & promised to behave better in future (Klein 1868).

No doubt Shiga (a.k.a. Schaka) applied the same skills of persuasion to her own son, 'Ali, and his protector, Shaykh Fandi al-Fayiz. A final attempt to throw off the Turks and collect *khawa* north of the Zarga River occurred in 1869, when the two shaykhs raided the town of Ramtha, intent on extracting two years of unpaid "brotherhood." The raid was successful, but the Turks sent an expeditionary force in pursuit of the shaykhs, who were eventually brought to heel. Abu Jaber (1989), drawing on diplomatic correspondence of the period, writes:

> Once the expedition was about to attack the 'Adwan, their chief, 'Ali Dhiyab, requested *aman* (safe conduct) which was granted on condition of the payment of 25,000 piastres, an amount representing both the expenses of the expedition and the value of the property taken at al-Ramtha. On submitting to the conditions, 'Ali was allowed to enter the camp. He gave as his reasons for the attack on al-Ramtha that the news of the war between Turkey and Greece, of the continued insurrection of Crete necessitating the withdrawal of troops from Syria and the wali's departure for Constantinople, had led both him and his ally, Fandi, to the belief that it was the most favourable time for obtaining their respective ends. His object was to rescue his father, who was a prisoner at Nablus, and Fandi's object was to re-establish his authority by levying the khawa (1989, 38).

Neither object was attained. Shaykh Fandi, who had fled south after Ali Dhiyab's surrender, was forced to choose between starvation and submission. He opted for "safe conduct," which was granted in exchange for 200,000 piastres and the relinquishment into government custody of one of his own sons, who would be kept hostage as a guarantee of Fandi's good behavior. On 2 June 1869 the Balga tribes forswore all rights to gather *khawa* from peasant villages and, in the presence of well-armed Syrian forces, ʿAli Dhiyab and Fandi al-Fayiz offered their allegiance to Rashid Basha, Wali of Damascus. "Thereafter," Abu Jaber concludes, "the shaykhs of Bani Sakhr and al-ʿAdwan alike found it more expedient to co-operate with the government, even becoming officials in its immediate service" (1989, 39). The ʿAdwan have chosen to forget this episode. It is not part of the oral histories they recount. In fact, I never heard the demise of *khawa* placed specifically in time. Tribesmen say only that *khawa* ended "when the government came" (*luma lafat al-hukuma*), though which government, Turkish or British, seems not to register as a significant detail. In other respects, however, the memory of *khawa* in the days before government remains surprisingly vivid. After a century's lapse, ʿAdwani men can still relate in detail which villages owed them *khawa*, which shaykhs collected it, and how the sums were divided among the principal ʿAdwani clans and their client tribes.

In Bedouin definition, *khawa* was a form of government based on brotherly inequality. When contrasting the tribal political order to that of the state, tribespeople sometimes use the term *himaya*, which means "protection" or "protectorate," as opposed to *hukm*, which means "judgment" or "rule." The protection tribesmen owed to peasants was an explicitly contractual matter. One had to pay for it, and despite the brotherly jargon, there was no pretense of fraternal amity with *fillahin*. The ʿAdwan assert without the slightest qualm—actually, with conspicuous pride—that *khawa* was imposed on peasants "against their will" (*ghasban ʿanhum*): "We were stronger; they could not refuse."

As stories in coming chapters will show, having taken *khawa* is a sign of strength; having paid it is proof of weakness. Thus, my ʿAdwani hosts were pleased when I read them the following passage from John Burckhardt's *Travels in Syria and the Holy Land* (1822): "[the Bani Sakhr] approached the Belka, and obtained from the Adouan, who were in possession of the excellent pasturage of this country, permission to feed their cattle here, on paying a small annual tribute" (1822, 368). The ʿAdwanis immediately recognized this tribute as *khawa*, and several men demanded photocopies of the passage. The rivalry between the Bani Sakhr and the ʿAdwan is notorious— ʿAdwani history is a litany of the wars between them—and the ʿAdwan now possessed "written proof" that the Skhur had once been subject to them. The find was a literary coup of sorts. I mentioned it, with utter politesse, to a gathering of Skhur, who vociferously denied it: "This Burckhardt got his

information from the 'Adwan. The Skhur never pay *khawa* to anyone!"
They then told me how the Bani Sakhr had expelled the 'Adwan from the
Balga, completely destroying them. They were mollified, and somewhat relieved, when I told them that what they said was also reported in Burckhardt's book. Several men demanded photocopies of the passage; ironically,
it was on the same page the 'Adwanis had clamored for.

The politics of *khawa*—a politics that exists now only in historical discourse—still shapes the contours of Bedouin identity. A well-known incident from 'Abbadi history, as told by Shaykh Salih al-'Abd of the Tawahia
clan, illustrates the range of social distinctions the remembrance of *khawa*
can engender today.

The Origins of the 'Abbad-'Adwan War

[Shaykh Salih waves his arm toward the north.]

[The people of] Jabal 'Ajlun, yonder—the 'Adwan imposed *khawa*
on them, on the peasants. They call them "peasants" (*fillahin*). The
'Adwan imposed *khawa* on them. They call them "our brothers"
because they protect them from 'Abbad and other people.

[Shaykh Salih moves freely between past and present tense.]

They gave *khawa* to the 'Adwan every year. They collected it like
the government collects money. Tribes, *khawa*: there was no state
except this. They gave them *khawa*, the peasants did. The peasants
are the people of the stone house. They don't ride horses or thrust
with the sword and lance. The Bedouin, people of the desert, lorded
over the peasant . . . because the peasant doesn't migrate, he doesn't
camp down. He just sits in his house. The weak gives *khawa* [to the
strong].

'Abbad came. They were camping down in the Jordan Valley,
Shaykh Ibn Khatlan and his Arabs. 'Abbad came to raid the peasants
of Jabal 'Ajlun. They came and took all their livestock: sheep, goats,
cattle. They took them [from the peasants] and divided them up.

The peasants went to Ibn 'Adwan and said: "You became our
brother, and you protect us from people. 'Abbad took our livestock."

[Here Shaykh Salih offers an explanatory note on events yet
to come. The 'Adwan will use this incident to break up the alliance
between 'Abbad and the tribes of Salt.]

Between us, between 'Abbad and the tribes of Salt, there were
no problems. We and the Saltiyya are friends. They are not 'Abbadis, no, but we are united. As for Ibn 'Adwan, that's another
matter. Ibn Adwan is a master of discord (*sahib fitna*). The 'Adwan

are good; their origins are good; they have the shaykhdom. We can't backstab them. They are shaykhs of the Balga, but they are not shaykhs over us: 'Abbad.

The peasants went to Ibn 'Adwan and said this [about the 'Abbadi raid] and he said: "You know that no one can return your livestock except the Saltiyya."

[He said this] so there would be discord between 'Abbad and Salt [who were allied against him.] That way Ibn 'Adwan could stay in the Jordan Valley. Because of the [opposition of the] Saltiyya, he could not endure in the valley; if it were up to Salt, the 'Adwan wouldn't survive.

[The 'Adwan taxed the people of Salt, the only urban population in the Balga at that time, and the two groups had already fought a series of wars in which famous 'Adwani shaykhs were killed.]

For the tribes of Salt, it was a disgrace that Ibn 'Adwan was still in the Jordan Valley. He had been expelled once before to Jerusalem, and 'Abbad had pushed him across the Jordan to Kawkab al-Howa.

Ibn 'Adwan said [to the peasants]: "No one can return your livestock but the Saltiyya. Go to the Saltiyya."

The peasants went to Salt.

They said: "O brothers, the 'Abbadis are your friends, and we enter before you and God, asking you to return our livestock."

The Saltiyya are called "the white gathering." Their clothes are clean, washed. But those 'Abbadis were wild; they didn't know anything but horses, slaughter, stealing, and fighting.

[Shaykh Salih's sons begin to laugh.]

It's the truth, by God. But at least they weren't cannibals.

[More laughter].

They'd kill a man just like they'd slaughter a chicken. There was no one to say, "it's a sin."

The Saltiyya came all dressed up [in white robes], with weapons and rifles. They descended on 'Abbad, on Ibn Khatlan, shaykh of all the 'Abbadi shaykhs who loose and bind [disputing parties].

The Saltiyya said: "O 'Abbad, you must return the livestock."

Ibn Khatlan said: "By God, O Saltiyya, forgive us. By God, everyone took his share and left. We can't collect them now. And that son of 'Adwan just wants confusion. Let's stay friends, neighbors, in-laws, like we are."

The Saltiyya said: "No. Those peasants have entered before us, [seeking our help], and you must return [what is theirs]."

'Abbad said: "Look. There are four guest houses in Salt. Each guest house has one hundred goats [which can be given to the peasants]. Let's forget this 'Adwani discord and stay together."

The Saltiyya said: "By God, there will be a return!"

They wanted to return the livestock by force of the rod. So 'Abbad rose up against them in the tents and seized all their weapons, like firewood. I heard this from the tongue of my father. My grandfather was present. He was there with them. He told my father and my father told me. This is not a far-off thing.

Ibn Khatlan started yelling, "Weapons without wounds!" which means seize their weapons, but don't slaughter them. Why? Because he didn't want to cause hostilities. The whole Balga would pour down on us. The Saltiyya got up and left without their weapons. The 'Abbadis waited for a week, hoping there would be no hostilities.

Ibn Khatlan said: "Return their rifles."

And they returned the weapons to the Saltiyya.

When they returned the weapons, the Saltiyya went to Ibn 'Adwan and said: "O Son of 'Adwan, we want to slaughter 'Abbad. We want to unleash the Balga tribes, all of them."

He said: "In what direction?"

The Saltiyya said: "Against 'Abbad!"

This was the discord Ibn 'Adwan wanted. He was happy.

The peasants then disappear from the narrative. The Balga tribes are un-leashed and, thereafter, all characters are Bedouin at war. The conflict itself is brought on by the moral obligations of *khawa*—which the 'Adwan ne-glect, and the tribes of Salt embrace—but the 'Ajluni peasants and 'Abbadi Bedouin, as political actors, are defined only by the essential qualities that make *khawa* necessary. Shaykh Salih al-'Abd assumes that Bedouin are wild, strong, warlike, highly mobile, and fully capable of exploiting or offering protection to the weak. The people of 'Ajlun, by contrast, are stationary, docile, impotent, and constantly in need of protection from the strong.

The implicit difference in all these traits is one of "governability." Ac-cording to the stereotype, peasants submit to state or tribal authority—even welcome it at times—whereas Bedouin resist any form of subordination. This image of free tribes and governed peasants, which became ever more obsolete as the twentieth century approached, was nonetheless accurate for much of the eighteenth and nineteenth centuries. Burckhardt's notes on the areas just north of the Balga, made during his travels of 1812, record a peasantry subject to the depredations of Bedouin shaykhs and Ottoman authorities alike; in fact, tribe and state joined forces in gathering taxes from villagers. When Burckhardt crossed south of the Zarga River, however, he entered a region that contributed nothing to the flow of Ottoman tribute. In 1812, the Balga tribes were at war; the Bani Sakhr had just pushed the 'Adwan into Jabal 'Ajlun; and the town of Salt, finally loosed from the 'Adwani grip, was prosperous and independent.

The local Bedouin were no strangers to the fiscal cravings of the Turks. Damascus levied a yearly tax on their livestock and dairy products, but without a permanent military occupation of Salt and its immediate environs, that sum was impossible to collect (Burckhardt 1822, 369). When the Turks finally marched into Salt in 1867, arrears were gathered, fines assessed, and new taxes imposed. In 1869, Turkish authorities invited the British consul in Damascus, W. Wood, on a tour of the newly pacified Balga, during which they explained the reasons for their invasion.

Salt is the second town of the Kaza or sub-Governorate of the Belka, but the first in a military point of view and may be considered as the eastern key to Palestine. Its position is strong as it is built on the declivities of a hill, which is almost isolated from the mountains that surround it. A castle on the summit commands the town and the ravines on all sides. The inhabitants are chiefly engaged in agriculture and are computed at 3,300 souls, of whom about 2,500 are Mohammedans and the rest Christians, mostly of the Greek Orthodox Church. Previous to Rachid Pasha's expedition in 1867, Salt was in the possession of the Adwan Bedouins, a small but courageous independent tribe. An inscription records that it was held 150 years by the family of Diab El Adwan, their Shaykh. Diab levied oppressive taxes on the inhabitants and offered a ready asylum to all deserters from the Ottoman army and to all the murderers and robbers in Palestine. Raids into the rich districts of Tiberius and Nablous were rendered easy by the safe retreat the marauders found in Salt. So long as their stronghold was in the hands of the Bedouins it was a matter of impossibility to maintain security in the Hauran and in the richest districts of Palestine.

The valley of the Jordan had been completely abandoned. The peasants in the district of Nablous, Tiberius and the Hauran were obliged to till the ground with their guns loaded. During the harvest season they seldom reaped the fruits of their labour, for, no sooner was the corn ready for the sickle than the Bedouins swept over the plains and extorted the khoue or protection tax. This tax was so heavy that the peasantry were kept in constant misery: in one instance the Beni Sakhr obtained 200,000 piastres from one village which contributes 40,000 piastres [to the government] for tithes. When the peasantry in their distress called upon the government either to afford them protection against such exactions or to relieve them from paying taxes, the authorities sent inefficient expeditions which served only to draw the vengeance of the Bedouins on the unfortunate villages. It was with a view to put an end to this state of things, which was causing deficits in the revenue and was deepening a feeling of contempt for a government which allows marauders to exercise sovereign rights in its territory, that Rachid Pasha determined on the capture of this stronghold [the Balga town of Salt] as a first step (Wood 1869).

In local Bedouin tradition, the facts are remembered differently: the security of Palestine has nothing to do with the arrival of the Turks; the importance of Salt as a regional stronghold is never mentioned; and the Balga itself is described as an unknown land, fractured by tribal in-fighting, of little interest to the Turks or any other government. In the following account, told to me by Shaykh Sa'ud Abu l-'Amash al-'Adwan, the Ottoman sultan sends his armies to the Balga only after three local shaykhs persuade him to do so.

The Coming of the Turks

Shaykh Dhiyab al-'Adwan grew old and [his son] 'Ali began to grow powerful. Who rose up and contested the shaykhdom of 'Ali and Dhiyab? Ahmad Abu 'Arabi.

This is based on the talk of the old men and the elders.

Abu 'Arabi went to Istanbul, he and Husayn al-Subih of the Salti shaykhs, ancestor of the Fawa'ir, a well-known man, courageous, a leader . . . and Kayid Ibn Khatlan, shaykh of the Khatalin, shaykh of 'Abbad, the father of all 'Abbad: Ibn Khatlan. They went straight to Istanbul, to the Ottoman sultan. The Ottomans called him sultan, even though he was just a king. They called him sultan.

Abu 'Arabi said to the sultan: "I'll let you rule the land. We want a state. Our land is ruined. There is no security, only tribes and raids and slaughter and theft and plunder. The powerful devours the weak. And those are the shaykhs of the land. I brought them with me."

He gave them a state and the *faraman* (royal decree).

The sultan said: "Who [among you three] is the [paramount] shaykh?"

They said: "The shaykh is that one, Abu 'Arabi Ibn 'Adwan."

The sultan said: "This *faraman* proclaims that the Shaykh of the State and the Arabs, the Judge, Shaykh of the Tribes, Judge in Matters of Government, whose opinion the State will consider, is Ahmad Abu 'Arabi. And you two who came here with him—Kayid Ibn Khatlan and Husayn al-Subih—will be recognized as well."

ANDREW: Where was Dhiyab at that time? Wasn't he shaykh of the 'Adwan?

SA'UD: Abu 'Arabi was attacking Dhiyab! Let me finish the story. He didn't bring Dhiyab [to Istanbul]; he opposed him. They were set against each other, struggling. Nothing personal. It was a matter of leadership, of who would become shaykh, the leader. There were no other tensions. They were bone and blood. Cousins by genealogy. [But] they both wanted to be the leader.

Each one said: "I'm the leader, and Allah is lord."

So how did Abu 'Arabi make his plan, he and those shaykhs?

He said: "If we brought the government, the Turks, and they sided with us and gave us the decree, it would mean that the rule and the power would be ours. Tribal power and the power of the state. We would rule in the name of the state."

They received the *faraman* from the Turkish sultan. Ahmad Abu 'Arabi returned with the state at his side and the shaykhs who had gone with him. 'Ali and Dhiyab were defeated. They fled to the south, to the Bani Hamida tribe, and became fugitives under the protection of Fandi al-Fayiz, shaykh of the Skhur.

Abu 'Arabi was victorious. He was made judge in Salt. The people say, those who talk about him, that he was judge in Salt. He judged in the name of the state, like an administrative judge, the judge of a district. He judged this, he brought in so-and-so, imprisoned so-and-so, searched out so-and-so; he did this and that. He did what he wanted. The state was at his command; the army was at his disposal. What he wanted to do, he did.

It is hard to find a loss of tribal sovereignty in these events, and Shaykh Sa'ud would be the last to admit such an outcome. The story, as he tells it, concerns a shaykhly coup d'état, and the Turks figure only as nondescript accomplices. The Ottoman sultan, 'Abd al-'Aziz, who is really "just a king," goes nameless, while the illustrious Rashid Pasha, who led the Army of Arabistan against Salt, receives no mention at all. It is the troika of Balga shaykhs, led by Ahmad Abu 'Arabi, that emerges victorious.

When Abu 'Arabi died two years after the Turkish invasion, Fandi al-Fayiz, Shaykh of the Bani Sakhr and protector of the dispossessed 'Ali Dhiyab, petitioned the Wali of Damascus on behalf of Dhiyab al-'Adwan, eventually producing a reconciliation between the parties. Dhiyab agreed to step down as shaykh, whereupon he was released from prison; his son, 'Ali, was officially instated as Shaykh of the Balga Shaykhs; and 'Ali's sister, 'Alia, was married to Sattam, the son of Fandi. The pact between the 'Adwan, the Bani Sakhr, and the state—all of whom are portrayed, in oral tradition, as equal parties to the negotiations—was thereby made complete: "The Turks gave 'Ali Dhiyab the *faraman*, and he ruled the Balga once again; only he was stronger than before."

This ability to disregard the Ottoman presence, to diminish and talk over it, is a constant feature of 'Adwani oral history. The "age of the Turks" (*zaman al-atrak*) is remembered today as having belonged to "the age of shaykhs," not the "age of government," and, judging from the stories people tell now, a disregard for Turkish sovereignty continued—in sporadic revolts, highway robbery, tax evasion, and the murder of Turkish soldiers—until the collapse of the Ottoman Empire in 1918. It is this tradition of dissent that prevails in colloquial memory. The following account, told by Haj 'Arif Abu l-'Amash, is typical of the way the 'Adwan, former overlords and takers of *khawa*, remember their own experience of taxation.

The Story of the Widow

In earlier times, the state came to us: Turkey. And the shaykh then was Abu 'Arabi, shaykh of the area around here [that is, the area around the highland village of Salihi], and the Turkish soldiers were with him.

Abu l-'Amash was in the Jordan Valley. He lived there [part of the year], and the Arabs [who were his clients] were living here with the rest of us [in Salihi]. So Abu 'Arabi came around [when Abu l-'Amash was away], and the Turkish army came with him. They came to collect the taxes, the head tax on livestock which the government had started.

They came first to a poor widow. This widow was a *gasira* (a protected person) of Abu l-'Amash. Just like you.

[Haj 'Arif points to me.]

There's no one who can harass you when we, the 'Amamsha, are around. Yes.

They came to this widow to collect the tax.

She said: "O my brother, I don't have it."

Abu 'Arabi said: "Confiscate her goats. Confiscate them!"

The soldiers confiscated the goats. The widow began to cry. She was a woman. She had no money. She started crying.

They [the tax collectors] dismounted near the tent of one of our relatives named Hindawi. They dismounted at his place, and he brought a goat and slaughtered it for them for dinner. So they ate dinner and the confiscated goats were there; there were soldiers standing near them, near the tent.

The next morning, Abu l-'Amash returned to Salihi with his supplies and his horses, with all his kin and the others who followed him. The little boys and girls saw them coming. They saw them approaching from afar . . . riding horses. The children ran to greet them because they knew Abu l-'Amash would bring sweets. And sure enough, Abu l-'Amash gave sweets and candies to all the children who greeted him.

There's a kinswoman of Abu l-'Amash. Her name is Loza.

She said to him: "O my uncle, you are dear to us. You came from the valley, from another land, and brought sweets to the hungry children, to the family of our uncle, to the family of our father, to the family of our brother. You gave to them all. By God, O my uncle, our *gasira* is crying."

Abu l-'Amash said: "Why is she crying?"

Loza said: "By God, Abu 'Arabi confiscated her goats; he wants her taxes, and she doesn't have it, that widow. And that's her, crying."

Abu l-'Amash was enraged. He was enraged because they'd come and made his *gasira* weep.

He tied his horse up at his tent and moved on toward the tent where Abu 'Arabi and the state were sitting.

Abu l-'Amash said: "Peace be upon you."

Abu 'Arabi said: "And upon you be peace."

Abu l-'Amash said: "Abu 'Arabi!"

He said: "Yes?"

He said: "God curse you!"

He said: "Why?"

He said: "How can you confiscate our neighbor's goats? If she owed a dinar or two, why didn't you pay it from your own purse?"

He said: "This is a matter of state."

He said: "God curse your father and the state!"

Abu l-'Amash pulled his sword. The state, they fled. Abu l-'Amash was a terror. He threatened Abu 'Arabi with his sword.

Abu l-'Amash said: "Bring me those ledgers [tax records] you have with you."

Abu 'Arabi said: "I'm coming."

He said: "Put them in the fire. Hurry up! Cursed of God is your father and this state you've brought us. You brought an invasion. You haven't brought a state; you brought invaders to raid us."

Abu l-'Amash broke the state and smashed Abu 'Arabi. Everyone fled from him.

That's the story of the widow. Yes indeed.

A New White Page: The Age of Government Begins

The power to break the state and smash its minions came to a decisive end in 1923, the year of the ill-fated 'Adwani revolt against the new, British-backed regime of the Amir 'Abdullah. The state of Transjordan was a political configuration quite unlike anything the Balga tribes had seen before. It combined the moral authority of the Hashemites—proponents of Arab nationalism and descendants of the Prophet—with the military brawn of Christian Europe. The Balga tribes were unable, and many of them were unwilling, to resist this new ideological and coercive partnership. The following story, told by Haj 'Arif Abu l-'Amash, recounts the series of events that finally brought the "age of shaykhs" to an end.

The 'Adwani Revolt

Turkey was defeated. The British joined sides with Husayn, Sharif Husayn of the Hijaz, and they defeated Turkey. Turkey was an oppressor. The Turks dispossessed the Arabs. All the lands they acquired, they gave to the Turkmans; they gave to the Circassians; they gave to the Chechens.[2]

So all the people rose up against Turkey and its oppression. The British and the Arab Amirs started a revolt. The Great Arab Revolt. And Turkey was defeated.

The Amir 'Abdullah came to Jordan and became Amir.

As for the tribes, each tribe in Jordan wanted to make its own government. There was chaos, and every man said: "I want to be shaykh!"

So they consulted each other and said: "Why not let 'Abdullah be our leader. He comes from the House of God [i.e., from Mecca]. He is a prophet. Let him be Amir over us."

He was an Amir at that time, not a king.

So 'Abdullah became Amir.

---

2. The Haj refers here to the Muslim tribal peoples of the Caucasus who were displaced by the czar's armies in the late nineteenth century. They were resettled throughout the Ottoman Empire; many of them were brought to the Balga.

The British, who was their representative at that time? A man named Peake Basha. He came to Jordan heavily armed, with a company of horsemen, all of them officers. He stayed for a while, then left.

He went to the High Commissioner in Palestine and said: "Those people are all desert Arabs in the throes of ignorance. I don't know how to live among them."

Another British officer, Abu Hunayk,[3] said: "I want to go see."

So Abu Hunayk came to this land and studied it. Just like you. "Who is shaykh of this tribe?" "Who is shaykh of that tribe?" And so on . . . until he knew Jordan.

He returned to the High Commissioner and said: "If you grant me two requests, I will rule them all."

The High Commissioner said: "What are the two requests?"

Abu Hunayk said: "Give me military backing and a blank check. If I want one million, 100 million, or 1,000 million, then I'm free to have it. I'll rule the land."

The High Commissioner said: "Go. You have a blank check. Use it in our interests."

So Abu Hunayk started to buy the shaykhs. That one he gave a truck full of sugar. That one he gave a truck full of flour; that one a truck full of coffee; that one a truck full of rice. He even gave the old women tobacco for their pipes. Until finally he ruled all the shaykhs of Jordan. He made an army for himself, the Desert Patrol, which exists to this very day. It was an army he alone controlled, and the English ruled the land.

Shaykh Sultan al-ʿAdwan and his son Majid were shaykhs of the Balga at that time. They were wealthy, and the English could not buy them.

They went to the Amir ʿAbdullah and said: "Ya ʿAbdullah, this Britain is placing taxes on our land. They've imposed a head tax on our livestock. A goat costs us five girsh; a cow costs us twenty girsh. Will this oppression never end? Turkish oppression has ceased. Now is British oppression its replacement?"

3. Abu Hunayk ("Little Jaw") is the Arabic nickname of John Bagot Glubb, Peake's second in command, who established the Arab Patrol in 1930 and served as commander of the Arab Legion from 1939 until 1956. Unlike Peake, whose long tenure in Jordan (1921–39) has already faded in the Haj's memory, Glubb Basha is still fondly remembered for his knowledge of Bedouin custom.

The entire Balga rose up. Their opinion was that of Sultan and Majid.

They began to say: "The British brought 'Abdullah here. Who consulted with us? Are we not the people of this country? Do we not have our own leaders? We want a Majidi state (*dola majidiyya*) [i.e., a state ruled by Majid al-'Adwan]."

They marched in protest to Amman. Why? Because of the British. The Amir 'Abdullah came to speak to them.

Sultan and Majid said to him: "You are Britain's representative. You are the key that opens and closes them. You made an alliance with them. Tell them not to oppress us."

Sultan's slave stood up in the tent, unsheathed his sword, and said: "Ya 'Abdullah, give Sultan his rights or I'll cut your head off!"

The others pulled the slave away, and 'Abdullah told Sultan and Majid that he would do what they said. But nothing happened; nothing changed.

Sultan gathered the Balga tribes and marched toward Amman. The British troops rallied. They had airplanes, tanks, armored cars. Great Britain she was called. What weapons did the tribes have? Primitive weapons: swords, pistols, rifles. Those were the people's weapons.

Sayil al-Shahwan, a shaykh of the 'Ajarma tribe, was one of Sultan's horsemen. He took part in the revolt. He rode up against a British armored car and struck it with his sword. The English shot him with a machine gun. The tribes did not know how to fight against these weapons. They scattered in all directions. Sultan and Majid fled to Jabal al-Druze [in Syria] and became fugitives under the protection of Sultan al-Atrash, Shaykh of the Druze. The government came and confiscated their wealth.

The Amir 'Abdullah said: "The 'Adwan will not be granted clemency. The cause of this discord is the 'Adwan."

Husayn heard about this. Husayn, the father of 'Abdullah and King of the Hijaz. He heard about the disturbances in Jordan, so he came. He gathered all the shaykhs of the land. They came and greeted him.

After they greeted him, Husayn said to Mithgal al-Fayiz, Shaykh of the Bani Sakhr: "Who is shaykh of the shaykhs?"

Mithgal said: "By God, ya Husayn, every tribe has its shaykh. But there is only one shaykh of shaykhs."

Husayn said: "Who is he?"

Mithgal said: "Ibn 'Adwan."

Husayn said: "Where is Ibn 'Adwan?"

Mithgal said: "By God, there was a misunderstanding between him and 'Abdullah, so he went off to Jabal al-Druze."

Husayn said: "Is he truly shaykh of the shaykhs?"

Mithgal said: "By God, he is shaykh of the shaykhs, and every tribe has its shaykh."

After they had feasted, the shaykhs left, and only 'Abdullah and his father remained.

Husayn said: "Ya 'Abdullah."

'Abdullah said: "Yes?"

Husayn said: "God curse you!"

'Abdullah said: "Why?"

Husayn said: "In the Hijaz you're known as 'The Pygmy Sharif.'[4] That's your name in the Hijaz. Your counsel is worth nothing."

'Abdullah said: "Why?"

Husayn said: "The 'Adwan have become your enemies, but the people say they are shaykhs of the shaykhs. You're leading the horse by its tail, not by the reins. You don't understand things. You're the one who's caused this to happen. I won't leave here until you've brought the 'Adwan back."

'Abdullah said: "Ibn 'Adwan put a sword to my neck and threatened to cut off my head!"

Husayn said: "The sword is his companion. Even had he wounded you, the sword is his companion. You don't understand things!"

So 'Abdullah sent for Sultan and Majid, and they came. They and Sultan al-Atrash, Shaykh of the Druze.

The Amir's men said: "The 'Adwan have arrived."

'Abdullah said: "Tell them to leave their weapons outside."

The Amir's men said to the 'Adwan: "Leave your weapons here, enter, and greet the Amir 'Abdullah and King Husayn."

Sultan said: "We don't want to greet them without our weapons.

---

4. The nickname Shurayf ("Little Sharif") was pasted on 'Abdullah at the Battle of Turaba in 1918, where the Arab Hijazi Forces he led—a detachment of over 1,300 soldiers—were wiped out in a nighttime attack by the Wahhabi armies of Ibn Sa'ud. 'Abdullah and a handful of officers managed to escape. The Wahhabi troops reportedly shouted "Ya Shurayf! Ya Shurayf!" as 'Abdullah fled into darkness (see Wilson 1987 and Shwadran 1959).

We don't lay down our weapons. Our weapons, we don't relinquish. We don't want your greetings!"

The Amir's men returned and said: "They won't come in without their weapons."

Husayn said: "Let them enter with their weapons."

They entered and greeted Husayn and 'Abdullah.

Husayn said: "What's this between you and 'Abdullah, ya Sultan?"

Sultan said: "By God, 'Abdullah is beloved and a friend to us. We received him when he came to Jordan. We received him warmly. We made him Amir over us. Amir of Jordan. He is the key that opens the British government. The government does what he advises, but he doesn't respect our requests."

Husayn said: "Why, ya 'Abdullah?"

'Abdullah said: "Because the 'Adwan want to kill me and become Amirs in my place. They want to be kings."

Husayn said: "Because they were kings in this land before you, man! Those 'Adwan were here before you. You came here yesterday. They were before you. I want you to break bread with them and open a new page. A new, white page. And when they make requests of the British, you relay those requests. Those are the people. The people! Those are the citizens of your Amirate. We ended Turkish oppression. Do you want to impose British oppression on them? Isn't that a sin?"

They said: "We will open a new page."

They worked out a pact, an alliance, that they would not attack one another again. The 'Adwan would be leaders of the tribes. 'Abdullah would control the government, the laws, and relations with other states. But the shaykhdom and the tribal leadership belonged to the 'Adwan.

Sultan, Majid, and 'Abdullah swore on the sword and the Qur'an that they were brothers, and they are brothers to this very day. The descendants of 'Abdullah control the government, and the 'Adwan are shaykhs of the Balga shaykhs. That talk still holds. Nothing in it has changed.

Since these oaths were sworn in 1923, change has been relentless, and Haj 'Arif, in other moods, was eager to criticize the hollowness of all modern claims to shaykhliness. The story of the 'Adwani Revolt was the last of the many tales he told me. After Sultan and Majid professed their loyalty to

Plate 8. The new order, 1923. Sir Herbert Samuel, High Commissioner of Palestine, stands in the middle. He is flanked by T.E. Lawrence (on the left) and the Amir 'Abdullah (on the right). Shaykh Majid al-'Adwan (extreme right) is no longer the center of political gravity. Here, he is barely within the frame. Photograph courtesy of the American Colony Hotel, Jerusalem.

the Amir 'Abdullah's government, they no longer produced the kind of history worth recording on tape. Their political universe was altered beyond its capacity to generate heroic events. Uncontested power, political agreement, and submission are not the stuff of legend. If "nothing changed" after 1923, it is because suddenly, in the land of domesticated shaykhs over which Sultan and Majid presided, *nothing more could happen* (plate 8).

Today, the old tribal territories are filled with peasants; the state has tightened its grip on ungoverned space; Islam and education have brought the knowledge of good and evil, law and order; and the Balga tribes continue to tell stories that, as the "age of shaykhs" sinks further back in time, are beginning to look ever more historical. These radical transformations are enabling some tribespeople to sense the perishability of their oral traditions for the first time. They are also inspiring new attempts to represent spoken history in written forms. These experimental projects—which explore a *continuity* with the past that tribespeople still perceive despite the change that surrounds them—are described by their authors in an idiom of personal struggle. As we shall see in the chapters that follow, the object of this struggle is the desire to distinguish two types of authority: oral and textual.

FOUR

Documentation
and the War of Words

We all know objective truth is not obtainable, that when some event occurs we shall have a multiplicity of subjective truths which we assess and then fabulate into history, into some God-eyed version of what "really" happened. This God-eyed version is a fake—a charming, impossible fake, like those medieval paintings which show all the stages of Christ's Passion happening simultaneously in different parts of the picture. But while we know this, we must still believe that objective truth is obtainable; or we must believe that it is 99 per cent obtainable; or if we can't believe this we must believe that 43 per cent objective truth is better than 41 per cent. We must do so, because if we don't we're lost, we fall into beguiling relativity, we value one liar's version as much as another liar's, we throw up our hands at the puzzle of it all, we admit that the victor has the right not just to the spoils but also to the truth. (Whose truth do we prefer, by the way, the victor's or the victim's? Are pride and compassion greater distorters than shame and fear?)

Julian Barnes, *A History of the World in 10 1/2 Chapters*

The History of Things Heard and Said

The oral histories I recorded from Balga tribespeople were based almost entirely on things heard and said, not on things seen or read. Before the 1970s, there was no indigenous tradition of history writing among the ʿAbbad and ʿAdwan tribes.[1] The "age of shaykhs" survived only in the talk of old men; indeed, it was the talk of old men that, from 1921 onwards, created the age as a distinct historical period. The emergence of a literate audience capable of *reading* Bedouin history—what the denizens of Amman's publishing houses refer to as the "market" for tribal literature—is a recent development in Jordan. According to Arthur Day,

1. If oral histories *were* written down by Balga Bedouin in the Turkish period or during the early days of the Emirate, no ʿAbbadi or ʿAdwani I met in 1989–90 had ever seen copies of these texts. Tribal poetry was occasionally written down in the past, genealogies were sometimes recorded, and legal documents were stored away in trunks, but the idea that such materials could be assembled and used to construct written accounts of the past seems to be—at least in the Balga—a product of the modern era.

95

A most revealing set of figures about educational advances was compiled by the Jordanian Statistical Bureau in 1974, when the generation from the early days of the state was still alive. It showed that men born in 1909 or before had an 18 percent literacy rate, while 5 percent of women of the same age bracket were literate. Men born in 1935–39 had a literacy rate of 50 percent; women, 30 percent. Those born in 1960–62, however, had a literacy rate of 83 percent for boys and 80 percent for girls. As a current measure of educational progress in 1974, 98 percent of boys and 93 percent of girls of ten years of age were in school in that year. By 1983, 820,000 Jordanians, one-third of the total population, were students (1986, 68).

Yet today, when literacy rates are higher still, the "age of shaykhs" remains a topic most Bedouin are content simply to talk about. Its persistent orality, its inability (or unwillingness) to be textualized, render it marginal to the "age of government" in which it evolved. The Hashemite era, which stands in Jordan for the *modern* era, entails a different historicity: one that owes its legitimacy not to the talk of old men, but to the powerful blend of literate religiosity, dynastic ideology, and Arab nationalism that prevails in Jordan's popular media and public schools. It was perhaps inevitable that educated Bedouin, when confronted with "bookish conceptions of history" (Eickelman 1977), would begin to see the spokenness of oral tradition as an impediment to be overcome by textuality.

For Muhammad Hamdan, an 'Adwani tribesman who has spent several years compiling material for his own history of the 'Adwan, the paucity of the written record is both an obstacle to his work and, at the same time, the most compelling reason to engage in it. Muhammad defines his task as the "documentation" (*tasjil*) of spoken tradition, and like other writers of tribal history, he imagines himself not as an *author*, but rather as a conservator and scribe.

> ANDREW: Have you discovered anyone else like yourself who has tried to write a history of the 'Adwan, now or in the past?
>
> MUHAMMAD: No. I am the only one doing this work. Do you know of anyone other than me?
>
> ANDREW: No. Not among the 'Adwan. People speak only of you.
>
> MUHAMMAD: See how things are? As for the past: in the Turkish period, before the Hashemite state, the people were illiterate. Even the 'Adwani shaykhs, who were powerful and sophisticated, most of them could not read or write. So we have no documents from that time, no memoirs. What shaykh ever wrote his memoirs? And the history of the entire 'Adwan tribe takes more effort than a memoir. The only documents I've found were pro-

duced by foreigners: the books of travelers, for example. Or Peake Basha's book, which has a summary of 'Adwani history and a genealogical tree. His information is incomplete of course, and there are errors in it . . .

ANDREW: And you collect old photographs as well. What . . .

MUHAMMAD: Yes. And those too are from outside. Look. If you want the details of 'Adwani history, you must sit with the elders and listen to their talk, then record it. That is my method. See? I create documents, and this is important work because when these old men die, their sons will forget their poems and stories; . . . not all of them, but each generation forgets until a century from now, What is left? That is the problem. We 'Adwan do not write our own history. Everything is talk and oral recollections (*haki wa sawalif*).

If history writing renders oral history problematic, it is equally true that the oral tradition isolates, and sometimes obscures, the written records that Balga tribesmen, even in the "age of shaykhs," occasionally left behind. The grave of the renowned warrior-poet, Shaykh Nimr Ibn 'Adwan (d. 1823), bears an epitaph in verse that, alone among Nimr's many works, has existed as a written text for nearly two centuries. When I first met Muhammad Hamdan in 1989, he had already transcribed dozens of Nimr's poems—most of them recited by old men, for whom tribal poetry is a verbal art—but despite his relentless search for documents, Muhammad had not yet recorded the inscription on Nimr's grave. Like most 'Adwanis, he knew that Nimr's tomb stood in Yajuz, and that a poem, dictated by the dying shaykh, had been carved into the headstone, perhaps with a date as well. The epitaph, I was often told, went something like this:

Death has taken you from your own country to another
The worm of the grave turns in your eyes,
And the eyes of the people watch over your campsites

I met no 'Adwani, however, who had gone to Nimr's grave to confirm whether these words were actually written there, or even to determine the year of the illustrious shaykh's death. In fact, this brief epitaph was among the small number of Nimr's poems that the ninety-year-old Haj Khalaf al-Fahd, a literate man, a living encyclopedia of 'Adwani lore, and the fourth lineal descendant of Nimr, could *not* recite. After a tour de force recording session in which the Haj delivered, almost effortlessly, hundreds of lines of Nimr's verse, I asked him to recite Nimr's final work.

I don't remember it. They say: "Death takes you from your
land / The worm of the grave turns in your eyes / the eyes of the
people dwell in your campsites." Like that. I'm forgetting a word.

[The Haj pauses and blesses the Prophet under his breath, to
jog his memory.]

It's just two words [i.e., it is not a long poem]. It's written on his
grave, in Yajuz; engraved in stone. I've seen it. But I can't remember
it now. You'll have to go there and record it. It's not far away.

I found the general ignorance of this epitaph as a text odd, and yet it
seemed consistent with the emphasis Muhammad placed on gathering *oral*
sources, and with his belief, which was widely shared among tribespeople,
that documentary evidence, if it existed at all, would be located somewhere
outside the local tradition. Only when I showed Muhammad the description of Nimr's grave published in Selah Merrill's *East of Jordan* (1881), did
he decide to accompany me to Yajuz.

Near . . . our camp is a kind of family burying-ground. There are not
many graves, however, and only one that is at all prominent. This is the
tomb of Nimr Adwan, the grandfather of Qoblan [who, in turn, became the
grandfather of Haj Khalaf al-Fahd]. This is well built, with an inscription
upon it in Arabic, and appears to be cared for by the descendants of the
deceased with more than usual attention. The year is given on Sheikh
Nimr's tomb as follows, the scrawl meaning *sanat*, or year, and the
characters indicating the date:

That is, 1238, which corresponds to A.D. 1823. Above it is some poetry, and
on the other end of the tomb is the mark of the Adwan tribe, as follows:

(Merrill 1881, 275)

Merrill's account, written in 1876, was of little use to us as a guide. The grave-
yard has long since filled up with prominent tombs, and none of them is especially well kept. Nimr's grave, now indistinguishable from the rest, lay
knee-deep in wildflowers and spring weeds, its headstone badly weathered.
The epitaph was still legible in the afternoon sunlight, when the raised let-
ters were made crisp by a thin, shadowy outline. Unfortunately, our visit

Plate 9. Muhammad Hamdan (in checkered head scarf) tries to decipher the epitaph on Nimr's grave.

fell on a cloudy day, and Nimr's poem, except during brief intervals of sunshine, was barely decipherable.

As Muhammad and I puzzled over the inscription, several men from a nearby household came to see what we were doing. Soon, everyone was disputing various readings of the text, cursing the lack of sunlight, and caressing the words in hopes of *feeling* their proper shape (plate 9). After much debate, Muhammad and I wrote the following version in our notebooks:

> The Year
> 1238
> Death has taken you from your country
> And fate has placed another house on your campsite
> The worm of the grave turns in your eyes
> And the eyes of the people watch over your land
> May the All-Merciful cover the sins of Nimr Ibn ʿAdwan.[2]

The locals from Yajuz (who were not ʿAdwanis) asked for a copy of the verse, which Muhammad quickly scribbled out. By way of thanks, one of them re-

---

2. The Arabic version of the epitaph, as best we could decipher it, is provided in Appendix A.

ferred us to an old man who, it was said, knew exactly how the epitaph read: "He can verify what you have written." Muhammad then walked over to his car, returned with a can of black paint, and before anyone could say a word, he sprayed a new epitaph around the vault of the tomb. It read simply, glaringly, and at a perfect right angle:

The deceased, Nimr Ibn 'Adwan

"Now," Muhammad said, obviously pleased with his work, "people will know who is buried here."

This peculiar homage to Nimr left everyone in a state of amazement. We stared uncomfortably at the paint, wondering out loud if we had witnessed an act of reverence or desecration. Muhammad, for his part, was unapologetic and eager to move on; he wanted to visit the old man who could "authenticate" our version of the epitaph. We were returning, much too quickly I thought, to the "talk of the elders" (*sawalif al-kubar*), to the very discourse Nimr's epitaph had finally allowed us to escape. The knowledgeable old man, it turned out, had never read the inscription; he was illiterate, and the poem he recited was simpler, less elegant, than the one Muhammad had taken from the headstone. No one, in fact, possessed a version as complete as our own; still, the knowledge we had gained—a firm date and some long-forgotten lines of verse—was insignificant when compared to the wealth of material on Nimr that Muhammad had already compiled from the oral tradition.

My preoccupation with Nimr's epitaph was, of course, a cultural oddity in its own right. If Muhammad had expected the elders to authenticate a written text, I had expected a written text to authenticate the talk of old men. My "search for the historical Nimr" was based on notions of textual historicity that were out of place.

"If you want documents from the age of shaykhs," Muhammad instructed me, "go to the archives in London."

Nimr's epitaph, which had stood 167 years in the Balga, seemed as far away as the Public Records Office. The extent of the text's displacement became vividly clear to me several months later. While rummaging through archives in England, I discovered that Nimr's epitaph had been recorded by a German traveler, Heinrich Frauenberger, in 1893 (see Spoer 1923).[3]

---

3. Frauenberger's German translation is as follows:

Der Tod führt dich aus deinen Lagerstätten fort;
Und das Schicksal führt dich von einem Haus zum anderen;
Und die Würmer des Grabes weiden in deinen Augen;
Und die Augen der Ueberlebenden schauen in deine Lagerstätten.

Muhammad was right: Nimr's poem had found its place, beside other such documents, in London.

Increasing the Confusion: The Interplay of Speaking and Writing

When Muhammad Hamdan creates historical texts, he is dependent on, and answerable to, the oral traditions he records. And yet the process of *writing a history*, that is, of constructing an account of the past that incorporates these newly made texts, demands a method different from, and often at odds with, the conventions of spoken history. The limits of this new method are still being debated among tribesmen, and even the (apparently) modest work of scribes and conservators is apt to become sensitive.

In the following exchange, an 'Adwani friend, Abu Firas, helps me explain my research to Haj Mahmud al-Talab Abu 'Arabi, from whom we hope to record stories about Ahmad Abu 'Arabi, the 'Adwani shaykh who "brought the Turks" to the Balga in 1867. Though Abu Firas and I both stress the importance of creating accurate historical texts, it is obvious that the next step, *writing a history*, means something different to each of us. Haj Mahmud, irritated by our mixed signals, suggests that we might find history elsewhere.

> ANDREW: Ya Haj, I want to record stories about your grandfather, Abu 'Arabi. The famous stories, like . . . when he went to Istanbul and brought the Turkish government to the Balga. I want to record this on tape, then write it word for word, just as you spoke it, without mistakes, God willing.
>
> [The Haj is uncertain. He picks up my tape recorder, looks it over judiciously, then returns it to its place.]
>
> HAJ MAHMUD: Do you want [information] from the time of Abu 'Arabi on?
>
> ANDREW: Well . . . from the time when he brought the government.
>
> HAJ MAHMUD: I don't know the year he went or how long he ruled in the Balga . . .
>
> ANDREW: That's not a problem. No one knows dates. I just want the stories you heard from your father, the stories you tell your sons.
>
> ABU FIRAS: We don't want years; we want details about him. Details that you know. You saw Abu 'Arabi. Didn't you see Abu 'Arabi?

HAJ: Me? No. He died long before me. I can't talk to you [about him].

[The Haj is reluctant to be recorded, but his reason for keeping silent is not convincing. Clan history is typically about men who died long ago, about remote times and unseen events. Abu Firas presses on.]

ABU FIRAS: Ya Haj, we all pass on a tradition (*kullina nangul nagal*). You transmit something that's been passed on [to you] and . . .

HAJ: Yes. Yes. We transmit but we didn't actually see.

ABU FIRAS: Even Talab, your father . . .

HAJ: He was in his mother's womb when Abu 'Arabi [his father] died.

[Here, the Haj introduces another disclaimer: namely, that his knowledge is not received directly from Abu 'Arabi, since Talab never his father or heard his stories. His knowledge is indirect. But Abu Firas learned much of his own history indirectly, from his uncle, Haj 'Arif, and he still is not convinced.]

ABU FIRAS: I'm telling you. Even Talab transmitted what had been passed on to him.

HAJ: Yes, indeed. Drink your tea! Turn off that tape recorder and drink tea for a while.

[Another round of hot tea is poured, and the Haj greets us as we sip:

"Welcome!"

"And welcome to you, ya Haj."

"The tea is delicious."

"There's strength in it."

"God give you strength."

For Haj Mahmud, the tea ritual is a pleasant escape from interrogation, but Abu Firas, who is tense and impatient by nature, finds the polite formulas annoying. He wants to get on with the recording. He signals me, and I flip the switch.]

ABU FIRAS: Ya Haj, Andrew has sat with other men and recorded. He went to Haj 'Arif, and the Haj talked until we were bored with the amount he told us.

HAJ: Yes.

ABU FIRAS: If you go to Haj 'Arif and ask him "Such-and-Such," he will respond like so: "Yes. They were. They went. They came." With plenty of details.

HAJ: By God, this man knows history then. 'Arif told him everything. We don't want to increase the confusion: "He said this, another man said that." And in the end, all is confusion.

[The Haj assumes that an account combining his knowledge with Haj 'Arif's would be confused and contradictory. The two accounts are unique; each comes from a different source. What is gained by comparing them? And what is our true agenda in recording: to compare and judge?]

ABU FIRAS: This is not increasing the confusion.

HAJ: Well then?

ABU FIRAS: We just want the talk, ya Haj. The talk. Because this man knows how to write, and he wants to transmit what you say. Do you know why, ya Haj?

HAJ: Why?

ABU FIRAS: Because the history you tell is not written down. The people don't know about it. No one knows a thing about it. He wants to take this talk from you in an organized fashion. Do you know what I mean? Like this:

"Abu Arabi went to Turkey and brought the Turks. The Turkish Army came to the Balga with him. They made him shaykh of the state and shaykh of the Arabs. He judged this and that. He did this and that. He divided the land among the people like so. Abu 'Arabi gave this region to this person or that person, and so on."

This is the history that is not written. If you tell it to him, he will know it and write it. It is known to you and me, but when tomorrow comes . . .

[Now the Haj is angry. Abu Firas is telling him what to say and how to say it—behavior which is disrespectful. The Haj should impart knowledge on his own terms. He should not be instructed by a younger man.]

HAJ: Ya Abu Firas! One thing at a time! This won't do. Don't pressure me.

[Feeling somewhat responsible for the situation (and still hoping to record narratives), I introduce a more positive tone.]

ANDREW: Ya Haj, talk to us as you wish. I just want to record from you because you are close to Abu 'Arabi and the people say you know stories about him. If we record your stories, then people in the future will remember Abu 'Arabi.

ABU FIRAS: Yes. For example, my father Manna' died, God have mercy on him. He went. He died. Didn't all his history die with him?

HAJ: But his history should have been passed from him to you, ya Abu Firas.

ABU FIRAS: Wasn't Abu 'Arabi's history passed on to you?

HAJ: Did I ever see Abu 'Arabi? I'm just sitting here transmitting what's been passed on to me. But you . . . when you sat with the old man, your father, you did not . . .

ABU FIRAS: I didn't pay attention.

HAJ: You didn't pay attention.

ABU FIRAS: I didn't, I'm telling you. The fault is mine. I'm disappointed in myself. I'm at fault and I've failed. The right thing is clear to me now. The right thing is this: *You must take history from its proper source.* Tomorrow, when I am seventy or eighty years old, the sons of my sons, if something like this happened, they would consider me history. I would be their reference. Why? Because I lived through the '50s, '60s, '70s, '80s, and '90s. If I live to the year 2000, long after your time (God preserve you), . . .

HAJ: God prolong your life, ya Abu Firas.

ABU FIRAS: . . . I will become history to them because I witnessed the second half of the twentieth century.

[Agreed: Haj Mahmud is the proper source. But hasn't he already argued that the line of transmission, in his case, is indirect and therefore weakened? The argument is going in circles. I opt for another approach.]

ANDREW: Ya Haj, I'm not recording only from you. I'm trying to record from many people because Abu 'Arabi was a famous shaykh, and all the 'Adwanis have something to say about him. So I record from many people, and in that way I can develop a more complete picture.

[Abu Firas throws a distressed look my way. Clearly, he doubts my comment was helpful.]

ABU FIRAS: Do you know why, Haj?

ANDREW: The truth is not in one place. I have to listen to many voices, then I can see the differences and . . .

[Abu Firas cuts me off, hoping to prevent further damage.]

ABU FIRAS: Yes. Then he will write "Mahmud al-Talab Abu 'Arabi." When he writes his research, he writes the source below: "From the stories of the Haj Mahmud al-Talab." You are the reference. Why? First, because you are one of Abu 'Arabi's grandchildren. You have received his history. Whatever Andrew takes from Haj 'Arif, he must return to what you say. If he goes to the

Jordan Valley and records from the Nimr and Salih clans, he must return in the end to what you say, as far as Abu 'Arabi is concerned.

HAJ: He goes from one old man to another and records so he can see what's right [i.e., the correct version].

[I am about to agree. Yes, I listen to many voices on the assumption that a more complete account is somehow more accurate. But Abu Firas senses another meaning in the Haj's words. He quickly extends his arm across my chest, as if to restrain me, and gives his own answer.]

ABU FIRAS: No. Not so he can see what's right. He has to consider *you* right.

[The Haj knows better. First, Abu Firas tells him how to speak, then I diminish his authority further by suggesting that his voice, the voice of Abu 'Arabi's own grandson, will be made equivalent to all others. The Haj brings the conversation to a halt in the customary manner: by invoking the name of the Prophet.]

HAJ: Bless the Prophet!

ABU FIRAS: Blessings be on him and peace.

[Now only the Haj can speak. He begins, as one does after such dramatic pauses, by greeting his listener.]

HAJ: Ya Abu Firas, an evening of goodness to you.

ABU FIRAS: And an evening of light to you, ya Haj.

HAJ: When my grandfather died, my father was in his mother's womb. I can pass along only what I saw and heard. The old men . . . those who were older than I . . . I would go to them and take their words and sayings . . .

ABU FIRAS: Yes! We just want what you've heard or what you know, and after that we'll take from the others.

HAJ: Yes. I used to love to ask the old men, "What happened in your time?" For example, "When Sultan al-'Adwan rose up against the Amir 'Abdullah and wanted to expel him from the Balga, how long had the Turks been gone?" Some said ten years, others said fifteen. That's old men for you.

[The Haj has just completed his argument. Not only has he disqualified himself, he now discounts the talk of the elders as well. We have lost him, but Abu Firas goes on.]

ABU FIRAS: The old men don't know dates. I know dates. That talk happened in 1923. When I tell you the date, I say 1923. Why? Because there were historians at that time, like Andrew here, who wrote and recorded. But the old men just say: "It happened in the

year of the ice." Or: "It came to pass when we were camped in the
Jordan Valley." But that history is in books—the time of the Amir
'Abdullah—and the 'Adwani Revolution is written about.

HAJ: No. I mean something else. You claim the old men say
"this happened in the year of the ice." Well, that's not worth
considering. But as far as you are concerned, the old men can't
verify the history they speak. So the reliable history, where is it?
I'll tell you. If you sit with X the Salti, he'll give you history. By
God, he'll bore you to death. He has a book from Lebanon on the
history of the tribes and . . .

[Once again: documents from outside the local oral tradition.
These are reliable in a way that plain talk is not.]

ABU FIRAS: The Salti is a liar. Have you seen his book?

HAJ: Yes, but I haven't read it.

ABU FIRAS: His lies are thicker than that book. He says the
'Adwan are descended from Abu l-'Amash. What kind of talk is
that? Was Abu l-'Amash the father of 'Adwan? Is he among the
first ancestors?

HAJ: No.

ABU FIRAS: Abu l-'Amash is my grandfather's name, but there
is no one else in the 'Adwan tribe with that name. No one ever! And
that's the proof that the Salti's information, even if it's written in a
book, is all lies.

[The book is subordinated to the spoken tradition. Now everything has been rejected. Nothing more can be said. The Haj has
won.]

HAJ: Well, let's not increase the confusion. You must eat with
us today. Let's eat now, and maybe later we can record stories.
Welcome. Welcome to you all.

Conversations of this sort were a common prelude to recording, but rarely
did speakers take up positions as bewildering and seemingly inconsistent as
these. Abu Firas, an advocate of written history, defends the oral tradition
against Haj Mahmud's appeal to texts. The Haj, an elder who speaks with authority on matters of 'Adwani history, suggests that reliable history is contained in a book he has not read. And I, in the role of conservator and scribe,
espouse a method that, to the Haj's mind, seeks out "confusion" (*harj*), then
openly embraces it. I will compare his testimony to that of other men, analyze the differences, and subject all versions to critical scrutiny. My relativism
made no sense to Haj Mahmud; indeed, it granted his testimony only the au-

thority I (as analyst) could bestow on it. But Abu Firas' response, which gave all authority back to the Haj, came as a shock to me: "He has to return to you, Haj. You have received Abu ʿArabi's history. *He has to consider you correct.*"

Like most ʿAdwanis, Abu Firas envisions a tribal history composed of "proper sources," in which each speaker passes on a tradition received from a chain of fathers and grandfathers. Thus, members of the Nimr clan should relate the history of Nimr and the generations of his sons; members of the Salih clan should tell of Salih and his male descendants; and members of the Abu ʿArabi clan, represented by Haj Mahmud, should do likewise. A history of this sort mimics the lineage structure of the tribe, and writing it consists of four basic procedures: collecting testimony from reliable elders, textualizing it, weeding out whatever is boldly offensive (either to the author or to the intended audience), and arranging what remains in genealogical form. This method of tribal historiography—which appears time and again in the works of Ahmad ʿUwaydi al-ʿAbbadi (1984, 1986), Ahmad Abu Khusa (1989), Ruks al-ʿUzayzi (1984), and others—treats history as a family tradition of memory and received historical speech. The technique is made difficult, however, by the fact that bringing oral testimony together and converting it into documentary evidence leads unavoidably to a comparative perspective in which the propriety of sources is suddenly much harder to define. According to Jack Goody (1977, 44), the literary mode

> makes one aware of the differences, forces one to consider contradiction, makes one conscious of the "rules" of argument . . . . Why? Because when an utterance is put in writing it can be inspected in much greater detail, in its parts as well as in its whole, backwards as well as forwards, out of context as well as in its setting; in other words it can be subjected to a quite different type of scrutiny and critique than is possible with purely verbal communication. Speech is no longer tied to an "occasion"; it becomes timeless. Nor is it attached to a person; on paper, it becomes more abstract, more depersonalized (1977, 44).

Among the Balga tribes, "difference" and "contradiction" have always been the substance of historical talk. The history of the Abu ʿArabi clan, for example, is told in opposition to other ʿAdwani clans. The "proper sources" speak not only *for* themselves, as Abu Firas imagines, but *against* one another. The history Haj Mahmud received from his father is inherently contentious. It concerns betrayal, war, and banishment (see chapters 3 and 5), and any attempt to combine it with other accounts, or even to juxtapose them in a single text, would provoke the very "confusion" Haj Mahmud hoped to avoid by silence.

An entry from my field notes, written just after our interview with Haj Mahmud ended, shows that the Haj's silence was, in fact, a prudent choice: apparently, he knew the nature of his audience—or, at least, the nature of Abu Firas—far better than I did.

> The limits on Abu Firas' theory of "proper sources" became painfully clear after our meal. At last, Haj Mahmud relaxed and began to talk about events from Abu 'Arabi's life. I was eager to record, but Abu Firas kept interrupting the Haj, throwing in contradictory details, stock phrases, and fragments of poetry he'd received from *his* "proper source": Haj 'Arif. Each narrative collapsed under the weight of picayune disputes; the tape recorder was constantly flipped on and off as Abu Firas and Haj Mahmud tried to negotiate an acceptable version. By the end of our eight-hour visit, I'd succeeded only in recording the genealogy of the Abu 'Arabi clan; the spirit was not good, and Abu Firas was exasperated: "You can't write a history based on this talk! It is impossible. Just write what Haj 'Arif tells you and forget the rest."

The textualization of clan histories does not force Bedouin to "consider contradiction" (Goody 1977) as if for the first time; more typically, the prospect of contradiction keeps them from writing (or even taping) any history at all. The new perspective gained by Muhammad Hamdan, who has recorded the oral histories of numerous 'Adwani clans, reveals only an irreducible pattern of discrepancies. Such literary devices as the "third-person account," the "neutral voice," the "master narrative," all of which are quite familiar to Western historians, are seen by Muhammad Hamdan, from his vantage within 'Adwani discourse, as neither possible nor desirable. Thus, after years of documentation, Muhammad has yet to publish a single page of his long-awaited "History of the 'Adwan."

> MUHAMMAD: I am not sure how to organize it. Each group tells a different story. They all say, "My ancestor was shaykh of the land." This is not a simple thing; there have been wars among us because of the shaykhdom. . . . If I organize it on the basis of genealogy, there are still problems. The genealogy is inconsistent from the first generation on, and some clans, like the X and Y, are not original 'Adwanis. But I can't write that in a book. Not at all. These are the problems of writing history.
>
> ANDREW: Perhaps you could present several versions, each from a different source, and not say, "This one is true, that one is false."
>
> MUHAMMAD: No. No way. It's not like that with us. If I present

different versions, they will accuse me of sowing discord. They will say, "He just wants to make problems." That's a sure thing. Besides, there *is* truth; there *is* lying. How can I treat all sources equally? By God, it would bring disaster!

Even in published accounts, Muhammad's concerns are rarely addressed. I remember my dismay upon purchasing Ahmad 'Uwaydi al-'Abbadi's *Jordanian Tribes: Land, People, History* (1986), only to discover that it was made up almost entirely of genealogies: hundreds of them. The bulk of the local oral tradition—the narrative history I had recorded from Balga shaykhs— was conspicuously absent, and in Ahmad's opinion, it would remain so for quite some time. The talk of the elders, he was always quick to argue, is based on a "backward mentality" (*'agliyya mutakhallafa*) that impoverishes literate history-making at every turn.

> ANDREW: You say you cannot write history, but I see your name in bookshops all over Amman. You've published at least ten books . . .
>
> AHMAD: More than that.
>
> ANDREW: Ten that I know of; on women, on tribal law, on ceremonies, on . . .
>
> AHMAD: These are books on customs and traditions, not on history.
>
> [We are sitting in Ahmad's library. His books are displayed prominently on the shelves.]
>
> ANDREW: Well, what about the *Jordanian Tribes*? You call it a history, and it's at least seven hundred pages long. What do . . .
>
> AHMAD: Do you refer to this?
>
> [Ahmad takes a copy of the *Jordanian Tribes* off the shelf.]
>
> AHMAD: This is nothing. I will show you real history.
>
> [He hands *The Jordanian Tribes* to me, then fiddles in his pocket for the key that opens a cabinet beneath the bookshelf. Inside this cabinet are dozens of notebooks and several hardbound volumes that appear to be dissertations. Ahmad refers to them as "drafts." What I am looking at is, in fact, Ahmad's cache of unpublished manuscripts.]
>
> AHMAD: This is the true history that cannot be written. What you read in *The Jordanian Tribes* is just the skeleton. Genealogy is skeleton history. But this is the muscle and nerve. I gathered it from

the best sources, the oldest men. Many of them are dead now, but I have preserved their talk, with names and dates and places, so people cannot say, "Ahmad is a liar." Any story you record, I am sure, is already recorded in these drafts.

ANDREW: This is absolutely incredible. What will you do with it all?

AHMAD: It cannot be published; the people are not ready for muscle and nerve. I keep it here as a resource for future generations. Perhaps my sons will publish it after my death. God knows best. This is the true history that cannot be written without a struggle. It is dangerous knowledge. My enemies, shaykhs and sons of shaykhs . . . fear it. They want to distort history, as they did in the past. They are masters of the old mentality, masters of ignorance. With this [Ahmad points to his store of drafts], I am changing the battle; they do not know how to fight the new mentality I will create.

In a war of (spoken) words, textuality is a new source of power, and the truth Ahmad keeps under the bookshelf—the ammunition for his revisionist attack on the ancien régime—does, in fact, seem dangerous to many. It inspires an almost occult fascination. Favret-Saada's reflections on witchcraft among French peasants are easily applicable to Ahmad's stash of tribal lore: "he who succeeds in acquiring such knowledge gains power and must accept the effects of such power; the more one knows, the more one is a threat, and the more one is . . . threatened" (1980, 11).

Yet Ahmad's inability to make written history of this material is not due solely to its sensitivity. Tribesmen expect such discourse to be offensive. Rather, the struggle of writing owes more to the fact that Ahmad envisions a tribal historiography modeled on (and against) speech. The truth in Dr. Ahmad's drafts is made up of oral testimony, and its truthfulness is determined by the authority of the elders who spoke it. The battle is indeed changing; the shaykhs and sons of shaykhs are astounded by the "new mentality" Ahmad espouses. But in the historical war of words, the rules of the "old mentality" still prevail, if only by keeping certain oral traditions out of print. These rules must be examined before current ventures in textuality begin to make sense.

Traditions of the Multitude:
The Structure of Historical Talk Among the Zyud

The Zyud are an 'Abbadi tribe composed of at least seventeen unrelated clans. The two principal sections of the Zyud, the Dwaykiyya and Sharrabiyya, are divided into the following groups:

The Dwaykiyya	*The Sharrabiyya*
1. al-Dwaykat (shaykhs of the Dwaykiyya)	1. al-Sharrab (shaykhs of the Sharrabiyya)
2. al-Harayza	2. al-Tarakia
3. al-Maghariz	3. al-Ghanmiyyin
4. al-Jabur (original shaykhs of the Zyud)	4. al-Shawafi'a (who include al-Fugara, al-Rataymat, al-'Aqil, al-Jaru, and al-Hamaydan)
5. al-Sawajina	5. al-Mawas
6. al-Shu'ar	
7. al-Bakhit	
8. al-Shiyyabin	

Today, these clans live west of Wadi Sir, in the villages of Badr al-Jadida municipality. Their histories, as one might expect, can be told from diverse points of view. Each family passes on its own traditions, and a shared Zyudi past, to the extent that one exists at all, is conceivable only in relation to the histories of other 'Abbadi tribes, such as the Afgaha, the Manasir, or the Bagur. The oral histories I present here focus almost exclusively on the shaykhly families of the Zyudi past and present—the Dwaykat, Sharrab, and Jabur—but each is typical of narrative genres common to all Bedouin history-making. These include:

- *Gass*: a colloquial term that means "division into parts." *Gass* refers to knowledge of tribal names and their interrelations. It can stand for "genealogy" (*nasab*) in the everyday sense—i.e., the recitation of the names of one's male ancestors—but it also entails an understanding of how genealogical groups are joined by patterns of marriage and political alliance. In the texts that follow, *gass* often appears in the form of questions asked not by listeners, but by the narrators themselves: "Who are the Zyudi clans?" "Who is the ancestor of the Dwaykat?" "Who are the offspring of the Jabur?" The answers to such questions (which are also supplied by narrators) come in the form of segmentary trees, lists of allied clans, and patrilineal chains of begetting and begotten. *Gass* is the "skeleton" of Zyudi history. Its categories inform a sense of place, identity, and time, and as such, *gass* is all that makes Zyudi points of view possible.

- *Gisas* (sing., *gissa*): these are the "stories" that take place within segmentary frameworks of *gass*. The Zyudi *gisas* offered here dwell on events from the "age of shaykhs": the origins of the Zyudi clans, their territorial disputes and power struggles, violent clashes with other tribes, and the deeds of shaykhs. Such topics are memorable because their memory is sharply contested; they relate episodes in which identities were, and still are, defined. A *gissa* is delivered (more or less explicitly) as an argument against other groups who, the narrator assumes, tell the same *gissa* differently. This is especially true of *gisas* about "origins" (*usul*), which establish the character and early relations of the Zyudi clans.

- *Gasayid* (sing., *gasida*): these are metrical, rhyming poems that commemorate significant tribal events. *Gasayid* are usually appended to *gisas*, apart from which they make little sense. The story and verse serve as mnemonics for each other; the *gissa* is the poem's "foundation" (*asas*), and the *gasida*, in turn, becomes the story's "proof" (*dalil*). These mnemonic pairings are quite old. They usually date from the nineteenth century, and most *gasayid* can no longer be understood without the "interpretations" (*tafsirat*) provided by old men. Like *gisas*, *gasayid* are confrontational. They are delivered either as taunts or in response to taunts. Only two short *gasayid* pertaining to the Zyud have survived the "age of shaykhs": the first, a taunt, was composed by a Zyudi poet; the second, a response, was composed by an 'Adwani. Other Zyudi *gasayid* are now lost to memory.

Rather than attempt to harmonize the multiple, contradictory accounts that make up Zyudi history, I have decided to arrange them in a way that preserves their polemical nature. Most Zyudis would reject this artifice: but not, as one might suspect, because it exposes internal disputes. To the contrary, it is my *refusal to take sides* that Zyudis would find strange. My own point of view, which lies outside local frameworks of *gass*, is not the point at which Bedouin would begin to construct their past. For Zyudis, the simultaneous display of Jaburi, Sharrabi, and Dwayki histories (without any concern for their truth or falsehood) comes perilously close to Haj Mahmud's sense of *harj*: the "confusion" that results when everyone speaks at once and no one controls the discourse. By remaking oral tradition in the form of comparable texts; by denying spoken authority the power to impose silence on ri-

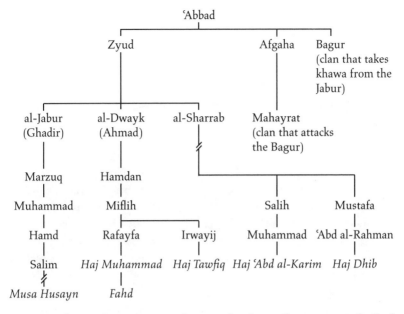

Figure 3. The Zyudi narrators in relation to the clans and prominent individuals they describe in their stories.

val accounts, I am writing *for* and *against* every account. Or as Dr. Ahmad al-ʿUwaydi might say: "I am changing the rules of battle."

The narratives that follow were meant to be heard by intimates and kin. They are thoroughly parochial. Most Zyudis would not expect foreign readers to find anything intrinsically interesting about them. At times, the stories can be difficult to read. The relationships between the narrators and the ancestors of whom they speak are shown in figure 3, but keeping the names straight will demand of the reader, as it does of the Zyudis who learn these tales, a great measure of concentration. My reasons for presenting Zyudi histories as I do will become clear only *after* the stories have been told. For now, the reader can use these texts to gain a sense of the narrative richness, the flood of detail, and the partisan multivocality I encountered as I tried to map out one very small portion of the tribal past.

Traditions of the Jabur

AS TOLD BY MUSA HUSAYN AL-JABUR (A PSEUDONYM)

[Musa's narrative was recorded on his verandah, beneath a thick canopy of grape vines. The tape recorder was tucked discreetly between the cushions on which we sat. Musa wanted no one to know I was recording from him: (1) because he is a young man who, by custom, should not be imparting the talk of the elders, and (2) because his testimony was directed against the Dwaykat, the family who had "stolen" the Zyudi shaykhdom, and the dominant place in Zyudi historical discourse, from its original possessors: the Jabur.

Musa's desire for anonymity stands in sharp contrast to the prideful assertiveness of Dwayki and Sharrabi narrators. As the Jabur have gradually lost their grip on shaykhly power, their spoken traditions have assumed a subaltern and increasingly secretive mien. Musa was the only Jaburi I met who would even consider being taped. This descent into political (and discursive) weakness, which took many decades in real time, is accurately reproduced in the shape of Musa's narrative. The first *gissa*, which deals with the origins of the Jabur, is delivered in a shaykhly voice. In later *gisas*, the Jabur are gradually moved to the periphery of their own history by the Dwaykat. As if to complete this process rhetorically, Musa entitled his talk, "The Story of Irwayij," after the preeminent shaykh of the Dwaykat clan.]

The origins of the Jabur

This is what used to be, in bygone days, maybe two hundred years ago or more.

The Jabur was the first man to come to this area, which, at that time, had no one living in it. When he came here, he was traveling from one place to another. He came here from Iraq. His name was Ghadir, and he came first to the Jordan Valley, to the lowlands. He settled there and started building himself up until he became a well known and famous man. There was another man with him, whose name was Imjalli. They say he was the cousin of the Jabur, but really he was not. He is from another origin entirely. They are not real Jaburis.

Soon afterward, a family called the 'Adwan appeared. They were a small family. They came and lived in the valley, and Ghadir held part of the valley, a big part. He had many slaves and other people working for him. He also begot two fine sons: Marzuq and another, whose name I forgot. Both were very good, very strong sons. The 'Adwan tried to gather people from all around, to make their family stronger than it was. They turned against the Jabur. But Ghadir stayed in the valley; he didn't listen to the 'Adwan. He had two brave sons [and he was not afraid]. But one day, when his sons were encamped in the mountains, the 'Adwan came and killed one of them. They shot him. After they shot him, Ghadir gave up on the valley entirely. He moved away.

The 'Adwan asked him for the valley: "We want this area; we want to live in it."

And the Jabur said: "I give you everything you ask for, except the share belonging to my slaves."

The Jabur had slaves, and the slaves, in the old days, had water and land [of their own] in the valley.

"As for the slaves, you will not touch their share."

And the slaves still have their share in the Jordan Valley, as they were promised; this was originally given to them by us, the Jabur.

Ghadir moved up to Wadi Shu'ayb. He pitched his tent on the south bank of the wadi. They say his tent was over 100 meters long; the ropes reached across the wadi, so great was the size of it. The Jabur had many goats and sheep. His name was Ghadir, the father of Marzuq. Many people joined him, to work and live with him. He was a great shaykh, the first shaykh. The others came after him.

Traditions of the Sharrab

AS TOLD BY HAJ DHIB 'ABD AL-RAHMAN MUSTAFA AL-SHARRAB
AND HAJ 'ABD AL-KARIM MUHAMMAD SALIH AL-SHARRAB

[The Sharrab are recognized among Zyudis as a shaykhly family, and Haj Dhib and Haj 'Abd al-Karim, both nearly eighty years old, are respected men. On the day I visited them, they had just returned from an *'atwa*, a "truce" between two disputing clans, at which they served as "guarantors" (*kufala'*) for the Zyudi side. They were sharply dressed in traditional garb and were the very image of tribal authority. Clearly, I would not be asked to stuff the recorder between the cushions: Dhib and 'Abd al-Karim were eager to talk. It was their shaykhly place to do so.

Like Musa's narrative, the Sharrabi account begins with the arrival of two fictive kinsmen, and though the precedence of the Jabur is granted, the claim that the Sharrab entered the land "before the others"—and especially before the Dwaykat—is essential. Dhib and 'Abd al-Karim assumed that I had already heard Dwayki history, and much of their testimony was offered

as a counterweight to the Dwayki view. While Jaburi traditions
recount a gradual loss of power to the Dwaykat, Sharrabi traditions
stress the emergence of two equally powerful factions, each led by
a Sharrabi or Dwayki shaykh. The best known episodes of Zyudi
history, however, center on Dwaykis, not Sharrabis, and this fact
becomes a rhetorical problem for Dhib and ʿAbd al-Karim in later
gisas.]

*The origins of the Sharrab
and the formation of the Sharrabiyya alliance*

HAJ DHIB: The first Zyudi was the Jabur. He is the foundation.
Then came the Sharrab and the Turki. They came from the Arabian
Peninsula. They were not brothers; each was from his own tribe.
They came to Jordan from Palestine. They became brothers and
crossed over to Jordan from Palestine. The Sharrab and the Tarakia
are like brothers, but we are not brothers.

[Tarakia is the plural of Turki. As the reader will soon realize,
Zyudi narrators often use the names of groups and individuals
interchangeably. He is they and they are he. Singulars are forever
turning into plurals and vice versa. This is especially true of
the Jabur, who are referred to in these accounts sometimes as a
person, sometimes as a collectivity. All of this tends to intensify the
identification between individuals and the clans and tribes to which
they belong.]

HAJ DHIB: The origins of the Tarakia are also in the Arabian
Peninsula. Our ancestor, the Sharrab, is originally from Midaʾin
Salih, which is in Arabia. He was called the Amir al-Salihi. His
ancestors were princes of the Inhas tribe, who live on the peninsula,
at Midaʾin Salih.

HAJ ʿABD AL-KARIM: The Sharrab are the only ʿAbbadis who
can properly be called by the name Amir. Our ancestors were
Amirs.

HAJ DHIB: Yes indeed. The Amir al-Salihi came to this land,
to Greater Syria, and we, the Sharrab, branched off from him and
settled here in the Balga. We received land, just as the Jabur had
land. They took a share, the Sharrab took a share, and the Turki
took a share.

HAJ ʿABD AL-KARIM: The Jabur had everything, even the
Jordan Valley. But he always had problems with the Bagur [a
neighboring ʿAbbadi clan], who were stronger than he.

When Sharrab and Turki came to this land, the Jabur said: "Come live with me. Take as much land as you can see from the border."

So they took land on the south bank of Wadi Shuʻayb, as far as they could see. The Sharrab and the Jabur were, from the beginning, guardians of the land. The other clans, the Dwaykat, the Harayza, and all those others—they came later.

HAJ DHIB: Yes. And we are the Sharrabiyya.

HAJ ʻABD AL-KARIM: And who are they, the Sharrabiyya? Who are their clans?

The Imwas belong to the Sharrab.
The Tarakia belong to the Sharrab.
And then the Shawafiʻa, who include

the Afgara,
the ʻAjil,
the Imhaydan,
the Jarru,
the Irtaymat.

They are all Sharrabiyya.

HAJ DHIB: And the Ghanmiyyin, who came later. Those are the clans who joined the Sharrab. They are not from one ancestor, but they are all one group. As for the Dwaykat, they are another group, and they have clans of their own. We are all Zyud. The Dwaykiyya and Sharrabiyya are all Zyud. The Zyud, it is said, grew and grew. They were small at first; they increased and became "The Multitude." They became a powerful tribe.

Traditions of the Dwaykat

AS TOLD BY HAJ TAWFIQ RUWAYIQ AL-DWAYKAT

[The Dwaykat are the dominant figures of Zyudi oral tradition; almost all Zyudi history is framed in relation to them or the set of political alliances they, along with the Sharrab, define. For Haj Tawfiq al-Ruwayiq, a shaykh in his early eighties, the Dwayki legacy is one of landed wealth and power, and his testimony conveys a sense of history that is obviously accustomed to its own importance. It is rich in heroic episodes and, rare among Zyud, even contains bits of poetry.

Like the Sharrab, the Dwaykat say they arrived in the Balga before all other Zyudi clans and were given land by the Jabur. Except for this strategic claim to territorial precedence, Haj Tawfiq does not spend his energy answering the "inaccuracies" of Jaburi or Sharrabi accounts. His narratives are often set in a larger context. They deal with Zyudi-Baguri relations, conflicts with the 'Adwan, Turkish suppression of the Bedouin, and, finally, with the emergence of "proper government," which brought the age of shaykhs, and Dwayki history itself, to an end.]

Origins of the Dwaykat and formation of the Dwaykiyya alliance

The ancestor of the Dwaykat came from Khalil, on the West Bank. No one was living here except the Jaburi: one man, one tent. And the Jaburi had a brother. That Jaburi was a clever man.

He said to my ancestor: "Let me give you one-fourth of the land and you can join me. I'll arrange your marriage."

So the Jaburi proposed on behalf of my ancestor and arranged his marriage. Later, the Jaburi killed his brother. The Jabur were two men, and the one killed the other. My ancestor banished the killer.

The Dwayk said: "This man is my brother, not yours. We became brothers when I joined your group."

As blood compensation for the dead Jaburi, the Dwayk took another fourth of the land. That was his right: one-fourth the land. So that made one-half of all Jaburi lands now in the hands of my ancestor. The better part was in his hands. He took all the good places, on all sides, from the Jordan Valley to the borders of Amman.

And all the other people, the Zyud, came after the Dwaykat. The Jaburi was the first, then the Dwaykat, and the rest came after. The Harayza, the Sha'ar, the Sharrab: they weren't here in the beginning. They came afterwards and joined together and entered the land. They increased and increased, grew and multiplied, and they were called "The Multitude," the Zyud. Like 'Abbad. Is 'Abbad [descended] from one ancestor? No. They gathered together and worshiped each other (*'ibadu ba'd-hum*) and were named 'Abbad. Each tribe was from another tribe, and whoever came here became brother to the rest. The Zyud, likewise, are not from one ancestor. They increased and grew, many families, and became the Zyud.

And who are they, the Zyud? There are two sections: the Dwaykiyya and the Sharrabiyya. We are the Dwaykiyya. And who are the clans of the Dwaykiyya?

The Harayza are Dwaykat.
The Jabur are Dwaykat.
The Maghariz are Dwaykat.
All the stronger clans are Dwaykat.

Traditions of the Dwaykat

AS TOLD BY FAHD MUHAMMAD RAFAYFA AL-DWAYKAT

[Fahd, a man in his fifties, spoke on behalf of his father, Haj Muhammad Rafayfa, who refused to be taped. Haj Muhammad was upset because I had recorded first from his lifelong antagonist, Haj Tawfiq, even though Haj Muhammad was older: "I have no *gass*; I have no talk. Just go back to Haj Tawfiq, who knows everything. But for me, no. Lying is forbidden." If I had considered Haj Tawfiq a "proper source," then Haj Muhammad would rather not be a source at all.

Fahd, ever the gracious host, made his own attempt at a summary of Dwayki history. His testimony is of interest because it is delivered in terms of *gass*, the most basic form of historical knowledge. Fahd had neither the confidence nor the authority to relate *gisas* or *gasayid* without the consent of Haj Muhammad.]

Origins of the Dwaykat

FAHD: When our ancestor first came here, his name was Ahmad. They say his name was Ahmad. Is that right, ya Haj?

HAJ MUHAMMAD: It's possible that his name was Ahmad. It's possible.

FAHD: It's said that he came from Bayta, Nablus. But God knows for sure. Ahmad begot whom? Hamdan.

Hamdan begot whom? Three brothers: Khanayfis, Miflih, and Filah.

Miflih begot Irwayij, and Rafayfa, and . . . [tape is not clear]. Rafayfa begot Muhammad, my father, who begot me.

And Irwayij, who was shaykh of all the Zyud, begot Tawfiq. Isn't that so, ya Haj?

HAJ MUHAMMAD: Yes. So they say.

FAHD: So the Dwaykat are three brothers, the sons of Hamdan: Khanayfis, Miflih, and Filah.

ANDREW: But the name Dwayk [which means "little rooster"] is a nickname. What is the origin of that name?

FAHD: As for the word "Dwayk" . . . well . . . the tribes used to fight among themselves, and our ancestor, Ahmad, would stand between them and break them up, and they would say: "See? You look like a little rooster to us. You [must] think you're a little rooster."

But we can't verify 100 percent where he came from: Bayta, Khalil, the Hijaz. That's something ancient. There are no documents that verify it. Is there anything to verify it, ya Haj?

HAJ MUHAMMAD: That . . . I can't help you. I can't be of use to you.

FAHD: But whenever there was a war between two tribes, or any disputes, he would separate them. He had, you might say, the "leadership position" (*az-za'ama*), and the people said: "You think you're a little rooster among hens." And that name stuck to him.

Traditions of the Dwaykat

AS TOLD BY HAJ TAWFIQ RUWAYIQ AL-DWAYKAT

The rise of the Dwayki shaykhdom

ANDREW: How did your father, Irwayij, become a shaykh?

HAJ TAWFIQ: His father was shaykh, and his father's father. They were shaykhs from the beginning. The first shaykh was my ancestor, Ahmad.

ANDREW: How did he become a shaykh?

HAJ TAWFIQ: I'll tell you now. When my ancestor came here, only the Jabur and the villagers of Mahis were living here. The Bagur [a neighboring 'Abbadi clan] took *khawa*, money, from them. My grandfather came to them as a guest.

He said: "What's going on?"

The Jabur said: "We are paying *khawa*."

My grandfather was surprised.

He said: "Are you strong men?"

They said: "Yes."

He said [to himself]: "Because they are strong men, I'll lead them."

The people of Mahis served the Bagur a slaughter-beast; they put all the meat on top of rice. [The Bagur ate it all] and nothing was left to the hosts.

Then the Bagur said: "Tomorrow we eat with the Jabur."

The Jabur were upset. My grandfather encouraged them.

He said: "Tomorrow you will be men. I will lead you."

The Jaburi said: "Do what you will, and I will support you."

The next day, everyone went to the Jaburi's place. They all sat down, [and waited for the Bagur to arrive].

When the Bagur came [into sight], my grandfather said: "When they dismount, loosen the saddles of their horses. Don't leave them tight; so that when they mount, they will fall."

The Bagur sat down on their mattresses.

They said: "Serve us what you have."

The Jaburi said: "You will not eat!"

He poured out all the broth and just ignored the Bagur.

One Baguri said to his brother: "He didn't give me meat. I deserve meat! Give us meat!"

The other said: "Let's strike this man down."

And my grandfather said: "We'll strike you down first!"

He called out: "Warriors!"

And they rose up against the Bagur with clubs and knives and blows. The Bagur fled from the tent and left their cloaks and boots and weapons behind. They tried to mount their horses, but they fell off. The saddles were loose. My grandfather chased them off, and they never returned.

The Jabur and the people of Mahis said to the Dwayk: "We give you all of Wadi Shu'ayb. We give you the wadi. All of it."

So he took it, and built a grain mill there and named it "the Dwayki Mill." He took all the land and built a mill for grinding lentils, and he put a slave in [charge of] it. Where was this? Down by the wadi. He pushed the Bagur out a second time, just chased them off. And where did they go? To Fahays village. He closed the road on them and forbade them to collect *khawa*. None of them ever came back again.

Your protection. [*Silamtak*; a benediction commonly used to end a story]

ANDREW: May God protect you, ya Haj.

Traditions of the Jabur

AS TOLD BY MUSA HUSAYN AL-JABUR

The story of the Dwayk

One day, the Jabur was sitting in front of his tent.

He saw a boy walking around, and he said: "Come! Eat with me!"

Then he said: "You look tired. You must be coming from a long way off."

The boy said: "I'm coming from Khalil, on the West Bank."

The Jabur welcomed him and said: "What are you doing in this country?"

The boy said: "I'm looking for work."

The Jabur said: "Why don't you work for me?"

Because all this land was his; nobody owned this land except the Jabur.

The boy said: "Good. I'll work for you."

He started working.

There is this 'Abbadi family, a big family, called the Bagur. The Bagur used to come and take money from the Jabur because the Jabur didn't have many people to help him in a fight. We call this *khawa*. The Bagur would come to him and take the *khawa*, and he would always give it to them. He was rich. They took goats, sheep, cows . . . anything he had.

So when that boy, the ancestor of the Dwaykat, came to the Jabur, the Jabur said: "Stay and work for me. Stay."

And the boy said: "Fine."

And every month the Bagur would come—through the moon they knew the time—and they would take *khawa*. They came at the end of the month. The Jabur would slaughter a sheep for them, and he would put the entire sheep in front of them, until they finished eating, then he gave the rest to the women and children. That boy, whose name was Hamdan or Ahmad, was working now as the Jabur's cook and coffee maker. He slaughtered the sheep, cleaned it, and cooked it. He cut it in half and put one-half in front of the Bagur.

They said: "Where is the rest?"

He said: "I left it for the women and children."

They said: "Hey little rooster, you must think you're brave."

He said: "No. I'm not brave. But that's your share, and it's all you get."

There was a boy from the Imjalli—those people who, as I told you, claim they are from the Jabur but they are not—and this boy's mother was from the Mahayrat clan.

The Dwayk told that boy, whose [maternal] uncles were from the Mahayrat . . . he said: "Go to your mother's family and tell them that the Bagur have come to take *khawa* from the Jabur, and they refuse to eat their meal unless your mother carries the platter on her head, so they can eat it off her head."

That boy ran to the Mahayrat and told them: "The Bagur are putting the platter on my mother's head and eating from it."

The Mahayrat were her family; she was their daughter. So they rode off [toward the Jaburi encampment]: many horses, many riders. When those Bagur saw them coming, they dropped everything and ran away. The Mahayrat fought with them and killed seven. They killed seven Baguris. Those Bagur . . . they never came back again.

The Jabur said to the Dwayk: "Why did you do that?"

The Dwayk said: "I just did it."

The Jabur said: "Good. You share with me whatever you want: money, goats, sheep, land, everything—you can have half."

Traditions of the Dwaykat

AS TOLD BY HAJ TAWFIQ RUWAYIQ AL-DWAYKAT

The damming of Wadi Shuʿayb

Things stayed like they were between the Bagur and the Zyud until my grandfather, Miflih, shut the waters of Wadi Shuʿayb on the ʿAdwan tribe.

ANDREW: Why?

HAJ TAWFIQ: They were at war: ʿAbbad and ʿAdwan. Always at war. So he clogged up the stream, and the ʿAdwan sat for a week in the valley without water. The valley dried up, and the water sank into the ground.

The Bagur took sides with the ʿAdwan. Some went with ʿAbbad, but the others went with ʿAdwan. They are traitors, the Bagur. At night, one hundred men came up from the valley, to where the dam was blocking the water. The Dwayk had dammed it up, and the water . . . they couldn't release it. The men stepped into the water up to their chests. They took off their cloaks and their clothes. They wanted to break the dam and release the water for the ʿAdwan. Miflih fired on them. He shot here and there and scared them off; ran them off naked. He grabbed their cloaks and boots, loaded them on mules and carried them away. And the Dwaykat kept the water. A poet from among us said:

> The Dwayk is son of the falcon, and you are pigeons.
> When he flaps his wings, he throws down flesh and game.

Abu Hariz struck terror in the mounts of screaming warriors.
He broke up your gathering, you disrespectful rabble.[4]

ANDREW: Who is Abu Hariz?

HAJ TAWFIQ: One of the Harayza, a clan belonging to the Zyud.
He was one of my grandfather's riders; he was one of the Dwayki
cavalry who fought alongside my grandfather.

Anyway . . . the 'Adwan came up from the valley and tried to
make peace. They offered the Dwayk land in the valley in exchange
for releasing the water. An 'Adwani poet composed a poem. He said:

O Dwayk, you aren't capable of 'Adwani warfare.
Come down to the *ghor* and grow gardens.
Your melon, O Dwayk, will fetch four quarters grain.[5]

[Just before] the 'Adwan agreed to give the Dwayk land in the
valley, God, in His power and majesty, unleashed the waters below
the dam, at a narrow point in the wadi. The waters gushed out from
beneath the earth and flowed into the valley.

The 'Adwan returned to the valley and said: "The Dwayk is on
his own now; let him keep his dam."

That's all. The matter ended just like that. Yes indeed. Your
protection.

ANDREW: May God protect you, ya Haj.

Traditions of the Sharrab

AS TOLD BY HAJ DHIB 'ABD AL-RAHMAN MUSTAFA AL-SHARRAB
AND HAJ 'ABD AL-KARIM MUHAMMAD SALIH AL-SHARRAB

The damming of Wadi Shu'ayb

HAJ DHIB: The Dwayk cut off the water, but that story . . . no.
It wasn't just the Dwayk. It was all the Zyud. The Sharrab and the
Tarakia took part. He did it alongside the Sharrab, whose shaykh,
in those days, was Tafish Hamdan.

ANDREW: But wasn't the Dwayk the leader?

HAJ DHIB: No. We were all together, acting together. They
brought a large stone and dropped it in the streambed, and the
water just disappeared. The 'Adwan sat in the valley one whole
week without water. There was no water.

4. This poem is transliterated in Appendix A.
5. This poem is transliterated in Appendix A.

ANDREW: I heard a poem about it. A Zyudi poet said: The Dwayk is son of the falcon . . .

HAJ DHIB: . . . and you are pigeons. Yes indeed. He said that.

[Haj 'Abd al-Karim, who is not about to waste his breath repeating Dwayki poetry, quickly invokes the 'Adwani response. His version, which he delivers with stentorian relish, contains a line ridiculing the Dwayk. This bit of "mockery" (*ta'lig*) is well known among 'Abbadis—more so, even, than the Dwayki poem—and Haj Tawfiq al-Ruwayiq, not surprisingly, had omitted it from his version.]

HAJ 'ABD AL-KARIM: And the 'Adwani answered. He said:

O Dwayk, you aren't capable of 'Adwani warfare.
Come down to the *ghor* and grow gardens;
Your melon, O Dwayk, will fetch four quarters grain.
O Dwayk, you aren't capable of 'Adwani warfare,
You whose likeness crows on the dung heap.
Make peace, O Dwayk, and grow gardens
Your melon will fetch four quarters grain.[6]

He answered the Dwayk with that *gasida*.
[Both men chuckle.]

ANDREW: And did the 'Adwan offer you land in the valley?

HAJ DHIB: The valley already belonged to the Zyud; from the valley to the highlands: it all belonged to the Zyud.

ANDREW: Really?

HAJ DHIB: Yes, by God! All that land which is now in the hands of Mijhim al-'Adwan [a prominent 'Adwani shaykh] used to be Zyudi land . . .

[At this point, Haj 'Abd al-Karim launches into another story entirely.]

The Zyud lose their lands in the ghor

HAJ 'ABD AL-KARIM: Look here. Three shaykhs—Tafish Hamdan and Salih al-Sharrab [both of the Sharrab], and Irwayij al-Dwaykat—went down . . .

HAJ DHIB: No. Irwayij was not with them. Don't say Irwayij. He has nothing to do with this story.

HAJ 'ABD AL-KARIM: That's the way I heard it. They went down to the camp of 'Ali Dhiyab al-'Adwan. The father of Sultan.

6. This poem, in its more complete form, is transliterated in Appendix A.

Sultan had just been born, and Shaykh ʿAli invited the tribes to a feast in the *ghor.*

The people saw the Zyud coming, and they went to ʿAli Dhiyab and said: "Hey! Those Zyud have come, and they want to give a present in honor of [the birth of] Sultan."

There were people who brought food, who brought stallions, who brought mares as presents for Sultan. But the Zyud didn't bring anything.

ʿAli Dhiyab was clever.

He said: "Everyone has given a gift to the father of Sultan. What are you giving, O Zyud?"

The Zyud were afraid the ʿAdwan would betray them, kill them, even though they were guests. They were only three men.

They said: "By God, what is it you want, Shaykh?"

He said: "I want a gift of land, according to custom."

The ʿAdwan had no land in the *ghor* above Wadi Shuʿayb; it was all Zyudi land.

So ʿAli said: "I want the waters of Nimrin [where Wadi Shuʿayb empties into the *ghor*]."

So they presented him with the waters of Nimrin, as he requested.

Later, when they returned to their lands, they said: "By God, our Arabs will kill us for sure. We just gave away our land in the *ghor*!"

They said: "Let's give Sultan our cloaks instead. Each one of us should give him a cloak."

They came back to the camp of the ʿAdwan with cloaks and said: "Take these in honor of Sultan."

But ʿAli Dhiyab refused the cloaks.

He said: "What is this? The gift of the ʿAbbadi doesn't cross the wadi."

And that saying is still known among the people: "The gift of the ʿAbbadi doesn't cross the wadi" (*hadiyyat al-ʿabbadi la tagtaʿ al-wadi*).

They went to a tribal judge and disputed it legally. And how were their rights decided?

The judge said to ʿAli Dhiyab: "In place of these cloaks, you will take the waters of the *ghor*."

So they belonged to ʿAli Dhiyab. Then ʿAbbad and ʿAdwan rose up against each other, and the Zyud dammed Wadi Shuʿayb, just as we told you, and no one could separate them until the government came.

Traditions of the Dwaykat

AS TOLD BY HAJ TAWFIQ RUWAYIQ AL DWAYKAT

The Zyud lose their lands in the ghor

The northern part of Zyudi territory belonged to the Jaburi, but the Jaburi was weak. He was a weak man. That was his property: from the Jordan River to Jabal Amman.

The 'Adwan said: "What can we do [to get that land]?"

They invited everyone to the camp of 'Ali, whose son, Sultan, was getting married.

'Ali said to the Jaburi—while the Jaburi was eating meat and rice—he said: "Make a gift! Make a gift! Sultan wants a wedding gift from you!"

The Jaburi hadn't brought any money. The 'Adwan wanted to betray him, to kill him.

So the Jaburi said: "I'll present him the waters of the *ghor.*"

The 'Adwan still wanted to kill him, so 'Ali said: "He's presented his gift. That's the end of it!"

The Jaburi gave it to them out of fear; there was no good will in it.

From the *ghor* upwards, the land still belongs to us. It's all Zyudi land.

Traditions of the Jabur

AS TOLD BY MUSA HUSAYN AL-JABUR

The rise of the Dwaykat and fall of the Jabur

The Jabur gave the Dwayk one of his daughters. Hamdan al-Dwaykat married the daughter of the Jabur, and after that the Dwaykat started taking the land . . . taking this, taking that.

[Musa tells, in great detail, of two land swindles. In the first, Hamdan al-Dwaykat convinces one of the Imjalli—"who are not true Jabur"—to exchange Jaburi land on the banks of Wadi Shu'ayb for the right to marry his daughter, "who was very beautiful."]

When Hamdan took the land, he married and begot many sons: like Irwayij and Filah, and . . . many, five or six.

The Jabur had many daughters, but only one son who lived; his name was Marzuq . . . or maybe it was Muhammad. I'm not sure. Marzuq, they say, was a good fighter, a horseman, a rider. We take

pride in these things. He owned Dabuk and Firdaws; all that land
was his. He used to send his cattle to graze there. He was very rich.
   So that Dwayk, Irwayij, he started taking pieces of land. He
moved the boundary stones. Marzuq got old; he begot Muhammad.
Muhammad was, how do I say it, a religious man. He didn't do
much. He lived about ninety years. Then Hamd came. Hamd begot
two sons: Salim and ʿAli.
   [Here, Musa tells, in great detail, of a swindle that deprived
Salim and ʿAli of their lands. Briefly: A Christian clan from Fahays,
acting in league with Irwayij al-Dwaykat, swore falsely before
a government surveyor that the land of Hamd belonged to them.
After the government decided the claim in their favor, the Christians gave half the land to the Dwaykat.]
   So the Dwaykat divided our lands. That's the story. That's all.
You can turn it off.

Traditions of the Dwaykat

AS TOLD BY HAJ TAWFIQ RUWAYIQ AL-DWAYKAT

Shaykh Irwayij al-Dwaykat and the Turkish Wali

My father, Irwayij, became even greater than my grandfather,
Miflih. My father took control of the land and the people. He
became shaykh in those days, and he ruled by the rod. It was a
time of the sword, not a time of law. Power. By power he ruled.
He was the complete shaykh: a judge, a horseman, a generous
man. He was an official in the Turkish government in Salt . . . like
representatives in the parliament are today. He owned land from
the *ghor* to the borders of Amman; all the property of the Zyud
was registered in his name.
   A shaykh, in those days, was responsible for his tribe: responsible before the people and before the Turks. The Turks were not
a proper government; they were oppressors who slew the people
and took their wealth. They despised the Arabs. The Turks brought
the Shayshan from Russia and settled them here on tribal lands.
   [The Haj is referring to the Chechens, a Muslim tribal people
who were driven from the Caucasus by czarist armies in 1859. The
Ottoman government relocated them in the Balga of Jordan, mostly
in the period between 1902 and 1907 (see Lewis 1987).]
   There was a war between the Arabs and the Shayshan. They
fought, and after they slew each other, the Turks imprisoned all

the Arab shaykhs in Kerak. There is a fortress in Kerak. The Turks imprisoned them there. Not just the shaykhs of 'Abbad; the shaykhs of all the tribes. My father was among them.

When they had sat in prison for a while, some of them tried to escape.

They said: "Let's go out the window."

There was a window, and beneath it was a drop-off. Four meters below the window was a rock they could crawl down from and escape. So they made a rope out of their head scarves, and lowered themselves to the rock. My father refused to go down. Shaykh 'Abd al-Mahsin of the Mahayrat, whose body was light, landed safely on the rock and got away. Shaykh Nihar al-Bakhit of the Manasir, whose body was fat, broke the rope and fell. He died. Several others died, and several escaped. The Turks tracked them down, one by one, and hanged them all in Kerak. They hanged six men in Kerak that day.

The Turkish Wali came down from Syria. He wanted to see this disaster. My father was put in chains—manacles—after the trial.

When the prison boy came to unlock his chains, my father said: "Don't loose me. I swear by my right hand that only the Wali himself will unlock my chains."

The boy returned to the Wali.

The Turk said: "Where is the Dwayk?"

He said: "He's chained up, locked up. He has sworn by his right hand the you alone will remove his chains."

The Wali said: "Peace be!"

He rushed out to see the Dwayk. He was hitched to the hitching post, just like the mules.

The Wali said: "Why didn't you let the boy free you?"

The Dwayk said: "My honor would not allow me. My dignity would not allow me. I did not go down in disgrace. Yet still they placed chains upon me. Do you consider me an animal?"

The Wali put the key in the lock and released him.

He said: "Because you have kept your dignity, I pardon you."

The Turks did something in Kerak that had never happened before. They gave my father a horse, and money, and they hosted a celebration for him when he returned to the Balga. It was unbelievable. Your protection.

ANDREW: May God protect you.

Traditions of the Sharrab

AS TOLD BY HAJ DHIB ʿABD AL-RAHMAN MUSTAFA AL-SHARRAB
AND HAJ ʿABD AL-KARIM MUHAMMAD SALIH AL-SHARRAB

The Dwayki-Sharrabi rivalry

ANDREW: Who were the shaykhs of the Zyud, from the first days till now? I ask you this because people say there was a rivalry between the Sharrab and the Dwaykat.

HAJ DHIB: Yes indeed. There was always rivalry.

ANDREW: Do you know the details of . . . that matter? Who were the shaykhs involved?

HAJ DHIB: At first there was Irwayij al-Dwaykat. He was a shaykh: shaykh of the Dwaykat. And among us, the Sharrabiyya, there was a man named Tafish Hamdan, who rivaled the Dwayk. Then came Salih al-Sharrab, and he, too, rivaled the Dwayk. They divided the Zyudi tribes between them—Salih and Irwayij. They went their way and we went ours. Yes indeed. When Shaykh Salih died, my father, ʿAbd al-Rahman, became shaykh. Today, there are no shaykhs.

ANDREW: What was the source of this rivalry?

HAJ DHIB: There was disagreement between them. What happened, happened. The shaykhdom has ended, my brother. Today there is government in Jordan.

HAJ ʿABD AL-KARIM: Irwayij was a good man. He didn't care if he slaughtered five, ten, or twenty sheep for his guests. He just slaughtered them. But later, Irwayij became poor, and the slaughtering ceased. He couldn't find a meal.

Who rose up? Salih al-Sharrab. Salih al-Sharrab got stronger, and Irwayij became weak. He had no wealth. See? They went to Syria, to the Wali, and divided the Dwaykiyya clans from the Sharrabiyya clans. That's the story from the beginning to the end. Irwayij was a good man. A man worth his weight. We can't curse him.

[An untold story lay beneath ʿAbd-Karim's careful synopsis, but no line of questioning could extract it. My only glimpse of the Sharrabi role in Irwayij's demise came, ironically, from a member of the Dwaykiyya alliance. When Ahmad al-Sawajina told me the story of his grandfather's investiture as *mukhtar* (headman) of the Dwaykiyya, it was obvious that his narrative captured a central episode in the rivalry between Irwayij and Salih al-Sharrab.]

Traditions of the Sawajina

AS TOLD BY AHMAD AHMAD AHMAD AL-SAWAJINA

The fall of Irwayij al-Dwaykat

Irwayij, God have mercy on him, was shaykh of the Dwaykiyya. As for the Sharrabiyya, their shaykh was Salih al-Sharrab, God have mercy on him.

One day, Irwayij was going about the Wali's business. Of course, the government center was in Salt, and he went with soldiers to the Arabs who, of course, were living down in the area of *al-humra*. He wanted to assess their taxes and count their livestock and assess the land taxes. Whoever had Majidi coins, or some other currency, paid.

To the people who didn't have money, Irwayij said: "You'll have to pay with your wife's gold, or the coins she has stitched on her dress."

He took the decorative coins and the women's gold earrings in exchange for the taxes they owed. After he took them, he got on his horse and left . . . he and the soldiers he brought with him.

When my grandfather, God have mercy on him, came upon the Arabs, he saw that they were upset.

He said: "What's with you?"

They said: "Irwayij came with soldiers, and he made the people without money pay with their gold or the coins off the women's chests."

My grandfather said: "Where did he go?"

They said: "He mounted and rode on."

My grandfather rode after him and found him; he overtook him near Wadi Shu'ayb. He called out to him and stopped him.

He said: "Ya Dwayk, the shaykh of the Arabs is supposed to protect the Arabs. It's not proper for him to oppress them and take what is rightfully theirs. Give me the money bag you've got."

Irwayij said: "No, I will not give it!"

My grandfather had a lance with him.

He pointed it at Irwayij and said: "You'd better get off your horse."

He got off.

My grandfather said: "Give me the money bag."

The Dwayk gave it to him. He took it by force and returned to the Arabs. The others knew there might be problems with the

Turkish government because of this incident. The adviser, Salih al-Sharrab, came and so did Husayn al-Faris. One of them was shaykh in Mahis, and the other was shaykh of the Sharrabiyya.

My grandfather said: "Here's what happened. What's your advice?"

They said: "Write a complaint. We'll go to the Wali and see how things stand with him, and you'll become *mukhtar* in Irwayij's place."

They wrote the complaint then went to the Wali in Salt and said: "Such-and-such happened; that's the story, and we want to put this man as *mukhtar* in place of Irwayij."

The Turks decided to put him in Irwayij's place, and he stayed there until he died. God have mercy on him, and your protection.

ANDREW: God grant you peace.

AHMAD: His name was Ahmad al-ʿAyan al-Sawajina.

Traditions of the Dwaykat

AS TOLD BY HAJ TAWFIQ RUWAYIQ AL-DWAYKAT

The challenge to Irwayij

ANDREW: They say there was a rivalry between the Dwaykat and the Sharrab.

HAJ TAWFIQ: Yes indeed. This rivalry happened in the time of my father, Irwayij. From the start, he was never stingy with them. He was in charge of tax collecting; he controlled all the money . . . from the government and from the people. The clans began to criticize him.

"This, that, this, that."

It was no use. They complained about him to the Wali in Salt. They all went [the disputing parties], as delegates to the legal proceedings. Shaykh ʿAli Dhiyab al-ʿAdwan was there, sitting next to the Wali, and he had shaykhs with him. My father greeted them, and they all stood [as a show of respect] except for Ibn ʿAdwan. Irwayij pulled his sword on Ibn ʿAdwan, right there in front of the Wali. Then chaos broke out.

"Aaaah! Aaah! Stop him! Stop!"

Everyone was startled; everyone jumped in to separate them. My father wanted to slay the one who would not stand and greet him. Those other Zyudis, when they saw my father draw his sword on Ibn ʿAdwan, they just fled.

The ones who had instigated the proceedings said: "God's pardon on you. We don't want [to press the case]."

They all left.

They said: "Just forget it. We forgive you because of your deed. You drew your sword in the presence of the Wali and tried to cut off 'Ali Dhiyab's head with it. We can no longer hold anything against you. You have God's pardon."

Your protection.

ANDREW: God protect you.

The end of the age of shaykhs

HAJ TAWFIQ: Irwayij was shaykh of shaykhs; he was the headman (*mukhtar*) of Mahis village and all the Zyud. Before him and after him, there were no shaykhs. When he died, God have mercy on him, the shaykhdom ended, and every clan had its own *mukhtar*. The Dwaykat have a *mukhtar*; the Sharrab have a *mukhtar*; the Jabur have a *mukhtar*. We can't backstab them. All the people are goodness and a blessing.

ANDREW: Yes. We don't want to backstab them.

HAJ TAWFIQ: But in former days, all the Zyud and the people of Mahis, their shaykh was Irwayij.

ANDREW: Are there shaykhs like Irwayij and Miflih today?

HAJ TAWFIQ: Nowadays *everyone* is a shaykh. There's a shaykh in every house. Before, there was only one, two, three . . . maybe four in the entire region. That was it.

But then the people split apart, and now everyone will tell you: "I am shaykh of my own group."

ANDREW: So why are things different now?

HAJ TAWFIQ: The [nature of] government rule has changed. The world has changed. The virtues of the shaykh that we take pride in—what are they? Generosity, the resolution of disputes, assistance to his family and neighbors, hospitality, protection of fugitives, and leadership on the field of battle. Such is the work of shaykhs. But where are such men today? Where are those days? The government came, and the shaykhdom broke down. That's what happened. Now we live in an age of law.

Despite my attempts to weave these traditions into one tangled fabric, they remain what they are: a collection of partial, fragmentary accounts that, even when strung together, have no unified story to tell. The Zyud are not

134 / Documentation and the War of Words

an "imagined community" defined by the communion or presumed similarity of its members (*per* Anderson 1991). They are, instead, (1) a political
response to the "imagined" (and always threatening) community of *other*
'Abbadi tribes—e.g., the "treacherous Bagur"—and (2) a partly rhetorical,
partly territorial space in which specific clans, each descended from a different man, have struggled (and continue to struggle) for dominance. Thus,
for Musa Husayn al-Jabur, a Zyudi history based on anything other than
his own tradition entailed disturbing possibilities, and like other Zyudis, he
lobbied against its construction.

> MUSA: If you want the truth, don't go to X. He's a liar; his
> whole group are liars. As for the Y . . . same thing.
> ANDREW: But everyone says that about everyone else. How can
> I learn about Zyudi history unless I take some from each clan? The
> history of the Jabur is not the entire history of the Zyud.
> MUSA: I'm just saying you will not get the truth. The Zyud
> are a single tribe. Yes. But we are not from one ancestor. We do not
> have the same blood. Our origins and characteristics are different.
> So we do not have one history. I have told you the truth I received
> from the tongue of my father, but the others will not tell you the
> truth about the past. They are all liars; if you compare what they
> say to the things I have told you, it will be obvious that they are
> lying.

A single Zyudi clan—the Dwaykat, for instance—is more easily imagined
as a community of shared "blood" (*damm*) or "ancestry" (*nasab*), but this
unity, too, is fractionated into multiple degrees of cousinage. The descendants of coeval brothers usually relate history in mutually offensive ways;
thus, Haj Muhammad al-Rafayfa and Haj Tawfiq al-Ruwayiq, both elders
of the Dwaykat, could not trust each other as "proper sources" because their
fathers, who were both sons of Miflih Hamdan, had vied for control of the
shaykhdom. There are, in reality, as many Dwayki histories (or Sharrabi or
Jaburi ones) as there are collateral lineages branching off from the first ancestor.
    Zyudi histories would appear, then, to be locked in an almost Newton-
ian discourse: each oral tradition engenders, or counters, an equal and opposite tradition; each truth is told against a lie, which is truth to someone
else, and so on. If the Zyud are seen as one unit within an abstract, segmentary structure—a view familiar to tribespeople and ethnographers
alike—such mechanical imagery is entirely accurate. The Dwaykiyya *do* relate history against the Sharrabiyya; among the Dwaykiyya, the Jabur *do*

speak against the Dwaykat; among the Jabur, the "true" Jabur *do* pit their traditions against the Imjalli: all in accord with the finest principles of "balanced opposition."

This binary rhetoric is real, and the farther I moved away from Zyudi sources, the more stereotypically oppositional it became. When members of the Afgaha section of 'Abbad learned that I was taping history from Zyudi shaykhs, many of them questioned my judgment. A man of the Y clan, whose wife and mother are both from the Zyud, spotted me walking one morning toward a nearby Zyudi village; he invited me to sit with him and drink tea. In the following dialogue, which is reconstructed from field notes, this man is called by a pseudonym: Najih.

[We are seated in the shade of the olive grove, where Najih's sisters and younger brothers are stringing tobacco. After the traditional exchange of greetings, Najih asks where I am headed and what business I have there. I tell him that I'm on my way to B, where I hope to record stories from Haj Y: "Because the people say he has history."]

NAJIH: Who told you he has history? He's senile, and he lies. Just stay here with us; drink tea and be happy.

ANDREW: Thanks. You are generous. But I have an appointment with him.

NAJIH: Ya Andrew, why are you going to the Zyud? What do you want from them? Isn't the history of the Afgaha enough?

ANDREW: I have to collect histories from all the people, not just the Afgaha.

NAJIH: But the Zyud have no history, by God. Listen, and I'll tell you their history right now. When the 'Abbad-'Adwan war happened, the Zyud stayed here. They didn't go to Baysan with the Afgaha; they didn't fight; they didn't drink the salty waters of the *ghor.*

[Najih is recalling a war between the 'Abbad and 'Adwan tribes that occurred in the first half of the nineteenth century. 'Abbad was defeated and fled to Baysan, a village on the West Bank of the Jordan. They remained in Baysan "for fourteen years," then returned to the Balga, where they defeated the 'Adwan and retook their lands. The Afgaha are eager to point out that the Zyud, rather than retreating to Baysan with their honor intact, surrendered to the 'Adwan and "came under their rule."]

NAJIH: They stayed here and took the land of the Afgaha and

became slaves to the ʿAdwan. They made tent pegs for Shiga [the wife of Dhiyab al-ʿAdwan] and we call them "tent pegs of Shiga" to this day. That's their history.

[Najih's sisters start giggling; the history lesson comes at the expense of their mother, who, after pretending not to listen, waves a dismissive hand at Najih and says to me: "Empty talk. Don't answer him."]

NAJIH: Ya Andrew, why aren't you writing this down? Get out your notebook and write!

[I produce my notebook and write the following aids to memory, which I read aloud in Arabic for effect: "The Zyud . . . have . . . no . . . history. They are . . . called . . . Tent pegs of Shiga." There is more laughter from the tobacco stringers, and Najih, who is enjoying the exchange, rewards me with another cup of tea.]

NAJIH: Bravo for you, ya Doctor! Now write: "The Zyud didn't go to Baysan."

ANDREW: I know. They stayed here. They say that themselves. But they do have clans, just like the Afgaha, and these clans have origins, just like the Afgaha clans have origins. Right?

NAJIH: Do you want to know about their origins? I'll tell you right now.

[Najih takes my hand in his and begins to count off the Zyudi clans, folding my fingers down one by one.]

The Shuʿar are *nuwar*.

[*Nuwar* (sing., *nuri*) is the Arabic term for "gypsies." As elsewhere, *nuwar* are a stigmatized group in Jordan; they are deemed to have neither "origins" (*usul*) nor "honor" (*sharaf*).]

The Harayza are *nuwar*, too.

The Jabur are *ghawarna*.

[The term *ghawarna* (sing., *ghorani*) means, literally, "valley dwellers," but its everyday connotation is more like "valley blacks." The *ghawarna* are the Afro-Arab inhabitants of the *ghor*. Like *nuwar*, they are deemed to have neither origins nor honor. Bedouin do not intermarry with them (or with gypsies), and being called a *ghorani* is, for any tribesman, a tremendous insult.]

ANDREW: But they don't look like *ghawarna*; I mean, they don't look African.

NAJIH: Just look at their eyes; their eyes are black; you can't see their pupils. This is the evidence that their ancestors were *ghawarna*. Not all of them. There are some original ones among them. Yes indeed. Now . . . how far have we gotten? Yes: the shaykhs.

[Najih continues to fold my fingers into my palm.]

NAJIH: As for the Sharrab, their ancestor came from Palestine. From Khan Yunis. He was a drunkard, always drunk. The word *sharrab* means drunkard, and that is their proper name.

As for the Dwaykat, their ancestor was a rooster from Palestine; a rooster peasant from Palestine. As the poet said: "You whose likeness crows on the dung heap."

[My fingers are now folded into a fist, which Najih returns delicately to my lap, as if it were a captive bird. More giggling. Najih's mother walks away with the empty teapot, muttering "God forgive! God almighty forgive!" under her breath. Now everyone is laughing out loud. "Where to, ya Hajja?" says Najih. Then to me: "Don't worry about the Hajja; she doesn't understand joking."]

NAJIH: So those are their "origins": gypsies, *ghawarna*, drunkards, and peasants. I know. They are my in-laws. Write *that* in your book.

ANDREW: Do you want me to write that?

NAJIH: Of course. Write it and *underline* it.

[I do so.]

ANDREW: And put your name?

NAJIH: No. No. I didn't say write my name. This talk is between us and you, even though it's true.

ANDREW: OK. Do you want me to write what the Zyud say about the Afgaha?

[We are still joking, but Najih assumes a slightly more serious tone.]

NAJIH: What do they say? Did they tell you something about us?

ANDREW: Well . . . not about you exactly.

NAJIH: About whom? Scoot over here!

[Najih draws me close; in a conspiratorial whisper that signals the end of all joking, he urges me to beware.]

NAJIH: Don't listen to their talk. They are liars, by God. They fart out their mouths and talk out their asses. Don't listen to them. Just erase their empty talk from your tapes. Burn it. You don't want lies. Do you want to write lies?

[There being no simple answer to this question, given the

relativity of such concepts as "lying" (*kidhib*), I assume the role of the methodical, indiscriminately honest scribe.]

ANDREW: God forbid! No. I just want to be accurate and reliable. I won't change people's talk. I just record what people tell me, then write it word for word.

[In other words: Yes, I will be writing "lies" . . . along with everything else.]

NAJIH: God help you, ya Professor. God smooth your path. The world is full of lies.

The sense that I was "writing lies" became especially acute several months later when, having settled down among 'Adwani tribesmen, I decided to record *their* version of certain Zyudi stories: namely, "The damming of Wadi Shu'ayb." Although this *gissa* is the most dramatic moment in Zyudi history, only a handful of 'Adwanis knew anything about it. For the few who did, nothing in the Zyudi account rang true. The timing of the incident, the names of the participants, the outcome: all were wrong. The following testimony, recorded from Haj 'Arif Abu l-'Amash, shows one style of argumentation used against the Zyudi account.

[It is my first visit with the Haj. I have just told him the Zyudi story of "the damming of Wadi Shu'ayb." He is greatly amused: partly by what, for him, are the obvious improbabilities of the Zyudi account; partly by the sheer oddity of hearing a foreigner tell such a story. I delivered the story in dialect. I had all but memorized it from Haj Tawfiq's tape, and like most tribesmen, Haj 'Arif was taken aback by my "old man's tongue." Throughout my recitation, he turned occasionally to his wife and said, as if amazed: "By God, he knows history!"]

HAJ 'ARIF: You are clever, my brother. You remember the recollections of the old men. Who told you that story?

ANDREW: An 'Abbadi shaykh. He also told me two poems about the story. One is from the 'Adwan side and the other is from the Dwayk.

HAJ 'ARIF: Do you remember them?

ANDREW: Yes. I will say them to you now. First the 'Adwani poet said:

O Dwayk, you aren't capable of 'Adwani warfare.

[The Haj recognizes the opening line and immediately takes over the recitation, which he completes at a brisk pace.]

HAJ 'ARIF: You whose likeness crows on the dung heap.

Come down to the *ghor* and grow gardens.
Your melon, O Dwayk, will fetch four quarters grain.

Yes indeed. The poet said that. By God, you are clever. And how did the 'Abbadi answer?

ANDREW: Perhaps you'll get angry if I say it.

HAJ 'ARIF: No. No. We don't get angry. Say it, and we'll listen.

ANDREW: OK. The 'Abbadi said:

The Dwayk is son of the falcon, and you ['Adwan] are pigeons.

HAJ 'ARIF: He's talking about the 'Adwan, that poet. Can you believe it?

ANDREW: Present company is excluded, ya Haj (*ba'id 'annak, ya hajj*).

HAJ: Finish it. Finish it.

ANDREW: [I begin again]

The Dwayk is son of the falcon, and you are pigeons.
When he flaps his wings, he throws down meat and game.
Abu Hariz struck terror in the mounts of screaming warriors,
He broke up your gathering, you disrespectful rabble.

HAJ 'ARIF: I haven't heard it before. What did he say? Abu Hariz?

ANDREW: Yes. Abu Hariz is one of the Zyud.

HAJ: No. No. The 'Abbadi botched the poem a little. The right name is Abu Hunayk, the English general: Glubb Pasha. Abu Hunayk is his nickname.

ANDREW: But I thought this story happened in the age of Turks, before the English. They say 'Ali Dhiyab was shaykh.

HAJ: No. Not at all. There are mistakes in that talk.

ANDREW: That's what I want to know, ya Haj. What is the story you heard? When did this thing happen?

HAJ: It happened after the Turks, at the beginning of the Amirate. Majid was shaykh at that time.

ANDREW: Not 'Ali Dhiyab?

HAJ: No. If the 'Abbad cut off the water on 'Ali, he would definitely have slain them all. In the time of 'Ali Dhiyab, no one could lift his hand against the 'Adwan. They ruled the land, from the Zarga to the Zarga. Majid came later. He is the son of Sultan, who is the son of 'Ali Dhiyab himself.

[Majid ibn Sultan al-'Adwan (d. 1946) was the grandson of Shaykh

'Ali Dhiyab, the principal 'Adwani character in the Zyudi version of the story. The two accounts occur as much as sixty years apart. My subsequent conversations with the Dwaykat—who remember but downplay the incident Haj 'Arif is about to relate—lead me to suspect that the Haj is simply not familiar with the earlier episode.]

ANDREW: What really happened?

HAJ: I'll tell you what's right. I was alive at that time. Is that tape running?

ANDREW: Yes. It's working.

HAJ: OK. In our country here, no one cultivated bananas; where were the bananas like we have today? Then Majid, God have mercy on him, brought a company from Palestine and started to plant bananas using water from Wadi Shu'ayb, water from Salt. And this is evidence that the 'Abbadi story is wrong. What did the poet say? He said:

> Come down to the *ghor* and grow gardens.
> Your melon, O Dwayk, will fetch four quarters grain.

In Turkish times, there were no melons in the *ghor*. That's a new thing. Before, we grew grain. That's all. There wasn't a lot of water available, except from the stream: Wadi Shu'ayb. So Majid brought a company from Palestine [to develop banana plantations]. Yes indeed.

After he started planting bananas, a handful of 'Abbadis near Wadi Shu'ayb brought a company [to divert water from Wadi Shu'ayb]. One of them, named Abu 'Ata, wanted to divert the water from whom? From Majid. From the *ghor*. The 'Adwan sent for their clans: the Kayid, the Nimr, the Salih.

Majid said: "What's your advice? The 'Abbad are diverting our water."

They said: "By God, the advice is yours to give, ya Abu Hamud [Majid, father of Hamud]."

He said: "My advice is this. Attack them! Attack them! Those 'Abbad want to return us to the past. I say attack them!"

The general of the local army post said: "No, ya Abu Hamud. Let's deal with this peacefully. I can settle the matter."

He contacted the Qayimaqam [district official] in Salt. Salt had a Qayimaqam at that time. The Qayimaqam contacted the Amir 'Abdullah. He was an Amir then, not a king.

He said: "This and that happened between the 'Adwan and 'Abbad, and the 'Adwan want to strike 'Abbad."

He sent a force, the Amir did, tanks and armored cars and military, and they stood between the two sides. And who led them? Abu Hunayk. Not Abu Hariz; not the 'Abaddis.

So Abu Hunayk [Glubb Basha, the English officer] said: "What's going on, ya Majid?"

Majid said: "By God, 'Abbad wants to cut off our water, and we have no water except from this stream."

He said: "No. [That won't happen.]"

The next day, the Amir brought the matter to a halt. He forbade 'Abbad to approach Wadi Shu'ayb. Even if they wanted to drink from it, they could not.

He said: "This water belongs to the *ghor*, or to the person who can pay the government a tax of 16,000 dinar for its use."

[A sum the 'Abbadis were incapable of paying.]

There was a poet who heard all this talk. His name was Hamdan Abu Hilayil al-'Ajrami, from the Shahwan faction. He composed this *gasida* about the water affair, and I carry it in my memory.

[Like many 'Adwani poems, the one that follows was composed by a member of the 'Ajarma, a small tribe loyal to the 'Adwan. In the past, the 'Adwan seldom composed *gasayid* in praise of themselves; that task was left to their slaves and political dependents. By reciting a poem composed by a non-'Adwani, Haj 'Arif is spared the task (as was Majid in his day) of fully engaging with 'Abbad, a tribe 'Adwanis consider beneath their own.]

The poet said:

The Dabta swells, a mighty roar,
and fills the saddles [with warriors].

[The Haj interrupts his own recitation to provide commentary. He asks: "And what is it, the Dabta? It is the "battle cry" (*nakhwa*) of 'Adwan. Yes indeed."]

From Mausers fire is flaring,
And the weak of heart takes flight,
When the young men are riding,
Those of sharpest deeds.
They come to confront you proudly,
O Abu Khanayfis, O weak thing.

[The Haj explains: "Abu Khanayfis, that's the one from the Dwaykat faction, about whom the poet said: 'your likeness crows on the dung heap.'" The Haj continues.]

It came to pass: war cries and trembling.
You'd say: "Dire straits indeed!"
The Mauser lit up when they fired it,
And they charged to attack them with swords.
They consulted the paramount shaykh:
"O Majid, what will transpire?"
He said: "Those ['Abbadis] are pigeons;
By order they'll come here in chains."
The army post feared a revolt
And informed the Qayimaqam,
Lest all those involved be hanged
On order, decisive, from the Sharif.
O shameful one: those are the 'Adwan,
Shaykhs of the Balga for ages.
There's little doubt you're guilty,
and your cover last night was weak.
The 'Adwan sired Majid, father of Hamud,
Nobleman of the Balga and upright pillar.
His stream is kept free of dams.
It's an ocean, not a dribbling of drops.

[In the verses that follow, the poet heaps lavish praise on 'Adwani notables. Most are brothers and cousins of Shaykh Majid.]

And 'Abd al-Hamid and 'Afash,
Each faces a throng [of attackers].
And the one who mans the machine gun
Is Majid, who makes the coward flee.
'Ali, he and Mansur,
Each, in the councils, a falcon of falcons.
Each is a fearless lion
From the lofty branches.
The brother of Shaykha, O Nawfan,
Comes forward, his likeness a stallion.
Nayif is a safeguard to the others,
and Salih is forever drawn to battle.
And Ahmad, though yet small,
Is among the predominant sons.
Sharper than the scimitar,
He comes from the lofty branches.
Madfi, he and 'Abbas,

And Abu 'Abdullah, all are superb.
They never stand down from the ramparts,
And they come from the lofty branches.
The Kayid joined in with their aid,
With rifles and warriors on horseback.
Those from among them are a barricade;
Each strikes terror [in the foe].
The Brothers of Mahara are magnanimous.
They charged them down from the right.
Fahd was a safeguard to the others,
And Barakat is ever drawn to battles.
Haj 'Ata straight away
Ran off like one gone mad.
He feared the unsheathed sword
And fled, his debts unpaid.[7]

Haj 'Arif's critique of the Zyudi account is a delicate mix of sober exegesis and incendiary poetics. He is not quick to cast accusations of lying; nor is he prone to the scandalous talk of younger men like Najih. The Haj leaves the brass tacks of challenge and riposte to the 'Ajrami poet. Still, for all his discrimination, Haj 'Arif's critique is scathing: the Zyudi account—which, in keeping with segmentary principles, the Haj depicts as a generic 'Abbadi account—is reduced to the status of *kidhib*, and the Dwaykat are reduced to a pack of cowards on the run. Haj 'Arif's testimony would, for that reason alone, seem as scurrilous to a Zyudi reader as would Najih's cutting remarks; indeed, his testimony would be offensive even to Najih, who, in keeping with segmentary principles, would read it as a criticism of the entire 'Abbad tribe.

The latter implication was not lost on Haj 'Arif's nephew, who had arranged our initial recording session. As we walked home later that night, he assured me that:

> If you record the Haj's talk, you will learn that the history of
> 'Abbad is mostly lies and exaggerations. They have no history in
> the proper sense. In my opinion, you have wasted your time by
> living with them. What great poems do they have? What famous
> stories? Believe me. The 'Abbad are not a real tribe. The history
> of the Balga is the history of the 'Adwan.

7. This poem is transliterated in Appendix A.

It would be hard to exaggerate the frequency and unrelenting sameness of such talk. It followed me, quite literally, wherever I went. And yet each time a speaker expressed these sentiments, he thought he was sharing something new with me, something I had never heard before and would be unlikely to realize unless he told me. The "structural relativity" of Haj 'Arif's historical argumentation—that is, the pervasive effect of *'asabiyya* ("clannishness") on the traditions he related—was not a self-evident proposition to his nephew. If it had been, his preoccupation with the veracity of the Haj's testimony (and the mendacity of 'Abbadi accounts) would have made little sense.

Such ideas as "balanced opposition" and "segmentation" were, for most tribesmen, perfectly apt characterizations of tribal structure. As principles defining historical truth and falsehood, however, these ideas necessitated a critique of oral history-making that tribesmen always found extreme. I met no 'Abbadi, no 'Adwani who would accept the "structural relativity" of his *own* received traditions. To repeat the words of Muhammad Hamdan al-'Adwan: "There is truth; there is lying. How can I treat all sources equally?" Which invites yet another question: How could Muhammad and I, both of us engaged in the collection of polemical testimony, arrive at such markedly different views of our material?

The circumstances that made "structural relativity" self-evident to me, for all its unacceptability to tribesmen, were rooted in two rather obvious aspects of method. First, I had no position to defend or assert within the tribal structure and, therefore, I had nothing at stake in the outcome of historical disputes. I was Bourdieu's ethnographer, "excluded from the real play of social activities by the fact that he has no place (except by choice or by way of a game) in the system observed and has no need to make a place for himself there" (1977, 1). Second, my textualizing practices—making tape recordings and taking notes—when combined with this marginality, allowed me to triangulate voices and events in ways tribal historiographers could not (and did not care to) accomplish: they, after all, were "real players" located within the system. This is not to say that I was *neutral*. Quite the contrary. I was *marginal*, and tribesmen sought to include me in their discursive agendas by means of textuality: that is, by telling me their historical truth, all the while disparaging the truths of others.

Thus, even though my antiphonal display of 'Abbadi and 'Adwani histories *in print* does accurately convey something of their substance, their polemical intent and tone, it also fosters a misconception. It instills in the reader a sense of *systematic* and *symmetrical* inconsistency that, however palpable to the ethnographer, is not experienced by tribespeople in quite this way. In the daily life of history making, the voices of Zyudi narrators do not confront one another as they do in the texts I have made of them: openly, at once, and all equally visible to the eye. Some traditions are more *audible* than others. Some speakers request anonymity; others insist that their full names be given. Some clans project their vision of the past vigorously; others are reluctant to say anything at all. Real historical discourse is shaped by a segmentary logic of truth and falsehood. It is also informed by notions of power and spoken authority that take all the "balance" out of "opposition." The contests that animate tribal history-making are taken seriously— which is to say, *not* in a spirit of relativism—because such disputes can, in fact, be lost.

Consider, again, the Zyud. If their histories are posed in the form of ongoing arguments, one might reasonably conclude that the Dwaykat are carrying the debate; the Sharrab are angling for a draw; and the Jabur are surely losing. This state of play is discernible along several dimensions, not all of them rhetorical.

- *Gass.* The Zyud are divided nowadays into two sections: the Dwaykiyya and Sharrabiyya. It is admitted by all parties, however, that the Jabur were once the central clan, the "foundation" (*al-asas*). Later, the Dwaykat, under Shaykh Irwayij, came to dominate the tribe. Finally, the Sharrab, under Shaykh Salih, successfully asserted themselves against the Dwaykat, becoming leaders of their own faction. The segmentary structure of the Zyud is not simply a constraint on discourse; it is an artifact of historical arguments that have been decisively won.
- *Gasayid.* Of all the Zyudi clans, only the Dwaykat have inspired heroic poetry, and this is taken, by the Dwaykat at least, as a proof of their historical weight. It can be argued, given the absence of *gasayid* among the Sharrab and Jabur, that their ancestors did not perform deeds worthy of verse. As one Dwayki put it (rather dismissively): "They have no mention in poetry" (*fish 'andihum dhikra bi-l-gasayid*), a comment meant to convey the prosaic quality of non-Dwayki histories.
- *Gisas.* Dwayki traditions are richer in stories than those of the Sharrab or the Jabur, and these stories often deal with non-Zyudi settings and characters. The incidents retold by other Zyudi clans tend to center on, or include, the Dwaykat. As a result, the Dwaykat wield a formative influence on Zyudi history that no other clan can match. They pervade the discourse.

- *Material correlates.* The shaykhs of the Dwaykat and Sharrab own the best (and the most) land in Zyudi territory. Jaburi holdings, by contrast, are small and scattered. The Dwaykat and Sharrab are also wealthier and better educated, on average, than Jaburis. The power of Dwayki and Sharrabi rhetoric is part of their political clout; likewise, the reluctance of Jaburis to be tape-recorded is part of their political weakness. A challenge to the Dwaykat, rhetorical or otherwise, has unsettling consequences; a challenge to the Jabur does not entail similar risks.

- *Historiographic remains.* The Zyud are seldom mentioned in the nineteenth-century travel literature, but when they are, the Dwaykat and Sharrab are the only clans noted. Conder's 1881 survey of the Balga contains perhaps the earliest reference to the Zyud. It reads: "'Arab ez Ziud, under Sheikh Ruweiyij el Muflah" (1889, 294). In 1908, Musil adds the Sharrab to this short description (1908, 110), but the Jabur still are not mentioned. This absence is reproduced consistently thereafter in works ranging from Peake's *History and Tribes of Jordan* (1958) to al-'Uzayzi's *Encyclopedia of Jordanian Folkore* (1984). Not until Ahmad 'Uwaydi al-'Abbadi's *Introduction to the Study of the Jordanian Tribes* (1984) do the Jabur finally enter the historical record.

- *Current politics.* In Jordan's 1989 parliamentary elections, the Zyud agreed to support a Sharrabi candidate, Hamud al-Jibali, the younger brother of Haj Dhib. A potential Dwayki candidate was rejected because, as the Sharrabi clans argued, it was now "our turn" to represent the tribe. Emphasis was placed on keeping the political balance between the dominant shaykhly clans. The Sharrabi insistence on taking their turn suggests, as does the oral tradition itself, that the Dwaykat are seen to be one turn ahead. The Jabur did not field a candidate, nor did they feel qualified to do so.

Though committed to talk of a bygone era, Zyudi oral traditions are linked metaphorically and genealogically to the present; they serve as commentary on *now* as it happened *then*. Hence, the Dwaykat are a prominent clan because they have been shaykhs "from the beginning"; the Sharrab are the progeny of Amirs and, by virtue of their present standing in the tribe, this claim still makes sense. The Jabur were once lords of the Jordan Valley, but they can no longer defend this lofty status. They have lost their ability to define the situation, and other Zyudi clans speak of the Jabur today as if they had *always* been weak. Should the Jabur try again to assert their shaykhly heritage openly, other Zyudis would accuse them of "lying," ridicule their pretensions, or ignore them altogether. My inclusion of Jaburi texts is, therefore, a victory for them; but it comes at the cost of the narrator's anonymity, a fact that deprives the victory of its value and implies (correctly) that the narrator lacks the courage to affirm what he says publicly. In the end, Musa's words still look like *kidhib* to his fellow Zyudis.

The subtle interplay of "lying" (which follows a segmentary logic) and "power" (which varies independently of it) gives rise not to a Newtonian pattern of call-and-response, but to a volatile din above which is discernible the clear, authoritative speech of a few men: figures like Haj 'Arif Abu l-'Amash, who possess the rhetorical strength needed to silence other accounts, or to speak effectively against them. This capacity obliges us to consider, once again, Abu Firas' commentary on historical truth: "Now I know what is right. You must take history from its proper source." Because it allows us to escape a structural relativity apparent only to the external observer, this advice can no longer be profitably ignored. Indeed, my own habit of making texts brought Abu Firas' theory continually into play. A tape recorder, despite all the suspicions it might raise, works remarkably well as a divining rod of spoken authority.

FIVE

Border Crossings

The stranger will not be considered here in the usual sense of the term, as the wanderer who comes today and goes tomorrow, but rather as the man who comes today and stays tomorrow—the potential wanderer, so to speak, who, although he has gone no further, has not quite got over the freedom of coming and going. He is fixed within a certain spatial circle—or within a group whose boundaries are analogous to spatial boundaries—but his position within it is fundamentally affected by the fact that he does not belong in it initially and that he brings qualities into it that are not, and cannot be, indigenous to it.

Georg Simmel, The Stranger

Outsider! Trespasser! You have no right to this subject! . . . We reject your authority. We know you, with you foreign language wrapped around you like a flag: speaking about us in your forked tongue, what can you tell but lies?

Salman Rushdie, Shame

The Social Construction of Proper Sources

Haj Salih Slayman al-'Uwaydi was about eighty years old when I worked with him in 1990. His knowledge of tribal history was legend among his clan, the Sikarna, and the authority of his testimony inspired strange patterns of deferential silence. Though most Sikarna eagerly related all the 'Abbadi history I cared to hear, few agreed to have their voices recorded on tape. At the first sight of a cassette, they would urge me (sometimes a bit nervously) to visit Haj Salih. The Haj, it was said, had a better memory for such things: "He will tell you the proper history." This went on for several weeks. Talk of the past was freely uttered, but my attempts to textualize it were put off time and again.

When at last I called on Haj Salih, he seemed to be expecting me, as if he had known all along that the silence of his kin would compel me, sooner or later, to consult with him. He offered no objections to being recorded on tape, but he prefaced his testimony with a cautionary note.

> If you want to record, then record. But people won't be constrained by recording. Everyone has his opinion. Your recordings won't come to one view. Because everyone speaks from his experience. We, when we are 15 years old, we listen to someone whose age

is 120, and we don't know if he's reliable or unreliable. You can't verify it. This one recollects and that one recollects. Our grandfathers recollect and our fathers recollect. We didn't see [these things]. We listen to people who listened to people before them. Because the kind of thing you're dealing with is like that: face to face. You can't verify it unless you say who told you.

Haj Salih's view was not like that of ordinary Sikarna, who were enthralled by more divisive historical themes. His intellectual tolerance brought to mind, instead, C.M. Doughty's laudatory image of Bedouin shaykhs: "men of ripe moderation, peacemakers of a certain erudite and subtle judgement." Haj Salih, speaking from the lofty vantage of old age, had seen the contours of his own discourse clearly, and he was ready to put away childish things: first among them, the bizarre notion that my "comparative method," as he understood it, would somehow enable me to reconstruct the tribal past *wie es eigentlich gewesen*. There was, for Haj Salih, no official version, only diverse lines of oral transmission, each fractured by memory and experience, each ending in a melange of contestable speech.

"The truth," he was fond of saying, "is known only to God."

The fact remains, however, that other 'Abbadis regarded Haj Salih as a reliable font of truth: so reliable, in fact, that it was not fitting for them to speak in his place. The Haj stood in a special relationship to the past. Not only was he willing to speak; he was expected to speak on behalf of (and potentially at the expense of) other tribesmen. He was a "proper source" (*masdar salih* or *masdar sahih*), and his words of warning, when seen in this light, are revealing: "You can't verify it unless you say who told you." In giving me permission to record his voice, the Haj was allowing me to say: "I received this on the authority of Salih al-'Uwaydi," a pronouncement that accomplishes all the verification the Haj deemed possible or necessary.

Had I been without a tape recorder—or had I stopped insisting on its use—I doubt that the significance of "proper sources" would ever have become apparent to me. The more immediate impression of tribal history-making is that related by Davis, who worked among Zuwaya Bedouin in Libya.

> All Zuwaya men . . . learned the basics of their history from an early age, and used them in conversation and argument from then on. The youngest person I heard reciting his genealogy was about ten years old, and two years later he was referring to an epic event in Zuwaya history in a discussion. Old men, it is true, both knew more and talked about it more often than younger ones; and poets also composed poems about the past,

usually about the past of the Zuwaya as a whole. But with these exceptions, talk about the past was not a specialism. . . . Most history speaking was informal, fragmentary, and it was the concern of all men, each a repository of facts and details, which often differed slightly from the next man's (1989, 107).

In the Balga, too, historical talk is not a specialism. Every mature 'Abbadi I knew—along with a surprising number of children—could propose a credible summary of the tribe's past. Older men, for their part, could spend hours on the subject without any risk of exhausting their material. Authoritative speech, however, was not the concern (or possession) of all Balga tribesmen alike. It was, in exactly the sense Davis puts forward, a specialism, and the men who had mastered it were distinguished by common features. These were put to me in formulaic terms by Haj 'Arif Abu l-'Amash.

> ANDREW: Ya Haj, how can I know who is reliable? How can I distinguish between truth and lying?
> HAJ 'ARIF: Do you want the truth?
> ANDREW: Yes.
> HAJ 'ARIF: The truth. Where is it? You must go to the old men who have seen with their eyes and heard with their ears. Don't go to the young men. They have no information. Go to the ones who have received it from the old men who were alive in that time. It is a chain, my brother, from elder to elder. I heard from my father, Abu l-'Amash, and he got it from his father, Slayman, until you arrive at Fawzan, the first ancestor. Yes indeed. That's the reliable chain; that's the proper history.

It was only much later, when I began to catalogue my tapes, that I saw how accurate Haj 'Arif's pronouncement had been. Of the fifty-three 'Abbadi and 'Adwani tribespeople whose voices I recorded, fifty-one were male and forty-eight were at least fifty years old. The people who had not flinched at the prospect of textuality were a strikingly uniform lot, and their similarity extended beyond the more obvious dimensions of age and sex. Most were the oldest surviving member of a set of brothers, and most were members of influential families. The authority of these "proper sources" was rooted, then, in the combination of two unrelated factors: they were the living men closest to the past, and they belonged to groups that cut a high profile on the tribal landscape. They were, to repeat Dr. Ahmad's phrase, "shaykhs and sons of shaykhs." The most authoritative forms of local historical knowledge—poetry, genealogy, and storytelling—tended to concentrate in their hands.

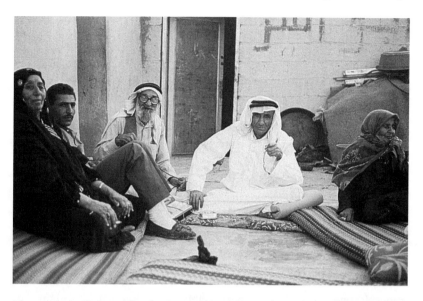

Plate 10. A "domain of authority" at the moment of speech. Five ʿAbbadis come together to hear the stories of Haj Mahmud Nisar Nasir al-Jarmi (the old man on the left).

Moving Through Territories of Discourse

Tribal history is a collective endeavor. It is not, however, a shared tradition. During fifteen months in the Balga, I saw no public occasions on which tribal histories were told; no communal ceremonies at which the old poems and genealogies were recited. The voices I captured on tape, no matter how widely respected they were, always spoke in private settings. Their audience was made up of sons and daughters, younger brothers, nephews, wives, screaming children, and a foreigner with a tape recorder. Their domain of authority might encompass entire clans, but at the moment of speech, it never exceeded the dimensions of a plush diwan, a cement verandah, the shade of an olive tree, or the warmth of a kerosene heater (plate 10).

This extreme localization of historical talk became, for me, a methodological fact of life. The "proper sources" I sought were arrayed like prominent (and immovable) objects on the landscape: Haj Salih was in Wadi Sir; Haj ʿArif in Salihi; Haj Musa in Marj al-Hamam, and so on. Their domains of authoritative speech comprised, in a literal sense, territories through which I was required to migrate, often under the escort of local guides. These border crossings—which I first mistook for "paying a visit"—entailed exchanges of a rather complex sort. Consider the following:

> I am living in the ʿAmamsha village of Salihi, the rhetorical domain of Haj ʿArif. I want to record from ʿAli Barakat, a member of the Nimr clan who lives in the *ghor*. I am taken by Abu Firas to visit a lawyer, X, who is a relative of ʿAli Barakat. X, it turns out, is estranged from his kin, so he arranges for another Nimri, Z, to drive me down to the *ghor*. After a week of planning, Z finally delivers me to ʿAli Barakat's house in Kafrayn.

Or:

> I am living in Swaysa among the Sikarna, rhetorical domain of Haj Salih. I want to record from Haj Zamil of the Slayhat, who lives in a tent near the *ghor*. Dr. Ahmad al-ʿUwaydi introduces me to Haj Zamil's younger brother, Musa, who invites me to his home. During my visit, Musa introduces me to his nephew, Y, who is the son of Zamil. Y escorts me to Zamil's tent.

In both cases, the use of intermediaries enabled me to pass from the domain of one "proper source" to another without subjecting members of one audience to the authoritative speech of another. Such arrangements, though cumbersome, were always helpful. They kept "domains" and "audiences" discrete, and discreteness was a prerequisite for tape-recording historical talk. Whenever the boundaries between separate domains and audiences were blurred in my presence, disputes were apt to occur, and these led either to *harj* (confusion) or, more often, to a diplomatic (and irreversible) change of topic.

My insistence on textualizing a broad range of authoritative speech gave rise to elaborate procedures whereby the rhetorical domains of respected men could be protected and, when necessary, circumvented. These procedures were reminiscent of tribal legal conventions that, in 1990, had no official place in Jordan's civil law codes: namely, "sanctuary" (*dakhala*) and "escort" (*rafaga*). During the "age of shaykhs," these customs ensured the safety of strangers who wished to move through the "protected areas of shaykhs" (*himayat al-shyukh*) or sought refuge within a shaykh's domain. Since I was the consummate outsider—neither Bedouin, nor Muslim, nor Arab—my movements through tribal space forced certain reenactments of the relationships forged between Balga tribesmen and European travelers in the nineteenth century.

"We will protect you here," I was told. "You are a guest with us. Our ancestors have always protected the Orientalists who come searching for ruins and knowledge of our tribes."

According to Haj Khalaf al-Fahd, tribal protection was extended to foreigners on terms negotiated by his grandfather, Goblan al-Nimr, and "the English government." I later found evidence supporting this claim. James Finn, British consul in Jerusalem from 1846–1863, writes in his professional memoir, *Stirring Times* (1878), of an agreement drawn up in 1855 with Shaykh Dhiyab al-'Adwan for the escort of English tourists east of the Jordan River.

> The disturbed state of the country did not prevent the chief of another Bedawy tribe from the East, Shaikh Deab, of the Adwan, from visiting me. He came with two of his people to arrange for the escort of British travellers to Jerash and the Ammon country, on the Eastern side of the Jordan. Hitherto that part of the country had been very little accessible to visitors, and our Arab friends were willing to enter into a treaty for the safe convoy of persons willing to pay a fixed sum in return. What mattered it to them that the Kings of the earth were in a state of agitation—that the Sultan and the Muscovite Emperor were at war? All this was very far off; but English travellers were known to the wild men, and they were prepared to make them welcome as guests in the territory over which they and their allies roamed, where neither Turkish Government nor European Powers could exercise any authority, but where nevertheless the code of Arab honour guaranteed perfect safety to the travellers who might venture to trust themselves to it (1878, 375).

And later:

> The Chief of the Adwan Arabs, Deab el'Adwan, came to Jerusalem on his own business, and sent me word that he was able and willing to arrange for the drawing up of the contract whereby the comfort and safety of English travellers might be secured. He announced that the Chief Abd'ul Azeez [of the Nimr clan, uncle of Shaykh Goblan] was ready to come if invited. This meant that the Bedawy chief and his suite were within reach somewhere on the east of the Mount of Olives, which serves as a barrier between the civilized world, having government authority, and Desert rule and territory. The wild men shelter in quiet nooks behind it, and there communicate with people who may give them the meeting. In a few hours the Shaikh appeared. He and his party are real wild Arabs—dirty, and forming a strong contrast to his cousin Deab, who is dressed as clean and as well as any Effendi of the town, but with a more magnificent sword than any Effendi. They are both tall fellows, with hawk eyes and noses. All the Adwan party were childishly curious about the house and furniture (so new to them) (1878, 470).

Their childish curiosity was short-lived. The Nimr soon got the upper hand in their dealings with Europeans, successfully extracting exorbitant sums from wealthy noblemen who wished to visit the ruined cities of Jerash and Amman. By the 1880s, Shaykh Goblan al-Nimr was well known to English readers of the Holy Land travel literature. He, his brother Filah, and uncle 'Abd al-'Aziz figure prominently, though not always positively, in the reports of Conder (1883, 1889), Tristram (1865, 1873), Merrill (1881), and Oliphant (1880).

When the Rev. F. A. Klein toured the Balga on behalf of the Church Missionary Society in 1868, he did so without first informing his old friend, Goblan, whose costly protection he hoped to elude. The following passage from Klein's journal is worth quoting at length; it reveals, in vivid detail, the sense of "domain" that underlay 'Adwani conventions of escort.

> Before I started for Burma two Bedouin horsemen of the Adwan tribe had come to my tent and inquired about the "Consul" as all gentlemen travelling in these parts are styled. They then informed me that Scheich *Gablan*, one of the chiefs of the Adwan, a daring & desperate fellow, was in the neighborhood and would be glad to see me. This was no welcome news to me as I was almost sure something unpleasant would occur, Gablan having hitherto considered it his exclusive privilege of escorting European travellers to these parts & pocketing the handsome bakshish due to him for his protection; only recently a gentleman who travelled in that country had to pay to Gablan upwards of £120 for his escort for 20–30 days besides sundry presents. But what could I do under the circumstances. I should not have liked to return to Salt, nor would it have been prudent to do it so I told the men to give my best compliments to Scheich Gablan who was my friend and to tell him not to give himself the trouble of meeting me, but if he chose to meet me somewhere on the way I should be happy to meet him. With this message the two horsemen went away. When, as I said we had passed Tekiddi whom should we see come down a little hill but Gablan armed as usual with pistols & a long spear and two of his men similarly armed. I saluted him in a friendly way & he very politely returned my salutation, but still he could not entirely conceal his anger, but on my guide saluting him [the guide was not 'Adwani] he began to abuse and curse him, lay hold of his pistol and advance a few paces towards him. One of our men took down his gun from his shoulder with the utmost coolness so as to be ready to fight if necessary; I entreated Gablan by his friendship to me not to go farther and to let his pistols remain in his girdle & I told him that if he hurt any of my men I would consider it as done to myself. You are my friend, he replied, I have no desire to hurt you but on the contrary will let you ride my own horse if you are tired on yours and protect you & accompany wherever you like but these dogs, turning to my men & chiefly the guide, what have they to do in my country, do they not know that it is my business to bring "Consuls" to this country, I'll kill them & drink their blood (Klein 1868).

Klein and Goblan assert their relationship to "this country" in very different terms. For the 'Adwani shaykh, the Balga is a closed space defined, in part, by his right to profit from the affluent foreigners who amble through it. For the Rev. Klein, the Balga is potentially an open space in which individuals possessing adequate local knowledge—"sons of the country"—should be allowed to roam freely. Thus:

> By dint of entreating him & representing to him that I was not a foreign Consul but a "son of the country" and that as such I was not encroaching on his rights by coming to this country without an escort & sundry Arab compliments & appeals to his friendship & generosity I at last succeeded in appeasing his anger and at last he said: Well this time I will forgive them but if another time they dare to bring "Consuls" to these parts without previous notice to me I'll kill them all. . . . This affair convinced me that it is not yet advisable for European travellers to visit these countries without first securing the protection of some powerful Bedouin chief, unless government be strong enough to put down the pretensions of chiefs & abolish their claims to the exclusive right of escorting European travellers to those regions at their own conditions, to which only Dukes & Lords, very rich gentlemen or very large parties can agree (Klein 1868).

By the turn of the century, the 'Adwan had lost their exclusive hold on the provision of escort. Gertrude Bell, it will be recalled, passed through the Balga in 1905 under the protection of Goblan al-Hamud, shaykh of the Da'aja, a small tribe allied to the 'Adwan (see chapter 2). When the "age of shaykhs" drew to a close in the 1920s, so too did the age of escort. Today, foreigners of all sorts move freely through the Balga, and city folk from Amman and Salt picnic in tribal territory on the weekends. Local Bedouin, if they pay any notice to these uninvited guests, are more likely to offer them a service of tea than to accuse them of trespass. The days of wild men and desert rule have decidedly passed away.

Yet when Bedouin talk about the "age of shaykhs," they attach themselves (metaphorically and by way of genealogy) to "wild men" who ruled an ungoverned country, and the foreign listener becomes, once again, a stranger in need of escort. I was led about this rhetorical landscape much as Victorian travelers had been led through a more obviously physical one. The tellers of oral history do not go in search of their audience,[1] nor did they ever seek me out. Their audiences return to them as one returns to a dic-

---

1. Wandering storytellers who perform for pay were once common in the Balga. Today, they are few and far between. I met only one such character: a sickly old gypsy who sang epic poetry at the social gatherings of a wealthy Christian family in exchange for alcohol. His repertoire was slanted toward pieces that could be performed in front of diverse company: mostly love ballads and tales of Arab heroes such as Abu Zayd. He avoided the local, historical poetry of the Balga tribes because, he told me, it was "political and full of insults."

tionary; people sit with them, ask questions, and learn from their talk. I was carried along on these secular pilgrimages. My neighbors in the villages of Swaysa and Salihi were always my principal guides, and the pilgrimages we undertook were confined to a select group of "proper sources," all of them close kin and affines of my hosts. I was actively discouraged from venturing further, since the oral traditions of other groups were "full of lies." Once news of my research spread, however, other tribesmen approached me in public spaces—at weddings and funerals, on the bus, at the market, in the post office—and they offered to escort me to other old men who, without exception, they believed to be more truthful and endowed with greater knowledge than the elders among whom I lived.

If "proper sources" were a uniform lot, the "escorts" (*rufaga*, sing., *rafig*) who led me to them were also members of a distinct social type. They were mostly younger men (only one was over fifty years of age); they were usually related by kinship or marriage to their "proper sources"; and, most markedly, they displayed a knowledge of oral tradition that was rare among men their age. They kept handwritten copies of tribal poetry in their wallets; they sat with old men at gatherings and asked questions about "the bygone days"; they mulled over the fine points of tribal history with their friends. With only one exception, however, my escorts refused to have their own testimony recorded on tape. They could not yet produce authoritative speech. Their goal, instead, was to increase the accuracy of the scholarly account I would create, and they accomplished this by taking me to the elders closest both to them and to the past. If, in the nineteenth century, a local strongman (Shaykh Goblan), acting on behalf of a more powerful shaykh (Dhiyab al-'Adwan), escorted foreigners through tribal territory for a fee; then in the late twentieth century, younger men, acting on behalf of older men ("proper sources"), led me through discursive territories that were no less tribal, expecting remuneration of another sort: namely, my agreement to textualize their version of historical truth and not some other.

Escapes and Entrances

Authoritative speech is jealously guarded. Only once did a "proper source" lead me directly to another "proper source," and then only the elder of the two men spoke. Afterwards, the younger man, who had temporarily placed himself in the subordinate role of guide, asked for a copy of the tapes we recorded: "So I can memorize Haj X's poems. That way I won't have to return to him all the time, and you and I both can benefit." His reasons for arranging the visit were similar to my own: he wanted to gain information that he could use to bolster his authority, thereby becoming a more proper source than he already was. Rarely did tribesmen manipulate my textualizing methods so creatively. It was easier to defend a man's spoken authority by obscuring, discrediting, or blocking access to the speech of his competitors. Thus, machinations of the following kind:

- The people of X, with whom I live, will not accompany me on a visit to the Y, nor will they arrange for a member of Y to escort me to the Y village: "You don't want to talk to them. They have no history, only lies about us." As far as the X are concerned, my interest in the Y portends an act of betrayal.

- The people of X will not even tell me who the authoritative members of Y are; instead, they send me to a Y in-law, Haj B, who is not willing to be taped. The knowledge that I have been sent by the X is enough to stifle him. He does, however, suggest that I visit Haj D, who "remembers all the history." I try to arrange this visit, perhaps with Haj B (or one of his sons) going along as my guide. Haj B demurs.

- I decide to visit Haj D on my own. The X advise against it: "He will think you are a spy; he will not talk to you." I go anyway. When I arrive at the house of Haj D, he admonishes me for not having visited him sooner: "If you hadn't shown up here by the end of this month, I would have sent my son to fetch you." I tell him how difficult it was to arrange a visit: "No one would come here with me." He responds: "By God, those X don't want you to know the truth; they will lead you only to liars." He urges me to go home, pack my things, and bring them to his village: "We are not like them; we can direct you to the best sources; we have history without limits."

The guidance of the Y would, no doubt, have proved equally tendentious. Like the Rev. Klein in 1868, I felt compelled to elude the exorbitant costs of escort, which in 1990 entailed not a loss of hard currency, but (ironically enough) a loss of mobility itself. I was forever being asked to stay put, to avoid the slanderous talk of others, to profess my loyalty by taking sides once and for all. Yet to preserve my marginality—my only defense against the co-optive power of 'asabiyya—I had to remain constantly in motion. I had to escape the confined spaces in which only the X could escort me and become, instead, a temporary fugitive in the rhetorical domains of other men.

The design for these escapes (though I did not realize it at the time) played neatly into local conventions of "sanctuary" (*dakhala*) or, as it is more commonly known, "protection of the fugitive" (*himayat al-dakhil*). In tribal custom, the *dakhil*, the "one who enters," is any person who approaches a man or group seeking refuge from others. In the past, the *dakhil* was usually a murderer who feared retribution, but the label applies, in a broader sense, to any "alien among us," any stranger at the mercy of his hosts. As a foreigner in search of oral history, I was just such a creature. If tribesmen wanted me to know the truth, they had to admit me to their domains of authoritative speech, lest I be ensnared in the lying talk of other clans. By protecting me from the *kidhib* of their rivals, tribesmen were protecting their own reputations. They were also strengthening the marginal position from which I observed, partook in, and now write about their past.

In the following narrative, Shaykh Saʿud Abu l-ʿAmash tells of the coming to the Balga of Fayiz and Fawzan, ancestors of the ʿAdwan. Their arrival provokes a famous incident of "sanctuary." I recorded this story during my first week in the ʿAmamsha village of Salihi, and Shaykh Saʿud delicately likens the status of Fayiz and Fawzan, strangers in a strange land, to my own standing as an outsider in need of patrons.

In the Tent of the Amir

[The principal characters, Fayiz and Fawzan, are brothers. They belong to the Swayt, the shaykhly lineage of the Dafir tribe. According to Shaykh Saʿud, they have been banished from their tribe for murdering their cousin. In keeping with Bedouin custom, they cannot return to their people for at least seven years. Now they must find a new place to live.]

Fayiz and Fawzan said: "We want to go to the Balga."

This area we are now living in, which is now our country, was at that time called the Balga. So they came to the Balga, and the Amir of the Balga was who? The Mahfud al-Sardi, ancestor of the Sardiyya tribe. They came to him as guests. They came at night. They came to the encampment to greet the people, but everyone was sleeping, so they went to the tent of the shaykh and slept there, in the tent of the Amir.

In the morning the slaves came to make coffee and tea and to wake people up. They saw how Fayiz and Fawzan looked. Their clothing was strange; their appearance was strange. They weren't from this country. Foreigners, like you. They also had swords of a strange kind, all of gold, and the look of their dress was strange.

The slave of the Mahfud al-Sardi went to his master who was inside the tent—he hadn't come to the diwan yet; he was with the women still—and said: "O Master, we have two guests, strangers, not from this country. Their appearance is strange; their clothing is strange. They have swords the likes of which I've never seen in my life. All gold."

The Amir said: "Go fetch me one of their swords. I want to look at it."

The Amir said that to the slave, who belonged to him. The slave went.

He said: "O guests, I want one of your swords. The Amir wants to look at it."

The older of them said to him: "When the Amir comes to the diwan, he can look at our swords. We don't give up our swords for people to look at."

The slave returned and told his master: "The guests refuse to give me their swords. When you come to the diwan, you can look at them."

He said: "No. Return to them. Bring one of their swords. If they don't give it willingly, take it by force."

The slave came a second time and said: "By God, O guests, the Amir wants one of the swords. If you don't give one willingly, we'll take it by force. It's better for you to give us one and let us look at it."

They said: "We won't give it. If he wants to see the swords, he's welcome to come here and see them. But we don't give our swords away."

The slave approached and grabbed the sword of the elder brother, Fayiz, and they started to fight over it: the guest, whose name was Fayiz al-'Adwan, and the slave who belonged to the Amir al-Sardi. Fayiz' brother got up; he got up but didn't speak. He drew his sword, struck the slave, and cut off his hand: the hand of the slave who'd grabbed his brother. He struck him again and cut off the slave's head.

They left the Amir's tent, the tent of the Mahfud al-Sardi. They fled.

The people sent news to all the shaykhs that those two, the guests, killed the slave, cut off his hand and killed him. The people all gathered round. The brothers fled to a nearby tent. They didn't know whose tent it was. They were guests, just like you are among us. They didn't know the people. The tent belonged to a man named Abu Haydar. His descendants are still living here. They are now few, but good men, sturdy men. They are small in number; they never grew. They were in the country before the 'Adwan. They went to his tent as fugitives. We have a custom that if one man kills another and enters a tent [other than his own], the tent becomes a protected area for him. Period. It's not possible for anyone [of those who seek him] to enter his presence.

Abu Haydar came and faced the people who were gathering to kill [the two 'Adwanis], and the Amir came up to him.

Abu Haydar said: "Where are you headed, all worked up? These men are in my tent."

The Amir said: "Those men killed my slave."

Abu Haydar said: "Your slave is my slave. I'll pay his blood money. It's not possible for that crowd to enter my tent. If any one of you enters my tent, it's not allowed for you to approach them."

Allowed or not allowed, the important thing is that the Amir backed down. He didn't try to enter.

Abu Haydar said: "I'll pay the slave's blood money, whatever amount you want: two-, three-, or fourfold. I'll pay it."

The people backed down before Abu Haydar. He was a respected man, a shaykh. He paid the slave's blood money to whom? To the Amir al-Sardi.

So the two came and lived with him: Fayiz and Fawzan.

Shaykh Sa'ud has harbored *dakhils* himself in the past—mostly women on the run from their families—but protective custody, especially that given to an accused murderer, is nowadays the prerogative of the state. When, during Jordan's civil war of 1970, an 'Adwani military governor gave refuge to Palestinian guerrillas who sought protection in his home, he was gunned down by Jordanian security forces who had no interest in the niceties of tribal law. Like conventions of "escort," those associated with "sanctuary" have lost much of their power in the age of government.

My own tenure as a protected person in Salihi had nothing of the danger or high drama conveyed in the story of Fayiz and Fawzan. I was a *dakhil* only in a figurative sense, but the manner in which I had come to Salihi did strike the 'Amamsha as an appeal for help. My first four months of fieldwork had been spent in the 'Abbadi village of Swaysa, where I recorded only 'Abbadi oral traditions. When I arrived as a stranger among the 'Amamsha, I was moving beyond the reach of 'Abbadi escort, which had, as 'Adwanis saw it, kept me prisoner in the rhetorical domains of 'Abbadi narrators. Shaykh Sa'ud took my appearance in Salihi as a request for security of a more intellectual sort: I was fleeing the "lies" 'Abbadi elders had told me and seeking refuge in a truth only the 'Adwan could impart.

Sanctuary, Escort, and
the Effects of Power on Historical Talk

In the "age of shaykhs," when raiding and warfare were common, the ability to lead outsiders through tribal territory, and offer them sanctuary within it, was a quality only the most powerful men possessed. Today, in an "age of government," tribal wars are still being fought in speech, and the tribesmen who led me through this contested rhetorical landscape, who gave me sanctuary in authoritative talk, were also men of power. Very often, they were the sons and grandsons of shaykhs who had been prominent in the days before government. Their ability to make proper history was a function of their ability to assert credibly (and for the record) their genealogical connection to the great tribal leaders of the past.

The radical effects of power on oral history-making, which were evident in Zyudi testimony (see chapter 4), are perhaps better seen in a comparison of 'Abbadi and 'Adwani discourse. This comparison, I should add, is one few tribesmen would ever draw themselves. It is the work of a *dakhil* who moved from one domain of authoritative speech to another, all the while creating and analyzing texts. Only Dr. Ahmad 'Uwaydi al-'Abbadi, who once pursued a similar career, was familiar with the contrasts I describe below. His response—that of a man bound to an 'Abbadi point of view—was to suppress them. He urged me to do likewise. My "indiscretion," as Dr. Ahmad labeled it, was to recognize the following pattern and, worse still, to persist in lending significance to it:

1. During my first four months of research among 'Abbadis, I succeeded in recording only four hours of spoken testimony. Proper sources were few and far between; their testimony was fragmented; their genealogical knowledge, which seldom extended beyond seven or eight generations, was meager; the poetry they recited was incomplete, seldom more than a few lines long, often with a botched rhyme. In fact, the poem I heard most often—the one urging the Dwayk to grow gardens in the *ghor*—was an 'Adwani composition!

2. Among the 'Adwan, I recorded four hours of testimony during my first week of fieldwork. Proper sources were everywhere, and they needed little inducement to speak. Their stories, though told as separate episodes, came together in a lengthy narrative called *sirat al-'adwan* (the "saga" or "epic" of the 'Adwan); their genealogical knowledge, which went back thirteen generations or more, was prodigious; their poetry was abundant, better remembered, and superior in quality to 'Abbadi verse.

I eventually recorded tribal history from thirty-six ʿAbbadis—as compared to only seventeen ʿAdwanis—but the pattern of greater ʿAdwani volubility had, by the end of my fieldwork, defined itself even more sharply. The testimony of the seventeen ʿAdwani elders accounted for two-thirds of my sample. The longest (and most artful) poems, the longest (and most elaborate) genealogies, the longest (and most intricately detailed) prose narratives: all belonged to ʿAdwanis. In the historical war of words, the ʿAdwan stood better equipped to fight. ʿAbbadis, by contrast, produced history of a modest sort. Even when they engaged in shaykhly poetics, their words seemed to deflate the heroic aspirations of that genre. Indeed, the longest ʿAbbadi poem I recorded on tape—a tribute to Kayid Ibn Khatlan, the last paramount shaykh of ʿAbbad, who died circa 1875—was uttered as a protest against the mediocrity of the ʿAbbadi shaykhs who came after Kayid. The version that follows was spoken by Haj Mahmud Nisar Nasir al-Jarmi of the Jaramna.

> Hey boy, saddle up my camel,
> And (throw on) the saddlebags, red of color!
> Your path leads down to the *ghor*,
> And you'll travel night and day.
> You will come to the suite of Ibn Khatlan.
> The tent flaps are raised (to receive you)
> Clarified butter (is kept) on the fire,
> In boiling vats (it is simmering).
> The mutton is piled high on platters;
> It looks like the Stones of Abu Tara.
> And why, O shaykhs of this age,
> Is there found in you no refinement?
> O shaykhdom that came after Kayid,
> O like a buzzard, it fled to its nest!
> Kayid's fame spread to the Haj Road
> When he went to . . . [unclear] . . . in Zara
> His fame spread to Istanbul,
> When he gathered the troops in his tent.
> O shaykhs (who came) after Kayid,
> Your council is held among maidens.[2]

A blunter report on the "state of ʿAbbad" was offered by Shaykh Saʿud Abu l-ʿAmash. When I asked him why ʿAdwanis were more willing to have their historical talk recorded than ʿAbbadis were—and why, for that matter, the

---

2. For an English transliteration, see Appendix A.

'Adwan seemed to have more history to talk about—he gave a reply that, like most 'Adwani rhetoric, was unabashedly imperious:

> The 'Abbad have no history. Why? First, no famous shaykhs rose up among them. Shaykhs of mighty deeds. So they composed no poetry to remember them by. Also, the origins of 'Abbad are mixed. We 'Adwan are from one ancestor. We are the only tribe in the Balga from one ancestor, and we have one history. But 'Abbad: no. 'Abbad is many tribes, and they have no common origin, so how can they tell you an organized history like what we tell you? It's impossible. They have no history, really, so they stay quiet.

The image Shaykh Sa'ud develops is a caricature. I knew many 'Abbadis, shaykhs and sons of shaykhs, who were eager to recount history for the record. More often, though, I found myself in situations that confirmed Shaykh Sa'ud's view. The following incident (marked by a clumsy border crossing, a failed appeal for sanctuary, and an atmosphere of deep suspicion) spun itself out, with intricate variations, in dozens of 'Abbadi homes.

> [As we approach the house of Haj Migbil 'Abbas, we see him sitting beneath an oak tree, cat-napping. I recognize this man; he sat next to me once on the bus to Wadi Sir. I am struck now, as I was then, by his appearance. A large, tumorous growth, the size and shape of a fig, rises on the end of his nose. The tumor holds in place a pair of antique spectacles. The lenses are thick and the frames, taped-over at every joint, seem as old and worn as the Haj himself.
> My companion, Zayd, calls out a greeting: "Peace be upon you, ya Haj."
> Haj Migbil's magnified eyes gaze up at us: "And upon you be peace."
> I have been sent to visit the Haj by Tirfa, first wife of my 'Uwaydi host, 'Ali Khlayf. Tirfa, always a kind woman, feels sorry for me. Two weeks have passed since I last recorded a tape in Swaysa. The elders have grown wary of me. Even 'Ali Khlayf, who allowed me to record several stories about his father, is suddenly unwilling to speak. After learning of a whispering campaign against us, my wife, Sally, asked Tirfa for advice: "Andrew is upset. He is not succeeding in his work. No one will tell him stories. What should he do?" Tirfa suggested that I visit Haj Migbil 'Abbas, an elder of the Jabur clan: "He has lots of talk. He will tell you many stories."

I was excited to hear this. Like Tirfa, Haj Migbil is a Zyudi, and I had not yet recorded oral histories from the Zyud. In fact, this would be my first venture beyond the "proper sources" of the Afgaha. Tirfa sent along her twelve-year-old son, Zayd, as my escort: "To guide you on the path. It's just down the hill . . . not a far walk."

I should have realized that, despite the shortness of our trip, certain unspoken rules of border crossing were being broken. Zayd was not a kinsman of these Jaburis, nor was he an in-law. He lacked a natural place in Haj Migbil's audience. The Jabur must have wondered: "Why did the American bring this 'Uwaydi boy with him? Who will be privy to what we tell this man?" I was entering the Jaburi domain indiscreetly. I had failed, in fact, to leave the 'Uwaydi domain behind, and my status as a "marginal stranger" was not to be trusted.

But all this is hindsight. Now we are here, in the ethnographic present, sitting with Haj Migbil beneath the oak tree.

I can tell Zayd is afraid of the Haj. As a young boy, he is not quite sure how to act as a go-between for two adults: one a foreigner, the other a fright to behold. He rushes through the greetings as if reciting his school lessons, then he gets down to business much too quickly.]

ZAYD: Ya Haj, our brother Andrew wants to record stories. Tell . . .

HAJ MIGBIL: I don't have stories. I don't know anything.

[The Haj is offended by the rush. Zayd gives me an anguished look. What now? I try to slow the pace.]

ANDREW: That's fine, ya Haj. You don't have to talk. Zayd's in a little bit of a hurry.

[I grab Zayd's shoulders and playfully shake him.]

He has no patience, this boy. No patience at all. We just wanted to visit you.

HAJ: Welcome. Welcome.

ANDREW: And welcome to you, ya Haj.

[For the next few minutes we discuss the comforts of his napping place: it is shady, the breeze is cool, the tree is a good rest for his back. Haj Migbil carefully refrains from asking me questions about myself; such are the manners of very old men. The conversation lulls, and the Haj returns to Zayd's request: "What did he say, this boy? You want stories from me?"]

ANDREW: Yes . . . because all the people say you have stories. They say, "If you want history, go to Migbil ʿAbbas; he knows everything."

HAJ: Who told you that? The ʿUwaydi?

ANDREW: Many people say it. You are known for this.

[Not exactly true, but the flattery seems to work.]

HAJ: Well . . . an old man of great age . . . he should know history. He should remember it. Could I pour you some coffee?

ANDREW: Yes.

[As we pass around the cup, two men amble over from the nearby houses. We stand and receive their greetings. They are Badr and Bilal, Haj Migbil's sons. They know who I am: "Aren't you the American who lives with the ʿUwaydi?" The tone is wary, but cordial. I have the vague impression that they have come to break up a scene, to put a stop to something illicit.]

BADR: What is it you want from the Haj?

ANDREW: With your permission, I want to record stories from him: the history of ʿAbbad; the history of the Jabur and the Zyud; stories about the famous shaykhs. That sort of thing.

BADR: Why do you want talk like that? The history of ʿAbbad . . . what does America want with that kind of information?

[Badr assumes I am a spy. And why not? I fit the type. The old men liken me, always a bit ominously, to Glubb Basha, British commander of the Arab Legion. Like him, I wander about the tribal areas writing down the names of people and places: recording, scribbling, asking questions. Like Glubb, I speak a Bedouin dialect. I am familiar with local customs. To many ʿAbbadis, such knowledge is odd and threatening. Whose power does it serve?]

ANDREW: I'm not in the American government. I work as a researcher . . . with Yarmouk University . . . here in Jordan. I'm writing a dissertation on the history of the Balga tribes. I want to record the Haj's talk and put it in my book.

[A likely story. Even I have trouble believing it. But now is not the time to draw nice distinctions between Fulbright, the National Science Foundation, and the CIA; or to distinguish my "local sponsor" from my "funding source." Such disclaimers would be meaningless to Haj Migbil and his sons. Besides, a judgment has already been made. As I speak the words above, Bilal flashes Badr a sign: he snips the air with his fingers, like scissors, or the flitting tongue of a snake. Zayd catches the message in route to Badr. The

gesture, he will later tell me, is a common one. It means: "He's
lying."

I, however, am oblivious to these local codes. I sense only that
my safe introduction will not suffice. Unlike old men, who consider
it rude to confront their guests with personal questions, Badr and
Bilal conform to the modern etiquette, in which the stranger—once
an "extra-ordinary" figure, anomalous, and surrounded by sacred
duties of hospitality (see Pitt-Rivers 1977)—becomes a plainly
secular type: a tourist or a spy. Since I claim to be neither, the
brothers are eager to discover my true identity. They ask me an
array of questions that, by now, seems almost ritualistic. It divides,
roughly, into queries of the following sort: (1) those concerning
how much money I have, where it comes from, and who, on the
local scene, has access to it; (2) those concerning my religious beliefs
and ethnic origins; and (3) those concerning my stand on the Arab-
Israeli dispute.

Amid this flurry of all too familiar questions, Badr asks one that
has never been put to me before. It seems a bit off-topic, but given
the popular equation of the terms "Jew" and "spy," the question
goes boldly to the point.]

BADR: Are you circumcised?

ANDREW: Yes. I am circumcised.

BILAL: [To Badr, confused and astonished] He's circumcised?

BADR: [To Bilal, equally confused and astonished] That's what
he said.

ANDREW: Yes. It's normal in America. Most men my age are
circumcised: Muslims, Jews, Christians. There's no difference. They
say it's cleaner.

[Badr and Bilal find my admission utterly bizarre. Jordanian
Christians, in accordance with the teachings of Saint Paul, refuse to
be circumcised, lest they be held accountable to Jewish law. Indeed,
they take pride in their unmutilated foreskins, which set them apart
from both Muslims and Jews. Is it conceivable, then, that an
American Christian would submit to circumcision; that millions
of them would submit to it?

No. Obviously I am not a Christian. Badr and Bilal have un-
cloaked me: I am a Jew and, therefore, a spy. I, and my little 'Uwaydi
accomplice, will not be given sanctuary today, only the obligatory
service of tea. Zayd understands fully what has just transpired. I,
once again, do not. The conversation, still as cordial as ever, turns

quickly to other things: life in America, marriage customs, the morals of Western women, my opinions of Jordan, the progress of my work. I try to elicit historical talk, but Bilal and Badr are not about to be duped into revealing their clan secrets to a Jewish spy.]

BILAL: Didn't you take information from those 'Uwaydi? [He points uphill, in the direction of Swaysa.] Dr. Ahmad knows everything about 'Abbad, and he writes it in books. Why don't you take information from him?

ANDREW: He knows a lot. But he doesn't write it all in his books. There is no chapter on the Jabur, on your ancestors, in his books. Not a word.

[Badr and Bilal look stung. Perhaps this is news to them. Both men are illiterate; they do not own Ahmad's books nor, I suspect, have they ever seen them. Perhaps Dr. Ahmad's omission will embolden them to speak?]

ANDREW: The stories I record from the 'Uwaydi are all about the Afgaha. They don't talk about the Zyud. When I ask about the Zyud, they say, "Go to the Zyud. Go to Haj Migbil." So I came to you.

BADR: They told you nothing about us? No. Not possible. What did they say about the Jabur?

[Plenty. None of it good. If Zayd were not with me, I might be able to play on this negative 'asabiyya; I might be able to prompt Haj Migbil to speak against the 'Uwaydi, as a corrective. But with Zayd sitting by my side, such gambits are totally out of the question. I try another approach.]

ANDREW: Well . . . as you know, people like to talk about themselves.

BILAL: That's true.

ANDREW: When I ask about the shaykhs of this area, "Who were they?" they say:

Fandi Abu Mahayr,
Sa'id Basha al-Slayhat,
Filah al-Dhib al-Hisami,
Khalaf al-Rashid al-'Uwaydi, . . .

BILAL: Eh! Khalaf was no shaykh. Those 'Uwaydi are lying to you. Khalaf was not a shaykh. No way. Don't put that in your book. No shaykh ever rose up among the 'Uwaydi.

[Zayd is glowering into the pile of dirt he has nervously scraped together with his feet. He is angry; he has been angry for some time now, but he says nothing.]

ANDREW: Many people say he was a shaykh.

BILAL: His own kin say it, that's all. Just his own kin in Swaysa.

ANDREW: Well . . . God knows best. The important thing is that all these men [the shaykhs I just mentioned] were from the Afgaha, not from the Zyud. Is it possible that the Haj tell me about the shaykhs of the Zyud?

[The Haj, who has drifted in and out of wakefulness, perks up.]

HAJ: Shaykhs of the Zyud?

ANDREW: Yes. Stories about them. Look . . . I brought a tape recorder with me, so I can record what the Haj says, word for word, without mistakes, just as he said it.

[I take the recorder from my backpack. Badr and Bilal are perturbed by the sight of it. They want nothing to do with this intrusive little machine.]

HAJ: What does he want me to say?

BADR: Nothing, Haj. We don't talk into tape recorders.

HAJ: The shaykh of Zyudi shaykhs, the true shaykh, was the Dwayk. Irwayij al-Dwaykat. And among us, the Jabur . . .

BADR: No, ya Haj. That talk is old. We don't want it right now. There are no shaykhs today.

HAJ: The shaykhs . . . all of them died.

[Haj Migbil returns to silence. He wants to talk, but his sons no longer fear him. They will not tolerate any storytelling in my presence. I am reminded of a similar incident, several weeks ago, when the sons of an old Hisami shaykh asked to listen to the tape their father and I had recorded earlier that afternoon. It did not please them, and they demanded that I erase it. Hoping to avoid an embarrassing reprise of that event—which left the old man feeling humiliated—I put the recorder away.]

ANDREW: Some people don't like tape recorders. That's no problem. I can write notes . . . in a notebook. I write everything in this notebook.

BILAL: Can I see it?

ANDREW: Of course. Look.

[Bilal, who is illiterate, thumbs officiously through my mostly English notes. This is not unusual; people very often ask to look through my notebook, or (without asking at all) will rummage through my backpack. The line between "mine and thine" is drawn differently here, and I have lost my initial unease with such behavior. I am the one, after all, who has made a profession of probing into other people's affairs. Bilal spots a page of Arabic.]

BILAL: Did you write this?

ANDREW: Yes. I learned how to write at my university in America.

BILAL: Eh! Read it to me.

[The entry is a proverb, which I read: "The shaykh must be strong, as our Lord is strong." Badr starts to laugh, the way a father laughs when his child reads to him aloud for the first time: a bit proudly.]

BADR: See, ya Bilal? This is really a dangerous man; he's smarter than you are.

[Badr laughs again. I join in; being called "dangerous" (*khatir*) is something of a compliment among Bedouin. Zayd is still glowering into the dust, and Haj Migbil, who knows that his sons will not let him speak, rises slowly to his feet, takes leave of us, and wanders off toward the house to pray. I have missed my chance.

The brothers, meanwhile, persist in their questioning. I have given up any hope of extracting useful information from them, but they have not yet abandoned their quest for knowledge. Badr wants to know the names of the people I have recorded from. I mention several, all of them from the Afgaha. Badr sniffs, then dismisses them as liars. He offers no "proper sources" of his own, however, and all my attempts to coax stories from him fail.

The current of information is flowing strongly in one direction: *away from me.* Bilal wants to hear a story I've been told. Any story. I am tired; Zayd is fidgety; it is time to leave. I want to say: "No. No stories. I have already told you a lot. I've given you access to my notes. I've named my sources. I've answered all manner of personal questions, several of which dealt with my most private parts, and you have told me nothing."

Yet even as I ponder this testy response, one of 'Ali Khlayf's stories comes to mind. When 'Ali (plate 11) first told it to me, I immediately took it for an allegory. I am paying 'Ali's family a generous rent, and the jealousy this inspires, along with the belief that 'Ali is aiding and abetting a Jewish spy, has led to some nasty talk in Swaysa. The gossip weighed heavily on 'Ali's mind when he related the following account, in which his father and uncles defend

Plate 11. ʿAli Khlayf al-ʿUwaydi: "We and they have eaten bread and salt. We and they have lived together, and they are dear to us and friends to us. . . . We will not betray them."

the wealth of Christians against a party of Bedouin intent on plundering it.]

"We must protect the wealth of the Christians until they return"

AS TOLD BY ʿALI KHLAYF AL-ʿUWAYDI AL-ʿABBADI

[This event took place in 1918, on the estate of the Bisharat, a family of well-to-do Christian farmers. ʿAli's father, Khlayf, and his uncles, Khalaf and Khalifa, are employed as watchmen on the estate. The First World War, now in its final stages, has only just arrived in the Balga. In March, 1918, and again in May, the British attacked Ottoman positions in the Balga, but heavy rains and Turkish reinforcements forced them, on both occasions, to retreat west of the Jordan. The Bisharat, like many other local Christians, were suspected of sympathizing with the British. Fearing for their lives, they fled to the West Bank, leaving everything behind. The ʿUwaydi watchmen now find themselves in charge of an immense, indefensible fortune.]

The Turks defeated the English. The English retreated and the Christians followed them and retreated with them. Then the Bani Sakhr rose up in power and strength, with the ʿAjarma alongside them, and took up their weapons and set out to plunder the wealth of the Bisharat.

The Bisharat had 100 Hollandi cattle [milch cows]. They had seventy plows and 80 mules to plow with. There weren't machines for plowing the soil in that day and age. There weren't any. They had 70 camels, 200 Shami goats, and some 250 she-camels. The house of the Bisharat was vast, a huge space, and it had two doors: a door that opened toward Mecca, and a door that opened to the north.

Then Khalaf al-Rashid, Khlayf al-Rashid, and Khalifa al-Rashid (God have mercy on them all) locked up all the wealth of the Christians, of the Bisharat, who were: Shakir, Raji, Bishara, and Nur al-Bisharat. All the goods, all the wealth of the Bisharat, everything was locked up in that building. Around it was a wall more than five meters high, and inside it were wells; inside was all the seed; inside were all their possessions.

The Bani Sakhr rose up and surrounded the building, they and the ʿAjarma alongside them, and said: "We're going to plunder this wealth."

And Khalaf stood on the wall and said: "We have eaten together . . . we and these Bisharat. We have shared bread and salt, and it's not possible now for us to betray them. It's not our custom to betray a man, whether he be Christian or Muslim. It's not our custom to betray a man. It's our duty to protect the wealth of the Bisharat, and we intend to see to it that when they return, they'll find all their goods, the large and the small."

The Bani Sakhr said: "Ya Khalaf al-Rashid, our brother, those Christians have seceded and fled from this country, and they won't be returning to this country. So let us plunder their wealth."

The 'Uwaydis said: "We'll repeat what we just told you. We and they have eaten bread and salt. We and they have lived together, and they are dear to us and friends to us. We have lived side by side, and we will not betray them. It's up to us to protect their goods until they return."

The Bani Sakhr tightened their reins [and moved forward].

The 'Ajarma tightened their reins, and said: "We are going to plunder this wealth, this plenty the Bisharat have stored up."

Now those 'Abbadis were Muslims, but they said: "The man who comes near either one of these doors will die."

And they aimed their rifles at them.

There was a section of the 'Ajarma, in-laws of 'Abbad, who were friends of Khalaf. They did not want to attack him, so they asked for a special favor: "Let us plunder that wealth."

Khalaf said to them: "It's not possible. We must honor you in our own tents and slaughter for you from our own herds and wealth. But the livestock of the Christians, no man comes near it. If we show you hospitality, it'll be from our own tents."

So they honored the Skhur and 'Ajarma nobly, happily, and obligingly . . . from their own wealth. And they were content. They honored them as guests and slaughtered sacrifices for them and showed them all due respect.

They said: "Farewell. Go safely. And forgive us, because those Christians are friends and loved ones to us. We ate bread and salt. We won't betray them. We have to protect the Christians' wealth until they return from the West Bank. If they don't return, we'll take whatever we want."

Then the Skhur and the 'Ajarma left . . . and, praise be to God, the wealth of the Bisharat was protected.

Peace be upon you and the mercy of God and His blessings.

[As I repeat my own version of ʿAli Khlayf's story to Badr and Bilal, our allegorical places within it become embarrassingly clear. My wife and I are the wealthy Christians, ʿAli Khlayf and (at the moment) his son Zayd figure as our dutiful protectors, and Badr and Bilal stand with the plundering horde outside the storehouse walls.]

BADR: Hmm. That's something that definitely never happened.

BILAL: Are you going to put that [nonsense] in your book?

ANDREW: Yes. And God willing, I'll have Jaburi stories to put beside it.

BILAL: God willing.

[As if shamed by ʿAli's talk of "bread and salt," Badr invites us to stay and have supper with them, but Zayd wants to go home. I politely refuse. Bilal suggests another pot of tea: "Just another glass before you go." Again, I decline and promise to return another day. Bilal presses on, as one does in these situations: "Are you sure? Just one glass." Now Zayd speaks up. His tone is frustrated, almost insolent.]

ZAYD: When Andrew says no, he means no. He's not like us Arabs, who say one thing and mean something else. The Americans say yes or no, and that's it. They don't like to lie.

[I often hear tribesmen say such things. Many seem eager to believe that Europeans, especially Americans and the English, are more truthful than they are, more direct, more apt to mean what they say, to keep their promises and appointments. I am always shocked to hear this, and I am doubly shocked now. Zayd's comment could easily be taken as it was intended: as an attack on the character of Badr and Bilal. We decide to let the outburst slip by unnoticed. After a barrage of cordial farewells, Zayd and I head back uphill to Swaysa, both of us relieved that our failed visit is finally over.]

Several months later, as I recorded ʿAdwani history in the luxurious sitting rooms of Shaykh Saʿud Abu l-ʿAmash, I finally came to understand my experiences with ʿAbbadis like Badr and Bilal. The Jabur had produced no "shaykhs of mighty deeds." They were strangers to power and the historical fascination it inspires. They were men who could not speak confidently, without fear of retribution. The ʿAdwan, even at their most reticent, were strikingly otherwise. Haj Mahmud al-Talab Abu ʿArabi, who proved highly evasive when placed in a situation similar to that faced by Haj Migbil ʿAbbas (e.g., a breakdown of rhetorical domains and a mixing of audiences) performed his evasive maneuvers openly, on tape (see chapter 4). Unlike Badr and Bilal, who stifled their father, Haj Mahmud's sons encouraged him to speak, and eventually the Haj did speak. Most 'Abbadis worked toward opposite goals: silence, concealment, and the avoidance of textuality.

> On our way home, Zayd criticized me for admitting I was circumcised: "Why did you tell them that? Now they will say you are a Jew." He thought I had been too friendly, too open with men who showed me no goodwill, who served lukewarm tea, and did not offer us meat: "They were laughing at you!" When we got home, Zayd catalogued every perceived insult to a rapt audience, which (to my embarrassment) included 'Ali Khlayf and Tirfa. The horrors of the visit, most of which had not been apparent to me, were embellished with every retelling, and my ears were soon blistered by hot curses against Haj Migbil and his sons:
> "Those people are descendants of *ghawarna*; they have no honor."
> "Do you know why Haj Migbil's nose is so big? Because he swore falsely on the Qur'an, that's why!"
> "It's a known fact that he has the evil eye, that old man, and his sons are thieves. They steal even from their own neighbors."
> "Why would you want to record from liars like them?"
> And on and on and on: a lava flow of *'asabiyya*.
> At the end of the evening, 'Ali pulled me aside and gave me some personal advice: "In the future, when you talk to people outside the 'Uwaydi, don't say Khalaf was a shaykh. Say he was a good man, a man worth his weight . . . or, better, don't talk about him at all. You see now that it brings trouble, or don't you?"

When I told 'Adwanis about this episode, they found only one word to describe it: *maskin*, a term signifying all that is pathetic, hapless, and low. The 'Adwan were no less concerned that I might be a spy; they suspected that other tribesmen might be privy to my tapes as well. But unlike 'Abbadis, who were often silenced by these concerns, the 'Adwan seemed to delight in the recklessness of their speech. Going "on the record" was a consummate show of strength for them. I once asked Haj 'Arif if he would like me to change his name before I published his testimony, much of which was highly inflammatory. Like most 'Adwanis, he was genuinely offended by the specter of anonymity: "Eh! Change my name? Why? I've told you the truth. The truthful one fears no one but God!"

If Badr and Bilal dreaded the thought that others might overhear their

Plate 12. An escort and his proper source. Faris Salih al-ʿAdwan and his grandfather, Haj Khalaf al-Fahd al-Nimr.

testimony, ʿAdwanis feared the possibility that certain others (perhaps those shadowy powers that had sent me to the Balga) might not hear it. The ʿAdwan, themselves important men, mistook me for a man of importance. For some, I was a statesman in training. I would return one day as U.S. ambassador to Jordan. Others thought I was related to prominent officials in the U.S. government. An imaginative handful argued that I would return soon in the front ranks of an invading Israeli army. An even smaller contingent believed that I was writing a book. Whatever the reality, it was necessary that I understand certain facts: the ʿAdwan were shaykhs of the Balga; they were men to be reckoned with. Concealment, even in the face of the enemy, was simply not the ʿAdwani style. As Faris Salih al-Nimr put it, a bit facetiously: "If you were a spy, I'd tell you about ʿAdwani history anyway. It's something any good spy should know. Then, after you'd written it all down carefully, I'd turn you in to Intelligence: you and all your notes and tapes. They need information like this."

When Faris took me to visit his grandfather, Shaykh Khalaf al-Fahd, the old man regaled us with stories about all the Western and Jordanian scholars who had come to him over the years, seeking knowledge (plate 12). Ruks al-ʿUzayzi had recorded the poems of Nimr Ibn ʿAdwan from him; Dr. Ahmad al-ʿUwaydi had asked the Haj to judge the correctness of variant ʿAdwani genealogies; an American historian—"or maybe she was French. God knows"—had taken down his memories of the 'Adwani Revolt of 1923. Haj Khalaf did not consider these visitations odd or threatening; it was only natural that scholars would seek his guidance. Had not the English Orientalists turned to his grandfather, Goblan, for escort and accurate information on the Balga tribes?

[Faris is explaining to the Haj, in a very loud voice, who I am. I have visited Haj Khalaf before, but two months have passed. I am not sure he remembers me. He seems entirely familiar, though, with the persona Faris is describing to him. I am "the foreigner in search of knowledge." Faris asks me to turn on the recorder.]

FARIS: Ya Grandfather, our brother Andrew wants to record your talk about the shaykhs of the 'Adwan.

HAJ KHALAF: The 'Adwan have many shaykhs. They are the princes of this country. The paramount shaykh of the Balga is Ibn 'Adwan. There are no shaykhs mightier than he. What do you want to know about us?

ANDREW: I want to know how the 'Adwan became shaykhs. What was the basis of their rule?

HAJ KHALAF: Good fortune (*haz*) and horsemanship. Their fortune was great, even though they were small in number. In the time of my grandfather, Nimr, they were only sixty riders, the 'Adwan, but they defeated the Bani Sakhr, who were a thousand men. The dominion . . .

FARIS: The poet said, "O Leader of the sixty, attack the thousand!"

HAJ KHALAF: . . . was theirs because they were intelligent in matters of politics. The 'Adwan, this is written in books . . . the Orientalists would ask them, as a test, "Do the English rule such and such a land?" They would say, "No." Then they would ask, "Do the English rule such and such?" They would say, "Yes." This was not news to us, who rules what.

[The Haj laughs.]

HAJ: But the foreigners would say, "The Bedouin, what does he know about such things?" And indeed . . .

FARIS: They were clever, the 'Adwan. Very intelligent.

HAJ KHALAF: . . . if the Bedouin said "France rules it," then France ruled it. Don't think the Bedouin are not aware of politics.

ANDREW: No. They are very aware.

FARIS: The English Orientalist said in his book: "I was surprised. A shaykh named Dhiyab, who lived in the Third World, beyond civilization, where no newspapers could reach him, nor magazines—this old shaykh explained to me the terms under which we occupied Cyprus."

[Faris is referring to a passage from Conder's *Heth and Moab* (1883), which appears in Arabic, along with excerpts from other travel books, in Suleiman Musa's *Kitab al-rahhala*. The same passage in English is given below:

> The aged Diab ("the wolf"), a modern Zeeb, was a little old man of commanding appearance, whom Goblan treated with the respect due an elder relative . . . The conversation on occasion of this visit was most instructive. The old gentleman, who came in a private, not in an official capacity, hobbled in aided by his grey junior, and leaned on his crooked cane, arrayed in a fine white and amber abba, with a warm lambswool jacket beneath. It was not long after the taking of Tunis by the French, and their war with Beni Helal, the "Sons of the Crescent," as the 'Adwan term the Arabs of North Africa, for whom they have a great respect. The English, he remarked, had as yet taken nothing in the east. I reminded him of Cyprus. "No," he answered; "you hold that as tributaries of the Sultan." He then asked if the French would take Tripoli also. I replied that it belonged to the Sultan. "So did Tunis," he dryly answered. I told him that the English, having a country as fair as that of the 'Adwan, and being a righteous people, did not desire to seize the lands of the Sultan or of anyone else, and this final announcement he received in silence, with an air of courteous incredulity.
>
> The interview was thus of considerable interest. It is not surprising that the Maronites and the Christians of Damascus and Jerusalem should be keenly watching the political horizon—that they should know Lord Beaconsfield and Mr. Gladstone by name, and approve the policy of the latter, because they consider it anti-Turkish; but it was somewhat startling to find in the wilds of Moab an old gentleman with a stiff leg, who had certainly not been over Jordan for several years, yet who understood the nature of our tenure of Cyprus, and dimly foresaw the probability of such an event as the occupation of Egypt (1883, 323–324).

I had not yet read Conder when I sat with Haj Khalaf; only later did I realize that his reference to *Heth and Moab* contained subtle instruction: "We are not politically backward. We know what you are up to. Do not condescend to us." Our positions were being defined, once again, by a carefully drawn analogy. I was Conder; Faris was Goblan; Haj Khalaf was Dhiyab.]

HAJ KHALAF: The 'Adwan know these things.

[He stares at me long and hard, trying to gauge my reaction. I am about to speak when he starts up again.]

HAJ: Nowadays . . . our government, all the Arab states, each
Arab state. I say they are all mistaken. We have in our history,
the history of the Arabs, we have the knowledge that no Jew will
be left outside; they will all return to Palestine. Palestine. How
many governments have ruled it? It is mentioned in the Qur'an:

> Then did we grant you
> The Return as against them:
> We gave you increase
> In resources and sons,
> And made you
> The more numerous
> In man-power.

FARIS: Yes. It is said in the Qur'an that the Jews will return to
their lands again.

> Bani Israel will twice do mischief in the land
> And be elated with mighty arrogance.

That's in the Qur'an.

HAJ KHALAF: It says in the Qur'an:

> If ye did well,
> Ye did well for yourselves;
> If ye did evil,
> (Ye did it) against yourselves.
> So when the second
> Of the warnings came to pass,
> (We permitted your enemies)
> To disfigure your faces,
> And to enter your Temple
> As they had entered it before,
> And to visit with destruction
> All that fell into their power.

[The abrupt shift to Palestine is not without purpose. Like Badr and
Bilal, Haj Khalaf cannot rule out the possibility that I am Jewish, or
a spy, or both. Nonetheless, he makes his suspicion known to me in
a way quite unlike the Jaburi concern for circumcision. His recitation of the Qur'an suggests that he fully comprehends the politics
of God—that he comprehends it better than "all the Arab states"—
just as his mention of Conder suggests that, as an 'Adwani shaykh,
he fully understands the politics of Man. He is at ease in either
realm. If it is truly knowledge I seek, the Haj seems to imply, then
I have come to the right place.]

Haj Migbil ʿAbbas and his sons could not recite scripture or travelogue, but they, too, were acting out strategies that had close analogies in the "age of shaykhs." During the nineteenth century, ʿAbbadis seldom gave escort to European travelers, in part because ʿAdwani shaykhs forbade them to do so, but more important, because ʿAbbad had gained, early on, a reputation for unreliable escort. When Buckingham toured the Balga in 1816, he enlisted the protection of two Bedouin from "the tribe of Beni Abad"; they abandoned him and stole his rifle (1825, 16). In 1847, a group of ʿAbbadis—"60 wild Arabs firing guns and throwing stones"—plundered the crew of the HMS *Spartan* on the banks of the Jordan after negotiations for safe passage through ʿAbbadi territory collapsed (Finn 1847). In 1855, when Consul James Finn entrusted the "comfort and safety" of English travelers to the ʿAdwan, the ʿAbbadis were known to him only as brigands and "low fellows" (1868, 19).

In 1990, the ʿAdwan entertained similar views. They doubted that ʿAbbadis could tell me anything worth repeating about the "age of shaykhs." Often, they questioned the propriety of my living with ʿAbbadis at all, and the paucity of the historical material I collected during my first stay with ʿAbbad was taken as proof that my research design was flawed. The implications of this critique were infuriatingly obvious to ʿAbbadis, yet the quantitative disparities between their own oral traditions and those of the ʿAdwan could not be casually dismissed as fraudulent propaganda. If the ʿAdwan had more poetry, if their genealogies were longer, if I had recorded more stories from them, this gave the impression that the ʿAdwan had a more illustrious past. The contrasts had to be rendered meaningless, or reduced to the status of *kidhib*, and ʿAbbadis always rose eagerly to this deconstructive task.

[I have just returned from a five-month stint among the ʿAdwan and have come to visit Dr. Ahmad al-ʿUwaydi, whom I have not seen since I left ʿAbbad. The diwan is full of tribesmen awaiting an audience with Ahmad, who is now a member of parliament. Ahmad's father, Haj Salih, is filling the air with greetings— "Welcome! Welcome to all!"—and pouring thimbles of cardamom-spiced coffee. I, meanwhile, am being quizzed about the ʿAdwan: "How were they?" "They were good to you, God willing, like us?" "How did you find their character?" "What do they say about ʿAbbad?"

Dr. Ahmad and his younger brother, Dr. ʿAbdullah, enter the room, businesslike and energetic. All stand and exchange greetings. Ahmad is surprised to see me. He bellows across the assembly: "What? Did the ʿAdwan throw you out?" Everyone laughs. We trade four kisses, two more than is customary, and Ahmad ushers me to a seat beside him. He is curious to know how he stands, politically, among 'Adwanis: "What do they say about me?" I give a mixed report: some disdain him, others are attracted to his nationalist message. Ahmad had hoped for better, but: "As you know, they have been against 'Abbad throughout history. They hate to see an 'Abbadi in parliament. They hate to see my 'Abbadi face on the television screen. Ha!"

Ahmad asks about my research: "Perhaps you found it difficult to get the truth?" I decide to be frank: "I can't say I got the truth, but I did record a lot: poems, stories . . . much more than I got from 'Abbadis. I hope I have better success getting 'Abbadi history this time." Ahmad tenses slightly. He had urged against my 'Adwani sojourn from the start, and he confidently predicted its failure.]

ANDREW: Some other time, when you're less busy, I'd like to talk with you about this.

AHMAD: What do you want to know?

ANDREW: How to get recorded testimony from 'Abbadis . . . you know . . . how to improve my methods. Otherwise, I won't have a good 'Abbadi sample. It'll all be 'Adwani.

AHMAD: 'Abbadis are not interested in the past; we are concerned with the future.

[Ahmad is now in his debating posture. He is trying to outflank me (and the 'Adwani past) by invoking the future. But his comment is inaccurate. The men sitting around us are engaged, even as we speak, in a heated discussion of 'Abbadi history and its effect on the recent parliamentary elections.]

ANDREW: Why, in your opinion?

[Ahmad shifts into English.]

AHMAD: Among us history is more political, more dangerous, because we are not from one genealogy. I think you have seen that?

ANDREW: Oh yes, definitely. You can't speak with one voice, whereas . . .

AHMAD: Exactly. I don't want to talk about so-and-so's genealogy, and I don't want him to talk about mine. It's not fitting that he do it.

[Another strange comment. Ahmad has built a career out of publishing other people's genealogies.]

ANDREW: . . . whereas the 'Adwan can speak with one voice,

theoretically I mean, even if it's only at a very high level in their genealogy.

[Ahmad grimaces and shakes his head.]

AHMAD: No. That is propaganda. They make themselves big through their genealogy. They say, "our ancestors were shaykhs." But we are through with shaykhs in Jordan; that history is dead. Today we want servants, establishers, constructors, brilliant leaders. We don't want parasites. A shaykh is a parasite.

ANDREW: Well, the 'Adwan say that too. Everyone says the "age of shaykhs" is finished. But they have this whole shaykhly tradition. The shaykhdom is still important to them, and . . .

AHMAD: There is no shaykhdom today.

ANDREW: . . . but the memory of the shaykhdom is still important, and, like you say, the unified genealogy is part of it.

AHMAD: I have proof that their genealogies are false.

ANDREW: In what sense?

AHMAD: Just compare them, from one 'Adwani to another, and you can see they are rubbish. I have shown this in my research, in a subtle way, so that all can see it.

[Ahmad is referring to the 'Adwan chapter in his book, *The Jordanian Tribes: Land, People, History,* in which he cites contradictory versions of 'Adwani genealogy, each taken from a respected 'Adwani elder. Ahmad usually publishes only a single version of a group's pedigree, and his reason for doing otherwise in the 'Adwani case is clear: "Behold! Their unified genealogy is a mess!"]

ANDREW: Well, the different genealogies are inconsistent, that's true, but even 'Abbadi genealogies are inconsistent. I'm talking about . . .

AHMAD: No. If it is true, it is consistent. There is proof the 'Adwan are definitely not from one ancestor.

ANDREW: Like what?

[Ahmad smiles confidently, knowingly, as if he has just glanced at a winning hand of cards.]

AHMAD: I have it. It is known to me. Someday it will be known to others.

ANDREW: Is there any chance that I could see it?

AHMAD: Perhaps. It is with my papers . . . somewhere. Perhaps later I will show you.

[Ahmad is politely declining my request. I am not surprised. He never lets me copy or browse through any of his unpublished material, even when it seems entirely in his interest—polemically at least—to do so. I suspect he is bluffing, but why press the point? Ahmad is most revealing when he attempts to obscure.]

AHMAD: Listen. The history of the 'Adwan is mostly exaggerations. It is known that they are deceivers and oppressors. If I wrote the truth about them (what is known among the tribes), they would definitely harass me.

ANDREW: I know how you feel. I don't see how I can write any of this down without offending someone.

AHMAD: It is better just to record their genealogy and ignore their lies and exaggerations.

ANDREW: Well, I can't just erase everything I recorded from them. It's most of my data. Besides, it's not all *kidhib*.

AHMAD: It is, I would say, 80 percent *kidhib*. Perhaps it is more.

[Like other tribesmen, Ahmad has a penchant for assessing truth in percentages.]

ANDREW: Are you saying the 'Adwan were not prominent shaykhs? I mean, there's plenty of proof in the travel literature that the 'Adwan were the really big shaykhs in the nineteenth century: Dhiyab, 'Ali, Goblan . . .

[A momentary recognition passes between us. We are about to discredit ourselves: I, by edging too close to an 'Adwani point of view; Ahmad, by committing himself to claims that 'Abbadi oral traditions, and a travel literature known to both of us, clearly do not support.]

AHMAD: They were, you might say, strong men. But 'Abbad was equal to them. They did not rule over us, as they claim, and what they took from us, they took by treachery, which is their way. Look. I have recorded their true history. I have it all, with the names of my sources and dates and places. But this information is private. Only I possess it. The important thing is: the history of the 'Adwan is a product of their complicated psychology. They are the most treacherous tribe in Jordan, famous for cruelty. They cannot trust their women. 'Abbad, as you have seen with your own eyes, is the most generous tribe, and Bani Sakhr, we say, is the bravest. These things are known. You should not contaminate your research by publishing 'Adwani exaggerations.

ANDREW: God willing, I won't contaminate it.

AHMAD: God willing. I know you hate lying.

[Ahmad turns abruptly to the man beside him and, speaking

Arabic once more, begins to fish for political intelligence on various ʿAbbadi clans. My audience has ended.]

If Ahmad sought to undermine ʿAdwani history by eliminating its exaggerated content, other ʿAbbadis—those who lacked Ahmad's knowledge of ʿAdwani oral traditions—sought to match the richness of ʿAdwani history by invoking against it all the ʿAbbadi traditions I had failed, by some fluke of method, to elicit.

[Mishrif and I are listening to the tape recorder. Haj ʿArif's voice, sonorous and rhythmic, delivers the last in a litany of boasts, insults, and curses. We stare intently at the machine.]

He who makes war on the ʿAdwan, limps away in chains.
The mighty swordsman makes play with his neck.

MISHRIF: Stop there.
[Mishrif checks the text, mutters something to himself, then crosses out a word.]
MISHRIF: Rewind and play it again. He's talking too fast.
[I rewind and push "play."]

He who makes war on the ʿAdwan, limps away in chains.
The mighty swordsman makes play with his neck.

MISHRIF: OK. That's enough. I got it.
[I pluck the cassette from the tape recorder while Mishrif scans the poem. We have been working together for several weeks now, transcribing and translating *gasayid*. Mishrif is himself a poet, highly literate in Arabic and English; he judges the piece we have just finished a rather fine one, even though Haj ʿArif "recites it like he's firing a machine gun."]
MISHRIF: Yes. It's very good. Listen:
[Mishrif recites the poem in Arabic, pronouncing each word deliberately for my sake. We then work out an approximate English translation, which, along with Haj ʿArif's prose introduction, is presented below.]

The Slaying of Sfug al-ʿAdwan

There was a boy, a warrior, the son of Dhiyab. His name was Sfug al-ʿAdwan. One day, when the horses met [on the field of battle], this boy was armed—he was only about fourteen years old—and he fell from his horse and was trying to mount her again. He pulled her reins. The horse refused to let him mount. The horse started to buck and refused to let him mount. So he backed away from her, and the enemy attacked him. The Skhur ambushed him. They slew him. He and Minawir Abu l-Ghanam of the Ghanamat, who was with him. Both were killed. The two of them.

When they slew them, news of it came to the ʿAdwan, that Sfug had been slain. And his mother, Shiga, was completely overcome by grief. The mother of Sfug mourned for him.

The people said: "What should we do? What should we do?"

Dhiyab said: "I want to raid them."

So the ʿAdwan raided them. And as revenge for the two they slew fourteen shaykhs. From whom? From the Skhur.

The poet says:

O rider atop a mare of pure color,
You'd say: "Like a bird diving toward its perch,
By God, like a hind startled by the wind,
Like a bird of prey hunting down the flock."
You come to a tent of seven columns,
And the sound of the coffee mill, before sunrise, invites you.
Go to him and tell him what's transpired,
And let your mind be alert to the reply.
Tell him your master, who reads and writes on paper,
Has sent him this missive from the Brother of Zahia:
"O Ibn Fayiz, don't prolong our absence.
Such behavior reflects poorly on those who condone it.
You owe us a debt you cannot bear.
Not all debts to the Swayti [Ibn ʿAdwan] are forgiven.
Ibn ʿAdwan comes to you atop a strong-legged mare,
Like a meteor amid earthquakes descending,
And his people, in unison, have drunk a cup of wrath.
Hellfire is the fate of the far-off one they seek.
The people of this country met in the wasteland
And knocked the sons of shaykhs from their saddles.
We took for the two shaykhs, shaykhs in abundance.
The scales again have tipped in our favor.
He who makes war on the ʿAdwan, limps away in chains.
The mighty swordsman makes play with his neck."[3]

---

3. For an English transliteration, see Appendix A.

[As we scribble out this translation, Mishrif's younger brother, Mis'if, and their father, Haj 'Isa, wander in from the houses next door. Perhaps they have overheard Haj 'Arif's voice. The tea service is rushed back to the kitchen, and while we await a fresh pot, conversation turns to the poetry at hand. Haj 'Isa is a lover of verse and a master of the *rababa*, a one-stringed fiddle that serves as musical accompaniment to the chant-like recitation of *gasayid* (plate 13). He has been monitoring our work from the start, and he, like Mishrif, has noticed that my collection of poems is heavy-laden with 'Adwani pieces.]

HAJ 'ISA: So . . . what are you writing now?

MISHRIF: A poem. An old poem.

ANDREW: I recorded it from an 'Adwani elder.

HAJ 'ISA: 'Adwani. Always 'Adwani. Recite some of it. I want to hear it.

[Mishrif begins to read the transcript. His father interrupts: "No. No. No. The tape. I want to hear his voice on the tape." I dutifully insert the cassette, rewind, and play. Haj 'Isa listens, now and then repeating the last word of a couplet, as if to acknowledge the rhyme. When the poem is finished, he feigns a contemptuous sniff. Haj 'Isa is an 'Abbadi—a Sharrabi of the Zyud, to be exact—but it is obvious that he has come, somewhat grudgingly, to admire Haj 'Arif's immense poetic recall.]

HAJ 'ISA: Who is that 'Adwani?

ANDREW: The old man from Salihi.

HAJ 'ISA: The same one we heard the other day?

MISHRIF: Yes. The same one.

MIS'IF: Let me see the transcript. I didn't understand all of it. He's speaking the old dialect—very fast—the Bedouin dialect. We don't talk like that anymore . . . in the present generation.

[I pass Mis'if the text, which he reads aloud with interest. Having free access to the poems of the enemy, like overhearing gossip about one's own group, inspires a strange mood of curiosity and irritation, a mood now shaping the expression on Mis'if's face. As he hands the text back to me, he repeats the phrase, "like a meteor amid earthquakes descending," and laughs: "Does that have a meaning?" He then asks Mishrif the inevitable question.]

MIS'IF: Isn't this *kidhib*?

MISHRIF: Of course. It's *kidhib*.

[The universal critique of an opponent's poetry. It has little to do with the quality of the work as oral literature. Mishrif has already

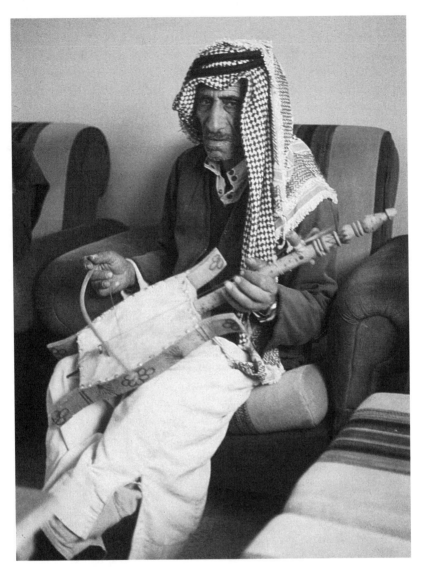

Plate 13.   Haj 'Isa al-Sharrab recites verse to the accompaniment of the *rababa*.

admitted to me—but not to his father or brother—that the poem is, aesthetically at least, a superior effort. It is also *kidhib*. Perhaps the Haj can elaborate.]

ANDREW: What's your opinion of the poem, ya Haj? Is it good or not?

[The Haj closes his eyes and waves a dismissive hand in my direction. Such questions annoy him. Do I honestly expect him to appreciate 'Adwani poetry? The *gasida* he has just heard is propaganda, a challenge, a violent threat, a verbal weapon. It provokes deep feelings of *'asabiyya* for and against its speaker. The Haj gives my ill-conceived question a rather brusque reply.]

HAJ 'ISA: 'Adwani *gasayid* . . . they are all alike . . . empty talk. Why haven't you recorded 'Abbadi *gasayid*? I'm tired to death of all this 'Adwani blather. Didn't you bring 'Abbadi poetry with you?

[Mishrif and I had, in fact, transcribed an 'Abbadi piece earlier that afternoon. Like most 'Abbadi poetry, it was short and easy to memorize.]

ANDREW: We wrote one today. I'll say it to you right now. There was a feast in the *ghor*, in the tent of Dhiyab al-'Adwan, and the 'Abbadis were all invited. While they were waiting to eat, one of the 'Adwan, a man named "Drawing-His-Sword" (*jarar sayfu*), started to insult 'Abbad.

He said, in front of everyone:

The beard of 'Abbad is matted like wool,
It needs a barber to clean it.

The 'Abbadis said: "Eh! What kind of talk is that?" And one of them, a man from the Slayhat, stood up and said:

'Abbad chased them down, two thousand warriors.
Two thousand plundered steeds they tow away.
'Abbad is fierce, O worker of the blade,
The flesh off your face, we'll skin it![4]

[Haj 'Isa laughs out loud.]

HAJ 'ISA: Yes indeed. He answered him like that. Yes.

[The Haj falls silent again. He had anticipated something grander. The 'Abbadi poem, though catchy, is clearly no match for the 'Adwani *gasayid* I have been subjecting him to.]

---

4. For an English transliteration, see Appendix A.

HAJ ʿISA: That poem is just a simple thing. Two words. It's
known to everyone. Haven't you recorded something better than
that?

[I feel somehow at fault. I have created this odd context of
explicit comparison: a context in which ʿAbbad so decidedly pales.
I begin to rummage through my tapes for something a bit more
elegant. Mishrif, who is similarly vexed by these poetic disparities,
comes to my defense.]

MISHRIF: He's looked for ʿAbbadi poetry, ya Haj, but there isn't
any. Most of it is like that. Short.

[I'm tempted to remind Haj ʿIsa that the only historical poem
I've recorded from him is an ʿAdwani composition. I decide not to
mention it.]

HAJ ʿISA: There is poetry. There is, by God. You must find
it. Take him to Haj Dhib or Haj ʿAbd al-Karim. They'll give you
poems.

MISHRIF: We went already and recorded from them. They
didn't have poems like this [he holds up the ʿAdwani *gasida*]. By
God, I've listened to his tapes, and it upsets me. You say there are
poems. Well then, where are the poems on the Sharrab? On the
Amir al-Salihi? On the Zyud? All my days and I've never heard
them.

HAJ ʿISA: What do you want me to tell you? They are forgotten, those poems. The people stopped remembering them.

ANDREW: But Haj, why did the ʿAbbadis forget their poems and
the ʿAdwan still remember theirs? What's the reason for that?

HAJ ʿISA: Not all of them are forgotten. No. Look here.

[The Haj pauses . . . a bit dramatically. We watch him. He is
about to make a definitive statement of some kind.]

HAJ ʿISA: Who made up those ʿAdwani poems? The ʿAdwan
themselves? No. Their slaves and followers made up poems about
them, praising them.

[The Haj is correct. With the exception of Nimr Ibn ʿAdwan, the
great ʿAdwani shaykhs of the eighteenth to twentieth centuries are
not remembered nowadays for their poetic acumen. The ʿAdwani
gasayid I heard most often were, in fact, composed by men of the
ʿAjarma and Bani Hasan tribes, or by the ʿAdwani slave-poet, Abu
Mismara. The ʿAdwan, by virtue of their power and wealth, were
targets of lavish praise in the days before government. ʿAbbad, with
few exceptions, was not. The Haj has gone to the heart of the

matter. He has obliquely (perhaps unwittingly) recognized
the political inequality that underlies the gulf between ʿAbbadi
and ʿAdwani poetics. He manages, nonetheless, to cast the fact in
a positive, egalitarian light.]

HAJ ʿISA: Ibn ʿAdwan, we say, is a stallion among mares (*hisan
bast ramak*). The ʿAbbadi is a stallion among stallions (*hisan bast
husun*). We are all brothers. Everyone says, "I am shaykh." There is
no one higher than the others. We don't praise our shaykhs. We are
all, you might say, on the same level. Even Ibn Khatlan, and he's
the foundation. He's the shaykh of ʿAbbadi shaykhs; he alone.

ANDREW: That makes sense. The ʿAbbadi poems I've recorded,
most of them are about Ibn Khatlan.

HAJ ʿISA: Kayid Ibn Khatlan. Yes indeed. If you want ʿAbbadi
poetry, go to the Khatalin. All the poems are with them. There's
an old man among them who, they say, has one hundred *gasayid*—
poems on Kayid and his sons, the shaykhs of bygone days—all
written down in a book. They say he has it; I myself have never
seen it.

ANDREW: What's his name?

HAJ ʿISA: I don't know. Go there and ask them . . . the Khatalin.

[This is familiar advice. A great cache of ʿAbbadi poetry is always
just beyond the horizon. My ʿUwaydi hosts in Swaysa have assured
me that an ʿAjrami tribesman keeps (in a locked trunk) thirty-five
gasayid on their ancestors Khalaf and Khalifa. They seem in no
hurry to retrieve the poems, however, and I can never manage to
elicit the man's name or arrange a visit to his home. When I asked
Dr. Ahmad—who is not among Khalaf or Khalifa's descendants—if
he knew anything about these poems, he scoffed at the claim: "Trust
me. The poems do not exist. Khalaf and Khalifa do not deserve
thirty-five *gasayid*."

Stallions among stallions.

The old Khatlani, with his mysterious book of poems, is probably
a fable as well. I have been referred to him many times, but have
never been able to track him down. He remains, in this elusive
form, the best defense against ʿAdwani poetics. The missing ʿAbbadi
gasayid, though forgotten, are not lost: they are preserved safely in
his care.]

The constant allusions to a secret history that is hidden away, or lost, or
suppressed; to a truth that cannot be openly retold: each recalls the polem-

ical style of Dr. Ahmad ʿUwaydi al-ʿAbbadi, whose critique of ʿAdwani dominance, though dressed in scholarly jargon, was no less evasive. The rhetorical forces Dr. Ahmad and Haj ʿIsa are trying to counter (or simply bluff
their way around) have a definite shape.

Dominant discourse	*Subaltern discourse*
More wealth and political clout	Less wealth and political clout
More likely to give escort and sanctuary	More likely to avoid escort and sanctuary
Authoritative speech	Silence and anonymity
Projection of oral traditions	Concealment of oral traditions
Longer genealogies	Shorter genealogies
More well-known stories	Fewer well-known stories
More poetry	Less poetry
ʿAdwani rhetoric	ʿAbbadi rhetoric

When ʿAbbadis dispute the claims of ʿAdwani history, they are compelled
to do so (1) in a subaltern voice or (2) from an imaginary point of strength.
How could it be otherwise? "Where there is power," Foucault observes,
"there is resistance, and yet, or rather consequently, this resistance is never
in a position of exteriority in relation to power" (1978, 95). The following
narrative shows the extent to which ʿAbbadi oral traditions are filtered
through, and effectively reproduce, the ʿAdwani hegemony they contest. The
narrator, who asked to remain anonymous, describes his tale as "a history
of ʿAbbad from beginning to end"; nonetheless, the presence of the ʿAdwan
is conspicuous throughout.

The story of ʿAbbad

AS TOLD BY FULAN AL-ʿABBADI

In the beginning, they say, Ibn ʿAdwan came: a boy from the Swayt
tribe. They said: "Where are you from, boy?"
He said: "I'm from the Swayt."
He came, and the Amir al-Mihdawi was ruling the lands of
Jordan.
He said to the Swayti: "What's your work?"
He said: "I'm a coffee maker."
So the Amir made him his coffee servant, but he was really a
horseman by origin. A rider. When the Amir went out to raid, the
Swayti raided with him, and they captured an enemy party; they
captured their livestock, their camels, and brought them back. He

was clever, that Swayti. They had captured a she-camel called *al-dabta*, a weak thing. He brought his spear and poked around in her saddle, and there was gold in it.

The Amir said: "Come, ya Swayti, take your share."

He said: "Give me *al-dabta*. That's all I want."

And they said: "Fine. You are keeper of *al-dabta*. Take it, O Keeper of the *dabta*" (*ra'i al-dabta*).

When he was alone, he took off the saddle. It was full of gold.

He began to gather the Arabs around him. He made them his Arabs, his fighters. He married them off; he bought them weapons.

After a while, he said: "O men of my gathering, ride beside me, forty horsemen. We want to greet the Amir al-Mihdawi."

When the Amir saw Ibn 'Adwan with forty horsemen riding beside him, he was furious.

He said: "What do you want?"

Ibn 'Adwan said: "I came to visit you, ya Amir."

The Amir said: "I'll give you three days and a third. I don't want to see you again until that time, when we meet on the field of battle."

Ibn 'Adwan made war on the Amir and his tribes. He defeated them. He conquered the land.

When he conquered the land, the 'Abbad were already living in it, but they were only a few Arabs. Ibn 'Adwan made war on them; he tried to rule over them and take livestock from them. He wanted to take *khawa* from them: "the two-year-old goat and the *'akka* coin." 'Abbad refused to give it. They increased in number and grew strong, and there were always clashes between them and Ibn 'Adwan. Neither side could win, [both were] defeated and defeating, but 'Abbad was seizing the hills—beautiful lands—from the Zarga River to Wadi al-Shitta. They seized it, and no one could invade that rugged country.

Then Ibn 'Adwan brought the Saltiyya tribes to his side, and the Bani Hasan, and the 'Ajarma . . . all the tribes of the Balga. The war between 'Abbad and 'Adwan began in earnest. Many people were slain. The 'Abbadis who survived, who kept fighting, went to Baysan, in the northern *ghor*, on the West Bank. The 'Adwan cast them out. For seventeen years they sat in Baysan. Refugees. They sat seventeen years, forsaking their lands, forsaking what was theirs.

When they had sat seventeen years in Baysan, their shaykh,

Kayid Ibn Khatlan, rose for the dawn prayer. After he prayed, he
sat on the hill and looked and listened. He didn't hear the sound of
a single baby crying, or a mother saying "hush" to her child. Why?
Because the women, in the heat of the valley, would carry their
babies seven months and then abort them because of fever, malaria.
The salty water was killing them all.

Ibn Khatlan said: "If we stay here another year, two years, we'll
be finished. There will be no one left."

He pounded loudly on the *mihbash* [a drumlike container in
which coffee beans are pulverized; the sound of coffee grinding
is a signal for the men of the camp to assemble in the tent of the
shaykh] . . . and the men gathered.

They said: "What is it?"

He said: "Come with me to the hilltop and see what I see. Hear
what I hear. I prayed the dawn prayer and didn't hear a single woman
say hush to her child. If we stay here another year, we are finished."

They said: "What's your opinion?"

He said: "My opinion is: We migrate. We return to our lands."

They sent out *mugalladat* to the tribes, a piece of black cloth
hung on the neck of a horse. Whoever cuts off the cloth becomes
a fighter beside you, becomes a member of your side. The Skhur
accepted the *mugalladat*, a section of them, the Jabur. They became
fighters beside 'Abbad.

When 'Abbad began to migrate away from Baysan, a poet was
with them, and he says to you:

I climbed atop Kawkab, east of Baysan.

[Kawkab al-Hawa is the hill on which Ibn Khatlan prayed. The
narrator knew only the first line of the poem.]

Who is he talking about, that poet? He is speaking of Ibn
Khatlan, their leader, the greatest among them.

So they returned to the Balga, the Skhur beside them, and
camped west of Salt.

The nephews of Ibn Khatlan came down from Salt and said:
"O uncle!"

He said: "Yes?"

They said: "Tomorrow the Saltiyya will ride down on you from
here, the Bani Hasan from there, and the 'Adwan from over there.
They will slaughter you all. We are telling you this because you are
brother to our mothers."

Ibn Khatlan said: "Try to avert this."

They said: "By God, we can't."

Ibn Khatlan had an 'Abbadi nephew named Sari; he was a rider. His horse was called Gazelle.

He said: "O uncle!"

Ibn Khatlan said: "Yes?"

He said: "Send half the walkers and half the riders against the 'Adwan, and the other half against the Saltiyya, and I'll face the Bani Hasan alone."

He by himself would fight Bani Hasan. When the Bani Hasan saw Sari, they feared him and fled. They did not enter the battle. When the 'Adwan saw that Bani Hasan wouldn't fight, they fled too, and the battle was left to 'Abbad and the Saltiyya. That day, 'Abbad slew forty Salti grooms, along with all the others they slaughtered: in one day, forty grooms, forty grooms who had newly entered their brides. That was the battle of Rabahiyya. 'Abbad utterly defeated them.

The tribes of the Balga wanted to slay 'Abbad in one great slaughtering.

Ibn 'Adwan said: "Don't leave one of them alive!"

There were battles upon battles between 'Adwan and 'Abbad. We can't count them all. If we wanted to count them, we could not. A battle took place in Rabahiyya: "The Slaughter of the Forty Grooms," as I told you. Another battle took place in Zilaga, and the poet said:

All my days in battle, I've seen not a battle like Zilaga.

[Again, the narrator remembered only the first line.]

And then the battle of Dhira'a happened, when the Skhur betrayed 'Abbad.

ANDREW: I thought the Skhur and 'Abbad were brothers.

FULAN: Not all the Skhur betrayed us, just the Fayiz clan. It is said: "After the battle of Dhira'a, no friendship remained" (*ba'd kon adh-dhira'a ma zal sadaga*) between us and the Fayiz. The rest, the Jabur and the others who rallied round us, they are still our cousins. We and they are still one fighting group.

ANDREW: Why did the Fayiz betray you?

FULAN: Because Sattam Ibn Fayiz, shaykh of the Skhur, married the sister of 'Ali Dhiyab al-'Adwan. Her name is 'Alia. The 'Adwan made the Fayiz their in-laws, and the two became one fighting

group. On the day the battle of Dhira'a took place, the Fayiz betrayed 'Abbad, in the midst of the fray . . . a surprise attack. They
slew the sons of Ibn Khatlan: two of them, they say. Yes indeed.

Then what happened?

Ibn Khatlan said: "This thing goes on and on; these wars hold
no benefit for us. We should go to Istanbul and bring a government
to this land."

So he and an 'Adwani shaykh named Abu 'Arabi, and a Salti
shaykh named Husayn al-Subih, went to Istanbul, to the Ottoman
sultan, and said: "We enter before you and God. We want a government to come to our land and rule a world which is slaughtering
itself. The situation is not just; each of us wants to return to what
is right."

They went—those three shaykhs—and brought the Turkish
government from Syria, brought it to this land, and said: "These
wars will not be permitted anymore. They are not lawful."

They brought the tribes from afar, all the tribes that had been
cast out, and they worked a reconciliation. They brought them from
afar, and everyone who came was settled on his own land. And all
those who settled on their land were reconciled, and the wars
between 'Abbad and 'Adwan ended.

That's it. Turkey came. They divided up the land among the
tribes and made a government in Jordan. Your protection.

ANDREW: God keep you, ya Fulan.

This account reveals its subalternness in many ways. First, it begins with
the arrival of Ibn 'Adwan, a man whose rise to dominance is retold in great
detail. 'Abbad, by contrast, first appears in the narrative as a nondescript entity: "a few Arabs." As a tribe, 'Abbad is commonly said to be older than
'Adwan, but its history, as told here, starts abruptly. The speaker does not
recount the origins of 'Abbad, or any events from earlier times; instead, the
deeds of Ibn 'Adwan serve as the backdrop against which 'Abbad, and an entire historical epoch, are distinguished.

'Abbad enters its own past as part of a larger 'Adwani story, and its subordinate position, though never explicitly stated by Fulan, can be seen in a
consistent pattern of anonymity, of namelessness, and—in a system that
renders names and the honor of names inseparable—of relative obscurity.
Kayid and Sari Ibn Khatlan, the only 'Abbadis identified in the tale, are heavily outnumbered by characters from other tribes: the Amir al-Mihdawi, the
Swayti, Dhiyab al-'Adwan, 'Alia bint Dhiyab, 'Ali Dhiyab al-'Adwan, Abu

'Arabi al-'Adwan, Sattam Ibn Fayiz, shaykh of the Bani Sakhr, and Husayn al-Subih, shaykh of the Saltiyya. The shards of poetry the narrator recites are likewise bereft of 'Abbadi names. Even the narrator, who claims no explicit genealogical ties to the 'Abbadi past, remains nameless. He reproduces, in the very act of asserting his own history, the silence my 'Adwani friends thought befitting 'Abbadis.

This subalternness is not a generic aspect of 'Abbadi tradition; it is a specific feature of the discourse they direct against the 'Adwan. The stories of the Zyud, which transpire within a single 'Abbadi tribe, are much richer in detail, and the narrators who relate them strive always to link themselves to heroic persons and lines of descent (see chapter 4). Yet when Tawfiq al-Ruwayiq, shaykh of the Dwaykat, recalled the 'Abbad-'Adwan War, the story he told me was similar to the anonymous account presented above. He made no attempt to link his illustrious ancestors to the events of that time. Miflih (who dammed the waters of Wadi Shu'ayb) and Irwayij (who drew his sword on Shaykh 'Ali Dhiyab), were never mentioned, though Miflih, and perhaps Irwayij as well, would have been alive when the war with 'Adwan was fought (ca. 1840–50). When Shaykh Tawfiq spoke as an 'Abbadi, not as a Dwayki, he submerged himself in a faceless mass: a mass bound together not by shared descent, but by a common opposition to the 'Adwan and a single allegiance to Shaykh Kayid Ibn Khatlan.

The difference between these two voices—between Shaykh Tawfiq the Dwayki and Shaykh Tawfiq the 'Abbadi—brings to mind Meeker's (1976) distinction between communal and segmentary notions of *sharaf* (honor). The Dwayki voice, in Meeker's scheme, is segmentary:

> Every man has a direct connection (his line) with the total sharaf of the society, and the uniqueness of this connection (his own ascendants) represents his own unique sharaf. . . . We see then that genealogy "exists", so to speak, because it mediates sharaf more or less like a transmission line in which father-son connections represent the nodes of this transmission line (1976, 264).

The 'Abbadi voice, by contrast, is communal, and the honor attaching to it does not

> involve the unique and dynamic aspects of men's acts. . . . Here, the historical significance is not primarily in terms of acting persons and collectivities, but of the career of the entire community. Men or collectivities with sharaf come into the purview of this exaltation of the community— they act for the community. Sharaf, in a sense, represents historical evidence for the existence of the community, not for the definition of its parts. . . . In segmentary societies, we have the notion that the essential

aspects of men are their acts: military exploits, bravery, generosity, vengeance, and so on. In communal societies, we have the notion that the essential aspects of men are their subjections to communal conventions derived from a historical significance in which men no longer directly participate (1976, 265).

The 'Adwani voice, as the reader should by now suspect, is uncompromisingly "segmentary." The following accounts, told by Haj Ahmad Yusif al-Waraykat and 'Abd al-Karim al-Waraykat, are digested from a three-hour session in which the two men recounted, in a rather scatter-shot fashion, the high points of their history in the Balga. They did not attempt to produce a single story that covered the 'Adwani past from beginning to end. That talk, I was told, "would take many years to tell." They focused, instead, on great men, heroic acts, and the Warayki line of descent. Their testimony, which endeavors from the outset to divide the collective into distinct parts, stands in dramatic contrast to the communalism of 'Abbadi rhetoric.

[Abu Firas has formally introduced me to Haj Ahmad and 'Abd al-Karim. Both men are kin to Abu Firas' mother, who also belongs to the Waraykat. We have just finished a meal of rice and mutton, and our unspoken pact is complete. The border between the 'Amamsha and the Waraykat has been properly crossed; sanctuary has been granted. We are bound now by ties of blood, bread, and salt.]

ANDREW: From the beginning.

ABU FIRAS: The talk about bygone days.

HAJ AHMAD: First. Welcome.

ANDREW: And two welcomes to you, ya Haj.

HAJ AHMAD: This talk is about . . . when our ancestors came to the Balga. The first one was called Fayiz. Fayiz came with his brother, Fawzan, who died and did not beget sons. Fayiz begot sons. Fayiz begot one named 'Adwan. 'Adwan had three sons: among them was Shadid, ancestor of the Waraykat; another was Subih, ancestor of the 'Assaf; and the other was Hamdan. I'll now count them off for you one by one.

Hamdan begot Nimr and 'Adwan. This second 'Adwan begot Kayid and Salih and Saqr and Lami and Nu'aym and all those clans . . . not our clans. As for us. The Waraykat.

Shadid begot Salih.
Salih begot 'Awda.
'Awda begot Lahim.

Lahim begot ʿIsa.

ʿIsa begot Slayman.

Slayman begot Dawjan.

Dawjan begot Minwar.

Minwar begot Yusif.

Yusif begot Ahmad, the one who speaks to you now.

ANDREW: Your memory is strong.

HAJ AHMAD: Yes indeed. And I begot one named Nayif, and Nayif begot one named ʿAyman.

ABU FIRAS: Good. Now. The tribes of the Waraykat. Who are they?

[At this point, Haj Ahmad Yusif recites the genealogies of the nine original Warayki clans (*al-asliyyin*). He also lists the ancestors of two client, or "follower" clans (*al-tabiʿin*). The Waraykat, "big and small; male and female," are nowadays about 1,500 to 2,000 members strong. Or so the Haj reckons. He is prepared to extend his lecture on Warayki *gass*, but I notice that side A of my cassette is already half full. I try to lead the conversation away from genealogy.]

ANDREW: Ya Haj, I want to change the topic a bit. A man told me that the Waraykat have been known, for ages, as the sword of ʿAdwan.

HAJ AHMAD: Yes. True. Because they were real men. They were the family of horsemanship. In times past, when the people were ignorant, when slaying and reconciliation were our custom, the Waraykat were in the first ranks of battle. Always.

ANDREW: And who were the famous ones?

HAJ AHMAD: The ones renowned for horsemanship? Hamad and Dawjan and Saʿad al-ʿAzzam. Those were the ones famous for horsemanship. Every clan produced great men, but those three were the main ones.

ANDREW: Good. I want to know more about them and the ones who came before them. For instance, Shadid. Ancestor of the Waraykat. Did he become shaykh of the ʿAdwan?

HAJ AHMAD: He became shaykh but not for long. They made him shaykh, but his shaykhdom did not endure. Then they made Subih shaykh, son of the second ʿAdwan, but they didn't prosper. Then Hamdan became shaykh. He and his maternal uncle, Abu Haydar. And the Mihdawi was Amir at that time.

The keeper of the Dabta

They raided the Haj caravan, Hamdan and the Amir al-Mihdawi.
When the pilgrims came from Syria and Turkey, the Ottomans
would mount them all on camels and migrate toward the Hijaz. In
the Balga, the Amir al-Mihdawi attacked the caravan and plundered
it. They took all the camels, even though they belonged to pilgrims
traveling to the House of God.

ANDREW: That's a great sin.

HAJ AHMAD: They were ignorant in those days. Hamdan, his
share of the spoils was a she-camel, and it was hobbled. The Arabs
call such a camel *al-dabta*. The Turks had put all the wealth of
the caravan on this old she-camel because she limped and no eyes
would covet her. This was Hamdan's share of the spoils. No one else
wanted it, so God granted it to him. When he lifted the saddle, what
did he find? Gold. He said nothing. He began to buy horses and
weapons. He would give so-and-so a horse or a javelin or a rifle.
He made the Arabs [loyal to him].

Our custom in the past was . . . on holidays, we would go to the
tent of the shaykh and feast together. So they all went, Hamdan and
the horsemen he had equipped.

As they approached, the Amir Mihdawi said to his men: "Those
horsemen. Who do they belong to?"

They said: "By God, they belong to Hamdan, keeper of *al-
dabta*."

They arrived at the tent. The Amir's slaves greeted them and
took their horses.

They entered the presence of the Amir, and he said: "Where did
you get these horsemen, ya Hamdan?"

He said: "By God, I borrowed them from you on loan" (*ista-
gradt-hum gruda*).

And that name stuck to them. They call them "Sons of the
Graydi" to this very day because he said, "I borrowed them on
loan." The Graydi is 'Adwan, and the Gruda are the families who
follow us. Our allies. And the "battle cry" (*al-nakhwa*) of 'Adwan
became, from that day to this day, *al-dabta*.

The Amir said: "Listen. You have, by Arab custom, three days
and a third. After that, if I see you, I will slaughter you. You and
all your horsemen."

So Hamdan left, and they met on the field of battle, and Hamdan

defeated the Amir. Then he defeated the Mahfuz al-Sardi. The
'Adwan slew him and his people scattered. Then they defeated Ibn
'Asira and the tribes that followed him. They pushed them out of
the *ghor*, and the *ghor* became part of the 'Adwan country. They
ruled it and completely dominated it.

All that history . . . it is better to record it from the Kayid, the
ancestors of Abu Firas, who sits beside you. Or the Salih or the
Nimr, who live in the *ghor*. They will tell you about their ancestors.

But what do I want to tell you now? About the champions of the
Waraykat and their deeds.

[At this point, Haj Ahmad recounts a series of heroic encounters,
duels, and challenges.]

The slaying of Abu Shinaf

There was a man called the Ziyadi. He made a government in
Jordan and oppressed the people. The government of the Ziyadina.
They had a governor in the fortress at Salt and a governor in the
fortress at Rabad, which is in 'Ajlun. They expelled the 'Adwan from
the Balga. Where did they go? To Palestine. The 'Adwan raided the
Ziyadina. They plundered the caravans going from Salt to Nablus
and Jerusalem. The Ziyadina gathered their men together and
pursued them into Palestine.

There was a man of the Ziyadina called Abu Shinaf. His mustache was so long he could tie the ends of it behind his ears. He was
a mighty horseman. The tribes feared him. There was a man named
Milhim al-Waraykat, brother of Lahim.

He said: "That Abu Shinaf is mine. I'll slay him."

So he rode up close to them, dismounted in a dense thicket
of trees, and when Abu Shinaf rode by, Milhim threw his spear at
him. Then he pierced Abu Shinaf with his lance, crushed his troops,
returned to the Balga, and ruled the land. They defeated the
Ziyadina and scattered them completely.

The slaying of the bandit

Later . . . there was a bandit who, whenever they brought goods
to the 'Adwan from Nablus and Jerusalem, he would attack the
caravans. He would plunder them and take everything. In those
days, the 'Adwan were few, not many. Maybe twenty or thirty
horsemen.

So they poured coffee into a cup, in accordance with Arab custom, and said: "This is so-and-so's cup."

Which means, the one who accepts the cup and drinks from it must slay the man [whose name was mentioned as the cup was filled].

My ancestor, Dawjan, said: "Give me the bandit's cup. I will drink it."

He drank the cup.

ABU FIRAS: He made a pledge, a covenant to slay the bandit.

HAJ AHMAD: Yes. He went and slew him. He killed him in Tayba, which is in Palestine.

He approached his camp and said: "I come to you a warrior seeking death. Meet me in combat. Armed."

Dawjan struck him down and slew him.

The slaying of the three Rubba' shaykhs

Then . . . the 'Adwan went and plundered the livestock of the Rubba', in the area of Irbid. And later, the three shaykhs of the Rubba' caught up with them.

They said: "Look! Those are the three great warriors: Hamad, Sa'ad, and Dawjan. Shaykhs of the Waraykat."

They challenged them; the six met on the field of battle, and the shaykhs of the Rubba' were slain.

The 'Adwan have a great past.

ANDREW: Yes indeed.

The battle of Um al-Summag

HAJ AHMAD: What else happened? There were wars between the 'Adwan and the Bani Sakhr. Not just Bani Sakhr.

Bani Khalid.
Al-Sirhan.
Al-Sardiyya.
Al-'Isa.
Al-Jabaliyya.
Al-Huwaytat.
Al-Salayta.

All the desert Bedouin were what? Enemies of the 'Adwan. The 'Adwan farmed. The areas they controlled were agricultural lands.

The Bedouin lived in the desert, migrating east and west. When they came west, they would eat the crops and battles would take place.

The greatest battle of all happened at . . . we call it the Battle of Um al-Summag. The 'Adwan slaughtered the Bani Sakhr completely. They say they slew them and dumped their bodies in the wells. That's what they say.

ANDREW: Do you know the *gasida*?

HAJ AHMAD: Yes. I remember it.

[Here, the Haj breaks with convention and recites the *gasida* without first laying its "foundation" (*asas*) in the form of a story.]

HAJ AHMAD: He says,

Yesterday, O tears of my eyes, I was sleepless.
Until the dawn, my waking did continue.
We marched and were made to march, many gatherings.
The night of the 20th moon we became their neighbors.
The gathering of Abu Rabi' on the march were moving,
The gathering of the Ja'afira in lines and files made way.

The Abu Rabi' and the Ja'afira, who are they? They are clans of the Bani Hasan, [a tribe allied to the 'Adwan]. The poet is from them. He is not 'Adwani. The Bani Hasan have marched south to fight alongside us. He says:

But credit for the deed was 'Adwan's on that day,
When they filled the dens, the caves and the wells.
The beasts with cleft lips abandoned their calves.
The yearling, the foal, were left wandering the fields.
Dablan, though wearing no armor, hunted down their leaders,
Hunted down their leaders who ride atop excellent mares.

Dablan is from the 'Adwan. A mighty warrior. Yes indeed.

Shaykh Fandi took flight as though on wing,
Till he reached the distance of Mafraq and beyond.

Shaykh Fandi is the Shaykh of the Bani Sakhr . . . of the Ibn Fayiz, who met us in battle.

You considered us, O Ibn Fayiz, contemptible in your sight.
This is the punishment for him who betrays God's creatures.[5]

---

5. For an English transliteration, see Appendix A.

ANDREW: That's good.

HAJ AHMAD: It's very good.

[Laughter]

'ABD AL-KARIM: I want to tell the story of Fahays.

ANDREW: All right.

['Abd al-Karim, who appears to be in his late forties, scoots over beside me. He seems a bit nervous. Haj Ahmad, clearly a man over seventy years of age, is the authority among us. 'Abd al-Karim looks to Haj Ahmad for support as he speaks.]

The Amir al-Mihdawi and the daughter of the priest

'ABD AL-KARIM: The 'Adwan, when they were expelled from the Balga, went to Um al-Fahm in Palestine. Right. And the Ziyadi was ruling this land. One morning he went hunting with his dogs and slaves, and they came to the waters of Fahays. He saw a beautiful girl fetching water.

He said: "That girl. Who is she?"

They said: "That is the daughter of the priest."

[I have heard this story before, and I can tell 'Abd al-Karim is botching it. Haj Ahmad intervenes.]

HAJ AHMAD: No. It was the Amir al-Mihdawi. Not the Ziyadi. The two are different.

'ABD AL-KARIM: Yes indeed. The Amir al-Mihdawi.

HAJ AHMAD: Don't just say "Yes indeed." Correct it. Tell it right.

['Abd al-Karim takes a deep breath.]

'ABD AL-KARIM: Anyway, as I was saying, the Amir al-Mihdawi, when he saw that girl, said: "I must have her."

The people of Fahays said: "Ya Amir, from ancient times, we Christians and Muslims have been brothers, living together. This is the priest's daughter. Make your request as you see fit."

The Amir said: "I must take her."

The people of Fahays consulted among themselves, then said: "Ya Amir, give us one week. The girl is in the middle of her [menstrual] period."

They said this so they would have time to contact the 'Adwan. The people of Fahays kept a fast breed of horse, the kind that cannot be overtaken in a chase. They sent a rider with a written message to the 'Adwan in Um al-Fahm.

It said: "The Amir wants to marry the daughter of the priest against our will. On the day of so-and-so, meet us in the forest outside Fahays, and we will make a plan to prevent this."

The 'Adwan came and said: "When the Amir and his men arrive for the wedding, take their horses and loosen the saddles, so that when they try to mount, they will fall off. And serve them food without salt in it. When you are ready to eat, fire a rifle, and that will be our sign to attack."

The people of Fahays served the food and said: "Help yourself, ya Amir. You and all your followers."

They fired a shot into the air, and the 'Adwan charged down from the forest and attacked the Amir, and the people of Fahays slaughtered his followers with swords and guns and other weapons. The Mihadia tried to mount their horses but they fell to the ground. Only two of them escaped: the Amir's son, Dawman al-Jawda, and another one. After that, the 'Adwan returned to the Balga and ruled it again.

The rest of the history is with Abu Nayif [Haj Ahmad Yusif] because he is greater than I am in [talking about] these matters.

ANDREW: That is a famous story. They say the priest in Fahays keeps a poem in the church; it tells what happened between the 'Adwan and the Amir al-Mihdawi. I should visit him.

HAJ AHMAD: Yes. Visit him. They have books and records. They document things. But with respect to poetry . . .

[Here, the Haj stays true to form and carefully lays the "foundation" of the *gasida* he wants to recite.]

The coming of the Turks

When Turkey came here to rule the land, the lands outside Syria were not ruled by the Ottoman state. . . .

[The Balga, Haj Ahmad explains, was torn apart by tribal wars. The shaykhly clans of the 'Adwan, incessantly feuding, would make peace only long enough to slaughter the Turkish delegations sent to arbitrate their disputes. According to Haj Ahmad, the Kayid clan—"ancestors of Abu Firas, who sits beside you"—were the cause of this unrest. Their campaign to seize the shaykhdom from the Salih clan had failed, and now they were about to be expelled from the Balga.]

So Abu 'Arabi, shaykh of the Kayid, and Ibn Khatlan, shaykh of 'Abbad, and Husayn al-Subih, shaykh of Salt: those three went to Syria and said: "Give us a state, and we and the tribes will join with you in slaughtering the 'Adwan. We will finish them off for the last time."

The leader was Abu 'Arabi. The Turks gave him a stipend and allowed him to equip twenty-five horsemen to ride beside him. So they all returned to the Balga; they and the Turkish army.

Who were the 'Adwani clans that resisted this new government? They were the Salih and the Nimr and the Waraykat. They fled to the territory of the Bani Hamida. South. And the Turks attacked them west of Madaba, at a place called al-Asila. They attacked them there, and the ones who distinguished themselves in the fray were 'Ali Dhiyab, Sa'ad al-'Azzam, Hamad, and Dawjan. They were the bravest warriors in that battle.

They say that a *gasida* was composed in their honor . . . on that day . . . by an Arab poet. He says:

Hey Boy! Make ready my steed.
Sit in the saddle of the famous mare!
Throw on the 'Agayli saddlebags,
And let the tassels dangle freely!
He betrays his kinsmen, Abu 'Arabi.
He brought the soldiers to this country.
He dispatched the horses of the Sagr,
And even the State of 'Ajila.

This place . . . the State of 'Ajila . . . is in Palestine.

In the morning a party of 'Adwan
[Were engaged in battle], west of Far' Asila.

Which is in Bani Hamida territory, around Madaba. I've never been there.

O you who trill tongues for 'Ali,
O you who let your tresses hang down.
Sa'ad, O keeper of al-Harsha,
Who brought his loot in a train behind him,
His loot, from the horses of the State,
Which you'd say: "They surely neigh greatly."
As for Hamad and Dawjan,
They were lions of the Arabian Desert
When together they charged on the Turks
And left them to scatter completely.[6]

6. For an English transliteration, see Appendix A.

That is a *gasida* from the poems of that time.[7]

ANDREW: It's new to me. I've never heard it before.

ABU FIRAS: Didn't I tell you to come and listen to the Waraykat? They are like a "spring" [a plentiful source of knowledge].

ANDREW: Yes. And they tell stories the Kayid [Abu Firas' clan] never tell.

[Laughter]

HAJ AHMAD: That's because the Kayid brought the government to this land.

ANDREW: They brought the Turks.

[I point at Abu Firas. More laughter]

'ABD AL-KARIM: But Abu Firas is from us. His mother is from us.

ABU FIRAS: Ask the Haj who are the maternal uncles of Hamad and Dawjan [the two great heroes of the Waraykat]?

[The answer, which everyone here knows but me, is the Kayid. The clan of Abu Firas. We have broached the topic of bloodlines and their effect on character. Haj Ahmad, accepting Abu Firas' challenge, leads me through the dense network of marriages that binds together the shaykhly families of the Kayid and Waraykat tribes.]

HAJ AHMAD: Look. In regard to those Waraykat. Lahim begot 'Isa. 'Isa took the daughter of Kayid [in marriage]. The daughter of Kayid himself, the ancestor of Abu Firas and all his relatives. Whom

---

7. The battle is also recalled in the correspondence of E.J. Rogers, who, in 1867, was Acting Consul General of the British Consulate in Damascus. The following report, now held at the Public Records Office in Kew, England (FO 78/1978), gives the official Turkish account of the battle.

Sept. 10, 1867

Sir, . . . I also have the honor to enclose a translation of a telegram from the Governor General reporting the destruction of the camp of the Adwan Arabs near Hasban.

Translation of the telegram from His Excellency Rashid Pasha to the Mutesarrif of Damascus.

"When we were informed that the rebellious Dhiab el-Adwan had fled from the Belka and had strengthened himself in the heights of a difficult mountain called Hajar-el-Mansub at a distance of 4 or 5 hours from Hisban, we sent about 800 soldiers and rural police for his apprehension, who on Thursday morning encountered him with a number of his followers armed with muskets———They fought desperately and bravely for about 4 1/2 hours till the rebels were dispersed in a sad flight, leaving behind them all their property, tents, furniture etc. with 50 mares and horses and a considerable number of cattle———Fifty rebels were killed on the field of the battle and the son of Dhiab was wounded in the shoulder, but we thank God that all the troops are safe excepting four who have been slightly wounded."

did she bear? She bore Slayman al-'Isa. Then 'Isa took the daughter of his maternal uncle. He took the daughter of Shibli. Whom did she bear? She bore Hamad and Dawjan. Then Dawjan took the daughter of Slayman al-Shibli, his maternal uncle, and she bore one named Fadil.

And so it goes. The people form a chain from one to the other.

ABU FIRAS: The 'Adwan did not take [wives] from anyone but themselves. They took and they gave to each other.

HAJ AHMAD: In the past, the people didn't give [wives] except among themselves. They didn't give to outsiders. But in this day and age, things are different. People are mixed. Not pure. A man goes to America and brings back an American. He goes to Turkey and brings back a Turk.

[The discussion now turns to the subject of clan boundaries. Haj Ahmad delineates the changing shape of Warayki territory over the span of three centuries. He maps out the holdings of the Kayid, Salih, and Nimr clans as well. I mention the fact that I have visited Nimr's grave in Yajuz.]

ANDREW: He is very famous because of his poems.

HAJ AHMAD: And he has books. He has books in Saudi Arabia, in Kuwait, in the Gulf, in Turkey. In every land where Arabic is read, he has books. Stories. He was also very intelligent and full of insight. Among the Arab poets, there is none more insightful than he.

[Now 'Abd al-Karim is excited. He grabs our attention and begins, without any introductory comment, to lay the foundation for one of Nimr's poems.]

Nimr and the leopard

'ABD AL-KARIM: One day Nimr came to Yajuz. The people said they saw gazelles feeding beside the waters of Hasban, so he mounted his horse and rode off to hunt them. He had his rifle with him.

As for his rifle . . . the French Consul who was in Jerusalem went to visit the ruins in Madaba, and he gave this rifle to Abu l-Ghanam, his escort. When Abu l-Ghanam came to the tent of Nimr, he knew that weapons were not allowed in the shaykh's tent, so he left it outside with the swords. When Nimr saw it, he took it.

He said: "Ya Abu l-Ghanam, take one of my horses in exchange for your rifle."

He took a horse from among the 'Adwani horses in exchange for his rifle. This rifle was with Nimr on that day. When Nimr arrived at the waters of Hasban, he saw another *nimr*. This one was not a man, but a beast. [In Arabic, Nimr's name means "leopard."] This other *nimr* had come to hunt as well. Nimr, the son of 'Adwan, crept up on the leopard, son of a leopard. He wanted to kill it. He took aim, fired, and slew the beast.

Later, he composed a *gasida* about it. He said:

I went toward the wasteland, my ammunition in tow,
And distinguished the prey; not one did detect me.
I looked and caught sight of one whose hide is spotted.
Death was approaching, and the fated day drew nigh.
Again I looked, and the gathering of prey had vanished.
The one who hunts cannot himself be hunted.
O my rifle, the one of rich descriptions,
I've crept in closer now, and unless it bolts, I'll strike it.
The rifle answered Nimr, saying:
"If you are terrified by death, and sore afraid,
Steady your sights; mark the wagging of its tail."
The leopard fell where once it had been standing.
The width of its paw, O my kinsmen, is amazing.
Its hide was placed on a mare of rich descriptions.
On the day of battle, its tail you still can see.[8]

So Nimr killed the leopard and put the hide on his horse.

[At this point we take a break for tea. The Haj is growing tired. When we resume our recording, 'Abd al-Karim, whose confidence was boosted by his successful recitation of Nimr's poem, tells two stories that will "add to the recollections you have recorded from the Haj."]

Shaykh Sultan al-'Adwan and the Wali of Damascus

When the war started between Britain and the Ottomans, and the Arab countries rose up against the Turks . . . the Wali of Damascus summoned all the shaykhs of the Arabian Peninsula. Where to? To Syria. When they got there, Shaykh Sultan al-'Adwan did not go to a hotel.

He said: "Where is the house of the Wali?"

8. For an English transliteration, see Appendix A.

They said: "The Wali's house is that castle over there. It belongs to him." He came to the guard and said: "I want to see the Wali."

He said: "And who are you?"

He said: "Tell the Wali that I am Sultan Ibn 'Adwan."

He said: "No problem."

He was allowed to enter. The first person he saw was the Wali's little boy. The boy stuck out his hand and Sultan gave him a gold coin. He put it where? In his pocket. The boy ran and fetched his brother. Sultan gave the second boy a gold coin too. The Wali brought Sultan a cup of coffee and he drank it.

Then he said: "I am Sultan al-'Adwan. Shaykh of the 'Adwani shaykhs, and paramount shaykh of the Balga."

The Wali said: "You honor me. I will see you tomorrow in the diwan."

In the morning, when the Wali brought the shaykhs together, they thought the Ottoman government wanted to give them money . . . so the Arabs would support the Turks in the war.

Instead, the translator said to them: "The Turkish government asks you to pay a special tax, to assist us in the war effort."

As you know, there was not much money among the Bedouin at that time. So each shaykh paid a riyal or two or five or ten. They were upset.

Our shaykh, Sultan Ibn 'Adwan, came late to the meeting. He entered the diwan and sat in the empty place next to the Wali. No one else dared to sit there. The Turks were collecting money from the shaykhs.

Sultan said to his slave: "Give me the saddlebags."

He brought the saddlebags.

Sultan said: "How much did the shaykhs contribute?"

The Wali said: "Two thousand dinar."

Sultan said: "Take two thousand dinar from my saddlebags, and return their money to them. The 'Adwan give; we never take."

So he gave the Turks an amount equal to the amount given by all the Arabian shaykhs.

The Wali said: "Go, ya Ibn 'Adwan. Indeed, you are the shaykh of all shaykhs and paramount shaykh of the Balga."

And that completes the story. We do not take; we give. And now I will tell you a final story.

Sa'ad al-'Azzam and Harb al-Huwayti

Sa'ad al-'Azzam was angry with his kin, the Waraykat, so he went to live with Ibn Hamid of the Bani Sakhr. As you know, we and they are enemies at war. Shaykh Ibn Hamid was a great horseman. His saddle had two belts beneath it. He rose one day and gathered his men and raided the Huwaytat. Sa'ad al-'Azzam went with them. They took the livestock of the Huwaytat, all their camels, and divided them into three herds.

As they were leading the herds away, Ibn Hamid said to his riders: "Has Harb overtaken us yet?"

There was a famous horseman from the Huwaytat named Harb. He rode a fast stallion.

They said: "No. He has not yet overtaken us."

He said: "You are safe. Keep moving"

A quarter of an hour later he said: "Has Harb overtaken us yet?" They said: "No."

He said: "Good. You are safe. Move on."

Not half an hour had passed before the men cried out: "Harb has overtaken us! Harb has overtaken us!"

Ibn Hamid was in the first herd. The shaykh is always in the first herd [the one farthest in front]. So Harb came and retook the third herd, the one behind. He killed all the men riding with it, then raced ahead and took the second herd, killing all the men who rode with it. The first herd, which was guarded by Ibn Hamid and Sa'ad al-'Azzam al-Waraykat . . . the horsemen abandoned it and scattered. Ibn Hamid did not want to flee because of Sa'ad.

He said: "It is not good to abandon one's companion, but our lives are at stake. If you stay and defend the herd, you can have it. I must go with my men."

Then Harb was suddenly upon them. Sa'ad turned to face him. They chased each other across the plain. When Harb saw that Sa'ad actually wanted to kill him, he fled. Sa'ad chased him until they came to a canyon. The Huwayti stallion jumped over it, but Sa'ad's mare stopped at the edge. So Harb al-Huwayti stood on one side and Sa'ad al-'Azzam al-Waraykat stood on the other.

Harb said: "Stranger. I'm asking you a question, by God. Are you from the group that dwells among lotus trees in the *ghor*?"

Which means, "Are you from the 'Adwan?"

Sa'ad said: "Yes, by God. I am one of them."

Harb said: "The plunder is yours, my friend."

Then he rode off, and Sa'ad rounded up the camels and led them away.

When he arrived at the tent of Ibn Hamid, what did the Bani Sakhr say?

They said: "By God, that's my she-camel! That's the camel I captured! This is mine. That is mine."

Like that.

Sa'ad tightened his reins and said: "By God, I will slaughter you all. You ingrates, cursed of both your parents!"

He declared war on them. A single horseman against an entire tribe.

Shaykh Ibn Hamid stood between them and said to Sa'ad: "These Bani Sakhr will now want to betray you and murder you. You are my guest."

Ibn Hamid feared the disgrace that would come if his guest was killed, so he said: "My advice is that you return to your people when night falls."

In darkness, Sa'ad broke down his tent, got all his things together, and crossed over to the Balga.

This is a story about one of the horsemen of the Waraykat. Your safety.

ANDREW: God keep you safe.

Haj Ahmad and 'Abd al-Karim drape their historical narratives in the lavish fabric of nobility. The 'Adwani identity they construct, which reveals itself in duels, long pedigrees, hunting tales, the equestrian arts, and displays of largesse, is fundamentally aristocratic. 'Adwani names, arranged in a peerage of cousin marriage and shared descent, outnumber all other names. Meanwhile, 'Abbad, the largest tribe in the Balga, is barely visible on the 'Adwani landscape. Unlike the 'Abbadi narrator, who knew a great deal about the history of the 'Adwan, 'Abd al-Karim and Haj Ahmad were unable to discuss the 'Abbadi past in detail. Such knowledge was of no use to them.

If 'Abbadis saw their history as an epic struggle against the 'Adwan, the 'Adwan were loathe to admit that such a struggle had ever taken place. When I asked Sa'ud Abu l-'Amash to tell me his version of the great 'Abbad-'Adwan War, he blithely dismissed the entire affair—the defining moment of 'Abbadi history—as *kidhib*.

What war? There was no war between us and 'Abbad. No. Our wars

were all with the Skhur. With Bani Sakhr. They were our enemies
from the start, our true enemies. The 'Abbad fought us in the name
of the Skhur . . . you might say, as their "clients" (*tawabi'*). But
'Abbad could not fight 'Adwan alone. No way. Don't pay any
attention to empty talk like that.

The desire, so strong among 'Abbadis, to match 'Adwani history, to answer
and equal it, was alien to Shaykh Sa'ud's way of thinking. Like most 'Adwanis, he felt no compulsion to engage 'Abbad polemically, and his refusal
to recognize them as a "true enemy" rose, it seemed, straight from the pages
of Bourdieu's Kabyle ethnography.

> To make someone a challenge is to credit him with the dignity of a man
> of honour, since the challenge, as such, requires a riposte and therefore
> is addressed to a man deemed capable of playing the game of honour, and
> of playing it well. From the principle of mutual recognition of equality
> in honour there follows a first corollary: the challenge confers honour.
> "A man who has no enemies," say the Kabyles, "is a donkey" (the symbol
> of passivity). There is nothing worse than to pass unnoticed: thus, not to
> salute someone is to treat him like a thing, an animal, or a woman. The
> challenge, conversely, is "a high point in the life of the man who receives
> it." It is the chance to prove one's manliness (*thirugza*) to others and
> to oneself. A second corollary is this: he who challenges a man incapable
> of taking up the challenge, that is, incapable of pursuing the exchange,
> dishonours himself (1977, 11).

When 'Abbadis challenge the 'Adwan, they assert an equality of honor that
'Adwanis fail to discern. The language in which the two tribes confront each
other is intrinsically unbalanced, and the rhetorical tools needed to build
historical truth—namely, poetry and genealogy—have accumulated, over
time, in the hands of dominant shaykhs. Thus, in the Balga today, colloquial
memory is composed of speech acts that reimpose power differentials located in a real, historical past. There is nothing in orthodox segmentary
theory, which takes either the moral or the political equality of tribes for
granted, that can explain why asymmetries of this sort should ever arise.
  Yet Haj Ahmad Yusif explains the origins of 'Adwani dominance with
perfect clarity: it is the handiwork of his ancestors, who made history in epic,
spectacular ways. Even 'Abbadis, who steadfastly deny the reality of 'Adwani superiority, find themselves heir to an oral tradition that explicitly accounts for it. The 'Adwan are great for precisely the reasons the anonymous
'Abbadi narrator makes known to us:

"Because their ancestor found a saddle full of gold."
"Because he banished the Amir al-Mihdawi and conquered the land."

"Because he turned the Balga tribes against us."

"Because he banished us to Baysan."

"Because he convinced the Skhur to betray us at the battle
of Dhira'a."

The entire historical discourse, like the tribal system itself, is a structure of power and pervasive inequality. It is not simply an ideal image of lineage structure projected backward in time. It is just the opposite: an ideal image of the past, an "age of shaykhs," told in the face of a world that is rapidly changing. Part of that change is the emergence of literacy among the Balga tribes. It is the advent of textuality, not the presumed mutability of oral traditions, that now allows for dramatic reconstructions of the past.

SIX

From Hearsay to Revelation

In speaking of revelation, vouchsafed first to the Jews, then to the Christians, and now to Muhammad, the Qur'an manifests a mystical view of the book. For all the revelations granted to men are regarded as messages culled from something we can call the first writing, a Celestial Book existing with God and brought to man's knowledge piecemeal through prophetic revelations. The Celestial Book is the materialized expression, as it were, of God's knowledge and will. Everything in heaven and on earth, and everything that happens, is recorded in the book . . . and all the duties that God has seen fit to impose upon man are to be found there: "We bind no soul beyond its capacity, and We have a Book that sets forth the Truth: they shall suffer no injustice" (Sura 23, 62).

J. Pedersen, *The Arabic Book*

The Diglossic Regime of Talk and Texts

The proprietors of Amman's publishing houses do a brisk trade in books about politics and religion. They have also, in recent years, begun to profit from a growing demand for "tribal literature." This new market, which emerged in the 1970s, expanded greatly in the 1980s. It includes folkloric monographs (al-'Abbadi 1989; al-'Uzayzi 1984), genealogical compendia (Abu Khusa 1989), Bedouin poetry (al-'Uzayzi 1991), introductions to tribal law (Abu Hassan 1987; al-'Abbadi 1982), and studies that, combining elements of all these genres, are packaged as "historical" works (al-'Abbadi 1984, 1986).

The advent of a popular literature about the Jordanian tribes written *by* and *for* local Bedouin has been hailed in Jordan's national press as a new form of "patriotism." The early works of Dr. Ahmad 'Uwaydi al-'Abbadi, for example, inspired an upbeat response. The reports below, reprinted in Dr. Ahmad's book, *Ceremonial Occasions of the Jordanian Tribes* (1989, 505–536), show the positive spin journalists gave to the ethnographic studies Ahmad produced in the 1970s.

THE BEDOUIN WOMAN: SYMBOL OF LOVE AND WAR
Special to the Jordan Times 1976

Amman—The bedouin woman is the mirror image of the man, a person to be consulted on certain matters. She can propose marriage and participates, in a limited way, in war. . . . These are some of the points that come to light through the intriguing research of poet-writer Capt. Ahmad Oweidi Abbadi. An expert on Bedouin affairs for he himself is one of their number, Capt. Abbadi deals with different aspects of bedouin life in a series of ten books that unfortunately are only in Arabic. . . .

Cites Bedouin Example
JORDANIAN EXPOUNDS BRAND NEW THEORY CORRELATING LIFE-STYLES WITH SECURITY
20/5/78
by a Jordan Times Staff Reporter

AMMAN, May 17 (JT)—A Jordanian student of Bedouin culture has come up with an intriguing theory that there is a direct correlation between styles of clothing and dwelling in each society and its state of security and need for protection.

Maj. Ahmad Oweidi Abbadi, a police officer and M.A. graduate of the Higher Islamic Studies Institute in Cairo, has had portions of his "Theory of Security and Protection" published in the Kuwaiti newspaper *Al Ra'i Al 'Am* and quoted by the French News Agency (AFP). It is to be published in a book entitled *Bedouin Rites*. . . .

BEDOUIN TO WRITE PH.D. THESIS ON HIS PEOPLE'S CUSTOMS
by Rami G. Khouri
Special to the Jordan Times

Amman— . . . How does one rationally explain Arab behavior and social customs? One way is to go back and trace the roots of contemporary social habits, an exercise that will inevitably lead one to the desert-dwelling bedouins. . . . One person who has systematically delved into the organization of bedouin life and tried to explain this to non-bedouins is Major Ahmad Oweidi Abbadi. . . . A bedouin himself, he spent the first years of his life, in the tradition of most pastoral nomads, as a shepherd, herding the family's goats and sheep.

While completing his education, he systematically explored the strict social organisation and habits of the badia (the arid desert regions inhabited only by the bedouins) and wrote a series of books and television series based on bedouin life.

Major Abbadi, a member of the bedouin tribe of the same name . . . has most recently received an acceptance to study for his PH.D. degree in anthropology at Cambridge University, where he will further explore the social structure and dynamics of bedouin society. His work at St. John's College will be supervised by the Arabist Professor R.B. Serjeant, of the Faculty of Archaeology and Anthropology. . . .

The habits of the desert Dr. Ahmad was exploring in print—modes of dress, poetry, heroism, rituals of hospitality, sexual decorum—are now commonly invoked as symbols of a distinctly Jordanian heritage (Layne 1989). The fact that the local Bedouin tribes existed long before the British established the Emirate of Transjordan in 1921 has not prevented local authors from using tribal materials to historicize what Dr. Ahmad calls "a new Jordanian national identity." The Bedouin lore now sold in Amman's bookshops is not exactly an invented tradition. Much of it is genuinely old. The context of popular nationalism in which it is written up, however, is utterly new, and attempts to nationalize the tribal heritage—or, as some would say, to tribalize the national heritage—are carried out with an eye toward the future as well as the past.

"My work," Dr. Ahmad proclaims in the introduction to *The Jordanian Tribes* (1986),

> springs from my deep belief in God almighty, and in my people, our history, our existence, our [tribal] structure, and [its] great importance . . . to coming generations, the youth, who will perhaps take pride in the heritage of their fathers and grandfathers, which is a part of them and their nature. That is, if it is indeed they who live atop this soil. Should other people, not from among our own sons and grandsons, come here, this book will be evidence and an argument against them: that there was in this land a people who loved it, built it up, protected it, and shed their blood on its fields. Without a doubt, the curse will fall on anyone who relinquishes it or sells it, or assists in the same. . . . For this is our land; we were created in it to endure in it . . . and it is of the utmost necessity that every generation document its family tree and place of residence, its important personages and accomplishments, so that they will not be credited to others in the absence of those who made them; so that they will not be credited to any people other than those who achieved and attained them (al-'Abbadi 1986, 15–16).

Nontribal Jordanians (who make up the nation's majority) are apt to find this "blood-and-soil" rhetoric threatening. It kindles nativist, anti-Palestinian sentiment and creates a privileged form of national identity that only those of tribal descent can claim. "Jordan," Dr. Ahmad informs us, "is distinguished from many other countries in that its people, all of them, are sons of the tribes" (1989, 10). The confident exclusivity of Dr. Ahmad's formulation marks a dramatic break with educated opinion, a discursive realm dominated by urban intellectuals who define community in a political idiom that equates tribalism with ignorance (*jahiliyya*), disorder (*fitna*), and backwardness (*takhalluf*).

The urban intelligentsia revealed their profound distrust of tribalism during the parliamentary elections of 1984 and 1989. The following editorial appeared in *Al Rai*, one of Jordan's leading newspapers, in the heat of the 1984 campaigns.

> We are not against extended family ties, nor are we against the family concept, we are not going to be enemies of family relations nor the ties of kinship nor marriage relations. But we are against all of this when it is used as a ladder upon which one climbs to a seat as representative or a way to a national position. As we tour through the towns, villages and cities we see to our amazement evidence of a strange return to a time before the 1940s. Now in the eighties the time and the people are different. . . . Tribalism was appropriate and good at the time of no state, it was one of the means for peaceful existence in the absence of a state. But today tribalism is a kind of illness and affliction which eats the fortunes and sustenance of the people (9 March 1984; cited in Layne 1986).

The belief that tribe and state should never merge—that their separation is the basis of "civil society"—is more keenly expressed in the personalized, either/or rhetoric deployed by Marwan Muasher, a columnist for the *Jordan Times* who joined other journalists in attacking the popular "return" to tribal loyalties that accompanied the 1984 elections.

> I wish to see people proud because they are part of a professional organization, not because they are members of a big tribe. I wish to see people proud because of their own personal achievements, not those of their cousins. And above all, I wish to see people proud because they are Jordanians, not only because of their surnames (19 January 1985; cited in Layne 1986, 130).

The "civilized Bedouin," an individual who is highly educated, professional, nationalistic, and, at the same time, unabashedly proud of his surname, his cousins, and his big tribe: such a person signals, for pundits like Muasher, an ominous perversion of Jordan's modernizing agenda. The market for tribal literature is fed by this same "malfunction," and the patriotism of Bedouin authors, which could be fondly indulged in the 1970s, when it seemed less ideological and more folkloric, is nowadays likened (in some elite circles) to a dangerous mingling of Bedouin *esprit* and government interests. A professor at Yarmouk University advised me not to waste my time working with tribalists or studying their research:

> The men who publish books on tribalism, you should know, are members of the military establishment; they are officers in Public Security. Almost all of them. They are a conservative group, very reactionary politically. Their research is propaganda for the most traditional forces in society. Of course, no one [in the government] is going to discourage them; this kind of work supports the status quo.

Given the nature of these attacks, it is startling to find that the harshest critics of the new tribal literature are local Bedouin themselves, who cannot agree on how or why the tribal heritage should be adapted to print. This disagreement—which betrays an inability (or an unwillingness) to imagine the tribal community in nationalist terms—is rooted not only in the oppositional character of tribal identities, but also in the "diglossic" model of historical truth that Bedouin pose as a solution to their endless historical disputes. The advice of Haj Salih al-'Uwaydi, who urged me to split historical discourse into high and low registers (see chapter 5), is worth repeating, since it accounts both for the immense appeal textual historicity enjoys among Bedouin and for the skeptical response the new tribal literature inspires among its readers. As the Haj stressed,

- *The truth is known only unto God.* There is a reality defined apart from human interpretation. The truth is not a matter of "we say/they say." Its substance can be known when God chooses to disclose it, as He did in the Holy Qur'an, the Torah, and the New Testament. This truth, received from God, is *divine* truth, and everything that is essentially true is revealed to us in scripture.

- *Everyone passes on a tradition. We can't tell if it's reliable or not. We didn't see these things. We heard them from people who heard them from people before them. You can't verify it unless you say who told you.* The truth of what tribesmen say, however, can be judged only by assessing the propriety of the "chains of transmission" (*isnad*) through which their knowledge was received. And here, in a world of things heard and said, one steps into the quagmire of *'asabiyya* (clannishness) that shapes and corrupts the historical knowledge tribesmen possess. The oral tradition is neither scriptural nor sacred. It is thoroughly profane.

It was the profanity of tribal history that led many Bedouin to reject it as a genuine form of knowledge and to wonder why I, an apparently learned person, would forsake the archives and sit at the feet of old men. To arrive at the truth behind the talk—and most tribesmen argued that such a truth did exist—one had to transcend the secular world of *kidhib*. One had to discover an unadulterated source; one had to receive a "revelation," and like the sacred revelations of old, this newly obtained lore would be conveyed in textual forms.

A young 'Abbadi boy told me that for only five dinar, a company in Lebanon would dig up your true genealogical roots: without lies, without exaggeration. I asked how this could be done. "They have ancient books and documents," he said. "The most reliable information, they have." It was not little boys alone who believed these things. Most tribesmen suspected that their true history was known to others in some faraway place. I was constantly referred to books stored in private libraries in Lebanon, or to government documents in London or Istanbul, or to old poems and genealogies stashed away in trunks: none of these *wathayig* (documents) had ever been seen by the men who spoke of them. It was as though tribalism (the "low tradition") possessed a canon of invisible scriptures, a textual truth that remained just beyond reach. Some men had actually caught glimpses of it.

> I met a Sharrabi today. He presented himself as the shrewd, worldly-wise
> type, a posture uneducated men sometimes assume in the presence of
> anyone they consider learned. After some preliminary inquiries into the
> nature of my work, he concluded that my various "proper sources" had
> been pulling the wool over my eyes. He then gave me an impromptu,
> advisory lecture on the dangers of historical research among Bedouin. First,
> the usual disclaimer: everyone is lying; nearly everyone's roots (except,
> of course, those of the Sharrab) are ignoble. Even the mighty 'Adwan, truth
> be known, are descended from gypsy tinkers. But then came something
> new. The Sharrabi gave me an account of his own encounter with the truth.
>
> He had worked as a truck driver in Saudi Arabia for several years,
> and one day a local genealogy buff, a Saudi Bedouin, invited him over to
> see the definitive statement on the origins of the Arab tribes. The Saudi
> led him to a diwan that had all the attributes of a shrine. It was set apart,
> locked up, used only on special occasions. On the wall, a vast, endlessly
> branching tree was displayed. It showed the precise connections of all the
> true Bedouin tribes. Beneath it, on a short-legged table, the same genealogi-
> cal tree, engraved in brass, was displayed on a large serving tray. It spread
> out before him like a metallic reflection of the fabric on the wall. He was
> greatly impressed by the sight of it. Surely this was true; surely it was
> more than the incessant *kidhib* that plagued the Balga.
>
> What made this artifact so appealing to him? It was not old, nor was
> it based on anything old (so far as he knew). Being unable to read or write,
> he was totally unable to evaluate it . . . which is strange because he seemed
> most impressed by the textuality of it all. The family tree was a kind
> of document. Not only was it written down, it was inscribed in metal.
> Moreover, it stood in the Nejd, in the Arabian Peninsula, ancestral home-
> land of all true Arabs. The entire experience conformed precisely to the
> tenets of the local epistemology: (1) our own knowledge is polluted by
> *kidhib*; (2) true knowledge exists elsewhere; and (3) it survives in docu-
> mented forms. For all he knew, the Sharrabi had arrived at a source of
> TRUTH, and its inaccessibility, his inability to evaluate it, only added to its
> appeal. Like the Qur'an, it was a truth he could not give shape to, indepen-
> dently analyze, or expound upon. It was safe from his own tendency, and
> that of fellow tribesmen, to corrupt it.

But why did the Sharrabi assume that this elaborate genealogical shrine was not itself an artful display of *kidhib*? Why was he willing to conclude that what he saw—but could not understand—was somehow superior to what he already knew? I put this question to Dr. K al-'Adwan, an administrator at Jordan University. Dr. K received his higher education in Britain. His wife is English; his children are bilingual. He has lived in an upscale neighborhood in Amman, somewhat removed from his village kin, for many years now. All these factors contribute to the urbanity for which he is known among his clan. Our visit was arranged, in fact, by one of Dr. K's village cousins, who thought I should see how learned men view the topic of my research.

Dr. K was fascinated by 'Adwani history, but he looked upon oral traditions (even his own) with all the skepticism of a man who has joined sides with literate civilization. He asked me the inevitable question: "Have you uncovered any documents that lend credence to the stories you're recording?" I mentioned sources from the European travel literature, and Peake Basha's *History* but then added: "If you're talking about local sources, like documents written by 'Adwanis during the age of shaykhs, no, I've not found anything." Dr. K suggested that documents of that sort probably do not exist.

> ANDREW: It's interesting that you ask, though, because most people, even the old men who can't read or write . . . even they have this idea that there is a written version of tribal history. It's out there somewhere. People are always telling me about these mysterious books and files and things that, if I could just find them, would prove what they're saying is true.
>
> [I tell Dr. K the Sharrabi's tale, along with several others. He nods sympathetically. He has heard similar stories all his life. "Why did the Sharrabi believe what he saw?" I ask.]
>
> DR. K: You must understand that among the tribes, writing, reading, literacy, getting a high school diploma or a college degree: these are new things, all within my lifetime. What you describe— the story that 'Abbadi told you—is part of the old mentality, which is still very strong among certain people. Writing has sacred connotations to the unschooled. It is part of religion in their minds. They associate it with the Qur'an, and with people who know more than they do, and they respect it. So if something is written, they are likely to believe it. They will say: "Look! It is written in a book. How can it be wrong?" We can, I am ashamed to admit it, we can be very gullible about some things.
>
> [Dr. K chuckles, then catches himself.]
>
> DR. K: But really, why do I laugh? Even books by learned

authors, the most sophisticated kinds of research, benefit from
Qur'anic associations. You will note that even nonreligious books
usually begin with a passage from the Qur'an . . . out of respect,
I think, and because it makes them part of a very prestigious, very
sacred tradition. You cannot go against it.

The argument had an almost Orientalist tilt. It brought to mind a world made
up, at one pole, of illiterate tribesmen who wore Qur'anic amulets around
their necks to ward off the evil eye and, at the other extreme, of learned men
who were intellectually paralyzed by their reverence for scripture and the
eternal verities of Islam. This was not the world I encountered in the Balga.
'Adwanis and 'Abbadis are intensely critical of tribal histories written by *local* figures like Dr. Ahmad 'Uwaydi al-'Abbadi (even though his publications
always come richly larded in Qur'anic citations). Muhammad Hamdan al-
'Adwan, who has not yet published his "History of the 'Adwan," assured me
that his work would be attacked if he wrote the truth. He, in turn, lambasted
the publications of Dr. Ahmad and others.

There is, however, a certain class of documents that, even among this fickle
readership, inspires a gullibility of precisely the type Dr. K described. It includes travel books written by European authors, genealogical treatises written by Arabs in foreign lands, and other antique texts (refreshingly new to
the Balga) that come from distant times and places. It is not the sacredness
of script per se that sets these documents apart from colloquial memory; it
is, instead, their *externality* to the Balga. Tribesmen consider them "objective" (*mawdu'i*) precisely because the men who wrote them have no place in
the local war of words. Thus, Dr. K reserved his highest praise for Frederick
Peake's *History of Transjordan and Its Tribes* (1935), a book written by an
Englishman. He deemed it "80 percent true." At the same time, he had nothing but contempt for the works of local historians:

> You will find that most of these books are biased and very unreli-
> able. A tribesman, by nature, cannot write an objective history.
> When someone like Ahmad al-'Uwaydi writes a history, what is he
> really doing? He is praising his own ancestors and defaming others.
> That's all. I haven't read his work, but I'm confident, even without
> seeing it, that he writes in that vein. I don't say this just because
> he's 'Abbadi. In my opinion, the same would be true of an 'Adwani
> author . . . even more true, since we 'Adwan are the proudest, most
> arrogant tribe in the Balga.

The spoken discourse, framed by *'asabiyya* and accusations of *kidhib*, is following the textualizers straight into print. It was bound to do so. The oral tradition, for all its divisive profanity, is made of more than "empty talk," and the authority that still resides in colloquial memory cannot be overcome, to recite Dr. Ahmad's phrase, "without a struggle." Even Col. Peake, whose narrative sensibility was not tribal, was compelled to reproduce (in writing) the essential structures of local historical talk. Dr. K's endorsement of Peake, though offered as proof of his own objectivity, is instead an effective measure of the extent to which Peake made ʿAdwani "pride and arrogance" compatible with his text.

The First Round of Textualization: Peake's History of Jordan and its Tribes

When *Tarikh sharqi al-urdun wa qabaʾil-ha* (History of Transjordan and its tribes) was first published in 1935, the fledgling Emirate of Transjordan lacked an official account of its own past. Col. Frederick Peake filled this vacuum with a piece of modern, quasi-nationalist historiography that was acceptably pro-Hashemite while being scrupulously uncritical of British policy in the region. Beha al-Din Tawqan, a local member of Peake's headquarters staff, prepared the Arabic edition. He supplemented Peake's work with copious notes and emendations of his own, greatly improving the quality of the original English manuscript. When it is read today, Tawqan's arabization has a quaint, period flavor. It was written before the creation of Israel; before Jordan's acquisition of the West Bank in 1948 and its loss of the same in 1967; before the massive transfer of Palestinians to the East Bank; before Baʿthism, Nasserism, OPEC, the Arab League, the Islamic Revival. In short, before the features of the modern Arab political landscape took shape.

The world portrayed in the *Tarikh* is, by contrast, archaic and utterly provincial. It is a colonial world, and the structures of power the British imposed "East of Jordan," though never candidly discussed by Peake, are perfectly visible in the 54 illustrations that decorate the text. The book is overflowing with pictures of tribal shaykhs, Hashemite royals, soldiers of the Arab Legion, policemen, British officers in Bedouin dress, and select shots of Transjordan's natural wonders and classical antiquities. Interspersed among these images are dozens of genealogical charts tracing the descent of local notables. The Amir Abdullah's pedigree is displayed on a large, foldout version of the Hashemite family tree, which extends back to the Prophet Muhammad, whose name is boldly illuminated at center page. The borders of the Amir Abdullah's domain, an unprecedented cartographic shape, are drawn on an oversized historical map, which Col. Peake labels (with no discernible sense of anachronism) "Transjordan, From Earliest Times to the Herodian Period."

This parade of images—some obviously designed for framing—sends a clear political message. Transjordan is an ancient patrimony controlled by an alliance of modern patrons: shaykhs, British officers, and Amirs of prophetic lineage. Not surprisingly, the book includes only one photograph of a member of Transjordan's civil administration: Ibrahim Basha Hashim, an early prime minister. Despite this outdated rendering of the Jordanian state (or perhaps because of it), the Arabic version of Peake's history has remained popular in Jordan over the years; it can still be found in most bookshops in Amman. I bought my own copy at a kiosk in the Queen ʿAlia International Airport (the most politically sensitive public space in Jordan) where, ironically enough, it was stacked next to several books by Dr. Ahmad ʿUwaydi al-ʿAbbadi.

Peake's original English manuscript was revised and published in 1958 as *History and Tribes of Jordan*. As the title suggests, the book is divided into starkly contrasting halves. In the first, Peake constructs a conventional history of what would become, in 1921, the Emirate of Transjordan. In accord with nationalist ideology, his treatment is retroactive: that is to say, all events that took place within the physical area comprising modern Transjordan (ca. 1935) suddenly become part of a uniquely *Jordanian* past. Peake moves from the Paleolithic to the early years of the Amir Abdullah's rule, visiting all the great civilizations in between. Tawqan's chapter titles are consonant with this grand, "march of history" approach.

Chapter One: Transjordan from prehistoric times until the invasion
    of the Assyrians
Chapter Two: The Assyrians, Babylonians, and Persians
Chapter Three: The Greeks
Chapter Four: The Romans
Chapter Five: Transjordan at the close of Roman times
Chapter Six: The Islamic Conquest
Chapter Seven: The Crusaders
Chapter Eight: The Mamlukes
Chapter Nine: The Ottomans
Chapter Ten: The Great War and its aftermath

The only logic that unites this epochal procession—the only logic that connects, say, the establishment of the Crusader states and the locust plagues of 1928–30—is the fact that all of it happened within a set of geopolitical boundaries drawn on a map in the 1920s.

The national community Peake asks his readers to envision was, in 1935, a new and alien thing; in many ways it still fails to capture the popular imagination (see chapter 8). The enduring appeal of Peake's *Tarikh*, among tribespeople at least, is attributable instead to the second half of the text, "Part II: The Tribes of Jordan," in which Peake, drawing on information gathered by officers of the Arab Legion, assembles an extensive catalogue of the origins and spatial distribution of Jordan's indigenous tribes. Unlike the nationalist historiography of part one, part two has:

1.   *No unified narrative.* The origins of each tribe and tribal section (hundreds in all) are listed separately. Peake divides the Balga, for instance, into fifteen tribes. These fifteen are then divided into their constituent sections, subsections, and client groups. Accounts of historical incidents, too, are dispersed under separate genealogical headings.

2.   *No unified chronology.* Most of the dates that appear in part two are rough estimates at best. The ʿAdwan are said to have arrived in the Balga around 1640 A.D.; the ʿAbbadi clans are routinely said to have arrived about four hundred years ago, or five hundred years ago, or three hundred years ago, all without verification of any sort. Peake makes no attempt to construct a time line on which significant tribal events could be organized. Since there is no unified narrative, what purpose would this time line serve?

3.   *No sharp distinction between oral and textual evidence.* Peake cites the works of Arab genealogists (e.g., al-Qalqashandi's *Nihayat al-ʾarab fi maʿrifat qabaʾil al-ʾarab* and al-Swaydi's *Sabaʾik al-dhahab fi maʿrifat qabaʾil al-ʿarab*); he draws heavily from the European travel literature as well. Still, the bulk of the local, tribal event-history Peake records is based on oral testimony. It stands or falls on the authority of the (unnamed) men who spoke it, and Peake does not question that authority.

It should come as no shock, then, that part two strikes nontribal readers as a folkloric mishmash of unfounded genealogical speculations. Peake's treatment of the ʿAjarma, the oldest of the Balga tribes, is typical of the expository style he affects throughout the *Tarikh.*

The ʿAjarma

Al-Qalqashandi and al-Swaydi agree that Bani ʿAjrama is a section of Bani Turayf of Judham. As for the ʿAjarma themselves, they say that their ancestor is Nawfal the ʿAjrami, who came from al-ʿAla in the northern Hijaz. They are now many tribes with different origins and lines of descent. . . .

[Peake accounts for only six of these tribes. The sketch that follows is among the more colorful.]

THE ʿAFASHAT

It is said that they are among the oldest residents of the Balga. Their tribe used to camp on the lands around Naʿur, and it is said that they came into conflict with the Amir of Khirbat Swayma, which is located near the Dead Sea. As a result, they were defeated and scattered. Three brothers went out from them. One settled among the Ziyadat, of the ʿAbbad tribe.

His descendants are known as the Khararba because when the Amir of Swayma's men attacked his family, he sought refuge in a kharub tree and hid among its branches. When he told his story to the Bedouin, they nicknamed him Abu Kharub, and his descendants have carried that name until this very day. The second brother fled to Kerak and his sons are now called the Sarayra. As for the third brother, he remained in Naʿur and was nicknamed "ʿAfash" because all the personal belongings (ʿafsh) his enemies plundered from him (1935, 369–371).

And so the entries continue, tribe upon tribe, clan within clan, page after page. The final product would appear, at first glance, to be nothing more than an annotated register of territorial and genealogical identities. Peake's juxtaposition of parts one and two is fascinating, however, in that it "nationalizes" two radically different images of Jordanian community. Part one is meant to be read by a general public. It is not simply a dynastic history of the Hashemites and their deeds. Col. Peake, though subject to a monarch of his own, seems not to have thought of history in dynastic terms. His audience and object are *national*, and Peake defines each in relation to the borders of Transjordan (ca. 1935), which mark the divide between "this country" and others surrounding it: Iraq, Syria, Saudi Arabia, and Palestine. Part one takes as given (and attempts to flesh out) a shared Transjordanian heritage: one which Muslim and Christian, Arab and Circassian, Hashemite royal and commoner subject, can all alike proclaim.

To argue that Peake's *History* was a self-conscious attempt to instruct Jordanians in the art of imagining their nation-state would perhaps be overly cynical. Still, it is important to note that an *Englishman*, a commander of the Arab Legion, thought it desirable to write this book at a time when the Amir Abdullah, to whom the *Tarikh* is dedicated, fancied himself a Muslim dynast whose proper sphere of influence was the entire "Arab East." When seen as an instrument of ideological encapsulation, the family resemblance between Peake's work and other colonial artifacts—for example, "the census, the map and the museum" (Anderson 1991)—becomes instantly clear. The *Tarikh* speaks of a Jordanian nation, newly bounded yet possessing an ancient history, at a time when most "Jordanians" still lived in a Qurʾanic world of "peoples and tribes" (*shuʿub wa qabaʾil*), a world overlain by the "protected areas of shaykhs" (*himayat al-shyukh*) and the "rule" (*hukm*) of hereditary dynasts. In "Part II: Tribes of Jordan," Peake acknowledges (and temporarily embraces) this other way of imagining the sociopolitical landscape. Part two is not written for a general public. Its audience is fragmented into hundreds of *specific* genealogical communities, all of which predate the boundaries of Transjordan. A man of the 'Afash clan might think of himself as a member of the 'Ajarma; on other occasions he might consider himself a Balga tribesman; on yet others he might call himself a Jordanian, but the latter identity owes nothing to the first three. In 1920, only fifteen years before Col. Peake's *History* was published, Jordan did not exist.

Part two takes as given (and attempts to flesh out) the unshared, always segmenting character of its audience. One could argue that this makes for a flawed nationalism—that it accentuates internal divisions at the expense of an imagined unity—but its appropriateness for a tribal audience can be seen in the way Balga tribesmen actually read the *Tarikh*.

'Amr came over to see my copy of Peake Basha, which he's always heard about but never had the chance to read. Dr. Ahmad has advised his fellow 'Uwaydis not to buy Peake's book because his own books are "more accurate and reliable"; besides, he killed demand for Peake by giving free copies of his *Introduction to the Study of the Jordanian Tribes* (1984) to every 'Uwaydi household. So 'Amr was eager to see my illicit text.

He handled it in the ordinary way. First, he flipped through the pages looking for pictures.

"Are there any pictures of 'Abbadi shaykhs?" he wondered.

"No," I said.

"There should be," he said, trying in vain to find one.

Except for the old photos, 'Amr was totally uninterested in the contents of part one; instead, he asked me to find the 'Abbad section, which is in the compendium [part two]. He thumbed through the lists of 'Abbadi clans and subclans until he found his own, the Afgaha. Directly beneath the Afgaha on the same page was the Zyud entry. 'Amr read them both aloud, and I tried to gauge his reaction. I didn't expect it to be positive. This is what he read:

VI. The Fuqaha'

This is a tribe composed of the following divisions:

1. The Mahayrat—It is said that their ancestor was a Christian who converted to Islam, and the Bedouin still remind them of it. Their campsites are in the area of 'Araq al-Amir. A branch of the Mahayrat split off from them and resides now in the village of Kufr Abil in the Kura district of 'Ajlun; the latter are now called the Bisharat. The Mahayrat number about 300 souls and are divided into three sections: the Mir'i, the Rayan, and the Salama.

2.   The Slayhat—They say their ancestor came from the Najd some 400 years ago. Their campsites are in the area of Wadi Sir, and they number about 400 souls.

3.   The Hisamiya—They claim that their ancestor came from the Najd some 400 years ago. Their campsites are in the area of Wadi Sir and they number about 150 souls.

4.   The Sikarna—It is said that they immigrated from the Najd some 400 years ago. Their campsites are in the area of Wadi Sir, and they number about 200 souls.

5.   The Mahamid—They say they came from the Najd some 300 years ago. Their campsites are in the area of Wadi Sir, and they number about 130 souls.

VII. The Zyud

This tribe is composed of two groups:

1.   The Dwaykat—It is said that they came from the village of Bayta in the area of Nablus some 300 years ago. Their campsites are in the area of Wadi Sir, and they number about 200 souls. They are divided into three clans: the Maghariz, the Harayza, and the Shu'a'.

2.   The Sharrab—It is said that they came from Palestine some 300 years ago. Their campsites are in the area of Wadi Sir, and their numbers are about 200 souls. They are two clans: the Sawalha and the Mawasi.

Peake's information on the Afgaha seems to have come from secondhand reports. It is probably based on oral testimony collected from 'Abbadis of other clans. As a result, it is generic and tedious. Only the Mahayrat entry, which mentions their possible Christian origins, resembles the oral traditions I recorded from Afgaha themselves. Moreover, Tawqan has arranged the Afgaha clans in order of precedence: the Mahayrat, who (in 1935) were the leading shaykhs of the Afgaha, are listed first; the Slayhat, strong arm of the Mahayri shaykhdom, come next; the Hisamiya, who stood as shaykhs over the lesser Afgaha clans, the Sikarna and Mahamid, are placed third; and so on.

I prepared myself for 'Amr's protests, but to my great surprise, he was actually pleased by what he'd read.

"See?" he pointed out smugly, "It says here that the Zyud tribes are from Palestine. But the Afgaha tribes are from the Najd. Ha! This is proof that our origins are nobler than theirs."

Tawqan's ranking of the Afgaha clans in order of shaykhly prestige slipped by 'Amr totally unnoticed. Instead, he enlisted Peake as an ally in the age-old rivalry between the Afgaha and the Zyud, a rivalry that had been supercharged by the parliamentary elections of 1989, in which Dr. Ahmad 'Uwaydi al-'Abbadi defeated a Zyudi candidate, Hamud al-Jibali, a member of the shaykhly lineage of the Sharrab.

After reveling in this "documented proof" of Afgaha superiority, 'Amr proceeded to look up the tribes of his in-laws, his friends in the army, and any other people he knew. He didn't read the section on the 'Ajlun tribes to the north, or the Kerak tribes to the south, or the desert tribes to the east, unless he knew someone from a specific tribe. He kept very much to the Balga, a region which, for him, is congested with actual relationships. As he flipped back and forth, 'Amr gradually imposed his own social universe on part two, which he would have to do anyway, since part two has no consistent order—alphabetical, geographical, or chronological— of its own.

Not only is part two compatible with the structure of the tribal community it seeks to textualize, it also reproduces the patterns of confident speech and deferential silence I explored in chapter 5. Peake gives an extended, richly detailed account of 'Adwani history—most of it appearing for the first time in print—along with divers speculations on their genealogical and geographical origins. For 'Abbad, the largest tribe in the Balga, he gives no synoptic history whatsoever, only notes on the putative origins of the principal 'Abbadi clans; indeed, the only discussion of incidents from the 'Abbadi past is contained *within* Peake's narrative history of the 'Adwan (pp. 168–172 of the 1958 English edition). Once again, 'Abbadi history is framed by a larger 'Adwani discourse. Likewise, Peake includes an 'Adwani genealogical tree that is fifteen generations deep; no 'Abbadi family, not even the shaykhly lineage of Ibn Khatlan, is given similar attention.

In the Arabic version, Beha al-Din Tawqan tries to offset this imbalance by moving a large chunk of Peake's 'Adwan entry into "Part I, Chapter Nine: The Ottomans." The result, however, is an even more striking hierarchy. The history of the Balga in the eighteenth and nineteenth centuries—the period corresponding to the "age of shaykhs"—is transformed into a history that belongs almost exclusively to the 'Adwan: which is just how 'Adwanis, nowadays, would have us remember it. Col. Peake, the archetypal outsider, leaves the reader no doubt as to who ruled the Balga. The tribal discourse he adapted to print in 1935 was a set of oral arguments that had already been decisively won and lost. After the first round of textualization, it was the 'Adwan, "shaykhs of the Balga for ages," who emerged victorious yet again.

When 'Amr returned my copy of the *Tarikh* after a week of showing it off to his army buddies—some of whom belonged to tribes Peake examines in much greater detail—he had obviously changed his mind about the colonel's work.

"Dr. Ahmad's books are better," he said. "They give more information on 'Abbad. Peake just writes two words on this family, two words on that family. That's not enough for a correct history. Dr. Ahmad gives the full genealogy."

Peake Basha and the Tribal Historiographers: A Love-Hate Relationship

I have discussed Peake Basha's work at length because his *Tarikh,* more than any other book, has influenced the way Jordanian tribesmen write history today. Even when they criticize Peake, Bedouin historiographers borrow heavily from his material. Ahmad Abu Khusa, author of *The Jordanian and Palestinian Tribes and the Ties of Kinship among Them* (1989), holds a dim view of Peake's scholarship; in fact, he envisions his own work as an effort to repair the damage Peake and other non-Arab researchers have done.

> I have embarked on a study of most of the books that treat the genealogies of the Jordanian and Palestinian tribes, in addition to my exhaustive study of the Jordanian books that deal with this topic, comparing what appears in the pages of these books so as to arrive at the truth and because of my belief that Arab authors should co-operate in filling the gaps that exist . . . [while at the same time] . . . correcting the deliberate, conniving, and defamatory errors that have been made in regard to the ancestral Arab tribes by foreign authors such as Frederick, the author of *History of Transjordan and Its Tribes,* who called some tribes "Jews" and other tribes "Crusaders." This is the matter that caused me to undertake immediate study, making local visits to the shaykhs of the tribes and the old men who witnessed the life of the tribe and to the Bedouin poets who still recall the poems that tell the story of the life and history of the tribe in its wanderings throughout its vast Arab homeland, since these men inherited many of the folktales that were passed on by the upright ancestors, generation upon generation (Abu Khusa 1989, 162).

Despite this scathing indictment of Peake, Abu Khusa's book consists mostly of long passages taken word for word (sometimes without adequate citation) from the *Tarikh.* His 'Adwan and 'Abbad entries, like many others, are lifted with minimal abridgment straight from Tawqan's Arabic text. Peake's secondary sources are recycled as well, and his division of history into two registers—the national and the tribal—is accepted without question. The criticism Abu Khusa levels at the *Tarikh* is not, in reality, as censorious as he would have us believe, and the results of his own fieldwork, which are sprinkled lightly over the text, add little to knowledge already in print before *The Jordanian and Palestinian Tribes* was published.

Upon closer inspection, the nature of Abu Khusa's love-hate relationship with the *Tarikh* emerges clearly in his response to Peake's treatment of the Layathna tribes of Wadi Musa (pp. 516–518 of the 1935 arabization), some of whom migrated to Abu Khusa's home region of Bir Sab' (Beersheba), which is now part of Israel. In discussing the origins of the Layathna, Peake refers to the fanciful observations of Palmer and Wolf (Palmer 1872, 432), who believed the Layathna were descendants of the Jews of Khaybar. He also speculates, citing the genealogist al-Swaydi, that the Layathna are "descendants of Layth bin Sud bin Aslam al-Hafi of Qada'a of Hamir," and thus are of "pure Arab lineage." But the specter of Hebraic origins has been set loose, and Abu Khusa, who is not about to have the "authenticity" of his own Beersheba tribes questioned, charges Peake with sordid motives.

> Frederick, the Englishman by origin, is trying to raise doubts about the Arabness of the ancestral tribes, but his testimony is false. It has already come down to us in *Saba'ik al-dhahab* by al-Swaydi that they [the Layathna] are from among the descendants of Layth bin Sud of Qada'a of Hamir, and they are pure Arabs (Abu Khusa 1989, 189).

The proof of Peake's "falsehood" comes, oddly enough, from Peake's own reference to al-Swaydi. Abu Khusa cites the *Tarikh*—or at least derives his sources from it—even when he attacks it.

Ahmad Abu Khusa judges part two as did my 'Uwaydi friend, 'Amr: namely, in relation to what Peake and Tawqan say about the tribes to which he has a specific connection. His negative reaction to the *Tarikh*, though intensely personal, fits neatly into a larger, fairly consistent pattern of like and dislike. Indeed, I found that tribesmen who approved of Peake's work ('Adwanis like Dr. K prominent among them) belonged to powerful tribes who had successfully injected their own oral traditions into the text. If a tribesman did not like the *Tarikh*, it was almost always because he objected to what Peake had written, or failed to write, about his own group, however broadly or narrowly defined that group might be. The difference between "80 percent true" and "absolutely worthless" amounted, in most cases, to the content of a single entry. The difference between good and bad content depended, in turn, on whether the tribe in question engaged in historical discourse from a dominant or subaltern position in the years between 1921 and 1935, when Peake and his Arab officers were assembling oral traditions.

Which brings us to our main characters: the conservator and scribe, Muhammad Hamdan al-'Adwan, and the much published tribalist, Dr. Ahmad 'Uwaydi al-'Abbadi. Unlike Col. Peake, who saw tribalism as an external object to be catalogued and systematized, Ahmad and Muhammad have grown up *inside* the zones of propriety and power that inform the his-

torical universe of tribes. As a result, they have textual agendas quite unlike anything a British officer of the 1930s might imagine.

Bracing the Pillar / Shaking the Foundations:
The Conflicting Agendas
of Muhammad Hamdan and Dr. Ahmad

In 1990, Muhammad Hamdan al-ʿAdwan, heir to a robust shaykhly tradition, found himself encapsulated in a modern, nontribal state, an "age of government" in which the strength of his tribe had been waning steadily for
decades. Even in 1935, when the *Tarikh* was first published, the ʿAdwan had
already lost their grip on the Balga tribes. Sultan al-ʿAdwan and his son,
Majid, attempted to overthrow the Amir ʿAbdullah in 1923—this was the
famed "ʿAdwani Revolt" (see chapter 3)—but they were easily defeated and
fled to Syria, where they sought refuge among the Druze. The rebel shaykhs
(plates 14 and 15) were eventually reconciled to the Amir Abdullah, who
thereafter ensured their loyalty by conferring grand titles upon them and
reserving a place for them in his government.

The following observations, drawn from the preparatory notes for
Muhammad Hamdan's "History of the ʿAdwan," describe Shaykh Majid as
he came to be known in the years after the ʿAdwani Revolt.

> Majid had the attributes of power. He was tall, white, strong, and blessed
> with talents from God. In his diwan, there was silence and respect. He had
> no need of women. His father, Sultan, married 69 times, but Majid lowered
> his head in the presence of women. He was literate and religious, coura-
> geous, a horseman, and never afraid. His mind was open and brilliant. He
> excelled in the art of politics. He was a nationalist who loved his country.
> He supported the anti-imperialist rebels in Syria and Palestine. He received
> the title "Shaykh of the Shaykhs of Jordan," from ʿAbdullah, as well as the
> title "Pasha." From King Faysal of Syria he received the title "Amir of the
> Liwa." The Amir Abdullah always took Majid with him on state visits
> abroad. He was a modern man, Shaykh Majid b. Sultan, respected by the
> Amir until the day of his death.

In 1946, when Majid died, the ʿAdwan were left without a great man to lead
them. It was in the same year that the Amir Abdullah became king of an
independent Transjordan, and the ascendancy of the Hashemites over the
ʿAdwan and other indigenous notables was at last made complete.

"In the days of Majid and Sultan," an ʿAdwani shaykh told me . . .

> the ʿAdwan had power of their own, and the government respected
> it. Abdullah feared us. When Majid entered the diwan, Abdullah

Plate 14. Shaykh Sultan al-ʿAdwan. Shaykh of all Shaykhs and Paramount Shaykh of the Balga.

Plate 15. Shaykh Majid Sultan al-ʿAdwan: he "had the attributes of power."

would stand to greet him: "Welcome, ya Majid! Welcome, ya Shaykh of the Balga Shaykhs!" Majid was the only person Abdullah would stand up and greet like that. He saw that Majid was a true shaykh. In reality, he was an Amir just like Abdullah. But after Majid, our luck was broken . . . our dominion was finished. No shaykh rose up to replace Majid. Today, we gain power by cooperating with the government and supporting it. That's it. The 'Adwan have only the power King Husayn lets us keep, and don't listen to any other talk.

This residual, co-opted power is still quite impressive. 'Adwani shaykhs continue to play a leading role in Jordanian politics, with members in both houses of parliament, in the upper ranks of the military, and in various government ministries. Still, the authority gained by way of plebiscites and royal decrees pales in comparison to the power wielded by 'Adwani strongmen in the glorious "age of shaykhs." Today, 'Adwanis sit decorously in government councils, but in the not-so-distant past their grandfathers cut off the heads of Turkish Bashas, routed Bedouin armies ten times their size, collected *khawa* to "the gates of Syria," and settled disputes between the mightiest shaykhs of the land.

Muhammad Hamdan (plate 16), our local historian, finds himself equidistant from the modern and the historical arenas of 'Adwani power. His sixth lineal ancestor, Hamud Salih al-'Adwan, was overlord of Salt, shaykh of all Balga shaykhs, and a scourge upon the Bani Sakhr, from whom he plundered three camel herds in one day. In 1990, Muhammad Hamdan worked as a clerk in a textbook warehouse in the Jordan Valley, and the bulk of his income came from agriculture. At certain times of year, I could find him selling lettuce from his irrigated gardens to passersby on the road. When I first toured his farm in the Jordan Valley, Muhammad left no doubt in my mind that he was, by trade and inclination, a committed agriculturalist. He wanted me to understand, however, that things had once been different.

[We followed the irrigation channel out to a squash field. Muhammad's father, brother, and sister-in-law were there, stooped over, picking squash, throwing them into Styrofoam boxes, loading them onto a pickup truck. We chatted with them for a while, tossed in a few squash ourselves, then headed back to the house. As we trudged across the field, Muhammad made the following observation.]

MUHAMMAD: In my grandfather's time, when I was just a boy, no 'Adwani would do this . . . farm like this. He would consider it beneath him; he would leave it to his slaves and field hands. Or

Plate 16. Muhammad Hamdan al-ʿAdwan, conservator and scribe, sips tea.

maybe he would let out his land to a client tribe on shares. But nowadays we all work in the fields and no one says *ʿayb* (disgrace).

[If so, then why bring the topic up in this obviously self-conscious way? I decide to probe for the stigmatized link between farm work and peasant origins]

ANDREW: Nowadays, everyone is a peasant. In an economic sense. What do you think?

MUHAMMAD: Ha! Peasant by occupation, Bedouin by blood. It's close to that. It's close. But don't use that word—"peasant" (*fillah*)—around the 'Adwan. It's like a curse. Say "farmer" (*muzari'*). It's nobler.

ANDREW: Sorry. I was just joking.

MUHAMMAD: We consider ourselves nobler than peasants, but if we were really peasants . . . by origin I mean . . . we would produce two, three, four times the crop we produce now. They have more energy for this kind of work. But the Bedouin, especially the 'Adwan—because we were the powerful shaykhs and had slaves and tenants—our heart is not yet accustomed to the farming life. In the past, what was the work of the shaykhs? Raiding, war, making feasts, sitting in councils, preparing coffee for one's guests, collecting *khawa* from weaker tribes. How can men like that ever become energetic farmers? It will take many, many years of development.

At moments like these, Muhammad seemed acutely aware of the gap in experience that separates the chivalric glory of his ancestor, Shaykh Hamud, from the comfortable (but rather mundane) existence of a farmer and clerk. That chasm, which opens wider with each passing generation, holds an intellectual puzzle Muhammad must solve: "If my ancestors were mighty shaykhs, and their blood is my blood, why then do I no longer resemble them?" For several years now, Muhammad has been recording oral history from old men, transcribing poetry, and assembling all the documents he can find concerning the "age of shaykhs." He goes about these scribal tasks in a mood of urgent nostalgia, as if, by his own textual intervention, he will be able to consolidate (even revive) a shaykhly legacy that today, in an age of literacy and forgetting, is more vulnerable than ever.

[I am sitting in Muhammad's office at the textbook warehouse. This is where we do most of our work, away from the racket of unruly children and the limitless sociability of Muhammad's neighbors. This dusty, cavernous building, which Muhammad and I jokingly refer to as the "Center for 'Adwani Studies," is empty now. It is mid-term; the textbooks have all been passed out to the teachers and Muhammad is blessed with an abundance of free time.

A mess of folders and notebooks, the remains of the day's

research, is spread out over the surface of Muhammad's desk. We have just spent two hours sorting through various accounts of the rivalry between Muhammad's ancestor, Shaykh Hamud, and Shaykh Nimr Ibn 'Adwan, the illustrious warrior-poet. Muhammad's data are not organized chronologically or by topic, so we've had to rummage back and forth between the testimony of various "proper sources," each of whom is catalogued under the name of his clan. The amount of data Muhammad has at his disposal is impressive: over thirty 'Adwani *gasayid* in multiple versions; detailed genealogies of all the major 'Adwani clans; notes for the grand historical narrative he hopes to complete soon.

Muhammad wants me to publish this material in English. Most of it, he fears, will never see print in Arabic. It is too sensitive, too polemical. For the last two weeks, he has been transferring great chunks of it to me, reading aloud from his papers as I dutifully take notes in English (so other 'Adwanis, who occasionally look through my notes, will not be able to understand them). In exchange, I have been supplying Muhammad with useful passages from the English travel literature, in which his ancestors figure as leading men of the country.

Muhammad has just sent the custodian off to prepare a service of tea. While we wait for him to return, I decide to ask Muhammad a simple question that, it suddenly occurs to me, I have too long neglected to ask.]

ANDREW: Why do you write history?

MUHAMMAD: Do you want me to explain my philosophy, or my goals, or my methods, or what exactly?

ANDREW: I'm asking you because . . . well, I look at all these papers and I think, "This is strange; this is a revolutionary thing." I spent four months in [the village of] Salihi [recording testimony from another 'Adwani clan] and I didn't see a single document. Everything was talk, talk, talk. Abu Firas always said, "I must write down Haj 'Arif's poems," but he never did, and he would never do what you are doing, collecting history from all over the tribe. So, basically, I want to know why you are sitting here with hundreds of pages of written material.

[Muhammad swivels back and forth in his chair, deliberating. He is an earnest person, not one to make hasty replies. Besides, his desire to create texts is something he would like other 'Adwanis to take seriously, since so many of his kin think his methods are obsessive. A taste for old stories is one thing, but Muhammad's need to write it all down, store it up, collate and catalogue it—these habits are beyond normal. My use of the word "strange" (*gharib*) to describe his work prompts a response that, I suspect, he makes very often.]

MUHAMMAD: There are two reasons. First, the tribal era has ended. It won't be long before all this history, the history of the 'Adwan, is forgotten. The elders are dying. I must save their recollections for the coming generations, because no one listens to them and writes down what they say. They don't realize that there is important history in their words.

ANDREW: That's true.

MUHAMMAD: And there is a second reason. We do not want other people, like Ahmad al-'Uwaydi, writing our history. He cannot be objective. He is 'Abbadi. He only wants to tear down our reputation. He envies the 'Adwan, envies our power and our high reputation among the tribes, so he distorts our history and makes people ignorant of it.

[Muhammad waits patiently as I write down his words, then summarizes.]

MUHAMMAD: Those are my primary goals. To preserve my own history because it is a noble history, and to protect it from other historians—people who just call themselves "historians," but are really liars—who just want to destroy the truth.

Dr. Ahmad 'Uwaydi al-'Abbadi, for his part, would find Muhammad's critique agreeably insulting, since it leaves his 'Adwani critic where 'Adwanis rarely find themselves in relation to 'Abbad: *on the defensive.* Whereas Muhammad Hamdan casts himself in the role of conservator, Dr. Ahmad (plate 17) is forever depicting himself as an innovator and iconoclast, as a "dangerous" man whose ideas will topple the powers-that-be. During his protean career, Ahmad has been many things: public security officer, media pundit, Bedouin folklorist, university lecturer. But he has always been a writer, and his textual agendas, which are brazenly political and self-aggrandizing, are dedicated to the reinvention of Dr. Ahmad al-'Uwaydi, the renovation of his clan, the Sikarna, and the creation of an exclusively tribal, anti-Palestinian model of Jordanian nationalism.

When I met Dr. Ahmad in 1989, he strongly believed that Jordan is dominated by a conspiratorial alliance of "traitors" (*khawan*) (i.e., old shaykhly families like the 'Adwan) and "outsiders" (*barraniyya*): Palestinians,

Plate 17. Dr. Ahmad receives congratulations after his 1989 election victory.

Circassians, Hijazis, Masons, and a motley assortment of others. His response to this alliance, and the impetus for his many books on tribalism, was to build up a populist coalition of "original Jordanians" (*urduniyyin asliyyin*)—a faction of authentic tribesmen, *abna' al-'asha'ir* (sons of the tribes)—for whom he could act as political spokesman, power broker, and unifying cultural symbol. When Ahmad was elected to parliament in 1989, he saw his victory as the fruit of "seventeen years of writing and research." His rise to national prominence was accomplished by the pen, and Muhammad Hamdan's belief that Dr. Ahmad writes history in order to demolish the ancien régime is not at all paranoid. As Ahmad himself told me: "Without a strong clan, you are nothing in Jordan." He might easily have added a corollary: "You cannot become strong unless you make other clans appear weak."

On election day, Ahmad put the latter principle brilliantly into effect. He defeated his 'Adwani rivals by wide margins and trounced nine 'Abbadi candidates as well, although each claimed descent from a shaykhly lineage (see Appendix B).

"When you vote for a shaykh," Dr. Ahmad told a ready electorate, "you give him the sword he will use to slay you. When you vote for me, you purchase a stallion who will speed you toward your goal."

In Arabic, the word for vote is *sawt*, which literally means "voice." The voice Dr. Ahmad denied his shaykhly opponents at the ballot box is not unlike the voice he has systematically denied them in print. Peake's *History* mimics the patterns of rhetorical power and weakness that inform the oral tradition; Dr. Ahmad's publications, by contrast, turn these patterns upside down. The textual fate of all proud-talking shaykhs is foretold in the introduction to Ahmad's *The Jordanian Tribes* (1986).

> I oftentimes encountered the person who wanted me to fill the pages with details about him, even though he did not provide me with any information except that he was a shaykh and the son of a shaykh, and that the others have no merit and no power compared to him. There is no doubt that the conduct of reliable scholarship makes it impossible for me to facilitate these deluded fantasies, for it is not my fate to place my sons and myself under the curse of history and of the people. I sing the funeral dirge for those who dealt with me arrogantly. They believe they are superior to history, despite the fact that history—in our view at least—is greater than individuals, and the pen is mightier than history itself. I will not be drawn into disputations of this kind because it is not consistent with my methodology, my mentality, or my inclination. It is a matter of no significance to me (al-'Abbadi 1986, 19).

The seriousness of this claim can be seen in the glaring exclusions for which Dr. Ahmad's *The Jordanian Tribes* is justly famous. His chapter on the 'Adwan (1986, 297–326), for instance, contains no sections on the Salih or Nimr, two clans that, for over three centuries, have produced the most powerful shaykhs in the Balga. In his Zyudi chapter (1986, 206–220), Ahmad limits the shaykhly Dwaykat and Sharrab clans—whose histories I examine at length in chapter 4—to six scant lines, and these he buries inside a six-page treatment of the Sawajina, a Zyudi clan of minor historical significance.

By depriving shaykhly rhetoric of its power; by making the pen "mightier than history itself," Dr. Ahmad has published his way into the front ranks of tribal society. His current notoriety is not a legacy inherited from illustrious ancestors—Ahmad's people, the Sikarna, have long been counted among the weaker 'Abbadi clans—rather, his fame is a creation of the print and electronic media. The dust jacket of Dr. Ahmad's *The Jordanian Tribes* bears the following information about its author, much of which resurfaced in Dr. Ahmad's 1989 campaign literature.

About the Author

He is Dr. Ahmad 'Uwaydi al-'Abbadi, a graduate of Cambridge University in Britain (1982), and a member of the Hawarith clan of the 'Abbad tribes of central Jordan. He hails from a family well known for its learning and sophistication. He enjoys a lofty scholarly and social standing in central Jordan and is famous in the Arab Middle East—academically, because of his many publications; popularly, because of his television serials. Dr. al-'Abbadi has won the respect of researchers in Western universities because of his book, *Bedouin Justice*, which appeared in English, and because of the articles he publishes in scholarly journals there. Dr. Ahmad 'Uwaydi al-'Abbadi is an expert on Jordanian affairs in specific, and Bedouin affairs in general. He is considered one of the very few specialists in these areas. He has numerous works in print and in progress, and numerous collections of poetry, Jordanian folk poetry prominent among them. He also has [scripted] numerous television serials in Bedouin dialect.

All of this was accomplished without the aid of shaykhly capital, symbolic or material. Dr. Ahmad is a classically self-made man. But unlike the self-made man of Western tradition, who boasts proudly of his humble origins and arduous climb to the top, Dr. Ahmad inhabits a world of *usul*, of roots and foundations, in which the low status of one's ancestors is conveyed, quite literally, *in the blood*. The vaunted reputation of one's opponents, too, can seem equally a part of the natural order. Like Muhammad Hamdan, Dr. Ahmad is confronted by an intellectual puzzle: "If my ancestors were not great men, and their blood is my blood, then why do I, who am now a great man, no longer resemble them?"

To make sense of his upward mobility (and to accelerate it), Dr. Ahmad sought to uncover *what must have been* his true, noble origins. He succeeded marvelously. After a period of feverish historical research in the 1970s, Ahmad discovered that his clan, the Sikarna, actually belong to the house of the Prophet. They are descended from Muhammad al-Harithi, "who is the ancestor of the Hawarith sayyids [now living] in the Arab World" (al-'Abbadi 1984, 229). Dr. Ahmad has changed the name of the Sikarna, accordingly, to the Hawarith. The most blessed of noble blood courses through their veins. Is it any wonder, then, that Dr. Ahmad 'Uwaydi al-'Abbadi, having eclipsed the old guard of shaykhly families, now occupies his rightful place among the influential men of Jordan? As Ahmad put it: "Does the donkey give birth to the lion? No. The lion is born of lions, and I, Dr. Ahmad 'Uwaydi al-'Abbadi, am a lion. That is why the hyenas fear me" (personal communication).

Of course, many tribesmen, including some of Ahmad's own kin, dismiss his genealogical findings as a blatant deception, as a predictable grab for prestige, or (to extend Ahmad's own metaphor) as the lionization of a jackass. But no matter how loudly they scoff, Dr. Ahmad's books, dozens of them, remain in the bookstores for all to see, and this kind of *publicity* is something entirely new to Bedouin historical discourse. In tribal circles, where the identities of groups are linked together by a process of relentless argument and opposition, Dr. Ahmad's rise to prominence (made with his entire clan in tow) comes at the expense of the shaykhly lineages who still consider themselves superior to the Sikarna; it calls into question the received historical discourse, which has its own, well established zones of propriety and power; and, most alarmingly, with Dr. Ahmad's books now outselling Peake Basha's *Tarikh*, the gains made by the 'Adwan and other shaykhs during the first round of history writing are now in jeopardy of falling out of print.

Our main characters, Muhammad and Ahmad, enter the realm of literate historicity from opposite ends of the *oral* tradition, and this fact, more than any other, determines the trajectories of their work. Muhammad Hamdan (starting from a glorious past) writes history against the present, in which the 'Adwan are slowly becoming just another tribe. Dr. Ahmad (starting from a glorious present) writes history against the past, in which the Sikarna, according to oral tradition, were a weak clan of low origins. Both men are united, however, in their decision to carry out these renovations *in print*. Textuality, for both of them, is a means by which the profane world of *kidhib* and false appearances can be transcended and a new form of knowledge, this one modeled on scriptural authority, can finally be established amid the chatter.

Liminal Prophets and Foreign Texts

How does one turn a profane, oral discourse into knowledge that bears the likeness of learned, scriptural truth? If "the truth is known only to God" and all else is hearsay, how does one induce tribespeople, whose loyalties are fractured by 'asabiyya, to accept a single rendering of the past? One answer to this question was expressed centuries ago in the writings of Ibn Khaldun, who argued,

> because of their savagery, the Bedouins are the least willing of the nations to subordinate themselves to each other, as they are rude, proud, ambitious, and eager to be the leaders. Their individual aspirations rarely coincide. But when there is religion (among them) through prophethood or sainthood, then they have some restraining influence in themselves. The qualities of haughtiness and jealousy leave them. It is, then, easy for them to subordinate themselves and unite . . . When there is a prophet or saint among them, who calls upon them to fulfill the commands of God, rids them of blameworthy qualities, and causes them to adopt praiseworthy ones, and prompts them to concentrate all their strength in order to make the truth prevail, they become fully united and acquire superiority and royal authority (translated by Rosenthal 1967, 120).

Note that the truth is defined, once again, by its *externality* to the tribal moral system. Ibn Khaldun lets us assume that the prophets and saints do not resemble the Bedouin they unify. They are *among* the tribes but not *of* them, and the Abrahamic tradition is, in fact, teeming with liminal holy men of precisely this sort.

1. Moses, liberator of the Hebrew tribes, was brought up in the house of Pharaoh.

2. The Prophet Muhammad, who pacified the quarreling tribes of Yathrib, belonged to none of them.

3. Abu Muslim, the 'Abbasid propagandist who incited the Arab tribes of Khurasan to revolt against the Umayyad Caliphs, was a man of unknown (perhaps Persian) origins.

4. Muhammad Ahmad Abdullah, who proclaimed himself the Mahdi and united the tribes of the Sudan against the British-Egyptian Condominium, was the son of a boatwright.

5. The Sanusis, who led the Cyrenaican Bedouin in their war against the Italians, were members of a Sufi brotherhood from the Hijaz.

The list could be extended to include Fatimids, Wahhabis, Hashemites, and myriad others. The scriptural ideas these men preached had the power to bind tribespeople *exactly insofar as* those ideas stood apart from (or transcended) tribal morality. The "hidden documents" and "invisible histories" to which Balga tribesmen constantly referred me acquire, in this light, an even more intriguing aspect: they, too, were assumed to be true exactly insofar as they originated (or rested) somewhere beyond the local world of ʿasabiyya and *kidhib*.

The appeal of liminal prophets and foreign texts has not been lost on Dr. Ahmad and Muhammad Hamdan. Both men realize that the migration from "mere talk" to "literal authority" is made, as it were, across the registers of a diglossic regime, and to pass successfully, they must (1) set themselves and their knowledge apart from the profanity of oral traditions and (2) imbue their work with higher authority (what Ibn Khaldun called "a religious coloring") by linking it to forms of truth that are remote and written. They must, in other words, take on the mantle of prophecy—albeit prophecy of a semisecular, allegorical stripe—and (not unexpectedly) Dr. Ahmad and Muhammad Hamdan bring to their textualizing practice a prophetic sensibility that is genuine and deeply felt. Like countless prophets before them, they spread a message of warning:

> The "age of shaykhs" has come to an end. Now we live in an "age of government." Our land is filled with people from elsewhere. They do not know our history. We are being forgotten in our own land. Soon we will have no claim to precedence in the country that belonged to our ancestors: "What good is it to me if I say my ancestors were shaykhs of the Balga for ages, but I cannot tell you the details of my history or offer you any proof that it took place?" (Muhammad Hamdan al-ʿAdwan).

Like countless prophets before them, they offer a means of salvation:

> We must write our histories down. Only then will we be remembered; only then will our claim to this land be known to future generations. In an age of literacy, talk is nothing: "a story from the lips will not suffice in itself. Thus, the importance of written documentation to our Jordanian tribes becomes clear; it will be a proof to present and future generations and a weapon in their hands" (al-ʿAbbadi 1986, 22).

If the reader cannot easily associate tribal historiographers with the likes of Jonah and John the Baptist, then consider the frontispiece to Dr. Ahmad's *Jordanian Tribes* (1986), on which appears an ornately gilded passage from the Qurʾan, Sura 26, "The Poets." It begins:

> In the name of God, the compassionate, the merciful.
> 201. They will not believe in it until they behold the painful doom,

202. So that it will come upon them suddenly, when they perceive
   not.
203. Then they will say: Are we to be reprieved?

It ends:

213. Therefore invoke not with Allah another god lest thou be one
   of the doomed.
214. And warn thy tribe of near kindred,
215. And lower thy wing (in kindness) unto those believers who
   follow thee.

Herein, Dr. Ahmad compares his own mission to that of the Prophet: "to
admonish and redeem." Why, though, should anyone heed Ahmad's warning? Most Jordanians are unmoved by his message; some are greatly offended by it. Those who find it compelling—mostly Balga Bedouin from
nonshaykhly clans—are drawn by the promise of a more respectable history, and they trust Ahmad to supply it. Because he is educated in classical
Arabic and familiar with authoritative Islamic texts, Dr. Ahmad has already
crossed the divide between local and universal knowledge, between sacred
and profane understanding. His training abroad, in Cairo and Cambridge,
has allowed him to amass symbolic capital that is of value far beyond the
confines of his own near kindred. These two avenues of intellectual transcendence—travel and textual erudition—enable him to invoke structures
of authority that, in Jordan, are of immense antiquity and profound psy-
chological appeal. They enable Ahmad to produce knowledge that, in the
eyes of some, bears the likeness of truth.

   The grounds on which that veritable likeness is established are by no
means mysterious. In the Islamic tradition, which sprang from the teachings of a prophet who could neither read nor write, the epistemological links
between textuality, revelation, and truth were conspicuously drawn from
the start. As Fazlur Rahman observes:

> The Prophet mentally "heard" the words of the Qur'an; but he also
> mentally "saw" the Qur'an being recited by the Spirit of Revelation—
> "Holy Documents containing Precious Books" (98:2). Again, "Say: This
> Qur'an is but an admonition; whosoever will may take admonition from it.
> [It is contained] in Noble Documents, exalted and pure in the hands of
> Divine Messengers [Angels or Spirits of Revelation], who themselves are
> noble and pure" (80:11–15). These are the Divine Messages that emanate
> from the "Preserved Tablet" in the form of the Qur'an (85:21–22). This
> "Preserved Tablet," from which all revealed Books take their rise, is also
> called the "Hidden Book" (56:78) and the "Mother of all Books [*umm al-*

Kitab]" (13:39) from which also comes the confirmation or cancellation
of revealed verses [and Books] (1980, 104).

The intellectual authority Dr. Ahmad claims is modeled on similar assumptions—that is, on the presumed remoteness and ultimate textuality
of truth—and it can seem equally compelling to members of a newly literate community. The place of sacredness is assumed, in Dr. Ahmad's work,
by the singularity of textual erudition itself. As Dr. K observed: "writing
has sacred connotations to the unschooled." The power of divine revelation,
likewise, is replaced by something equally numinous: "documentary evidence not produced by us."

['Ali Khlayf and I are making the long trek back to Swaysa. We've
spent the day at 'Ali's tent in *al-humra*, the empty, unvillaged
grazing area that lies between the Jordan Valley and the Balga
highlands. 'Ali's second wife, Fatma, lives in the tent year round,
managing the family's livestock and keeping watch over the wheat
and tobacco fields. The nearest bus stop is two miles uphill, so 'Ali
and I will have plenty of time to talk along the way.

'Ali is especially curious about my latest tape-recordings. He
knows I've been visiting the Mahayrat, shaykhs of the Afgaha,
and he's burning to hear what they've told me.

"Who talked to you?" he asks, trying not to seem overly
inquisitive.

I list several Mahayri names, then say nothing more. My tactical
silence is well disguised in the emptiness of *al-humra*. Here, voices
are swallowed up in dead air; even the most animated conversations
seem oddly quiet.

We continue walking uphill. Neither of us speaks. I suspect 'Ali
is pondering my list of Mahayri names, locating them on the vast
grid of marital and blood ties he carries around in his head, piecing
together, on the basis of these connections, what each Mahayri
might have told me and why. Once his deliberations are complete,
he decides to test his conclusions.]

'ALI: God willing, you benefited from their talk.

ANDREW: Yes. I benefited. Praise be to God. I recorded a lot
from Shaykh Dawud al-Talab. He told me about the origins of
the Mahayrat and the famous shaykhs who . . .

['Ali interrupts. He already knows what the Mahayrat say about
their own clan. It's arrogant bluster as far as he's concerned, and
he'd rather not hear it from my mouth. 'Ali is a member of the

Sikarna, the clan Dr. Ahmad is now trying to recreate as the Hawarith. He has other historical concerns.]

'ALI: What did they say about us?

ANDREW: About the Sikarna?

'ALI: Yes. What did they say?

[More silence. The Mahayrat have a special contempt for Dr. Ahmad, who defeated a Mahayri candidate in the 1989 parliamentary elections. They regard him as a usurper, a *faux* shaykh, a scholarly fraud. Haj Dawud al-Talab, father of the defeated Mahayri candidate and ranking traditional shaykh of the Afgaha, punctuated his oral history of 'Abbad with scornful attacks on Dr. Ahmad and his clan, the Sikarna. Haj Dawud's opinions on this matter are well known, so any attempt to conceal them from 'Ali Khlayf would suggest that I am trying to protect the Mahayris, something I would do only if I had gone over to their side. I decide to be blunt.]

ANDREW: Do you want the truth?

'ALI: Say it.

ANDREW: They say the Sikarna are good men, respectable men . . . but they are not shaykhs, their ancestors were not shaykhs, and they are not *ashraf* (descendants of the Prophet). They say Dr. Ahmad just made it all up . . . that he is the biggest liar in Jordan.

['Ali laughs out loud. I am sure that he also suspects, at some level, that Dr. Ahmad is making it all up. But then again, Dr. Ahmad is obviously getting away with it, and if other people believe Dr. Ahmad is a descendant of the Prophet, well . . . that means 'Ali Khlayf is one too. As long as Ahmad's political success continues; as long as his present status seems consistent with its noble past, then 'Ali Khlayf and other Sikarna are eager to play along, even to believe. The only alternative is to affirm the old tradition: that is, to claim the Sikarna came to the Balga from the West Bank (not from the Hijaz) and are descendants of the Ta'amira, a tribe of mixed Bedouin-peasant origin. This older tradition, when compared to the new, luxury model Dr. Ahmad offers, lacks nobility and grandeur. 'Ali sees no doubt as to which version of the past he must embrace and defend.]

'ALI: The Mahayrat are cursed of both their parents. Do you know why they say such things?

ANDREW: Why?

'ALI: Because the Sikarna won the election. You ask them: "Ya Mahayri, Where did your shaykhdom go on 8 November? Where did it go [on election day]?" Their shaykhdom is finished. They are just troublemakers now. Don't answer their ignorant talk. Just write what Dr. Ahmad tells you. He knows how to separate the truth from lying.

ANDREW: Maybe. Yes. But there's a problem.

ʿALI: What is it?

ANDREW: The stories I've recorded from the old men of the Sikarna are not like the stories I've read in Dr. Ahmad's books. There are differences; there are inconsistencies. When Haj Salih [the father of Dr. Ahmad] told me the history of the Sikarna, he never said anything about the Hawarith. Not one word. He said: "I don't know about them. Ask Ahmad." Does it make sense to you that a descendant of the Prophet would forget his origins?

ʿALI: It's possible.

ANDREW: How? If you were from the *ashraf*, wouldn't you pass that information on to your children?

ʿALI: I would tell them and make them proud of it.

ANDREW: But the old men say they don't know anything about it . . . about the Hawarith and the *ashraf* and all that . . . so how can it . . .

ʿALI: We didn't know about it. Dr. Ahmad discovered this information, like something new, and brought it to us. But the old men, they never asked their grandfathers about it, and when they died, the history was lost. Nowadays, a sixty- or seventy-year-old man: what has he seen? Not much. All this talk happened hundreds of years ago. People forget what happened in the long-gone eras. People forget the names of their long-gone ancestors.

ANDREW: That's true. But what I mean is . . . there's agreement between the old men on certain things. They say the first ancestor, the ancestor who came to the Balga, was Ahmad al-Sikran.

ʿALI: Yes indeed.

ANDREW: And Dr. Ahmad says his name was Ahmad al-Harithi, and al-Sikran was only his nickname. Now, if Ahmad al-Sikran knew his proper name was al-Harithi, and he knew he was from the *ashraf*, why didn't he pass that knowledge on to his sons?

[ʿAli gives me an exasperated look, which says, "You are badly missing the point." Like most Sikarna, ʿAli is not prepared to second-guess Dr. Ahmad; nor is it in his interest to do so. If Dr. Ahmad is shown to be a fraud, ʿAli Khlayf will participate in Dr. Ahmad's shame. Besides, ʿAli is not willing to scrutinize

the message when the messenger, now a member of the Lower
House of Parliament, is so powerful and compelling.]

ʿALI: Look, ya Andrew, the *Duktur* [Ahmad is often called
by his academic credential] . . . the *Duktur* is a learned man. He is
educated. We should believe what he says. He went to Britain and
returned with new knowledge; he discovered documents among the
English that prove that what he writes is true . . . not like the old
men who just recollect on the basis of talk.

ANDREW: I've not seen these documents yet. Have you?

ʿALI: Can I read? Am I an educated man? Go ask Dr. Ahmad. All
the evidence is with him. He will show it to you.

ANDREW: God willing.

[I have already asked to see Dr. Ahmad's documentary evidence
several times, but the documents—if they exist at all—repeatedly
fail to materialize. Since ʿAli is weary of my skeptical tone, I decide
to keep this observation to myself. The idea that these textual
sources exist *somewhere* is enough to satisfy ʿAli's criteria of truth.
The truth, after all, is remote and inaccessible to ordinary men. Dr.
Ahmad's (invisible) texts open up a frontier beyond the mnemonic
reach of the elders, a new territory from which the forgotten
greatness of the Sikarna can at last be retrieved.]

When I asked Dr. Ahmad to account for the differences between his own
historical understanding and that possessed by his father, Haj Salih, the
"proper source" of ʿUwaydi oral tradition, I prepared myself for an answer
that would amplify ʿAli Khlayf's ideas. I expected Ahmad to say: "I am trained
in scholarly methods," or "The Haj is not educated," or "I have documentary evidence." Instead, he gave an oracular response that contained no explicit reference to formal learning.

"The Haj can only give you narrations," he said. "I can give you *interpretations*. I know the true meaning behind the stories he tells."

This answer, which turned Ahmad from a secular prophet to a gnostic sage,
left me puzzled. Dr. Ahmad's principal historical work, *The Jordanian Tribes:
Land, People, History*, did not seem overly interpretive to me. In fact, with
the exception of its introduction—in which Dr. Ahmad argues for the importance of documentary history—*The Jordanian Tribes* comes across as a
scrupulously nonanalytical study. The approach Ahmad follows resembles,
instead, the one endorsed by the great Muslim historiographer, Abu Jaʿfar b.
Jarir al-Tabari (d. 310 A.H./923 A.D.), who prefaced his *Chronicle of Prophets
and Kings* with a willing subordination of his own authorial voice.

Let him who studies this book of ours know that in everything I say about
the subjects I have decided to recount there, I rely only on what I transmit
from explicitly identified reports (*akhbar*) and from accounts (*athar*)
which I ascribe by name to their transmitters. I do not achieve understanding through rational proofs nor do I make discoveries by intuition (*fakr al-
nufus*), save to a very limited degree. For knowledge about the men of the
past and current news about men of the present cannot be obtained by one
who has not himself witnessed these men or whose lifetime does not reach
back to theirs. [In the latter situation knowledge can be obtained only] by
the statements of reporters and transmitters, not by rational deduction or
intuitive inference. And if we mention in this book any report about certain
men of the past which the reader finds objectionable or the hearer offensive,
to such a degree that he finds in it no sound purpose or truth, let him know
that this is not our fault, but is rather the responsibility of one of those who
has transmitted it to us. We have presented (such reports) only in the form
in which they were presented to us (cited in Humphreys 1991, 73–74).

The concern of al-Tabari's method, one could argue, is threefold: (1) it con-
signs hypothetical reasoning to the lower register of contestable human
knowledge; (2) it locates truth in the accurate transmission (whether oral or
written) of eyewitness accounts; and (3) it grants the historian, who traffics
in polemical recollections, a strategic distance from his own texts. These points
of method, as well as the wary mood that pervades al-Tabari's disclaimer, are
equally pronounced in Dr. Ahmad's work. He repeatedly lectured me on the
importance of carefully documenting the situations in which oral testimony
was collected. It seemed almost a fetish to him, and whenever he spoke of
proper citation, he did so in defensive (rather than collegial) terms.

> I always give the name of my source, the time and date we met,
> the place where I recorded his testimony, his tribe and family, his
> genealogy. Always. That way, they [the shaykhs and sons of
> shaykhs] cannot accuse me of lying. They cannot attack me, even
> though my writings destroy their shaykhdom, and this infuriates
> them (personal communication).

The "true meaning" Dr. Ahmad discovers in the stories of old men is revealed not in didactic narratives of his own construction (nor in what al-
Tabari calls "rational deduction") but in a subtle language of juxtaposition
and exclusion. Like al-Tabari, who was certainly no stranger to political controversy, Dr. Ahmad possesses a gift essential to the creative use of an *isnad* methodology: namely, the ability to arrange and omit oral testimony
(in written form) such that his interpretive agenda—which is critical and
reformist—seems to issue not from his own authorial voice, but straight
from the "proper sources" themselves.

In a historical discourse that still exists largely in speech, the editorial temper of this gift is not hard to detect. It allows Dr. Ahmad to enclose, abridge, manipulate, reconstrue, and co-opt a brand of authoritative speech that, until very recently, lay in sole possession of the elders. This unlettered priesthood of narrators has ample reason, as did the "scribes and Pharisees" of another time, to fear the disruptive authority of prophets in search of truth. Although most Bedouin still respect the folkish erudition of old men, the new historiographers warn their "tribe of near kindred" not to seek refuge in oral authority when the larger society has entered a literate age. Those who ignore this admonition are likely to find themselves on the losing end of historical arguments they once were accustomed to winning.

[As we drove through downtown Shuna, Faris spotted Haj Muhammad Zayd al-'Abbas. The old man was sitting near the drugstore, across from the South Shuna Municipal Building, where 'Adwani elders—as if to emphasize their estrangement from modern politics—often gather to pass the time. The Haj was alone, and Faris thought we should greet him and encourage him to quote poetry. Along with Faris' own grandfather, Haj Khalaf al-Fahd al-Nimr, Haj Muhammad is considered one of the great reciters of 'Adwani verse.

I was unsure about this venture, since the Haj already knew me from an earlier visit to his home, during which I made the mistake of telling him that he was everywhere praised as a "famous poet" (*sha'ir mashhur*). The Haj was visibly offended.

"I am not a poet!" he said, his voice pregnant with disgust. "I recite verse. I recite. Composition is for gypsies and slaves."

Muhammad Hamdan, who had brought me along on this visit, assured the Haj that I meant no harm. He then turned to me and delivered, as though the Haj were no longer in the room, a concise lecture on poetics and power.]

MUHAMMAD HAMDAN: Among the old men, it is still considered disgraceful to compose poetry or to perform it for others. The term "poet" was used in the past to describe the one who sings to the accompaniment of the *rababa* for pay. That is not honorable work. Among the 'Adwan, it was fitting for other people, like slaves, to compose poems in your honor. You shouldn't have to do it yourself.

ANDREW: But what about Nimr al-'Adwan? He is famous for his poems.

MUHAMMAD: He is the only one. In all our history, he is the only one. And he did not sing his poetry or perform it for pay. He was a gifted artist.

[Several months later, as I thumbed through old travelogues in the Bodleian Library at Oxford, I was surprised to discover that Haj Muhammad Zayd's own lineal ancestor, 'Abbas Salih al-'Adwan, had been celebrated as a creative poet in his own right. When the Austrian explorer Ulrich Seetzen toured the Balga in 1806, he visited the camp of Shaykh Nimr al-'Adwan, hoping to record some of Nimr's "more than 100" poems. The great shaykh was away, but the people of his camp told Seetzen that their kinsman, "Abbas el Szalehh, is also renowned as a poet among the 'Adwan" (1854–59, 327, 380).

Such are the ironic (dis)continuities of Balga history. In 1990, the two 'Adwani elders best known for their ability to *recite* poetry (and most reluctant to be called "poets") were descendants of the two 'Adwani shaykhs who, in 1806, were best known for their ability to *compose* poems of love, war, and the hunt.

As Muhammad Hamdan spoke that night of honorable and dishonorable poets, the phone rang. A blood dispute between Muhammad's clan, the Hamud, and another 'Adwani family, the Mindil, had just been settled, and Muhammad and I were expected to attend a meeting with the "guarantors" (*kufala'*) of the Hamud faction, at which the "ceremony of reconciliation" (*sulih*) would be planned. Within minutes, Muhammad and I were out the door and speeding toward Rama, where local police and tribal dignitaries were already gathering. Our visit with Haj Muhammad Zayd had ended on an abrupt (and not entirely pleasant) note.

But today, as Faris and I exchanged greetings with Haj Muhammad Zayd, it was obvious that he had forgiven me the blunders of my first audience. He even seemed glad to see me.

"I've been waiting," he said, "to give you the history of the 'Adwan. But you never came back."

When Faris suggested that we tape-record Haj Muhammad's talk, the Haj quickly agreed. He asked only that we follow him into the drugstore, which was air-conditioned and away from the street. The pharmacist, he added, would probably bring us a free service of tea, "to honor our American guest."

The 'Adwani history Haj Muhammad related gave unusual weight to his own ancestor, 'Abbas al-Salih. After an orthodox rendering of the events that occurred in the first five 'Adwani

generations—those of Fayiz, 'Adwan, Hamdan, 'Adwan, and Salih—
the Haj offered the following testimony.]

HAJ MUHAMMAD: After Salih died, the shaykh of shaykhs was
'Abbas. My ancestor. Salih had been a friend to Ahmad Basha Jazzar.
Have you heard of him?

ANDREW: Yes.

[Ahmad al-Jazzar, "The Butcher," is best known in the West as
the Ottoman Pasha who, along with his British allies, successfully
resisted Napoleon's siege of Acre in 1799. He is best known to
Jordanian Bedouin for his legendary cruelty. Ahmad al-Jazzar
died in 1804.]

HAJ MUHAMMAD: Ahmad Basha Jazzar, who cut off the heads
of shaykhs. He called for 'Abbas. Two men from the Nimr had
already come to Ahmad Basha asking him to recognize them
[instead of 'Abbas] as shaykhs of the 'Adwan after Salih.

Ahmad Basha said to them: "Hasn't Salih begotten sons?"

They said: "He only begot a few."

He said: "I want to see for myself."

He sent a messenger to the Balga and told him to ask about the
sons of Salih.

He asked them, and they said: "This is the tent of 'Abbas; this is
the tent of Hamud; this is the tent of 'Ali al-Kayid; this is the tent
of so-and-so."

Our ancestors.

The messenger grabbed 'Abbas and took him to see Ahmad Jazzar.

Ahmad said: "Why is everyone coming to ask me to recognize
them as shaykh, and you are the son of Salih? By God, if I didn't
love your father, I'd cut off your head!"

[At this point Faris, a bit confused, interrupts with a question.]

FARIS: Was 'Abbas the oldest son?

HAJ MUHAMMAD: Yes. He and Hamud were brothers.

Ahmad Jazzar said: "I'm coming to the Balga, and I want your
tent to be just like the tent of your father. I want to visit you in
a month."

'Abbas got his tent in order, and when Ahmad Jazzar came
to visit the Balga, he said: "You are the Shaykh of Shaykhs from
Shawbak to Syria."

Of all the land, not just the Balga. He became shaykh.

Hamud, brother of 'Abbas, said: "You, O my brother, are the
shaykh, and I am the warrior."

So Hamud became a fighter and 'Abbas was lord of the tent. When they brought back plunder from their raids, they would bring them to the tent of 'Abbas, and he would divide them up among the tribes. Yes indeed.

Later, Hamud died. Dhiyab, son of Hamud, became shaykh. The son of 'Abbas passed away, so he gave the shaykhdom to Dhiyab, son of Hamud.

He said: "You, O Dhiyab, take the sword of the shaykhdom."

The son of Hamud. The son of his own brother. Yes indeed.

[This version of events is not consistent with other 'Adwani traditions, in which 'Abbas figures only as the older, less heroic brother of the great Hamud al-Salih. It also denies Nimr al-'Adwan, the celebrated warrior-poet, his central place in 'Adwani political history. According to the descendants of Nimr and Hamud, the two men struggled three years for control of the shaykhdom, a contest that weakened the 'Adwan and allowed the Bani Sakhr to expel them from the Balga.

According to Haj 'Ali Barakat al-Nimr, Hamud and his followers were banished to Palestine, while Nimr became a fugitive under the protection of Shaykh 'Awad Ibn Fayiz of the Bani Sakhr. Nimr sent poems of reconciliation to Hamud, but Hamud's slave, Sha'ayl, who read them aloud to his illiterate master, changed Nimr's poems into slanderous tirades. When Nimr finally got wind of Sha'ayl's treachery, he sent Hamud the following *gasida* by way of another messenger. Upon hearing it, Hamud immediately agreed to reconcile with Nimr, and together they forced the Bani Sakhr out of the Balga. The poem, recited by Haj Khalaf al-Fahd al-Nimr, is as follows:

Move, O pen, and write what we desire,
And mark it on good paper, in the finest of inks.
Greetings from me to my cousin who raids us.
Hamud is beloved in this country, and we take pride in him.
By God, when these words came to us,
They burned in the heart; they fed flame and fire,
[These words] from Ibn Shibli, my longtime friend,
To whom I am also dear, and a source of pride.
O Ibn Sha'ayl, O you untrustworthy creature.
For a long time now you've fanned the flames.
Three years I've admonished you, O malicious talker.

You've done deeds the Devil wouldn't do.
I led you down this path, I led you down another.
I let you remain coffee boy to the shaykh, but for naught.
From your friendship, O Hamud, no one could divert us,
Except those men of evil whispers and empty talk.
If you inquire as to my health, I'm living in happiness here.
Around me are Men of the North, whom no one can defeat.
We speak of a shaykh who sold you out and bought us off:
'Awad, who in times of need is always there.
O Hamud, you are helpless without us,
And without you, we have no respect.
O Hamud, Sha'ayl has been a traitor for ages.
Sha'ayl is cursed, for he's a traitor at heart.
Our first blindness was an absence of foresight.
On a clique of slaves we depended for advice.
Our beards are torn between Hana and Mana.
He ran us through, that master of awls and needles.
The second blindness was an absence of foresight,
When my advice went unheeded by one who sought bad counsel.[1]

If, as Haj Muhammad Zayd al-'Abbas claims, Hamud was never shaykh, then this struggle for power could not possibly have taken place, and the existence of the poem that ended it would be hard to explain. It was for this reason that Faris, who belongs to the Nimr clan, asked the Haj to clarify his position.]

FARIS: In the time of 'Abbas, when you say he was shaykh, was Nimr, the Father of Poems, . . . was he living among the Bani Sakhr?

HAJ MUHAMMAD: Nimr got mad at his kin and went to live with the Skhur.

ANDREW: He was upset with Hamud, they say. Or . . .

FARIS: Yes. It was Hamud. The shaykhdom belonged to Hamud.

HAJ MUHAMMAD: The shaykhdom . . . no. Hamud was not shaykh.

FARIS: In the poetry of that time, it is mentioned that the poems were sent from Nimr to Hamud.

HAJ MUHAMMAD: Hamud? Which Hamud?

FARIS: Hamud son of Salih, younger brother of 'Abbas.

---

1. For an English transliteration, see Appendix A.

HAJ MUHAMMAD: Hamud died before 'Abbas.

ANDREW: Really? He died before 'Abbas?

HAJ MUHAMMAD: By God, before 'Abbas. Hamud died and 'Abbas was shaykh.

FARIS: But they say 'Abbas abdicated in favor of Hamud.

HAJ MUHAMMAD: He didn't abdicate until later, when Dhiyab got older. Dhiyab, son of Hamud. When Hamud died . . .

[Faris interrupts. I expect him to recite Nimr's poem, but instead he refers to John Burckhardt's *Travels in Syria and the Holy Land* (1822), a book I had shown him the week before. I had read him all the passages I could find pertaining to the 'Adwan.]

FARIS: There is a book. Andrew brought it here a little while ago. The year was 1812. It says, "I came to the Balga. . . . " He was an American, the author, right?

ANDREW: No. He was Swiss. A Swiss working for the British.

FARIS: He was British. He came here dressed up like someone from Syria, and he called himself Shaykh Ibrahim.

He said: "I came to the Balga in 1812, and the 'Adwan had not a single man in the country. I went to the mountains of Jabal 'Ajlun, in the north of Jordan, and I found there a section of the 'Adwan, the sons of Salih, and their shaykh was named Hamud. I asked them, "Is this the entire 'Adwan?" They answered, "No. There is another group, the Nimr, who number twelve horsemen. Nimr and his brothers and his sons and the sons of his uncles. Twelve riders, or thirteen."

That is the talk of . . .

[I am stunned by the liberties Faris is taking with Burckhardt's text. He has, in effect, turned it into an eyewitness account of the sort any *isnad* methodologist would admire, and the content of Burckhardt's testimony has been refitted so that it neatly matches the oral tradition. What Burckhardt actually wrote is this:

> The chief tribe in this province, for many years, was the Adouan, but they are now reduced to the lowest condition by their inveterate enemies the Beni Szakher. The latter . . . approached the Belka, and obtained from the Adouan, who were then in possession of the excellent pasturage of this country, permission to feed their cattle here, on paying a small annual tribute. They soon proved, however, to be dangerous neighbours; having detached the greater part of the other tribes of the Belka from their alliance with the Adouan, they have finally succeeded in driving the latter across the Zerka, notwithstanding the assistance they received from the Pasha of Damascus. Peace had been made in 1810, and both

tribes had encamped together near Amman, when Hamoud el Szaleh, chief of the Adouan, made a secret arrangement with the Pasha's troops, and the tribe of the Rowalla, who were at war with the Beni Szakher, to make a united attack upon them. The plot was well laid, but the valour of the Beni Szakher proved a match for the united forces of their enemies; they lost only about a dozen of their horsemen, and about two thousand sheep, and since that time an inveterate enmity has existed between the Beni Szakher and the Adouan. The second chief of the Adouan, an old man with thirteen sons, who always accompany him to the field, joined the Beni Szakher, as did also the greater part of the Arabs of the Belka. In 1812, the Adouan were driven into the mountains of Adjeloun, and to all appearance they will never be able to re-enter the Belka (1822, 368).]

ANDREW: Basically, there were ʿAdwan living with the Skhur, but we don't know for sure if . . .

FARIS: When the slave, Shaʿayl Abu Mismara, sent poems back and forth between these two factions . . . They were estranged for three years, Nimr and Hamud. And Nimr sent poems to Hamud, and the slave read them because Hamud was illiterate. And the slave would change the meaning. He would say: "You're this, you're that." Insults. Nimr was sending Hamud greetings; he wanted to make peace, but the slave changed his words.

HAJ MUHAMMAD: By God, I've heard that talk. That . . .

FARIS: It's mentioned in the book. "I sat in the tent of Hamud . . .

[Now Burckhardt is actually sitting in Hamud's tent!]

HAJ MUHAMMAD: I've heard that talk.

FARIS: . . . in the year 1812."

HAJ MUHAMMAD: I've heard that talk, and I saw it on the television, too.

[The Haj is confusing Burckhardt with a Bedouin soap opera based on the life of Nimr al-ʿAdwan. The serial, *Wadha and Ibn ʿAdwan*, which aired on Jordanian television several years ago, was written by Ruks al-ʿUzayzi. He based his screenplay on the testimony of Haj Khalaf al-Fahd, whom he interviewed extensively. Most ʿAdwanis are still highly critical of this serial, since the author was compelled to sanitize Nimr's poetry and to change the names of prominent historical characters in order to protect himself (and others) from controversy. The ʿAdwan, as we shall see in chapter 7, are a hard audience to please.]

FARIS: The British traveler didn't mention anyone except Hamud. So perhaps ʿAbbas died before?

HAJ MUHAMMAD: Before whom?

FARIS: Before Hamud. If 'Abbas was alive, the eldest brother is always mentioned . . .

HAJ MUHAMMAD: I want to tell you the truth. Nimr and Hamud weren't even alive at the same time. Nimr and Hamud weren't alive at the same time. Nimr was before Hamud. Nimr . . .

FARIS: But it's mentioned in . . .

HAJ MUHAMMAD: Who cares? That's all made up for the television serials. That's all lies.

FARIS: No, ya Haj. The foreign traveler came to the tents of the 'Adwan just as Andrew here is coming to you. He will say, "I came to Muhammad Zayd al-'Abbas, who told me that his sons are Ja'far and Zayd." It's the same situation. That foreigner had no interest in changing what was said to him. Because he was British.

[Complete silence falls over the room; the air conditioner seems painfully loud. Haj Muhammad, who now wears a look of slight confusion, is clearly impressed by the last bit of logic. By making reference to a discovered text composed by a stranger without local interests, Faris has outflanked Haj Muhammad, a man to whom he owes deference and respect. Realizing this, Faris is suddenly embarrassed. I try to alter the mood by introducing a modicum of doubt.]

ANDREW: Well . . . God knows best.

HAJ MUHAMMAD: God knows best.

The following day, when I told Muhammad Hamdan about this exchange, he made sure I understood that Faris was correct: Hamud (Muhammad's own ancestor) was the true shaykh, not 'Abbas.

"But what," I inquired, "do you make of a young man like Faris using a book as evidence against the testimony of a respected elder?"

Muhammad shrugged, then said, "The old men are merely reciters. They cannot evaluate what they say or give any proof to support it. In the opinion of educated people, they do not possess reliable knowledge."

Muhammad can never fully endorse this view without discrediting his own work, since the material that spills from his notebooks and file folders was collected from old men whose knowledge he obviously respects. Still, Muhammad is himself one of the educated people. His ability to evaluate and give proof of historical claims is based on a literate methodology the elders do not comprehend or even aspire to possess, and the personal archive he has compiled is, in precisely the sense Goody intends, "the prerequisite of history" (1977, 91). As the set of comparisons below indicates, the intellectual authority men like Muhammad and Dr. Ahmad proclaim is based on their ability to *transcend* local oral traditions, not on their ability to reproduce them in stockpiles of text. The authority of the old-style narrators is represented in entry (A) by Haj 'Arif Abu l-'Amash; entry (B) belongs to the advocates of literate history, Dr. Ahmad and Muhammad Hamdan.

EMBODIED VERSUS TEXTUALIZED AUTHORITY

(A) Haj 'Arif's authority is expressed in his willingness to speak on behalf of his group. His credibility depends on prodigious displays of genealogical memory and the ability to tell stories supported by the recitation of arcane poetry. As the Haj put it: "The story without a poem is a lie" (*al-gissa illay ma 'ind-ha gasida kidhib*). Historical knowledge is *embodied* in Haj 'Arif. As long as he is alive and alert, it is all but inseparable from him and can be *properly* conveyed only through the medium of his voice. Other 'Amamsha felt obligated to escort me to him; they were reluctant to speak for Haj 'Arif in his absence, since that would entail a usurpation of his authority, which is manifest not only in his eagerness to speak, but also in his capacity to render others silent.

(B) Although I worked more closely with Dr. Ahmad and Muhammad Hamdan than with any other tribesmen, neither of them allowed me to record his voice on tape; instead, they referred me to their texts, gave dictation, and read to me from notes. "You will find the truth," Dr. Ahmad often said, "in my books." Neither man was an artful storyteller; neither could recite much poetry. The total corpus of poems, stories, and genealogies available to them in written form, however, was certainly greater than that stored up in the memory of Haj 'Arif. This accumulated knowledge is separable from them; it can be alienated from the immediate and highly contextual realm of voices and spoken authority. Rather than escort me into Dr. Ahmad's presence, most tribesmen simply plucked one of his books from the shelf, or dug it out of the trunk, and showed it to me.

THE AUTHORITY OF AGE VERSUS FORMAL LEARNING

(A) Haj 'Arif is not illiterate, but he has had little formal schooling. In the 1920s, when he was already a young man, he was taught the three R's at a mosque school in Um Ruman, a nearby village that was then inhabited by Turkmans. The Haj can still speak a smattering of Turkmani. Most tribespeople over fifty cannot read or write, and this makes Haj 'Arif, who is approaching ninety years of age, a rarity among Bedouin. No one, however, would consider him a learned man, and the Haj himself often disparaged the grand aspirations of Jordan's public school system. "The [tribal] gatherings," he would say, "are better than the schools" (*al-majalis ahsan minn al-madaris*). The Haj's historical knowledge is respected not because it is scholarly, but because it was taken directly from men who are now dead, men like Abu l-'Amash, whom no living 'Amashi except Haj 'Arif has seen or heard speak.

(B)   Both Dr. Ahmad and Muhammad hold college degrees. Dr. Ahmad received his B.A. from the Arab University in Beirut, his M.A. in geography from the Institute of Islamic Studies in Cairo, and his Ph.D. in anthropology from Cambridge. Muhammad received a B.A. in history from the University of Jordan and an Advanced Teaching Certificate from the Arab University in Beirut. He taught history in the public school system for several years, while Dr. Ahmad has served, off and on, as an adjunct lecturer at Yarmouk University. They are both considered learned men. Each has gained access to what remains, for many Bedouin, an esoteric, exclusive, and highly prestigious world of scholarly texts. Their knowledge of the tribal past is no longer dependent solely on what their grandfathers have seen and heard.

PAROCHIAL VERSUS COSMOPOLITAN AUTHORITY

(A)   Haj 'Arif draws his knowledge of 'Adwani history from a narrowly defined tradition. His purview is the Balga; what happened to the ancestors of the 'Adwan before they entered Jordan is of little interest to him. Haj 'Arif knows only *where* his tribe came from and *why*. He received this knowledge from his kin; the chains of oral transmission, the so-called *isnad*, are entirely local, the content of the event-history he tells is local, and Haj 'Arif himself is a structurally fixed, highly territorialized authority. He is sought out—he does not go in search of a general audience—and the people most likely to consult him on matters of tribal history are his own kin, a constituency that is linked both to him and to the line of ancestors whose knowledge he transmits.

(B)   Dr. Ahmad and Muhammad try to situate the Balga within a larger tribal and national world; to do this, they must collect data from sources outside their own kin-based *isnad*. They must discover history as well as receive it. Whereas Haj 'Arif is a localized source of authority, Dr. Ahmad and Muhammad base their authority on mobility. They seek out old men from as many different clans and tribes as possible. They refer to external documents; they go to foreign lands in pursuit of knowledge; they translate the inaccessible works of English travelers. By various modes of border crossing, they have amassed in a few short years a body of historical knowledge that, in the traditional system, could not be amassed in a lifetime. It is not by chance alone that Dr. Ahmad (in his mid-forties) and Muhammad (in his mid-thirties) are young men, whereas Haj 'Arif is the oldest member of his group.

By posing as links between spoken discourse and the external world of texts, Dr. Ahmad and Muhammad can momentarily control the interface between oral history and the literate tradition from which it has carefully been excluded. They decide what will become proper history and what will remain empty talk, and the authority they seek is modeled on that which tribesmen so easily ascribe to travelers like John Burckhardt, whose mobility and otherness allowed them to escape the downward pull of parochial entanglements.

It would be wrong to assume, then, that the mechanics of literacy are the only (or even the most important) factors allowing men like Dr. Ahmad and Muhammad Hamdan to encapsulate the colloquial memory of the elders. The historical world of the Balga tribes, as we saw in chapters 2 and 3, has *already* been encapsulated in myriad ways. In 1869, just two years after the Turks captured Salt, the conquering Rashid Pasha led W. Wood, then British consul in Damascus, on a diplomatic tour of the Balga. In his final report to London, Wood offered his thoughts on the fate of the newly subjugated tribes.

> When these restless nomads become fully aware that the Government can punish them severely they will desire to be on good terms with it and if the local Authorities taking this desire into consideration were loyally to maintain the conciliatory policy, which Rachid Pasha has adopted, for the space of 10 or 15 years, it would have the effect of calming their restless spirit and by accustoming them to a sense of tranquillity would develop further personal wants: when these increase and have entered as a habit in their mode of life, they would find it difficult to forego them and would prefer submitting to harder terms than to take to a course of life which they had forsaken. They would in time exchange a nomad for a settled life (Wood 1869).

After World War I, the arrival of aerial reconnaissance, radio communications, and mechanized transport made the punishment of "restless nomads" a simple task. The ability to surround them militarily was further reinforced by a development Wood, writing in 1869, could not have foreseen: the collapse of the Ottoman Empire and the creation (along Western lines) of new Arab nation-states. By 1935, it was possible for Frederick Peake, in his capacity as historian, to locate the Balga tribes within a specifically Jordanian world and, in his capacity as military administrator, to keep them there.

This physical and conceptual encirclement of the Balga has, since the 1930s, brought about other changes. The matrix of genealogical time in which tribal entities such as 'Abbad and 'Adwan exist has been effectively parochialized by a state-centered political system that gauges its continuity against Christian and Muslim chronologies, a set of temporal measures that link Jordan to a past far deeper than any Balga tribe can claim. Local space, too, has been situated, *via* the ubiquitous Mercator grid, within a truly *global* geography. In 1816, when John Silk Buckingham passed through the Balga, the chance that the Bedouin might effectively transcend local points of view, temporally or spatially, was still remote.

> Among the many ridiculous questions that were seriously proposed to me, when talking of the different countries that I had visited, I was asked, whether I had ever been to the Belled-el-Kelb, where the men had dogs' heads? and, whether I had seen the Gezirat-el-Waak, or the island on which women grow on trees, budding at sunrise and becoming mature at sunset, when they fall from the branches, and exclaim, in the language of the country, *Waak! Waak!* "Come and embrace me!" The opinions entertained by the people of Assalt [the town of Salt] on all matters beyond their own immediate sphere of observation, are like those that prevailed among the most ignorant of the ancients; and their is no fable of antiquity, however preposterous, that would not find believers here. Even now, places not a league distant from the town are made the scene of miracle; and the people seem not only to believe but to delight in the marvellous (1825, 36).

If, in the "age of shaykhs," the lands beyond the Balga were alien and obscure, nowadays they are quite familiar. The modern world is mapped out in newspapers, on TV shows, in classrooms, in the stories of family members who have traveled abroad to work and study. Most local Bedouin, as Wood predicted, have exchanged a "nomad for a settled life," but their world of experience, which was never exactly small, is larger now than it has ever been. It even includes an obscure book, Burckhardt's *Travels in Syria and the Holy Land*, which, at the time of its first publication in 1822, no Balga tribesman could possibly have read.

In this cosmopolitan setting, where the architecture of time and space are greatly expanded, the ability of Dr. Ahmad and Muhammad to transcend the talk of the elders is not exactly impressive. Instead, it is their relentless fascination with tribal history, their inability to let it remain a low tradition, that is strikingly at odds with the ideological demands of national politics in contemporary Jordan. As we shall see in the next chapter, it is also at odds with the views of many tribespeople (ordinary and influential) who, though acknowledging their own encapsulation in an "age of government," still see real advantages in preserving the intellectual marginality, and the safe distance from textual domination, that only the spokenness of the received historical discourse can grant them.

SEVEN

Publication and
the Redistribution of Power

All profound changes in consciousness, by their very nature, bring with them
characteristic amnesias. Out of such oblivions, in specific historical circumstances,
spring narratives.

> Benedict Anderson, *Imagined Communities*

Externality and Odd Reversals

In their efforts to appropriate the intellectual authority of travelers, prophets, and other liminal types, it was inevitable that Dr. Ahmad and Muhammad Hamdan would see *me* as a valuable resource. I was a stranger, ostensibly without parochial interests, who would eventually produce alien texts
of my own. And the West, for both Ahmad and Muhammad, was a place
where I could plead their case before the world's most influential academic
and political communities. I might even be convinced to carry out archival
research that would prove, once and for all, the essential truth of their own
historical visions.

Dr. Ahmad expected me to spread his reputation in America, where he
and his ideology deserved to be better known. "I will make an excellent topic
for your dissertation," he assured me. Muhammad Hamdan wanted me to
write the uncut version of 'Adwani history he feared he would never be able
to publish in Arabic. Each man warned against my collaboration with the
other, and I succeeded in maintaining my partnership with *both* of them
only by convincing *each* of them that their textualizing agendas would be
studied, as comprehensively as possible, in my own work. The line between
analyst and accomplice, by unspoken agreement, was never precisely drawn:
I was compelled to maneuver on both sides of it.

As my collection of oral testimony grew, however, I came to resemble a
"proper source" in my own right, and despite my externality to the tribal
system—a social fact that led many tribespeople to assume, a bit paradox-
ically, that objectivity and suggestibility were my natural state of mind—
despite all this, I began to pursue a textualizing agenda steeped in the subjectivity of my own marginal position. More and more, I found myself

caught up in the evaluation of historical arguments Dr. Ahmad and Muhammad Hamdan were making, and I assessed their credibility not only in relation to extant tribal arguments, but against the version of the past I was developing by my own method of "escapes and entrances" (see chapter 5).

It was the pursuit of this critical agenda that finally awakened me to the strangeness of an analytical position that is simultaneously detached from, and informed by, parochial interests. All that I read and recorded led me to believe that ʿAdwani oral traditions were remarkably accurate, whereas the same body of evidence led me to doubt the veracity of Dr. Ahmad's writings about his own clan. And yet, in 1990, it was Dr. Ahmad's publications that filled Jordan's libraries and bookshops, while Muhammad Hamdan, his work languishing in the form of handwritten notes, was thwarted by an intrinsic misfit between oral and textual means of expression. This odd reversal, which is draining real discursive power from the hegemonic view shared by external observers and ʿAdwani elites, is the subject of the present chapter.

Outflanking the Shaykhs: Dr. Ahmad's Quest for Altitude and Distance

In 1984, Dr. Ahmad published his most ambitious work to date: *An Introduction to the Study of the Jordanian Tribes.* It was the sixth volume in his popular series, "Who are the Bedouin?," but unlike its five predecessors, which placed Bedouin in the folkish milieu of "manners and customs" (ʿadat wa taqalid), the *Introduction* portrays tribalism as a distinct sociopolitical form. Dr. Ahmad spends much of his intellectual energy elucidating the structure and function of the dozens of kin-based and territorial groupings that comprise the tribal order in Jordan. He locates terms such as *fakhadh* ("lineage"), *hamula* ("clan"), and *hilf* ("alliance") in dictionaries of classical Arabic, in the Qurʾan and *hadith* (sayings of the Prophet), in tribal law documents, Bedouin poetry, and proverbs. The method tends toward the philological and away from the ethnographic. Indeed, if Dr. Ahmad were not so proudly Bedouin himself, his style might easily be labeled Orientalist, but the author's intention is to show that tribespeople can, *and must,* carve out a niche for themselves in a modern culture that reproduces historical knowledge in textual forms. The stakes, Ahmad reminds his readers, are high.

> By way of example, I begin with the difficulty of knowing anything about the origins and descent of many Jordanian families and tribes, a difficulty which, because of the absence of written documents in the period before the establishment of the Amirate of Transjordan, cannot be overcome. If we do

not come to realize the importance of documentation now, the coming generations will end up in the same condition as past generations, and that will be a great misfortune. The time has come for us to realize the importance of knowing the history of the tribe, of the family, of its members, and the changes and shifts in ownership of the lands that once belonged to them. This is important now in population studies, in order to understand how the settlement pattern [in Jordan] has been altered and changed, and in [studies of] population movements in space, time, and direction. [Dr. Ahmad is alluding to the loss of tribal land—most of it by way of sale— to Palestinians. The latter are never mentioned by name, but Ahmad's next sentence, which alludes (even more circumspectly) to a sudden exodus of Palestinians from Jordan, would be immediately understood by his tribal readers.] And should there arise circumstances that we do not anticipate or know about now, nor even expect in the foreseeable future, I say: "If these circumstances should come to a tribe in one advantageous and secure moment, [a knowledge of history] would help immensely in developing a model that could be used to establish for a second time the structure [that existed in] the past (al-ʿAbbadi 1984, 10).

As a "service to future generations," Ahmad concludes his *Introduction* with a detailed tribal register, modestly entitled: "An Appendix of the Names of Some of the Jordanian Tribes." This appendix, which doubles as a not-so-subtle attempt to distinguish indigenous Jordanians from outsiders, extends the list of names that appeared some fifty years before in Peake's *Tarikh*, but the sensitive topic of clan origins, which has made Peake's work so beloved and maligned, is carefully avoided. It must be avoided, Dr. Ahmad argues, since what passes for "history" among the tribes is, all too often, insubstantial and unsubstantiated talk.

Dr. Ahmad does, however, permit one notable exception. In a lengthy footnote (1984, 228–230), he unveils his new history of the Sikarna (a.k.a. Hawarith), wherein he links himself to multiple generations of highborn, prophetic descent. This genealogical charter, pieced together "over a period of ten years, which began in 1973 and ended in 1984," is based on "reference to ancient and highly specialized books, and long and numerous correspondences with specialists in the region of the Hijaz" (1984, 23). Ahmad's meticulously reconstructed pedigree, at eighteen specifically named generations— and many more left unnamed—is one of the longest in Jordan. It appears in the *Introduction* not to impress others but, as Ahmad tells us, to demonstrate "how difficult it is to arrive at the truth."

Dr. Ahmad's new identity was revealed to his reading audience in the plainly constructed narrative that follows.

> My fourteenth lineal ancestor, ʿAmr b. Malik b. Nasir b. Ahmad b. Muhammad al-Harith, came from Holy Mecca in the Hijaz, and seven of his sons

were with him. He left behind his eighth and ninth sons, who were content to remain in their land, and their mother (the junior wife of ʿAmr) stayed there with them. ʿAmr had already been quarreling with his paternal cousins, so he retreated to the area of al-ʿArid in the Najd. He then settled in a village called al-Kharma, and life there did not please him. So he returned to his original territory in the Hijaz (the region of Holy Mecca), only to see the dispute between himself and his relatives intensify. He killed one of them and went into exile, as is the ancient custom of the Bedouin. Then he and his sons settled in Maʿan in the south of Jordan, where they killed a man from Maʿan and fled to Shawbak (72 kilometers north of Maʿan). Life there was good to them, and ʿAmr's seven sons dispersed into the land. Some of them went to Palestine (Bethlehem, Khalil, and Ghor al-Shimali); some went to Egypt; some of them remained in Shawbak. There is still a Harithi family living there today, and they are our kin. In Bethlehem, the nearby Wadi Hawarith is named after them. As for my seventh lineal ancestor, Ahmad (who was nicknamed Sikran), he was among those born in Palestine (Wadi Hawarith/Bethlehem). It is said that he sold their land to the Christians while his brother was away on pilgrimage. When his brother returned, he was greatly enraged. He drew his sword to kill Ahmad, and he slashed Ahmad's hand, saying: "Are you drunk (*sikran*), selling our land?" It became his nickname. Ahmad fled east of Jordan, the land of his ancestors (. . .) as was fitting. It was Muʿti, the grandfather of Ahmad, who had gone from Shawbak to Palestine and lived with his cousins, the Hawarith, in Bethlehem. He still has descendants there.

Ahmad, who was nicknamed Sikran, settled among the Windiyyin [a clan of the ʿAwazim tribe] in the area of Madaba, and there he married a second woman. He was already married to his first paternal cousin, who had born him two sons, ʿAbd al-ʿAziz and ʿAbdullah. When his family discovered that Ahmad had married again from the ʿAwazim, they came after him and forced him to return to Palestine [and abandon the new wife]. His ʿAzimi wife was already pregnant, and after she delivered, her family sent the child to its father. They arrived in the morning, when Ahmad was praying the dawn prayer, and they named the child Subah (Morning-time). Ahmad did not linger long in Palestine but returned east of Jordan, where he settled among the ʿAbbad tribes and became an ʿAbbadi.

As for Subah, he married a girl from the family of Abu l-Ghanam in Madaba, and she bore for him two daughters, then she gave birth to a third child: a son. And the people said, "God has returned to him," and they named the child ʿUwaydi (The Little Return). . . .

As for the complete pedigree of this author, accurately ascertained, it is: Ahmad b. Salih b. Slayman b. Qasim b. ʿUwaydi b. Subah b. Ahmad (who was nicknamed Sikran and is ancestor of the Sikarna clan now living in the area of Wadi al-Sir, and is the one who joined ʿAbbad and became an ʿAbbadi) b. ʿIsa b. Muʿti (who left Shawbak for Palestine) b. ʿAwayda b. ʿAwd Allah b. Muhammad b. ʿAskr b. ʿAmr (and he is my fourteenth ancestor, who came to Jordan as we said) b. Malik b. Nasir b. Ahmad b.

Muhammad al-Harith (who is ancestor of the Hawarith sayyids [descendants of the Prophet] in the Arab World) (1984, 228–229).

When Dr. Ahmad passed out free copies of the *Introduction* to his fellow 'Uwaydis, advising them to commit their true history to memory, they were astonished to learn of their noble descent. Many Sikarna, including some members of Dr. Ahmad's own household, are still reluctant to endorse his findings, although no Sikrani I met was prepared to reject them outright. Haj Salih, Dr. Ahmad's father, expressed what (among Sikarna) is perhaps the majority opinion on the Hawarith story: "the truth is known only to God."

If the information Dr. Ahmad published in the *Introduction* was "difficult to arrive at," this is because:

1. *The Hawarith story is not part of the received oral tradition.*

The elders of the Sikarna trace their descent to Ahmad al-Sikran, whom they routinely call "the first ancestor" (*al-jidd al-awwal*). He is said to have come from the Ta'amira, a tribe that still resides on the West Bank, near Bethlehem. If Ahmad al-Sikran carried the blood of the Prophet in his veins, no Sikrani elder ever mentioned that fact to me. The eleven names Dr. Ahmad affixes to the pedigree of the first ancestor were, before he discovered them, completely unknown to other members of his clan.

2. *The Hawarith story is not based on, or supported by, material drawn from antique travelogues or from any specifically cited textual sources.*

Ahmad fashioned his pedigree out of materials he found in "ancient and highly specialized books," but the exact content of these works is never shared with his readers. His correspondence with Hijazi genealogists, likewise, is nowhere displayed in print. The English travel literature of the nineteenth century—with which Dr. Ahmad is quite familiar—could not have been the source of his discoveries, since the Sikarna are not mentioned in it by name.

The absence of any conventional evidence *for* Dr. Ahmad's argument is of little concern to him, since the evidence *against* it is also scant. The oral testimony of the elders, after all, can be dismissed as "empty talk" whenever one likes, and the European travel literature, Dr. Ahmad informs his readers, "does not go into details on the tribes, their sections and genealogies, on individuals, events, stories, or places of residence. It does not cover the topic in a complete or comprehensive manner" (1986, 13).

Still, a comparative analysis of oral tradition and travelogue—a method

Muhammad Hamdan embraces in practice and Dr. Ahmad carefully avoids in print—does, in fact, support an interpretation of the past in which the Sikarna appear to have been an inconspicuous clan. By way of example: (1) the most knowledgeable Sikarna elders can recite genealogies only five or six generations deep, as opposed to the twelve generations (or more) commonly remembered among the 'Adwan; (2) the stock of anecdotes dealing specifically with the Sikarna is meager even by the standards of their own subtribe, the Afgaha; (3) there is no poetry—at least none that I could find—commemorating the deeds of Sikarna shaykhs; and (4) among the Afgaha, the Sikarna are still described as a clan belonging to the fourth rank, who lived beneath the rule of the shaykhly families of the Mahayrat, Slayhat, and Hisamiyya.

Peake Basha's *Tarikh*, which was published before the Sikarna were noble Hawarith, preserved this ranking in a crystalline, textual form. It, too, must be firmly discredited lest Dr. Ahmad's new history—and his status as a man of venerated descent—be characterized as a fabrication. Thus, Ahmad writes:

> The foreigners have taken up the study of tribes, even though they are not of the Arab race, nor are they Bedouin in the least. The first to write about Jordan specifically was Frederick Peake Basha, Englishman and early commander of the Jordanian Army, who wrote *History of Transjordan and Its Tribes*. The book was translated into Arabic by Beha al-Din Tawqan. . . . The second part deals with the study of the Jordanian tribes, and we find in it superficial talk which does not jibe with the truth regarding origins and descent. . . . [It has] misinformed and made ignorant insiders and outsiders as to the origins of the families and the tribes. This book has become (to my great distress) the only [popular] source from its publication until now. I have not read a book about the tribes of Jordan published since [it appeared] that is not based on it, and which does not describe it in a dim-witted way totally at odds with the scholarly spirit, as if it were a source one could not dispute (1984, 32).

Ahmad's good standing as a Bedouin of "Arab race" has not shielded him from attacks similar to the ones he launches against Peake. The tribesmen who read Dr. Ahmad's books understand perfectly well that his (selective) attempts to discredit the oral tradition, the travel literature, and the work of Peake Basha are all essential to the success of his own political agenda. For Haj Musa Nihar al-Bakhit, a leading 'Abbadi shaykh, Dr. Ahmad's agenda could be summed up rather bluntly: "He wants to piss on the heads of the elders."

Such desecratory acts can be accomplished only from a certain altitude (and a safe distance), and Dr. Ahmad's revisionist history of the Sikarna is a platform designed to provide both. The manner in which the Hawarith story elevates the Sikarna and sets them apart from other ʿAbbadi clans is best seen when Dr. Ahmad's published account is compared to the old model of Sikarna history, a spoken tradition that, for all Ahmad's efforts to stamp it out, is still current among the clan elders.

[Haj Hamdan Fanash al-ʿAyash is about eighty years old. He is among the last of the traditional Sikarna shaykhs. From his tent, which stands in front of his house, he presides over the valley, and for his regal manner—which is definitely out of style—he is called "the king" behind his back. I visit Haj Hamdan often, since he and his elderly wives make excellent conversation. He has allowed me, on several occasions, to record stories about his father, Fanash, who was "shaykh of all the Sikarna in his time." Haj Hamdan never seems unwilling to speak.

When I asked him to tell me the story of the Sikarna, however, he was not exactly sure how to proceed. The Haj knows I work closely with Dr. Ahmad, a man he greatly respects despite his youth. Dr. Ahmad, for his part, knows I work closely with Haj Hamdan, and he recently paid the Haj a visit. I have reason to suspect that, during this visit, instructions were given regarding the manner in which the Haj should relate the Sikarna story to me. By now, Dr. Ahmad is well aware of the gaps that have opened up between his official version of the Sikarna past and the version I have pieced together using the oral testimony of ʿAbbadi elders. As I record Haj Hamdan's story of "the first ancestor," I sense that he, too, is aware of the gaps, but his narrative retains a shape that, despite his care not to contradict Dr. Ahmad, differs significantly from the account that appears in the *Introduction*.]

ANDREW: Ya Haj, I want to know about how the Sikarna came to the Balga, because there are things that are written about it, as you know, and there are things the elders say. I want to know where he really came from, the first ancestor.

HAJ: He was not from this land. Ahmad Abu Sikran. It came to pass that he settled here. First he settled among the ʿAdwan, but they didn't get along well. Then he settled here among the Mahayrat. Abu Mahayr. There was no one in this area except Abu Mahayr and the Slayhat. The two. Abu Mahayr was the leader, but Abu Sikran quarreled with him.

He said: "By God, Abu Mahayr, I think I'll leave this country, but first I'll plunder your livestock and leave you with nothing."

See?

ANDREW: I see.

[Haj Hamdan has not told me *where* Ahmad came from: an unusual omission in a story of this sort. Has he been told not to mention the Ta'amira? Whatever the reasons for his silence, the Haj has clearly stated that the Mahayrat and Slayhat were already living here when the Sikarna arrived, a fact which, because it suggests precedence in matters of power as well as place, Dr. Ahmad ignores in print.]

HAJ: Abu Mahayr was afraid of him. So Ahmad al-Sikran went to the shaykh, Kayid Ibn Khatlan. He broke camp and moved on. When he got to Wadi Sir he saw the horses, the cavalry of Kayid. Ahmad mounted his horse, tightened her reins, put on his armor and shield, drew his sword, and rode toward them.

Ibn Khatlan said: "O men of my gathering, that man yonder is a warrior. He has many livestock. But he's never satisfied, no matter where he goes. [If things continue like this,] either we will kill him or he will kill us."

So they came to a stop and got off their horses. They hoped they could convince Ahmad to become an 'Abbadi. If he became 'Abbadi, it would be a gain for them, since in those days people always wanted to make their tribe bigger.

They said: "O Abu Sikran, where is your [rightful] place?"

He said: "I don't have land. Wherever I find good pasture, I settle down."

Ibn Khatlan said: "Prosper and become 'Abbadi."

Abu Sikran said: "And what will be my rank among the warriors?"

Ibn Khatlan said: "Horseman."

Abu Sikran said: "I have lions behind me [i.e., I am a man of proud lineage]. Do you want people to say I joined you only to become your henchman?"

Ibn Khatlan said: "Prosper and become 'Abbadi."

Abu Sikran said: "And what will be my rank among the warriors?"

Ibn Khatlan said: "Abu Mahayr is *'alim* (learned counselor) and you are *hasib* (noble counselor)."

He said: "Now I will become 'Abbadi."

Ibn Khatlan said: "'Abbadis, come on! Let's pitch this 'Abbadi's tent."

So they pitched his tent and gave him land.

The same story appears in Dr. Ahmad's *Jordanian Tribes*. Ibn Khatlan's recognition of the Mahayrat, however, is omitted.

> When our ancestor, Ahmad al-Harithi, settled in the area of Khirbat Sar (or Khirbat Sara) . . . [having come] from a western direction, Ibn Khatlan and a delegation from 'Abbad received him and requested that he join them and become 'Abbadi. And prior to [his agreement], Ibn Khatlan bestowed special distinctions upon him and gave him land in the highlands, the forests, and the grazing areas (1986, 230).

This minimalist rendering of the origin story, with its strategic elimination of all references to Palestine, the Ta'amira, and the Mahayrat, is now the one preferred by Dr. Ahmad. The long version he put forward in the *Introduction*, he told me, contained minor errors and "too many details with which people could disagree." Its true meaning lay in the Hawarith pedigree (which Ahmad has amended slightly since its 1984 debut), and contestable details should not be allowed to detract from that message. As my interview with Haj Hamdan continued, it became obvious to me that the Haj and Dr. Ahmad had come to an agreement on these matters.

ANDREW: This Ahmad Abu Sikran came from . . .

HAJ: The west.

ANDREW: Bethlehem, they say.

HAJ: From over there.

ANDREW: From over there. Was he from the Ta'amira or . . .

HAJ: Those people, brother of mine, just forget about them. Forget about those people. We don't want to talk about them or bring them up in any way. Enough. He came from over there. Your safety.

[During a previous visit, the Haj had freely admitted that Abu Sikran came originally "from among the Ta'amira." I simply want him to recite that same information now, on tape. His reluctance, which has never shown itself before, is surprising. Despite a mounting sense that we are treading on forbidden ground, I press forward.]

ANDREW: There's a wadi over there called Wadi al-Hawarith, and they say it is named after the ancestors of the Sikarna.

HAJ: No. Bless the Prophet! They were two sets of brothers. The ones who came to our country . . . one of them became the Amir al-Harithi when he entered the land. The other went to Wadi Musa. Those are the ones who entered the land at that time.

ANDREW: Those are the Hawarith?

[I am not sure I understand the link between these brothers and Ahmad Abu Sikran, but the Haj will not tolerate further probing.]

HAJ: They are . . . good people. They are . . . Praise be to God.

ANDREW: Praise be to God.

Haj Salih al-ʿUwaydi, in his dual role as Dr. Ahmad's father and "proper source," could afford to be less compliant. In fact, Haj Salih believed that a hankering for long pedigrees and prophetic descent had led his son astray, but "God knows best." In the following account, the Haj relates the origin story as he received it from his grandfathers (with a brief allusion to his son's book), and in so doing, he breaks all the rules Dr. Ahmad has set for a proper telling of the Hawarith story.

HAJ: Our ancestor, when he came from among the Taʿamira . . . Have you seen Ahmad's book? The gigantic one?

ANDREW: Yes.

HAJ: When they came here from there . . . and came here . . . they settled among the Taʿamira. There were three of them at first. One of them went somewhere . . . I don't know where. One went to the Taʿamira, and one went to Shawbak. Three. So he settled down there and . . . the az-Zayr family, shaykhs of the Taʿamira, are our kin. I don't know what happened . . . some problem. He fled from his kin and came to Abu Windi. Here.

ANDREW: Ahmad? That was Ahmad?

HAJ: Ahmad. The first ancestor. He had a wife there who bore him two sons, and when he fled, he left the woman and her children with his family and went to the Windiyyin. He settled in Maʿin and married a girl from Maʿin, from Abu Windi's group. He married her and lived with her and made a tent, and so on and on. He was in exile there for seven years. Later he returned to his family, and he left his new wife here. She and her son, who is the ancestor of the ʿUwaydi.

When he returned to the Taʿamira, he said: "By God, I can't live here. I want to return to the Balga."

The Balga was a land of hospitality, and fresh meat, and wide open spaces, and many blessings. But life in Palestine was cramped.

He said to his first wife: "I'm going to the Balga. Do you want to come with me or not?"

He brought her to the Balga. The other wife, the one from the Windiyyin, gave birth to Subah, and Subah begot 'Uwaydi. 'Uwaydi is the ancestor of our tribe, and the rest of the Sikarna are from that other woman. Yes indeed. So they were all together.

ANDREW: I want to return to the beginning of the matter. Ahmad al-Sikran. They say he was *hasib* of 'Abbad, *hasib* of the Afgaha. What do you know about that talk?

HAJ: That . . . yes. I can't give you anything. 'Abbad, in the old days, was a shaykhdom of Arabs. The shaykh was Ibn Khatlan, and the *hasib* was Abu Bagr . . . and Abu Mahayr was *hasib*. We want to tell the truth. The rest were horsemen. All of them were people of chivalry and horsemanship. None was more distinguished than the others in the ways of mounted warfare. Your safety.

ANDREW: God protect you.

After a parallel reading of these texts, one can easily imagine ways in which all three could, with minor adjustments, be collapsed into a single story. Dr. Ahmad, however, found the spoken versions totally unacceptable, and he asked me not to publish them.

"They are part of the old mentality," he said. "The elders are simple men. They do not want to bring attention to themselves. They fear the consequences. The present generation needs strong men who are not afraid to tell the truth. And this old mentality . . . we should burn it."

The retrograde thought Dr. Ahmad seeks to obliterate is discernible only in opposition to the new mentality he seeks to establish in its place. The latter frame of mind, which Dr. Ahmad grandly designates "the new Jordanian national identity," springs from the union of nationalism and the premodern conceptual geography of the Balga that was discussed in chapters 2 and 3. Ahmad calls this new mentality an ideology, and its fine points are spelled out in the introduction to *The Jordanian Tribes: Land, People, History* (1986), wherein Ahmad espouses a "Jordanian philosophy" committed (with varying degrees of frankness) to the following principles:

1. *The severance of all links to Palestine.* "As for origins and descent . . . I do not concern myself with the mention of origins if they are [traced to] any area that is not inside Jordan, since we are, in the end, Jordanians: one family and one substance" (al-'Abbadi 1986, 17). Despite the generality of this claim, the area outside Jordan that most troubles Dr. Ahmad

is Palestine. His distaste for West Bank origins, which is widely shared among the Balga tribes, is partly a function of the Arab-Israeli wars, which have left two million Palestinians on Jordan's East Bank. It is also, and more inherently, a result of Palestine's long association with peasantry and political subordination: two modes of human existence which, among Bedouin, are still held in contempt.

By contrast, origins in the Arabian Peninsula—which Dr. Ahmad asserted on behalf of his entire clan in the *Introduction*—are cause for great pride among Jordanians, since this region is homeland of the pure Arab tribes as well as the family of the Prophet and his companions. In *The Jordanian Tribes*, Ahmad does not explicitly mention his roots in Holy Mecca, which is not "inside Jordan"; instead, he endows his sixth lineal ancestor, Ahmad, with yet another nickname. This Ahmad al-Harithi, who was called al-Sikran, is now dubbed Ahmad *Abu Hijaziyya* al-Harithi. The Hijaz is built into the pedigree, and the geographical point is made.

The nobility of Dr. Ahmad's *usul* (origins) can only be tainted by association with the Ta'amira—a tribe he admits his ancestors lived among, "but never became part of it"—since the Ta'amira have acquired, at least in the minds of the Balga tribes, the twin stigmas of Palestine: peasantry and the dilution of their pure Arab bloodlines. An 'Abbadi shaykh of the Hisami clan, a man with no affection for Ahmad, put it this way: "The Ta'amira are really descendants of the French Crusaders who raped the local peasant women. I read that in a book. Yes. Those are Ahmad's true ancestors. The Europeans."

This is but an exaggerated rendition of commonly held views. Ahmad's presumed kinship with peasants is continually used by "shaykhs and sons of shaykhs" to deflate him, and corrosive rhetoric of this sort is by no means a recent innovation. Lt. C.R. Conder, who conducted his famed survey of western Palestine in 1873, was lending authority to local opinions when he observed,

> A study of the Arabs is carried on with difficulty west of Jordan. The great tribes are found either east of the river, or in the desert of the Tih, and in order to form a really good estimate of Arab character, it would be necessary to live in these remote districts for many years, following the migrations of the great tribes. The Arabs of the Jordan Valley are probably not of pure blood, and seem in some cases to have been mixed up with negroes, flying to the deserts from Damascus and other towns. The tribes are very small and scattered; many are offshoots of the Sugr and 'Anezah nations, whose countless tents stretch far away into the Eastern desert; others have migrated from the north, and one tribe—the T'aamireh— is of Fellah [peasant] origin, though now nomadic (1878, 272–273).

And elsewhere:

> The north part of this desert [the "Judaean Desert"] is inhabited by
> scattered groups of the Taamireh. . . . The Taamireh, or "cultivators,"
> are not true Arabs, but villagers who have taken to desert life. They
> wear turbans [instead of head scarves], and resemble the villagers in type
> more closely than the Bedu (1891, 38).

By refusing to obscure their links to this "Palestinian tribe," the old men
of the Sikarna decline to embrace a nobility that, in Dr. Ahmad's view, is
rightfully theirs to proclaim. When I asked Ahmad why it was necessary to
erase one entire chapter of his family history and replace it with material
that non-Sikarna would simply dismiss as lies, he was genuinely shocked
by my disregard for noble ancestry, especially descent from the Prophet,
which is a testament to "good origins and good behavior."

> DR. AHMAD: Why should I say I am a Ta'amiri? Only two of my
> ancestors are buried among them. Many more are buried here. Why
> say I am from the Ta'amira when I was first living in Shawbak?
> Why say Shawbaki when I was first living in Wadi Fatma? Why say
> Fatmi when my ancestors were the Hawarith, Amirs of Mecca?
> ANDREW: Yes. I agree with that. You shouldn't limit yourself.
> But why do you leave certain parts out? All of those places you
> named are part of your history.
> AHMAD: No. My history is a continuity. It is not important to
> give it all. I should only give what proves the continuity of my
> descent. I give only what is original and essential. It begins in Mecca
> and ends in Jordan: that is the reality of my identity and my
> history.

This concern for moral continuity is linked to a second tendency in Dr.
Ahmad's "ideology of the new national identity":

*2. The attempt to define Jordan as an essentially tribal nation, and the
tribes as essentially Jordanian.* If Jordanians are "one family and one substance," then recording genealogies can be construed as a patriotic act, since
it gives shape to a national community defined in an idiom of patrilineal descent. The most authentically Jordanian citizens, according to Dr. Ahmad's
ideology, are those who can plunge their roots deepest into Jordanian soil.
The people without long and local genealogies—immigrant and refugee
Palestinians, *ghawarna*, peasants, gypsies, Circassians, and others—will always be less surely Jordanian than the Bedouin, and are therefore of less
use to Ahmad in the construction of his "new Jordanian national identity."

This bias is clearly reflected in the focus of *The Jordanian Tribes*, which all but ignores the peasant communities of north Jordan, who make up the majority of the country's indigenous inhabitants.

The fact remains, however, that many 'Abbadi clans came to the Balga from Palestine only within the last three centuries—this, in a world of genealogical origins, is but the twinkling of an eye—and Ahmad himself, in the old version of Sikarna history, could claim only five ancestors who were buried in the political entity that is known today as Jordan. Other Jordanians (including certain peasant families from the north) can easily lay claim to twice that many. These awkward facts are answered in Dr. Ahmad's work by a demographic pattern he discovered, quite unexpectedly, while pursuing his research.

> From listening to the traditions and tales of the Jordanian tribes, we find that many of them have branches and offshoots that went to Palestine and lived there for the span of a generation or two, or three, or four, and we find evidence and true stories concerning the sacrifices the Jordanian tribes have made on behalf of Palestine, whether on its soil or outside it, a fact that has made us understand clearly that Palestine has been shaped, in its natural extension and population, by Jordan throughout history. And from Palestine, Syria, Lebanon, Egypt, and Iraq some of the families and tribes of Jordanian descent returned during the 19th century and the beginning of the 20th, from which sprang the false notion that they are not from the land that fathered them. But [to the contrary] they are, in all truth, Jordanians by blood, flesh, and history (1986, 22–23).

The Sikarna story, as the clan elders tell it, begins with Ahmad al-Sikran. It is meant to account for his arrival in the Balga, not his nationality, and neither Haj Salih nor Haj Hamdan pays much attention to the comings and goings Dr. Ahmad describes above. In the new Sikarna story, as Ahmad tells it, the first ancestor is already a Jordanian by "blood, flesh, and history," since *his* ancestor, Mu'ti, had come to Bethlehem from Shawbak only two generations before. The Sikarna described in Ahmad's publications are, in a sense immediately understandable to most tribesmen, *more authentically Jordanian* than the Sikarna described in the recollections of old men.

Dr. Ahmad is convinced that the same proto-Jordanianness applies to many other clans who, because they have not escaped the old mentality, are content to place their origins in Palestine, thus adding fuel to "the lie . . . that the majority of the inhabitants of this land are not native to it, or are not Jordanian" (al-'Abbadi 1986, 3). In all of this, the idea that one might become a Jordanian citizen by virtue of birth or legal convention is implicitly denied—as is any a priori basis for the legal equality of all citizens—

and nationality can be legitimately assessed only in terms of genealogical depth.

"If a man has not lived here for at least five generations," Dr. Ahmad told me, "I do not consider him a true Jordanian."

The latter definition of Jordanianness, which I heard many tribespeople offer as a rule of thumb, is politically insidious—Ahmad described it as a "very dangerous idea"—since it casts both the Palestinian majority and the Hashemite elite in the role of outsiders, now and for years to come. It would be wrong, however, to imply that the Hashemites (or the Palestinians) live in fear of such nativist sentiment. The "new Jordanian national identity" Dr. Ahmad espouses, for all its populist xenophobia and racial innuendo, is motivated by a personal desire he shares with Hashemites and Palestinians alike:

3. *The will to create a political identity that effectively transcends and recombines the solidarity of tribal groups, thus eroding the power of the shaykhs who control them.* The genius of Ahmad's ideology lies in its ability to accomplish from below—that is, from a position of real historical weakness—what the Jordanian government has endeavored, since 1921, to accomplish from a position of strength: namely, the encapsulation of local identities within collective ones of a higher moral order. These new affections, which are inevitably portrayed as nationalist, originated in a messianic sense of purpose: the creation of an independent Arab nation-state under Hashemite rule in the wake of the First World War. This vision of a unified Arab kingdom, though it prevails today only in one small country, is still portrayed in Jordan's popular media and public school textbooks as a grand, pan-Arab movement, and its appeal is inseparable from the personal authority of the man, King Husayn, who currently espouses it.

The Hashemite capacity to submerge parochial interests within more inclusive images of community—in the Jordanian state, the Arab nation, and the house of Islam—is a function of the same moralistic drama that has inspired political revitalization throughout Arab-Islamic history. The leaders of the "Great Arab Revolt" unified the tribes of Greater Syria and the Hijaz in their struggle against the Ottomans, but the Sharif Husayn and his sons were not themselves Bedouin. They were members of Mecca's urban elite, much as their ancestor, the Prophet Muhammad, had been. The Hashemite rise to power was a reenactment of a cultural schema of great antiquity—the liminal holy man who unites the tribes (see chapter 6)—and it is not at all surprising that Dr. Ahmad, in his own attempt to gain power through the unification of Bedouin tribes, would cast himself as leading man in the same historical script. His tribal antagonists are quick to read his claims to prophetic lineage as an exercise in political role-playing, and it is precisely Dr. Ahmad's Harithi descent, not his xenophobia or his tribal chauvinism, that the "shaykhs and sons of shaykhs" find morally offensive.

[The week before the elections, Hamud al-Jibali's offices in Biadr were teeming with campaign aids and a legion of hangers-on. The mood was festive, and Hamud confidently predicted victory. Now, two days after the votes were cast, he sits alone in his apartment, receiving the condolences of the few visitors who happen by. The legion of hangers-on has moved en masse to the celebration tents of the victor, Dr. Ahmad 'Uwaydi al-'Abbadi, where they are now listening to poems composed in Dr. Ahmad's honor and consuming great piles of rice and meat.

By the standards of Amman's fifth district, Hamud's campaign was conducted on the high ground. He rarely appealed to his tribal identity, which he considered a divisive (and highly volatile) theme. He even formed an alliance with a Palestinian candidate, as well as a Circassian: a strategic move Dr. Ahmad successfully used against him.

An engineer by training, Hamud made Jordan's need for technological advance and educational reform the central motifs of his campaign. Neither idea caught fire. Hamud's true appeal came from his membership in the Sharrab clan, one of the shaykhly families of the Zyud, and his most loyal supporters were Zyudi. He was loathe to admit this, since it smacked of the feudalism he spoke so loudly against.

Hamud has lived most of his adult life in Sweden, where his wife and daughters remained during the campaign. Many tribesmen found his living arrangements morally suspect, and malicious gossip about his unattended wife and children—who were doing God knows what in the land of the heathen—was of no help to his election efforts.

As we discuss the campaign, I suggest that a certain estrangement from local political culture might have contributed to his loss.]

HAMUD: Right now, I am considering a return to Sweden. If that is what you mean by estrangement, then I agree with you completely.

[Hamud smiles wearily.]

ANDREW: That's not what I mean. Let me give you an example.

Ahmad told me that his most effective campaign strategy was his use of the name al-'Abbadi. He told people he was the only candidate proud enough to use it.

[Of the ten 'Abbadi candidates who ran for seats in Amman's fifth district, Ahmad was, in fact, the only one to advertise his full tribal name. This allowed him to tap into a larger "group feeling" than any of his rivals, who, in a classic miscalculation, guessed that use of a tribal moniker would *cost* them votes.]

ANDREW: I heard him say it in a speech. He said: "On election day, we want the name 'Abbad to be honored. On 8 November, we do not want our women to weep. We want them to trill their tongues for joy. Whoever else you vote for, cast one vote for 'Abbad."

[Voters in the fifth district of Amman were allowed to cast five votes, one for each contested seat. This encouraged voting across clan lines, and Dr. Ahmad's decision to use his tribal name was intended to draw support from multiple 'Abbadi clans.]

ANDREW: What do you think of that?

HAMUD: It's nonsense.

ANDREW: That's what I thought, too. But when I asked people why they voted for Ahmad, that's one of the reasons they gave over and over again.

HAMUD: That's one of our problems. *'Asabiyya.* I tried to rise above it because it is a false ideology. It leads people away from important issues. Ahmad uses it the same way he uses his descent from the Prophet. It is meaningless. I do not believe that is why he won.

ANDREW: But I heard one man say, "Even a false sharif is better than a crooked shaykh."

HAMUD: I am a crooked shaykh? Was he referring to me?

ANDREW: No. He voted for you *and* for Ahmad. But you are the son of shaykhs, and Ahmad turned the people against the shaykhs. They represent . . .

HAMUD: Ahmad makes himself a sharif because he wants to get close to the King.

ANDREW: That's a dangerous game.

HAMUD: For a sane man, yes. For Ahmad, no. I have a saying for him. "Ahmad is allowed what others are forbidden."

[The urge to dismiss Ahmad as a fool is strong among intellectuals like Hamud. When I told professors at Yarmouk University that

Ahmad was a credible candidate who stood a good chance of winning his race, they laughed out loud: "But he's an absolute idiot!" Hamud's aphorism—that Ahmad is allowed what others are forbidden—is also meant, here and now, to imply that Ahmad is "crazy," a *mahbul,* a deviant whose challenge should not be dignified by a response (*per* Bourdieu 1966).]

ANDREW: Maybe that's true. But still, he's a member of parliament.

HAMUD: The people get what they deserve.

[Hamud takes a long drag on his cigarette and dramatically exhales, affecting disdain. My last comment came perilously close to "rubbing it in," so I assume the more detached, professorial tone in which Hamud is accustomed to talking politics.]

ANDREW: I think Ahmad makes himself a sharif so he can be higher than the shaykhs. He gives the people a kind of authority that is traditional but not like the power of the shaykhs.

HAMUD: Ahmad makes himself a sharif because he is *not* a shaykh, and none of his ancestors were shaykhs. If he were from a powerful family, we would not be discussing this now. The Sikarna . . . and this is the truth . . . the Sikarna never attained the third serving.

ANDREW: The what?

HAMUD: Whenever a feast was served to the tribes, the Sikarna were the fourth group to eat. They ate the scraps. That is what 'Abbad elected to parliament: a man of the fourth rank.

What Hamud attacks is the altitude (i.e., closeness to the nobility of the king and the Prophet) and the distance (i.e., no investment in the baggage of shaykhly descent) that enable Ahmad to piss on his head. If these qualities were merely imaginary; if they had no real basis in power, then men like Hamud al-Jibali could afford to ignore them. But Dr. Ahmad, who once was content simply to write the shaykhs out of history, is now denying them seats in parliament, and the sons of shaykhs are at a loss to account for Dr. Ahmad's success.

The candidates I interviewed in the months after the 1989 elections believed (to a man) that Ahmad won by fraud; that he attracted Palestinian votes by secretly claiming to be one of them; that he swore false oaths on the Qur'an in exchange for votes; that he sold his soul to the government; or (in a theory that comes much closer to the truth) that he convinced the clans of "second rank" to align themselves with someone low in order to defeat someone high.

One candidate even accused me of bankrolling Ahmad's campaign with CIA funds. Defeat at the hands of Dr. Ahmad was a political mystery, or a grand deception, and its true origin—just like truth in general—was as alien to the Balga as were the ancient books in which Ahmad had discovered his venerable ancestry.

Dr. Ahmad did everything in his power to enhance this mystique. Whenever I asked him to account for his meteoric rise, he usually responded with a single word: *haz*, "good fortune." God's will had also played its necessary role in his success, along with "good origins and good behavior." Ahmad believed deeply in these things, but his providential cant was also meant to protect his success—itself rooted in a mimetic variation on the life of the Prophet—from the imitation of others. On one occasion, however, Dr. Ahmad suddenly let down his guard and allowed me to glimpse what he fondly called "the genius of the 'Uwaydi mind."

[Zayd is banging on the door, breathless. He has come running to tell me that Ahmad is here for a visit and wants to talk to me. As I walk over to the olive grove where the house of 'Ali Khlayf entertains its afternoon guests, I can see Ahmad lecturing to a rapt circle of young men, who look at him in wonder. His chair is sinking into the soft earth, but he manages, by his physical and oratorical magnificence, to seem always a bit grander than everyone else.

We exchange profuse greetings as Zayd runs off to the kitchen to fetch Ahmad a water glass. Ahmad refuses to drink tea out of a small cup. His glass must always be the largest. He insists on it.

"I want a glass that resembles me," he says. "I stand out in every way, and my glass should be equal to my measure."

The gathering of supporters laughs respectfully. I recall Jonathan Raban's description of a younger Ahmad, which appeared ten years ago in *Arabia: A Journey through the Labyrinth* (1979, 325).

He looked like a body builder; his pectoral muscles rippled under his shirt and his biceps were the size of melons. He had been born a nomad, living on dates and camel's milk, going barefoot to school, and herding the family's goats, camels and sheep. Now he was a major in the police, he edited the Police Gazette, he had an M.A. degree in anthropology, and the telephone on his desk rang every two minutes. He had made a long strange crossing from one culture to another, and his pride in himself was at once innocent and overwhelming. "I am a Bedu," he said. "There is the material civilization, and there is the spiritual civilization. The Bedu man is the highest peak of the spiritual civilization."

Today, Ahmad is still a proud blend of spirituality and bulging musculature. As he sips at his oversized glass of tea, he asks me his favorite question.]

AHMAD: What are the people saying about me?

ANDREW: You are very popular. They call you the modern shaykh.

AHMAD: That, as far as I'm concerned, is a curse on my honor. [Laughter all around.]

ANDREW: Why?

AHMAD: It is comparing me to a dinosaur, an extinct thing. I am one of the "influential leaders" (*al-giyadat al-mutanaffidha*). That is what I call myself. I invented the term. I want you to use it when you describe me in your book.

ANDREW: What do you think people mean, though, when they call you a modern shaykh? You ran against the shaykhs. Do they think you're becoming like one now?

[Ahmad is often criticized—even among his devout followers—for his insatiable egotism, and the young men are silently titillated by my question, which they perceive as an oblique criticism of Ahmad's style. Ahmad appreciates it as well, since it allows him to assert himself with even greater force.]

AHMAD: I do not care about ancient vocabulary. Do not encourage this talk. Listen. I have committed my life to the destruction of the shaykhs, and I think you have seen that my plan has been successful. It is all part of my goal.

ANDREW: And what is that?

[Ahmad hesitates and smiles. He asks me to take out my pen and notebook. As he gives dictation in English, the young men, who resent being excluded but are too embarrassed to admit their inability to follow our conversation, gradually begin to talk among themselves.]

AHMAD: Let me show you the genius of the 'Uwaydi mind. Our family decided when I was still a child that we would become educated. We would not sell our land for a living. We would be doctors and engineers and writers. These are professions the government and the people need, but we don't need the people or the government. You see? Independence through education.

[Ahmad's brothers are all engineers, technicians, and medical men. His younger brother, Dr. 'Abdullah, is a widely respected hematologist and Dean of Medicine at Jordan University. Ahmad's family is often portrayed in the Jordanian press as a moral example to the nation. In a newspaper article published in the mid-1970s, "From Shepherd Boy to Medical Specialist Was a Long, Difficult Task but Perseverance Paid Off," an unnamed reporter turns 'Abdullah's career into a parable of upward mobility.

> Dr. Abbadi's parents are both illiterate but so far, out of seven sons and one daughter, they have managed to produce four university graduates. Ahmad, his older bother, has a degree from a police academy, Mahmoud is concluding his masters work in electronics engineering in Manchester and Abdul Karim is finishing medical school in Roumania. So it seems that there is a lot that could be said for sheer determination. When most people only see the difficulties and shirk, it is encouraging to see someone who forges ahead into the unknown with very little help, many difficulties and just a lot of will power. But it paid off for Dr. Abbadi. And yesterday's poor bedouin shepherd is today's haematologist (reprinted from the *Jordan Times* in al-'Abbadi 1989, 515).

The final sentence, with its Horatio Alger twist, gives salience to the humble origins of the Bedouin hero. Dr. Ahmad understands the appeal this narrative device has for Westerners, but as he continues to weave his own success story, it is the lowliness of those around him, and the perspicacity of his own kin, that enables him to rise.]

AHMAD: My father was always seeing the future. He was not a dominant man, the Haj. But he was very intelligent. The people here in Swaysa persecuted him. The Bedouin love toughness, not brains. He moved to Wadi Sir to get away from them. He bought land there, and put us all in school, and the others ridiculed him and said this was proof of his weakness. But now they see how stupid they were.

[Ahmad shoots a condescending look at the assembly of young men, who are no longer listening to us.]

ANDREW: And while you were in school, the shaykhly families were . . .

AHMAD: . . . were selling their land to Palestinians, and the money went in a day because they were ignorant. They bought cars and wives and built houses and ate meat every day. They did not become educated, like the 'Uwaydi. See the genius of my plan? The shaykhs still need the government and the people. But now the people do not want them; the government does not want them. This is why they fail, and I succeed.

[Ahmad leans back in his chair, smiling proudly. He awaits my reply.]

ANDREW: That's interesting. In a way, it was your family's lack of power and privilege that encouraged your father to invest so much in your education. You really had nothing to lose and a lot to gain, but the shaykhs already had power back then, and wealth, so they . . .

[Ahmad nips my "rags to riches" trope in the bud.]

AHMAD: We were a house of blessing and good fortune. Poverty is not the same as weakness.

ANDREW: No. I apologize. I didn't mean to imply that.

AHMAD: We are not of low origins. We are from the house of the Prophet. Our success is proof of that. In my house, I receive fifteen guests a day. They come to me for favors, to solve problems. And I can do what no shaykh can do. Look . . .

[Ahmad holds up the hem of his ankle-length gown. It is splattered with mud. Before he drove out to Swaysa, he had been watering the plants that grow around his house in Wadi Sir.]

AHMAD: This is what they see. A man with mud on his clothes. Such a man will not eat their wealth. They know I am humble. I am one of them.

The proper ratio of good origins, education, and mass appeal was, as much as anything else, the secret of Dr. Ahmad's electoral success. The ʿAbbadi shaykhs of Amman's fifth district—four families that produced all the ʿAbbadi candidates *except* Dr. Ahmad—were not short on lofty ancestry; in the case of Hamud al-Jibali, they even boasted impressive professional careers. Still, none of them was an ideologist by trade, and they proved themselves strangely incapable of generating popular attachments. Haj Dawud al-Talab Abu Mahayr, whose father had been the last paramount shaykh of the Afgaha, and whose son, Muhammad, was soundly defeated by Dr. Ahmad in the 8 November elections, summed up the state of the Mahayri shaykhdom in the following terms.

HAJ DAWUD: In the age of my grandfathers, there were wars, and rallying round (*fazʿa*), and the rule of the sword. People would rally round you.

They would say: "Who goes beside me? Who belongs to me?"

And the Mahayri would say: "The Zawatin are with me. The Mahamid are with me."

And so on. Entire clans. Today, if you have a son, or brother, or a few relatives, that's enough to keep you out of trouble. There are no alliances today.

ANDREW: No rallying round.

HAJ DAWUD: Why rally round? Today, government has come over the people.

ANDREW: Yes. No wars, no danger like before. That's right.

HAJ DAWUD: Ah . . . but in the past, you could buy and sell the people. I used to . . . but now I'm weaker [for my age] . . . when I had a lot of wealth, a lot of money, I would give a man ten or fifteen dinim [about three acres] and say this is your land, this is your horse, this is your stipend. Why? So he would rally to my cause. But today, your own son doesn't need your money.

The factors that have slowly eaten away the political significance of men like Haj Dawud—a powerful central government, public security, and a pervasive cash economy—are the same factors that allow Dr. Ahmad to siphon off the charisma that once belonged to the ʿAbbadi elite. In the "age of shaykhs," the Mahayrat gave ordinary tribespeople things they could not do without: physical protection, military equipment, and the means to make a living. In an "age of government," Dr. Ahmad (who began his career as a Public Security officer) can offer his clients a more valuable range of services: access to government officials and sources of employment, mediatory efforts on their behalf in case of legal problems with the police, and (with the help of his brother, ʿAbdullah) a better chance of admission to Jordan's universities, colleges, and military academies.

Dr. Ahmad's rejection of the label "modern shaykh," at a time when the might of real ʿAbbadi shaykhs is becoming ever more vestigial, is entirely in keeping with his reformative agenda. Ahmad aspires to much more than shaykhliness, and the new history of the Sikarna he uses to endow his current status with antique legitimacy is well made for this purpose. Its discovered contents—the prophetic lineage and the Hijazi origins—originate (and largely remain) outside the boundaries of the received oral discourse. Indeed, this act of radical transcendence is the only means by which Dr. Ahmad can (re)articulate the continuity of his past and present. The *spoken* tradition, after all, is a discursive contest the Sikarna, lacking poetry, heroic anecdotes, and elaborate genealogies, have already lost and, without revelations from elsewhere, will never be able to win.

Textual Cat-and-Mouse

If Ahmad sets himself above and beyond local knowledge, then we are left to ponder a basic question: in what historical realm does he now operate?

His Cambridge dissertation, "Bedouin Justice in Jordan" (1982), conforms fully to the cosmopolitan style of Western-based anthropology, but the works he produces for the Jordanian market seem to be written by another man entirely. This Other Ahmad, who described himself to me in the third person as "the ideologist," is devoutly nationalistic, though not exactly in the modular, Western sense Benedict Anderson (1991) and Ernest Gellner (1983) so insightfully analyze. Similarly, his books are constructed in a temporal and spatial frame that encompasses the Balga—and, indeed, the Jordanian state itself—but the lack of chronological dating in his new Sikarna history would suggest that Dr. Ahmad's personal identity and the national identity he preaches are located in an ideological space not exactly conformable to the "homogeneous, empty time" (Benjamin 1973, 263) in which academic history is now being written in Jordan.

It was in this conceptual half-world that Ahmad and I—two scholars who stood in a (constructed) relationship of externality to local oral traditions—struggled to arrive at a consensual understanding of the past. We did not succeed. Dr. Ahmad wanted me to accept his account of Sikarna history as true and to endorse it in print. My willingness to explore its meaning in relation to the discursive agendas of other tribesmen was not good enough. Ahmad wanted my unequivocal support, which, given my own notions of what counted for historical truth (in both the tribal Balga and the academic West), I simply could not give.

Dr. Ahmad understood my plight: I was held back by my desire for "proof." Thus, he sought to assuage my doubts by claiming to possess documentary evidence that proved the veracity of his work. But he never showed it to me. When his youngest brother, Husayn, joined me in asking to see the documents—Husayn was eager to peruse them as well—Dr. Ahmad told us they were locked in an old suitcase. He had lost the key. As compensation for these hermetically sealed texts, Ahmad escorted me to the apartment of a wealthy sharif (descendant of the Prophet) in Amman. The man was an expert genealogist, originally from Iraq, who had pieced together a minutely detailed version of the Prophet's family tree. As the beautifully crafted document was gently rolled out before us on the living room floor, Dr. Ahmad directed my eye toward a single name (plate 18).

"Here he is," he said. "This is 'Amr, my fourteenth ancestor. The one whose name appears in my books."

I bent over and looked closely at the name. A mild shock raced through me. This 'Amr had no sons. He was a genealogical dead end. I began to suspect the worst: that Dr. Ahmad had chosen 'Amr as the point at which he

Plate 18. Dr. Ahmad points out his fourteenth ancestor, 'Amr, as the author and the genealogist look for signs of the other thirteen.

would graft himself onto the holy lineage. Dr. Ahmad, for his part, seemed unperturbed by this implication.

"Of course 'Amr has no descendants," he reassured me. "This tree was prepared in Mecca after 'Amr was expelled from the city. His kin did not know about him or where he went. He concealed his identity from them. But I have found the connections."

We were back, once again, to the mysterious documents in the suitcase. I was beginning to feel like a character in a cheap spy novel; my game of textual cat-and-mouse with Ahmad was leading nowhere.

When I finally discovered an alien text of my own, proof of Dr. Ahmad's Harithi descent was the last thing on my mind. I was browsing aimlessly in the research library of the American Center for Oriental Research in Amman, when I stumbled across *Northern Najd: A Journey from Jerusalem to Anaiza in Qasim*, an account of Carlo Guarmani's 1847 trip to the Arabian Peninsula, where he hoped to find Bedouin with pure Arabian horses to sell. He rode across the West Bank on his way inland, and his local escorts were men of the Ta'amira tribe, of whom he offers the following account:

> The Taamris owe their origin to the Beni-Hares of the Uedi Mussa in Arabia Petraea. It is related that some Beni-Hares abandoned their *duar* at a date impossible to ascertain, migrated with their families, and finally

settled, after partially having rebuilt the ruins, at Bet-Tamar, an ancient Judaean city, about half an hour from Bethlehem. It seems they left their country owing to bloody combats with their own brothers, though not before having tried in vain to effect a reconciliation and thus evade the ban of outlawry.

The new inhabitants of Bet-Tamar rejected the ancient name of Beni-Hares and called themselves Taamri. It is said they were blessed by God on account of their extreme morality. They multiplied rapidly and contrived to make themselves respected by their turbulent neighbors, the *fellahin* of the Ebron mountains.

The Taamri have never been known to betray a guest, or to fail in their given word or a sworn alliance. They decided to go back to a wandering life again after a new fratricidal combat, which one day left more dead than living inhabitants in Bet-Tamar. . . . Although they till the land like peasants, they live in tents like Bedouin (1938, 65).

In a state of excitement, I made a quick xerox of Guarmani's account and hurried off to catch the next bus to Wadi Sir. I held in my hands a gift to Dr. Ahmad and, I figured, an apology for my relentless skepticism. The Beni-Hares Guarmani mentions—complete with the West Bank pronunciation of *th* as *s*—were Dr. Ahmad's Bani Harith, and Uedi Mussa was merely an Italian transliteration of Wadi Musa. Everything fit. There was no talk of prophetic descent, but the original link to lands east of Jordan, which Ahmad prized so highly, was clearly supported in the text.

Ahmad, it turned out, had never heard of Carlo Guarmani, but he was obviously delighted by what he read. He poured over the text, pointing out the various ways in which it agreed with his own version of events. Then, in a mood of relief and momentary candor, he acknowledged (for the first time) that he had based his account, in part, on the testimony of certain Ta'amiri elders now living in Jordan. Guarmani's positive depiction of the Ta'amira was surprising to Dr. Ahmad, and his link to them became, at least in the privacy of his own home, more palatable. Dr. Ahmad folded up the xerox and tucked it away. As he walked me to the door, he happily announced that now I could endorse his new history without reservations.

"Yes," I said. "And now you can show me the evidence for your Harithi descent."

Ahmad let out a booming laugh, then said, "We wanted you to discover it for yourself. We knew that only then would you believe it."

Later, as I mulled over our parting exchange, I realized that the game of cat-and-mouse was still being played. My textual discovery was not, in fact, the conversion experience Dr. Ahmad thought it should be. The Ta'amira are not a genealogically unified tribe; they are, like 'Abbad, a gathering of unrelated families who embrace a common name. Not all Taʿamira come originally from the Bani Harith, or from Wadi Musa; not all of them belong to the family of the Prophet. The genealogical skeleton of Ahmad's story (on which everything else depends) had yet to be fully articulated, and the witness of Carlo Guarmani would not be adequate to that task.

A few days later, I received a message: Dr. Ahmad wanted to see me. He, too, had been thinking about Carlo Guarmani, and he had decided, upon further study, that the Italian's account was not as attractive as it had initially seemed. He asked me not to publish it. I argued that Guarmani's testimony actually bolstered his claims: "Not 100 percent, but at least it doesn't go against what you say." My argument fell on deaf ears. Dr. Ahmad had turned adamantly against the text, and the reasons he gave for censoring it were exactly the reasons he gave for modulating the talk of the elders.

1. Guarmani does not distinguish between Ahmad's line of descent, which is noble, and the Taʿamira in general, who, everyone knows, are an ignoble tribe.

2. Guarmani gives the impression that Ahmad's ancestors lived in Palestine for many centuries, whereas they really spent only two generations on the West Bank and never became part of the larger Taʿamira tribe.

3. Guarmani does not specifically mention Ahmad's prophetic descent, which is the most important part of the Harithi identity.

The passage from *Northern Najd* could not be included in my book, Ahmad said, because it would damage "my national ideology and the party I am building. It can be used against me, my family, and my tribe. These things, as you know, are important to the future of Jordan." I told Ahmad that ignoring Guarmani's text was out of the question, but I was willing to abide by the following terms: I would not show the text to anyone in Jordan—Dr. Ahmad possessed the only photocopy—or discuss it; and when I published it, I would do so only in English. The matter was closed.

Or so I thought.

Over the next few weeks, I was occasionally stopped on the street by young ʿAbbadi men with news to share: "Dr. Ahmad says you found an Italian document that proves what he says is true."

"Yes," I would answer, "I did find a document. Dr. Ahmad has the only copy. If you want to see it, you'll have to ask him."

Suddenly, I was an accomplice in Dr. Ahmad's project. I had made my own unwitting contribution to his storehouse of invisible texts.

The Textual Liabilities of Power

> The photograph, fine child of the age of mechanical reproduction, is only the most peremptory of a huge modern accumulation of documentary evidence (birth certificates, diaries, report cards, letters, medical records, and the like) which simultaneously records a certain apparent continuity and emphasizes its loss from memory. Out of this estrangement comes a conception of personhood, *identity* . . . which, because it cannot be remembered, must be narrated (Anderson 1991, 204).

Dr. Ahmad has constructed his own identity without the aid of these documentary prompts. The new history of the Hawarith, which he narrates against the obscurity of the Sikarna past, makes no explicit reference to textual remains of any sort. In contrast, the "History of the 'Adwan," a book Muhammad Hamdan has been struggling for years to write, is supported by an abundance of documentary evidence. Europeans who traveled in the Balga during the Victorian era wrote colorful accounts of their 'Adwani escorts, shaykhs of the Nimr and Salih clans. Some travelers took photographs of these men as well. Now, over a hundred years later, the 'Adwan are engaged in disputes about the veracity of this material, the extent to which they can claim it, use it to boost their own clans, and keep others from doing the same. Because these alien documents concern local identities that, unlike those Benedict Anderson describes above, *are not yet lost to memory*, they must somehow be attached to narratives that already exist. This enterprise, which makes texts answerable to authoritative talk, is seldom accomplished smoothly.

Getting the Dates Right

'Ali Barakat and I went to Haj Khalaf al-Fahd, grandson of the great Goblan, in search of poetry and "the book." The first was easy to come by; Haj Khalaf was accustomed to reciting poetry for foreign scholars, and his ninety-year-old voice was still deep and resonant. The second item, "the book," was harder to extract. When 'Ali Barakat asked to see it, the Haj pretended not to know where it was. He had let Muhammad Hamdan borrow the book before, and it had taken him months to retrieve it. 'Ali Barakat did not press the issue.

A few minutes later, when our conversation turned to Goblan, the Haj swiveled abruptly and began to rummage through a box that was stored in the closet drawer behind him. Out of this box he drew a tattered copy of *Kitab al-rahhala*, or *The Book of the Traveler*, a collection of excerpts from the English travel literature that had been translated into Arabic by Suleiman Musa, a leading Jordanian historian. The book contained a passage from *Heth and Moab,* in which Lt. C.R. Conder extols the virtues of his companion, Shaykh Goblan al-Nimr. The book was ceremoniously passed around the room. When I got my chance to thumb through it, I noticed that Conder's dates, every last one of them, had been meticulously blotted out.

ANDREW: Ya Haj, what happened to the dates?

HAJ KHALAF: I rubbed them out. They are all wrong. Conder makes mistakes. Mistakes can happen.

ANDREW: How do you know the dates are wrong?

HAJ KHALAF: If Qoblan were alive in 1880, like Conder says, then X would have seen him . . . because X was 120 years old when he died a couple of years ago. I took history from him, and he said to me, "I never beheld Qoblan."

[I didn't dare argue with the Haj. The authority of the entire system of *isnad,* as he understood it, was at stake. The truth of the received oral tradition is buttressed by the great age of eyewitnesses, old men who are often said to have died twenty years or more after the century mark. By suggesting that X could not have been more than 100 years old when he died, I would only be placing his credibility, and that of Haj Khalaf, in doubt.]

ANDREW: That's very old. Not many people live that long nowadays.

HAJ KHALAF: Yes. The food was better in the past. Everything was fresh. We drank fresh milk every day; we slaughtered meat from our own herds. Today, our food is imported in cans.

['Ali Barakat interrupts.]

'ALI: Yes. This is true. My father Barakat, God have mercy on him, lived to be 93 years old, and he took his knowledge from his father, Filah, who lived 126 years. Filah was one year old when Nimr, the Father of Poems, passed away. He said to my father, "I remember beholding Nimr as though in a dream." See how things are?

ANDREW: Yes.

'ALI: So the history you receive from the Haj and me . . . we took it from men whose fathers saw Nimr himself. Isn't that right, Haj?

HAJ KHALAF: Yes. All the great battles . . . our grandfathers witnessed them.

All these numerical ages—93, 126, 120—were, like the great battles Haj Khalaf's grandfathers had seen, fully detached from chronological time, and as Muhammad Hamdan had already concluded, any attempt to bring tribal personages or events into calendrical time, Muslim or Christian, would be immediately resisted, since 'Adwanis cherish the great antiquity of their grandfathers' speech.

> MUHAMMAD: If I start to arrange things by date, everything will become confused. "This happened in that year." "No. My grandfather was alive at that time, but he never saw it." And so on. I think it is better to deal with periods and generations, because the order of the genealogy is known . . . with some exceptions.
>
> ANDREW: What would people think if you wrote in your book that Qoblan died in 1890, or that the Turks came in 1867 . . . because these are fairly certain dates.
>
> MUHAMMAD: The dates are certain. Yes. But the elders passed on their history without dates . . . so you can't make them fit, and they think that you are trying to say Haj X is a liar. If you try to use dates, that's what they think.

In fact, Muhammad, a university-trained historian, seemed as little concerned with dates as the old men. His history of the 'Adwan, which he read to me aloud over a period of three weeks, contained only approximate dates—most of them surprisingly inaccurate—until 1923, the year of the failed "'Adwani Revolt," when the Hashemites prevailed over the Balga elite and the modern era began.

By rejecting the chronological nature of textual history, Muhammad and Haj Khalaf were, in different ways, protecting a rhetorical space in which the words of certain men, most of them long dead, could still be conveyed with authority. Tribal space has already been reconfigured to fit the demands of a postcolonial state that must map and measure every inch of soil over which it is sovereign. Once the "age of shaykhs" is rendered conformable to the temporal standards by which modern governments map and measure the past, it can be administered with the same effectiveness.

[As we were preparing to go, 'Ali Barakat asked to borrow Haj Khalaf's copy of *The Book of the Traveler*. The Haj, acting as our host, was in no position to refuse, but he relinquished the book with obvious reluctance, as if he were losing control of a sensitive document that should not be allowed to circulate widely.

By scratching out the erroneous dates, Haj Khalaf had succeeded in making the book fit for the eyes of other 'Adwanis he knew. Yet as his grandson Faris pointed out to him: "Ya Haj, you cannot keep other people from seeing those dates. Will you go from house to house in Jordan and erase them all? These are things one person cannot control."]

Six months later, when I left Jordan, 'Ali Barakat had not yet returned Haj Khalaf's book.

Provocative Photos

Next, 'Ali Barakat took me to Haj 'Abd al-Jalil in search of "the picture." This artifact, 'Ali informed me, was something I absolutely must see. It was not currently hanging in the Haj's diwan, but he gladly fetched it from a back room and placed it, with curatorial delicacy, in front of us. It was a striking photo, sepia-toned and enlarged several times to accommodate its gold, rococo frame. The subjects were three young Bedouin seated before a stone edifice, armed with swords, daggers, and pistols. Each was attired in flowing cloaks; one wore a pair of fine leather boots. Their head scarves were held in place by unusually thick camel-hair braids, and they were affecting the sullen, "dangerous" look that Bedouin admire (plate 19). I stared at the picture while 'Ali Barakat and the Haj remarked on the regal comportment of the three men.

"They are 'Adwani shaykhs," said 'Ali. "Look at their appearance!"

Haj 'Abd al-Jalil proceeded to tell me the picture's story.

"It is a copy," he said. "The original came from Britain. They say three names were written on the back of it: Goblan, 'Abd al-'Aziz, and Fayad al-Bakir. These men, as you know, were famous shaykhs of the Nimr, which is our clan."

"*Ya Salam* (Peace be)!" I exclaimed, and the Nimris in the room were pleased by my excitement.

I was eager now to see the original. Haj 'Abd al-Jalil told me it was hanging in the house of Nawfan Sa'ud al-'Adwan, retired member of the Upper House of Parliament. I privately doubted that these three men were really Goblan and company, since camera work was not done in the Balga before the 1860s, and Goblan and 'Abd al-'Aziz were, by then, already old men. The figures in the picture looked young; moreover, the fat camel-hair braids they wore over their head scarves would not come into vogue until the early years of the twentieth century.

Muhammad Hamdan was a distant cousin of Haj Nawfan, so I asked him if he would accompany me to the house of the old senator, "to look at the

Plate 19. Portrait of the three 'Adwani shaykhs. A source of contention.

picture of the Nimri shaykhs." Perhaps, I suggested, there would be names and dates written in English on the back.

[Muhammad begins to laugh.]

MUHAMMAD: You mean the picture of the three men sitting together?

ANDREW: Yes. Do you have a copy?

MUHAMMAD: No. But I've seen it. Who told you those men were from the Nimr?

[I rehearse the details of my visit with Haj 'Abd al-Jalil. Muhammad, all the while, shakes his head in disagreement. Once again, I have stumbled into someone else's argument, and Muhammad, who is always trying to save me from misinformation, wastes no time in setting the record straight.]

MUHAMMAD: I will tell you the story of that picture. It comes from Spain. Not from Britain.

ANDREW: From Spain?

MUHAMMAD: Yes. Muhammad 'Afash [a member of Hamdan's own clan, the Salih] was ambassador there, and someone in the government gave it to him as a gift, and he gave it to Ahmad Sa'ud [Haj Nawfan's younger brother, who has since assumed Nawfan's seat in the Upper House.]

> The men in the picture are not from the Nimr. They belong to the Salih. To us. The one sitting in the middle is Dhiyab Fayiz 'Ali; the other two are —— and ——. They say those names were written on the back of the picture, but they had to cut them off when they fit it for its frame.
>
> ANDREW: Do you think they would let me take a picture of it?
>
> MUHAMMAD: A picture of the picture? You don't have to do that. Just go to the studio in Shuna. The photographer keeps a negative. He'll make a copy for you if you want one.

At that point, Muhammad disappeared into the next room and returned with one of his many folders. In it were newspaper and magazine clippings about the 'Adwan, and several snapshot photos. Muhammad plucked one out of the pile and submitted it for my inspection. It had been colorized. The subject was another heavily armed shaykh. He wore the same fat camel-hair braids and the same cloak; the same gun and scabbard belts ran across his chest (plate 20). This photo and that of "the three shaykhs," I thought to myself, must have been taken in the same period. Only the artificially blue eyes, the lightened skin, and pink lips, set this man apart from the sepia-toned Nimris Haj 'Abd al-Jalil had shown me.

"This man," Muhammad said, "is Dhiyab Fayiz 'Ali al-'Adwan. I took this picture from his family. One of the old widows remembered his likeness. She remembered seeing him when she was a little girl, before he was killed by his cousin [ca. 1915], and she said to me, 'That man is Dhiyab Fayiz 'Ali.' Take this picture to the studio and have a copy made. You can put both pictures in your book . . . along with the proper names that belong on them."

The contested area I was preparing to enter began to take shape when I delivered Muhammad's picture to the studio. The antique photo of "the three shaykhs" was, to my surprise, framed and on display in the small waiting area at the front of the store. I held the colorized photo up against it, comparing the "man in the middle" with Muhammad's recomplected "Dhiyab Fayiz 'Ali." They seemed, indeed, to be the same man. The hilts of their daggers were identically embellished. Or were my eyes playing tricks on me?

The shop owner, discerning my interest in Bedouin pictures, brought out several well known photographs of 'Adwani shaykhs. Occasionally, 'Adwani customers would request that he enlarge these photographs and frame them, or shrink them to wallet size, so he always kept a few copies on hand. The picture of the "three shaykhs" was the most popular of his collection. I asked who the men in the picture were.

"Well," he said, with a sly twist in his voice, "that depends on which family you belong to: the Salih or the Nimr."

Plate 20. The recomplected shaykh. Who is he?

"They say their names were written on the back of the original. Did you ever read those names?" I asked.

"No. I don't know anything about that," he said.

His attention was focused now on Muhammad's colorized photo. He had never seen it before, and he was eager to add it to his lucrative collection. Little did he know that my obsession with these nameless photos would bring him a fresh round of 'Adwani business. Once I mentioned the fact that these photographs might appear in my book, establishing the identity of "the three shaykhs" and professing one's genealogical attachment to them became something of a cause célèbre for members of the Salih and Nimr clans. Divergent accounts of where the pictures came from, how they got to the Balga, who was in them, who said so and why, began to spring up everywhere. Buying the pictures and hanging them on the walls of one's own home turned out to be the most decisive means by which a person could gain control over what was considered, by everyone involved, a kind of documentary evidence.

But "evidence" in support of what?

The answer to this question lay in the political significance of photography itself. For most 'Adwani men, cameras were meant to preserve images of propriety, solemnity, and power. They balked at my attempts to take casual, unposed shots. They insisted on wearing their best clothes, donning a pair of "scholarly" glasses (sometimes my own), or placing a service of tea or a coffee thermos in front of them as a sign of hospitality. Only in recent years have people begun to smile at the camera, and many of the older men still meet the lens with an imperious scowl. Photographic representation is, for them, a context in which individuals should present their noblest, most public face. The nobler the face—and the more public its expression—the more likely it is to merit photographic attention.

When European travelers introduced photography to the Balga, I was told, they used it to preserve the likenesses of those who were strong: those who were the most noble and public of men. Thus, when I asked a member of the Hamud clan to identify the men who sat in the picture of "the three shaykhs," he responded by naming the ancestor who, in his view, was most worthy of the lens.

> FULAN: The one sitting in the middle is Hamud, son of Salih.
> My ancestor. The other two are . . . God knows best.
> [Hamud Salih was almost certainly dead before 1840, the year
> in which photography was invented. It is hardly possible, then, that
> "the man in the middle" could actually be Hamud. I decide to keep

this conclusion—which derives, once again, from an odd form of chronological reasoning—to myself.]

ANDREW: I thought the three men were shaykhs of the Nimr.

FULAN: No. No. The foreigners always came to us, the Salih. Hamud was shaykh of the entire Balga. The Nimr were just escorts. Do you understand? Escorts. Hamud was above this kind of work, but he knew about it . . . because it was done under his protection.

The Nimr were indeed escorts, but nothing in Fulan's statement can prove that the men in the picture of "the three shaykhs" are descendants of Salih. The logic of the argument, as Fulan wanted me to understand it, works in the opposite direction: *given* the structure of power that existed in the "age of shaykhs," when the Salih were ultimate protectors and the Nimr were only escorts, the fact that the Salih would appear in a photograph taken by Europeans *rather than the Nimr* was already proven.

Insofar as it could be.

The photographs that are nowadays attached unequivocally to known 'Adwani shaykhs—to Majid and Sultan, for instance—were taken *after* the Amirate of Transjordan was established in 1921. Like the chronological dates that had to be scratched out of Haj Khalaf's *Book of the Traveler*, the documentary apparatus that defines fully modern portraiture is constituted so as to deny certainty to the historical attachments tribesmen create using the photographic residues of the shaykhly era. When Faris al-'Adwan hung up his new, lavishly framed portrait of "the three shaykhs," he placed a posterboard caption beneath it, which read: "These men are shaykhs of the Nimr tribe: X, Y, and Z." The caption could be discreetly removed whenever friends from the Salih came by to visit. Yet Faris' attempt to fix the identity of the shaykhs *in writing* was vigorously resisted by members of his own clan, who had different ideas about whose ancestors these three Nimr might be. When his own father accused him of using the picture to "sow discord," Faris decided to throw the caption away. His experiment in textuality—*detachable* textuality—had failed.

Muhammad Hamdan, meanwhile, was creating his own monument to the shaykhly past. It was characterized by the same indefiniteness that the Nimr had imposed on Faris' creation. Yet in Muhammad's case, the sense of indefiniteness was oddly accentuated. He placed his photograph—an enlarged, framed copy of the pastel shaykh—in the public guest room of his home, and in hanging it, he produced a shrinelike space in which very different representations of time, identity, and power could all be simultaneously displayed. The picture of the (nameless) shaykh was placed in the company of a framed passage from the Qur'an, a clock, and an official portrait of King Husayn (plate 21).

"What will you tell people when they ask who the shaykh is?" I asked after complimenting his arrangement.

"I will say he's an 'Adwani shaykh," he said, "possibly from the Salih. That's all."

I had seen Muhammad's gallery in other Bedouin homes. It always contained the same elements: (1) the Qur'an (emblem of eternity, sacred truth, and the authority of God); (2) the clock or calendar (marker of humanity's passage through profane, earthly time); (3) the king (master of secular time and steward of God's authority on earth); and (4) the ancestor (link to a tribal era that exists now—and has always existed?—only at the margins of the universe calendars, dynasts, and sacred texts create). In some cases, the ancestor is represented only by his sword or pistol, and these artifacts, too, are subjected to the same contestation that surrounds old photographs: "They say that sword hanging on the wall is the sword of Dhiyab, but truth is, they bought it in Syria a few years ago." No one, however, suspects that the clocks, the Qur'an, or the king are anything other than what they appear to be.

This discontinuity in the nature of historical certainty is unselfconsciously embraced by 'Adwanis themselves. The temporal hinterland, where clocks and calendars have nothing to measure, belongs to them. They can exclude others from it, or retreat into it, as easily as their ancestors moved through a Balga landscape that was more literally remote. The allure of old photographs—which are much more popular than those taken within living memory—lies in the struggle to make them one's own and deny them to others. The rhetorical spaces in which these struggles occur, because they are spoken and as transitory as a passing comment, cannot be controlled by the dictates of textual historicity. Names are cut off, dates are scratched out, squares of posterboard are reluctantly thrown away. The appeals to "textual evidence," in spite of it all, continue undiminished.

Muting the Power of Authoritative Speech

Marginality exacts its price. The rhetorical power 'Adwanis exercise beyond the intellectual reach of the modern state cannot be similarly exercised within the ideological space the state controls. This explains one of the more startling ironies of the current tribal literature: members of the Balga's shaykhly lineages—the men whose ancestors figure so prominently in the documentary accumulations of the nineteenth and early twentieth centuries—are nowhere to be found among the authors of popular books about the Jordanian

Plate 21. Muhammad's gallery. A shrinelike space.

tribes. Muhammad Hamdan al-'Adwan (plate 22), for all his manuscripts, antique photos, and excerpts from English travelogue, has yet to publish any of it. His creative block, which has continued for several years, is not reducible to the personal travails of an individual author. It is symptomatic, instead, of a more general 'Adwani attachment to forms of power and identity that, although they still flourish in speech, cannot be easily adapted to print. Indeed, Muhammad's urge (and inability) to reissue this identity in textual forms can be taken as evidence of the on-going "domestication" of 'Adwani power under the Hashemite regime.

In the "age of shaykhs," Muhammad's ancestors could afford to leave their publicity to others. Slaves and client tribes glamorized the deeds of 'Adwani heroes in epic verse, and the shaykhly names that surface time and again in the travel literature are grandiloquently preserved in the poetic consciousness of the Balga tribes. The great shaykh Dhiyab "draws his sharpened sword / He makes the corpses pile up in mounds / He makes them pile up like piles of stone." The infamous Qoblan al-Nimr "On his yellow steed, like a bird swooping down, . . . slew the star of their horsemen / The best of their horsemen is flesh now for birds." The verses below, composed in the mid-nineteenth century, commemorate an 'Adwani victory in battle.

> I ask a gift from the Lord of Creation,
> Lord of the throne and honor of those who seek Him.
> They grant the gift, the Sons of the Graydi [the 'Adwan],
> Who in their giving are fertile as a meadow.
> The gift is given by a generous shaykh,
> The light of our land, whose name is Dhiyab.
> How many legions has he scattered completely,
> With swings of the sword and strikes of the dagger?
> In his hand lies a Yemeni saber
> That cuts off the head at the tip of the spine.[1]

These images of martial prowess and godlike generosity, when recalled by 'Adwanis today, provoke a mood of prideful (sometimes wistful) reminiscence. The Yemeni sabers hang austerely on living room walls, relics of another time, and most 'Adwanis, should they ever find themselves on horseback, would probably not bring to mind the majesty of "falcons swooping down on their prey." The art of politics has changed dramatically since the days of Dhiyab and Qoblan (ca. 1830–90), and the bellicose poetry composed in honor of long-dead 'Adwani shaykhs, with its valorization of swordplay

---

1. An English transliteration of this fragment is given in Appendix A.

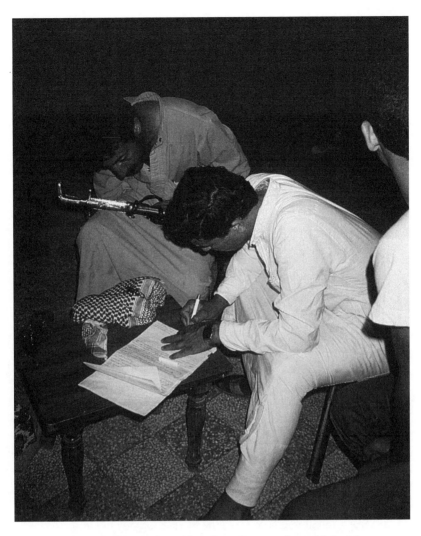

Plate 22. Muhammad Hamdan adds to his collection of unpublished documents.

and slaughter, can sound like resurgent barbarism even to Muhammad Hamdan's sympathetic ears. The debonair love poems of Nimr Ibn ʿAdwan have already been published in English (Spoer 1923; Musil 1928) and in Arabic (al-ʿUzayzi 1991), but Muhammad doubts that his stack of "battle day" poetry, by far the most common variety of ʿAdwani verse, will ever be (or *should* ever be) published in Arabic. The political messages it sends are delivered in a voice that is no longer fit to print.

In the following treatment of the Bani Hasan tribe, which Muhammad Hamdan read to me aloud from his "History of the ʿAdwan," the political scaffolding on which Shaykh Dhiyab towered above the lesser Balga tribes gives way, and his descendants are reduced, with the coming of the Hashemites, to a guarded silence.

> MUHAMMAD: I received this information from Ilyas Ishdayfat, one of the shaykhs of the Bani Hasan, and he himself received it from his grandfathers.
>
> The ʿAdwan took *khawa* from Bani Hasan, who were a very large tribe.
>
> The shaykhs of Bani Hasan got together and said: "We are many and the ʿAdwan are few. Why do we pay them *khawa*?"
>
> They planned a feast at which they would assassinate Dhiyab, who was shaykh of ʿAdwan at that time. But when Dhiyab stood before them, and they gazed upon his countenance, they could not bring themselves to kill him. They feared and respected him. Dhiyab knew their hearts.
>
> He said: "What is it you were intending to do?"
>
> The shaykhs of Bani Hasan told him the truth: "We were planning to kill you because of the *khawa*. O Shaykh Dhiyab, isn't it better to use our great numbers [to your advantage] than to oppress us?"
>
> Dhiyab laughed and was pleased with them and said: "From this day on, we will no longer take *khawa* from the Bani Hasan. There is an alliance between us."
>
> That is the testimony of one of their own shaykhs.
>
> So the alliance between the two tribes grew stronger, and the Bani Hasan proved their loyalty to the ʿAdwan at [the battle of] Um al-Summag, when they joined sides with Dhiyab against the Bani Sakhr.
>
> [Muhammad gives a thumbnail sketch of the battle, quotes several lines of poetry associated with it, then jumps three generations ahead in time, to the period of Majid al-ʿAdwan.]

MUHAMMAD: In 1923, some of the Bani Hasan clans betrayed the 'Adwani Revolt. They abandoned Majid [who led the rebellion against the Hashemite government] and became spies for the Amir 'Abdullah. After that, the Bani Hasan grew apart from the 'Adwan, but they remember their alliance with us from the time of wars. To this day, we speak well of them in our history, and they are pleased by this. But the old structure of the shaykhdom is gone. Today there is only respect and exchange among the tribes.

[Muhammad used this phrase, "respect and exchange" (*ihtiram wa tabadul*), to conclude his brief accounts of the 'Abbad and Saltiyya tribes as well. I am not sure exactly what it means, or how it will figure in his written text.]

ANDREW: Respect and exchange?

MUHAMMAD: Yes. What I'm giving you now is the general pattern of 'Adwani history. First we dominated the other tribes completely. A relation of strong to weak. Then we became like parts of a single body, with 'Adwan at the head. Then dominance was taken by the government, and we all became, as they say, one family. King Husayn is the father of that big family. *Today there is only respect and exchange.*

This moralistic incantation, which Muhammad would utter several times more before his recitation ended, was clearly meant as an act of deference: not to other tribes perhaps, but certainly to King Husayn and the patriarchal order on which his government is established. The etiquette of respect and exchange is the manner "sons" (the Jordanian tribes) should adopt in the presence of their "father" (the Hashemite monarch), and the observance of this etiquette turns certain historical topics and modes of expression into evidence of disrespect.

Of the seventeen 'Adwanis who spoke to me on tape, only five were willing to discuss the 'Adwani Revolt of 1923. Of those five men, all but one had been alive at the time. Their accounts were an antique blend of personal experience and uninhibited political expression heard nowadays only among very old shaykhs, who "say whatever they want." The version of the 'Adwani Revolt told to me by Haj 'Arif Abu l-'Amash (chapter 3) was, in the opinion of the 'Abbadis who helped me transcribe it, as raw and unpublishable as the poetry commemorating the battle of Um al-Summag. One man dropped his pen in a fit of incredulity and said, "This talk, ya Andrew, belongs to the Original Ignorance (*al-jahiliyya al-'ula* [a term used to describe the time before Islam]). The old man's brain is ripe. Do you really want me to write this?"

Muhammad Hamdan shared this readiness to censor the old mentality. He had not yet decided how he would deal with the 'Adwani Revolt in his own book, but he will certainly avoid Haj 'Arif's defiant tone. Muhammad's notes on the revolt were taken largely from *The History of Jordan in the Twentieth Century* (1959), wherein Suleiman Musa presents what has become, over the years, the official version of the revolt. Its causes, according to Muhammad (and Suleiman Musa), were:

1.   The 'Adwani resentment of favors the Amir 'Abdullah bestowed on their traditional rivals, the Bani Sakhr.

2.   The 'Adwani desire to purge the Amir's government of outsiders (Syrians, Iraqis, Palestinians, Lebanese) and replace them with local officials.

3.   The mistaken 'Adwani belief—which, Suleiman Musa contends, was encouraged by certain English officers—that British forces would not intervene on 'Abdullah's behalf.

The revolt, as presented here, can be blamed on things that everyone, in 1990, could agree to condemn: tribal jealousy, gullibility, and reliance on outsiders. As a teacher in Jordan's public schools, Muhammad was trained to break these debilitating political habits, and he accepted the muting of tribal consciousness—in classroom settings at least—as a pedagogical fact of life.

Please Refer to Your Textbooks

Muhammad was busy with teachers and paperwork, so I spent the morning sitting on a crate of biology textbooks, reading *Notes on the Modern History of the Arabs* (Ministry of Education, Hashemite Kingdom of Jordan: 1990), one of the textbooks Muhammad and company were preparing to ship.

"It's a new text for high school students," one of the teachers told me. "It presents Jordanian history in a larger, pan-Arab context."

Muhammad and I had been comparing notes on the 'Adwani Revolt when the flood of teachers arrived. The revolt merits several pages of close analysis in Musa's oft-quoted, and politically orthodox, *History of Jordan in the Twentieth Century*. Peake's *Tarikh* also mentions the 'Adwani Revolt, along with several others that occurred in the early years of the Amir 'Abdullah's rule. I was curious to see how the secondary school curriculum dealt with these events.

The 'Adwani Revolt, I soon discovered, is not mentioned at all in the *Modern History*, nor are any of the other uprisings. I should have expected such official silence in a government-issue textbook. The fact that King 'Abdullah was assassinated is not mentioned either, nor is the brief reign and abdication of King Husayn's father, Talal. The catastrophic civil war of 1970–71 merits only six cryptic lines. Such topics, which are common knowledge to most Jordanians, are obviously considered inappropriate for high schoolers to study or discuss in class. They belong to colloquial memory, which, like colloquial Arabic, is the responsibility of teachers to correct.

Still, as I skimmed the section on Jordan that forms the core of the text, I found myself unprepared for the total absence of the local Jordanian tribes from the national history. In the "Great Arab Revolt" chapter, there is a brief quote from (of all people) T.E. Lawrence, in which the bravery and toughness of nameless Bedouin are extolled, but thereafter, the tribes disappear without a trace. The principal characters of the text are Hashemite royals: the Sharif Husayn of Mecca; his son, King Faysal of Syria and (later) of 'Iraq; 'Abdullah, first the Amir, later the king, of Transjordan; and 'Abdullah's grandson, King Husayn of Jordan. These men, the book instructs us, are the heroes who have made history on behalf of the "Arab Nation." They are the true, unwavering champions of Arab unity, and their dynasty still governs "the Jordanian Arab people."

This monarchical history, I saw as I read on, is a thing of policies and programs, each of them forward-looking, democratic, and successful. The "Jordanian and Palestinian people" are portrayed in the text as a body of Arabs and Muslims whom the king protects. No further *internal* differentiation of the Hashemite political domain is explicitly acknowledged. Jordan's Bedouin heritage, so prominently advertised by the Ministry of Tourism, cultivated (and sanitized) by the Ministry of Culture, printed and sold for profit by Amman's private-sector publishing houses, and debated in the national press (see Layne 1989), is conspicuously absent from the *Modern History*.

The conclusion the student is meant to draw from this text is rather obvious: the *modern* history of the Arabs has nothing to do with tribes, nothing to do with subnational loyalties, nothing to do with political identities that are not inclusively Arab or Muslim. The modern era is defined by the progressive march toward Arab-Islamic unity. This march began with the "Great Arab Revolt," which was conceived and led by the Hashemite Sharifs. It continues under the enlightened leadership of King Husayn of Jordan, who has brought to his people the full array of modern blessings: "democracy," "free and compulsory education," "military strength," "economic development," "international prestige," and so on.

As I flipped back and forth through the text, looking for anything related to the Bedouin tribes, I remembered the incredulous reactions of 'Abbadi students when I asked them if they were taught anything about Jordan's tribes in school. One girl, an eleventh grader, wagged her finger as if to scold me.

"No," she said. "Of course not. There are no tribes in school."

Given the endless mental coaching boys and girls receive in matters of unity, my question had a subversive ring. Dr. Ahmad al-ʿUwaydi, a man always attracted to the most "dangerous" interpretation, explained the tribeless curriculum in terms colored by anti-Palestinian sentiment.

> AHMAD: I assure you that the Ministry of Education is under the domination of Palestinians. They control the universities, the schools of education. They write the textbooks; most of the teachers are from them. This is a well-known fact.
>
> [In 1990, the Minister of Education was Dr. Muhammad Hamdan, a man of Palestinian descent. It should also be noted that, in 1990, Dr. Ahmad's brother, Dr. ʿAbdullah, was Dean of Medicine at Jordan University. Academia is by no means an exclusively Palestinian habitat. It is, however, a field of high Palestinian achievement, and the belief that Palestinians control the schools and universities, as they control the media, is firmly entrenched among tribespeople.]
>
> AHMAD: Do they want the tribal nature of the Jordanian national identity to be known? No; because they are not true Jordanians. They know this. I am the one who struggles against this conspiracy, and I do it outside the schools.

Muhammad Hamdan lacks Dr. Ahmad's melodramatic flair, but he too was well aware of the silences and accentuations that pervade Jordan's textbooks. After the crowd of teachers had gone away and the paperwork was finished, I asked Muhammad what he thought about the tribeless curriculum and the textbook I had been reading.

> MUHAMMAD: I haven't seen that edition. It's new. But I will tell you that it's not in the interest of the state that we emphasize tribal matters in the schools.
>
> ANDREW: Why?
>
> MUHAMMAD: I'm telling you why. The schools are administered by the state, and who established the Jordanian state and governs it to this very day?
>
> ANDREW: The Hashemites.
>
> MUHAMMAD: Exactly. And we respect them. Don't say that we don't respect the state. But the Hashemites are from another genealogy and another region. They came from the Hijaz. They have a history of their own; they have ancestors and origins of

their own, and that's the history they want students to know about and admire.

A fascinating observation. I had been reading the textbook as a simple exercise in nationalist ideology. Muhammad, however, immediately picked out the premodern threads that held the fabric of the *Modern History* together. The textbook could, in fact, be read as a high-powered family history. It reproduced, at its core, a genealogical image of political power that most 'Adwanis, who base their own shaykhly prestige on noble birth and purity of descent, would instantly recognize. The *Modern History* was the story of a nation wrapped around a dynastic lineage, and Muhammad had merely assumed that the Hashemites, like any other dominant clan, would see no point in sharing the center stage of history with others.

The logic at work here is by no means unique to Jordanian politics. It is part of a more general relationship between discourse and power, one in which authoritative expression is defined by its ability to render other forms of expression mute. Hisham Sharabi, discussing the "monological discourse" that characterizes the official political language employed by modern Arab regimes, captures the spirit of *Notes on the Modern History of the Arabs* perfectly.

> Monological speech (and writing) typically never exhibits hesitation or doubt—attributes that delimit or undermine monological authority—but relies on general and unqualified affirmation. The fundamental type of monological truth is absolute truth and its ultimate ground is revelation. . . . While the structure [of this discourse] reinforces authority, hierarchy, and relations of dependency, it also produces oppositional forms . . . : gossip, back-biting, storytelling, and silence. For discussion or opposition in these settings [the family, the school, the tribe, the religious organization, and the state] can only be carried out behind the back of authority, or underground, never face to face in open exchange (1988, 88).

In developing the critical potential of his own argument, Sharabi chooses to underplay the extent to which "silence," instead of being willfully imposed, can be built into the fabric of certain modes of expression. As we saw in chapter 5, the subaltern quality of the "monological discourse" 'Abbadis deploy against the 'Adwan is pronounced even when 'Abbadis speak under the protection of anonymity. The *oral* tradition contains no position of strength from which the 'Adwan, speaking today, must willfully exclude 'Abbadis, since 'Abbadis, speaking today, cannot conjure up the rhetorical props—genealogy, poetry, heroic narrative—needed to occupy that position. Thus, Dr. Ahmad al-'Uwaydi has been forced to counter this inability *not* by writing against the 'Adwan directly, but by ignoring their oral history in print and constructing a new, more impressive one of his own.

It is also true that weakness can, in certain contexts, provoke "modesty" (*hishma*) and quiet admiration in the presence of "proper sources," men like Haj Salih al-'Uwaydi, who speak confidently on behalf of their group. Respect is not begrudged these men, and silence in their company is its own reward. Writing on women, young people, and other "status inferiors" among the Awlad 'Ali Bedouin of Egypt, Abu-Lughod observes that, "what is voluntary is by nature free and is thus also a sign of independence. Voluntary deference is therefore the honorable mode of dependency" (1986, 103–104). When silence is chosen, it is a proper form of deference, a legitimate source of honor.

These qualifications aside, the authoritarian tone of Sharabi's formulation, which links dependency with sullen compliance and corrosive gossip, is (at least in the Balga) a fitting representation of the relations that prevail among men, women, and young persons who wish to portray themselves as honorable and strong. For the 'Adwan, as for the Yemeni tribes studied by Dresch (1986, 47), the autonomy of "persons and collectivities" is the ideal. All forms of dependency—even those in which a subordinate position is assumed only temporarily—give rise to feelings of ambivalence. Even the relationship between host and guest, as it existed in the "age of shaykhs," is described today as if it were authoritarian, even dangerous. The feast at which the guest will be killed by his hosts (or the host will be killed by his guests) is a common motif in local oral tradition, and the diwans of powerful shaykhs are not remembered, generally, as carefree places. The stiffness and tension that sometimes marked shaykhly gatherings are attributed, appropriately enough, to the muting effect of powerful men.

"In the tent of Majid al-'Adwan," several elders told me, "you could hear a coin hit the carpet, even if the person who dropped it sat with the slaves, 100 meters away. No one lifted his voice in Majid's presence."

This same respectful silence—imposed by fathers on sons, by men on women, by the strong on the weak—was imposed on the 'Adwan by force. Majid's uprising of 1923 was soundly defeated, but his shaykhly self-image was not similarly crushed. Majid's continued "arrogance" in the face of 'Abdullah's rule has given rise to endless speculation about the cause of his death. The following anecdote, which was told to me in confidence by dozens of 'Adwanis, revolves around the entrenched distrust of hierarchy and powerful hosts, whose ability to silence their guests can sometimes be final.

The Amir 'Abdullah threw a feast, and he invited all the shaykhs of Jordan. Majid sat next to him, in the place of honor. When they finished their meal, the Amir told Majid a secret.

He said: "The British are going to make me King. What do you think?"

Majid said: "You should stay an Amir. It's better for you."

The Amir said: "Why?"

Majid said: "Because a king should have his own army and control it. You don't. A king should have his own mint and stamp his own coins. You don't."

The Amir was enraged and accused Majid of jealousy.

He said: "Do you want to be king in my place?"

That same night, Majid died. He just slumped over and died. Blood flowed from his nose. We cannot be sure, but many people believe, to this day, that he was poisoned. God knows best.

Muhammad Hamdan found this story hard to credit.

"They also say," he told me, "that Majid is still alive. The Amir 'Abdullah drugged him and sent him away to England where he is kept in a secret military prison."

I admitted to Muhammad that several 'Adwanis had told me the same thing.

The Indignity of Dignified Silence

That the death of the last great 'Adwani shaykh and the coronation of Jordan's first king took place in the same year, however, did not strike Muhammad Hamdan as a simple coincidence of history. The passing of Majid al-'Adwan signified, for him, the end of the tribal era, and the shift to new forms of political consciousness has not yet given birth to new forms of 'Adwani historical narrative. Muhammad's "History of the 'Adwan" closes abruptly, in 1946, with the following observation.

> After Majid's death, his oldest son Hamud was named shaykh of the Balga shaykhs. He had clamored for the position. It was his dream. But the title no longer conveyed official rights or duties. Hamud disappeared from the scene. He has no weight in tribal affairs. He became a private person. He is still alive, but many people think he is dead. The new power was Nawfan Sa'ud, who was appointed to the Upper House of Parliament upon Majid's death. He was close to the Hashemites and favored by them. His strength grew through cooperation with the government, just as Majid's had grown through opposition to it.

As a historian, Muhammad finds himself in a no-win situation. If he eliminates from his work all the themes and events that undermine the contemporary spirit of "respect and exchange," then he partakes in the domestication of his own tribe. If he chooses, instead, to assert the grand, domineering themes of the "age of shaykhs," he risks offending other tribes (who now consider themselves equal to the 'Adwan); he risks upsetting his fellow 'Adwanis (who have their own versions of the past to assert and protect); and he risks offending the government (which cannot allow other sovereignties, even historically eclipsed ones, to take root in its domain).

In all of this, Muhammad is a victim of the *real historical power* of the 'Adwan. His identity is firmly grounded in the shaykhly era, and the memory of local power—now reduced to a kind of haughty nostalgia—makes new identities hard to imagine in any terms other than loss. For Muhammad, a history recounting this loss is not desirable. Certainly it would be undignified. The only options that remain, in publication as well as politics, are to play a supportive role in the governance of Hashemite Jordan, as Senator Nawfan Sa'ud has done, or cling to the majesty of another age, as Paramount Shaykh Hamud Majid has done . . . and slowly fade away.

Publish or perish.

Whichever path Muhammad decides to follow, he will contribute to a political enterprise whose business, since it was introduced to the Balga in the 1920s, has been the reconfiguration of identity and the redistribution of power.

EIGHT

Popular Genealogical Nationalism

A country is a composition of many families; and as a family is communally supported on the principle of self-love, when one has no opposing interest, he extends the same self-love to his town or his village, which is called his country. The greater a country becomes, the less we love it; for love is weakened by diffusion. It is impossible to love a family so numerous that we hardly know it.

Voltaire, *Philosophical Dictionary*

If not altogether premodern, Voltaire's definition of "country," which appeared in 1764, is certainly prenationalist. One is immediately struck by the discontinuity between the particularizing, familial model of community he envisions and the uniform, anonymous citizenry that comprises the modern nation-state. According to Benedict Anderson, "nationhood" draws its strength from a peculiar act of imagination, and the figment of that imaginative act is a political community that, in the very words of the philosophe, is "so numerous we can hardly know it."

> The members of even the smallest nation will never know most of their fellow members, meet them, or even hear of them, yet in the minds of each lives the image of their communion . . . [and] regardless of the actual inequality and exploitation that may prevail in each, the nation is always conceived as a deep, horizontal comradeship. Ultimately it is this fraternity that makes it possible, over the past two centuries, for so many millions of people, not so much to kill as willingly to die for such limited imaginings (Anderson 1991, 5–6,7).

However badly it may jar against Anderson's model of psychic communion, Voltaire's parochialist dictum—"the greater a country becomes, the less we love it"—goes straight to the heart of nationalizing and tribalizing projects in Jordan. The urge to render oral histories textual and (somehow) national is part of an on-going reaction to Jordan as a political idea. It is an attempt to embrace and, at a deeper level, to resist "Jordanianness" as an official identity designed to co-opt, supersede, and sometimes even replace popular attachments based on allegiance to family and kin.

Because it renders all Jordanians "citizens" of roughly the same type, state-sponsored nationalism serves to homogenize a social landscape that, for the Balga tribes, is rich in essential contrasts: between noble and ignoble tribes, between Bedouin and peasants, between "real Jordanians" and Palestinians, between Arabs and Circassians. These distinctions are often thought of, among Bedouin at least, as attributes of blood that make one group superior to the other. Clearly, there is no (official) place for such ideas in Jordan's popular media or public schools. The state-sponsored vision of national unity threatens to turn the Balga tribes, many of whom deem themselves the only true "people of the land" (*ahl al-balad*), into equal and anonymous members of a Jordanian community that is too big to love.

Local responses to this homogenization are immersed in what would appear, on the surface, to be an equally nationalist frame of mind. Dr. Ahmad ʿUwaydi al-ʿAbbadi writes books about the *Jordanian* tribes, not Syrian or Saudi ones, and the possibility of being a Bedouin as well as a Jordanian makes an explicit articulation of the two identities politically expedient. It is interesting, given these ideological parameters, that Dr. Ahmad's attempt to create a "new Jordanian national identity" has not yet given rise to a uniform historical master narrative, a shared story that would allow his new identity to be embraced—as, say, the national identity put forward in Peake Basha's *Tarikh* was intended to be—by all Jordanians. Instead, Dr. Ahmad has seized on another, more atomizing theme: the determination of who is and is not a "true" Jordanian.

Indeed, the bulk of the recent tribal literature—that which appears in print and that which slumbers in private manuscripts—is marked by Lyotard's diagnostic sign of the postmodern: namely, "incredulity toward metanarratives" (1979, xxiv). Metanarratives, of which stories of national progress are but a peculiar, modernist type, are hard for tribal authors to construct, since other tribesmen do not willingly grant them the privilege of combining or juxtaposing received oral traditions in novel forms. Moreover, the kinds of metanarrative now available for historiographical use—most of them, except "Islam," being imported from the West—seem to be intellectually unappealing to authors who write as tribesmen. Muhammad Hamdan's "History of the ʿAdwan", for instance, is the story of his own line of descent and its relationship to other ʿAdwani and non-ʿAdwani groups, each spoken for by its own narrators. He hopes to construct a master narrative based on the idea of "shaykhdom," but this experiment, he suspects, will be rejected by most ʿAdwanis.

"Because everyone," Muhammad notes, "says *his* ancestor was the real shaykh."

Likewise, Dr. Ahmad's *The Jordanian Tribes* is an elaborate genealogical register that makes no claim to synthesize a shared, tribal point of view. Such points of view, the reader should realize by now, do not exist. Or they can be taken up only in contradistinction to nontribal points of view: hence, the anti-Palestinian flavor of the "Jordanian philosophy" Ahmad elaborates in the introduction to *The Jordanian Tribes* only to abandon in the body of the text, where no Palestinians appear to reanimate it.

All of this is based ultimately on a *genealogical* model of community, a model that renders "anonymous communions" very difficult to imagine. It would be easy, and totally in keeping with anthropological fashion (see Abu-Lughod 1989), to confine this sensibility to tribal quarters. Recent ethnographic work clearly suggests, however, that the tendency toward contentious multivocality and genealogical opposition is present in a variety of nontribal, nontraditional settings throughout the Middle East. Dwight Reynolds's (1992) attempt to chart the histories of Andalusian musical schools in the Algerian town of Tlemcen, for instance, was greeted warily by local artists who were concerned that he not portray rival schools as authentic. Each school was defined (by itself at least) as a community whose techniques and repertoire had been received, by means of face-to-face transmission, from certain Andalusian ancestors and not others. Points of style and fidelity were disputed among these groups in ways that constantly focused attention on the genealogical position of individual musicians.

Walter Armbrust (1993), in his study of popular culture in Egypt, illustrates the manner in which luminary figures of the Egyptian film and recording industries establish their own artistic authority by citing, and sometimes fabricating, *isnad* ("chains of transmission") that link them, via face-to-face relations, to great artists of the past. How one interprets the talents of a singer like 'Abd al-Wahhab depends largely on how one judges the *isnad*, the musical genealogy, of which he claims to be part, and that judgment, in turn, will be colored by the opposition of "elevated" and "vulgar" artistic traditions. As Armbrust contends,

> The principles of agonistic opposition and authenticating genealogy are so marked in popular culture and in the way people discuss and consume it that to ignore them would be to misrepresent the phenomenon. . . . Indeed, it is likely that our failure to fully appreciate the importance of [these two principles] in urban Middle Eastern society is one of the reasons that there is almost no Western literature on popular culture, which is by far the most ubiquitous form of cultural expression in the modern Middle East (1993, 7).

Those who suspect that a willingness to leap back and forth between Bedouin storytellers, international pop stars, and folkloric musical guilds will lead to a brand of analysis that is essentializing, or at best reductive, have every right to object. Discretion is in order. The three instances I invoke here do, however, share common features: (1) they bespeak a desire to interweave identity, authenticity, and authority in persuasive ways and, at the same time, to keep specific others from doing likewise; (2) they are concerned directly with matters of performance and social representation; and (3) they make one's position within structures of intellectual (and biological) inheritance central to the differentiation of true and false performances. These agendas, which are often inseparable in practice, help explain the prominence such themes as "lying," "honor," and "opposition" have acquired in the ethnography of Middle Eastern societies. The ethnographic encounter is itself congested with performances and representations—some made by "us," others by "them"—which strive, oftentimes against one another, for authenticity and authority. This representational striving was directed, in my own work and the work of many others (Gilsenan 1976; Rabinow 1977; Herzfeld 1987), by a genealogical sensibility that was relentlessly oppositional.

Some anthropologists have gone so far as to claim that the sensibility is itself an exaggeration based on the collusion of external (male) observers and local men, whose mutual obsessions with masculinity and violence have caused them "to slight other aspects of experience and concern" (Abu-Lughod 1986, 40). "Insistence on the essential segmentariness of Arab societies," Abu-Lughod contends, "seems to facilitate their representation as especially divisive and violent" (1989, 287). The people I lived with in Jordan did not consider themselves to be like other Arabs. They were Bedouin and, therefore, superior. Nor, despite wanting to seem tough on occasion, were they especially violent; but "divisiveness," in the form of 'asabiyya and accusations of *kidhib*, was entirely familiar to them. Indeed, it was among the defining features of their historical identity as tribespeople.

One can, of course, write against this androcentric, agonistic discourse, as Abu-Lughod has recently, and beautifully, done (1993). But this, too, is a literary commitment that slights a world of experience and concern; moreover, it renders much of intellectual and political life in the Middle East immediately unintelligible. Or inexplicable. Thus, when the critics of Orientalism come up against local instances of "contentious multivocality," its cultural roots can seem oddly opaque to them. A recent exchange between Salman Rushdie and Edward Said is, in this respect, quite instructive:

> SALMAN RUSHDIE: This is one of the things that you criticize
> from within Palestinianness: the lack of any serious effort to
> institutionalize the [national] story, to give it an objective existence.
> EDWARD SAID: That's right. It is interesting that right up to

1948, most of the writing of Palestinians expressed a fear that they were about to lose their country. Their descriptions of cities and other places in Palestine appeared as a kind of pleading before a tribunal. After the dispersion of the Palestinians, however, there was a curious period of silence until a new Palestinian literature began to develop in the fifties and, above all, the sixties. *Given the size of this achievement, it is strange that no narrative of Palestinian history has ever been institutionalized in a definitive masterwork.* There never seems to be enough time, and one always has the impression that one's enemy—in this case the Israelis—are trying to take the archive away. The gravest image for me in 1982 was of the Israelis shipping out the archives of the Palestine Research Centre in Beirut to Tel Aviv.

SALMAN RUSHDIE: In the context of literature rather than history, you argue that the inadequacy of the narrative is due to the discontinuity of Palestinian existence. Is this connected with the problem of writing a history?

EDWARD SAID: Yes. There are many different kinds of Palestinian experience, which cannot all be assembled into one. One would therefore have to write parallel histories of the communities in Lebanon, the occupied territories, and so on. That is the central problem. It is almost impossible to imagine a single narrative: it would have to be the kind of crazy history that comes out in *Midnight's Children,* with all those little strands coming and going in and out (1991, 178–179; emphasis added).

Tribal historians in Jordan, too, have found it hard to imagine a single narrative that tells the story of their communities. In fact, they actively resist such narratives. My own attempts to textualize spoken traditions ended in precisely the sort of crazy, multistranded narrative Said describes (see chapter 4). Yet the Balga tribes are not part of a diaspora. They have lived on the same thousand-square-mile patch of earth for hundreds of years, and they have no archives to steal.

The tendency to resist (or simply not to write) definitive masterworks of the type Said anxiously awaits is not, of course, proof that a sense of community is absent. Rather, it indicates that a community exists, for certain Palestinians and Jordanians alike, in ways that are not quite imaginable in the idioms favored by nationalist historiography in the West. Yet the belief that *we,* because we are a nation, should possess a story—an *objectifiable, institutionalizable* story—and, more significantly, that the lack of such a story is a failure to be overcome by specifically *historical* writing: these assumptions motivate the work of intellectual figures as diversely situated as Edward Said (who writes in the metropole for a metropolitan audience) and Dr. Ahmad 'Uwaydi al-'Abbadi (whose place and thought are, by comparison, utterly marginal).

In other words, history is being posed as the answer to the diverse array of challenges nationalism proposes. Those challenges are moral and political; they are intimately concerned, as Hayden White has argued, with "law, legality, and legitimacy" (1987, 14). The close correlation in the West between the development of modern historiography, nationalism, and the belief that rational law should provide the moral foundation for human communities leads White to speculate that the growth of historical consciousness

> has something to do with the extent to which the legal system functions as a subject of concern. If every fully realized story, however we define that familiar but conceptually elusive entity, is a kind of allegory, points to a moral, or endows events, whether real or imaginary, with a significance that they do not possess as a mere sequence, then it seems possible to conclude that every historical narrative has as its latent or manifest purpose the desire to moralize the events of which it treats. Where there is ambiguity or ambivalence regarding the status of the legal system, which is the form in which the subject encounters most immediately the social system in which he is enjoined to achieve a full humanity, the ground on which the closure of any story about which one might wish to tell about a past, whether it be a public or a private past, is lacking (1987, 14).

It is fascinating, bearing White's reflections in mind, to note that Dr. Ahmad's early ventures in historical writing—which came together in his doctoral thesis, *Bedouin Justice* (1982)—dealt with the changing status of tribal customary law in Jordan. His more recent attempts to write history against the "shaykhs and sons of shaykhs" are no less consistent with a desire to moralize the past. Unlike his dissertation, however, which has a beginning (the coming of government), a middle (the establishment of civil and tribal law codes), and an end (the triumph of civil law in theory and the merging of the two codes in practice), his latest works lack all sense of narrative closure. The national identity he writes about seems dangerously up for grabs: its past is undocumented; its future is uncertain. Like Edward Said, who looks with alarm at the growing discontinuity of Palestinian experience, Dr. Ahmad is also writing against the clock. What would constitute moral victory for him—apart from tribal dominance over outsiders—is unclear, and much of this uncertainty springs from the ambiguity and ambivalence that accompany attachment to a Jordanian state that, even after seven decades in place, is not yet the source of any moral community Dr. Ahmad is willing to imagine.

The "Deep Structures" of Nationalist Rhetoric in Jordan

My decision to interpret the advent of tribal historiography in Jordan as an adaptive response to nationalism is influenced not only by the testimony of tribespeople, but also by arguments put forward in Benedict Anderson's *Imagined Communities* (1983), an insightful essay that, over the last decade, has reshaped anthropological thinking on the topic of nationalism. Perhaps the most intriguing aspect of Anderson's work is his analysis of the early stages of nationalism's development in Europe: that is to say, its gradual speciation within a world dominated by (1) the "religious community," of which Christendom and the Islamic *umma* are representative types, and (2) the "dynastic realm," the political ambient in which Hapsburgs, Bourbons, Ottomans, and other imperial lineages flourished.

One of the factors that enabled nationalism to distinguish itself in relation to these older, better established forms of community was, Anderson claims, the advent of print technology and the growth, over the course of the sixteenth to eighteenth centuries, of "print capitalism," an economic and intellectual virus that spread through the medium of Europe's vernacular languages. The burgeoning market for vernacular literatures became a zone in which new forms of community could evolve. These new, "national" communities grew up apart from the spiritual boundaries of Christendom, which defined itself in the idiom of Church Latin; they multiplied in and across the polyglot domains of Europe's hereditary dynasts.

In contemporary Jordan, literacy and "print capitalism" have played an essential role in the construction of national identity as well, and massive government expenditures on education are the best proof of that link. This investment in schooling for all—which holds the promise of a properly indoctrinated, modernizable populace—is specific to the postcolonial era, and the intellectual repercussions of mass literacy, in Jordan as in other Arab states, are only now being felt (Eickelman 1992). The promotion of a uniquely Jordanian national identity, too, is recent. It began in earnest only after King Husayn came to power in 1953, and the content of that identity, which refers ultimately to a bounded political entity the Jordanians did not themselves create, has always been somewhat diffuse. Layne contends,

> A number of themes are discernible in official nationalist rhetoric: the role of Jordan's leaders in the Great Arab Revolt, the Hashemites' genealogical

links to the Prophet Muhammad and their traditional role as protectors of Islam's holy places, and Jordan's tribal character. . . . The first two strengthen the legitimacy of Jordan's administrative and legal ties with Palestine, especially the holy city of Jerusalem and the West Bank. Bedouin tribes have come to symbolize Jordan's national identity in contrast to Palestine's traditionally more settled population: thus the tribal character of Jordan tends to be used to accentuate the autonomy of the two nations. In both cases, formulations of Jordanian national identity are informed by Jordan's special relationship with Palestine and Palestinians (1989, 24).

In 1988, King Husayn officially severed Jordan's legal and administrative ties to the West Bank, preserving (as a personal obligation) his role as custodian of Jerusalem's holy sites. The two nations, Palestine and Jordan, belonged suddenly to separate jurisdictions, and the opposition of the two national identities *within* Jordan—one Bedouin-like, the other peasant-like—was viewed, during the time of my own fieldwork in 1990, as a recipe for political instability. What remains of the Jordanian national identity, as it is promulgated in government textbooks, centers on themes of Arab-Muslim unity and loyalty to King Husayn. The Jordan of today is still very much a "dynastic realm" embedded within a "religious community," and its nationalist rhetoric is shaped by a tense exchange between advocates of practical modernism, the Islamic Movement, and Hashemite dynasticism, all of whom disseminate their ideas in the nation's print market.

This ideological landscape, defined as national by those who occupy and strive fitfully to nationalize it, is marked by a feature Anderson's European model of national development does not take fully into account: namely, the presence of tribalism and pervasive clan organization, a form of community that imagines itself *genealogically*, in terms of identities based metaphorically (and oftentimes actually) on shared substance. Though ruled by hereditary dynasts, Western Europe, the geographical locus of Anderson's origin myth of nationalism, was an area that, in the sixteenth century and after, had little of what could profitably (or carelessly) be described as "tribal" or "clan" structure. Within the Middle East, however, these forms of community were (and are) so common that the genealogical component of tribalism is rarely singled out as its distinctive feature. Instead, the tribes of the Arab-Muslim world have traditionally been characterized—by those with the power to make such characterizations—as (1) backward people who adhere to legal customs that run counter to Islamic law; and (2) marginal groups that maintain a (potentially) antagonistic relationship to the state. The intelligentsia of the region have, throughout the Muslim era, posed tribal society as the antithesis of proper Islam and just government, and even today, tribes (and tribalism) are eagerly portrayed by the same learned elites as an obstacle to "full participation in a modern nation-state" (Layne 1989, 26).

By arguing that tribalism is archaic and should not be tolerated among citizens of the state, its opponents take up a position that, for all its apparent novelty in the context of national politics, is in fact extremely old. The community they envision consists of a governed space that must be kept intellectually (and physically) separate from the savage domain of tribes. The contrast between these domains is a moral one. The governed space is associated with high traditions, and its superiority as a form of community is justified by explicit comparison to local alternatives. The sociopolitical world of tribalism, which the keepers of governed space assume is organized only by kinship and marriage—not by Islam and law—has consistently served this comparative, moral purpose in the imagining of Arab-Muslim communities.

The idea that communities are made in the contest between tribal and supratribal identities can be traced back (or projected back) to the earliest historiographical traditions of the Islamic era. In *The Rise of Historical Writing among the Arabs* (1983), 'Abd al-'Aziz al-Duri argues that the earliest historical works by Arab-Muslim authors were shaped by two very different tendencies: (1) the "Islamic perspective," which gave priority to the collection and authentication of *hadith* [sayings of the Prophet], and (2) the "tribal perspective," which concerned itself with *ayyam* [glorious accounts of "battle days"]. The Islamic tendency, al-Duri argues, was driven by a new concern for "spiritual principles and activities"; tribal historiography, by contrast, found its inspiration in the factional loyalties that prevailed in pre-Islamic Arabia.

> Each of these two perspectives had a cultural center in which it was predominant: the Islamic perspective thrived in Medina, the abode of prophetic *sunna* [tradition], and the tribal perspective in Kufa and Basra, the two new garrison towns which were centers of tribal activity. All three cities were centers of vigorous cultural activity in early Islamic times. Each perspective developed its own school of historical writing, and each school exerted its own influence upon the other. In the end, however, the Islamic perspective prevailed as the viewpoint of the scholars of *hadith* rose to a dominant position in historical writing (al-Duri 1983, 22).

The neatness of al-Duri's formulation has been criticized by Western historians (see Humphreys 1991). I find it fascinating, however, because it accomplishes, in the guise of academic argument, the same marginalization of tribalism that has so often been the goal of learned, urban-elite scholarship. Al-Duri fails to discern the extent to which the tribal perspective shaped (and even survived in) the historiographical habits of the new Islamic community. Early accounts of Muhammad's career, the *maghazi*, clearly resemble the storytelling genres of the Jahiliyya; in fact, the word *maghazi* simply means "raids." The Muslims of the first and second centuries A.H., one could safely argue, were shaping their community by conventions that pervaded Islamic and tribal historicity alike, and those conventions—as displayed in the works of Ibn Ishaq (d. 761 A.D.), al-Zuhri (d. 741 A.D.), and Abu Mikhnaf (d. 774 A.D.)—are remarkably similar to the ones I encountered in 1990 among tribesmen in the Balga: great importance is given to the accurate, face-to-face transmission of historical reports, to the recitation of poetry and genealogy, to the commemoration of raids and battles, and so on. The continuity of this narrative tradition over time is itself stunning.

It is also true, however, that by the time al-Tabari (d. 923 A.D.) and al-Baladhuri (d. 892 A.D.) compiled their universal histories, the Islamic community was already constructing itself in ways that were less stereotypically tribal. Muhammad was no longer depicted as a divinely inspired leader of an Arabian political alliance, but instead as the last prophet in a unified prophetic tradition that encompassed all of Jewish and Christian history. Islam had transcended its tribal origins (or, more exactly, it *parochial* origins) and become a "religious community," a learned tradition. But once again, the intellectual habits of an earlier time were preserved and passed along: (1) a respect for knowledge gained through proper *isnad* (that is, "chains of transmission"); (2) a preference for the *oral* transmission of even textual traditions (hence, the importance of formal recitation); and (3) a tendency to think of society as a framework of discrete human linkages of power and intellectual authority reproduced *genealogically*. These ideas are concisely illustrated in Hourani's (1991) description of *tarajim*, or "biographical dictionaries," a form of historical writing common to Arab-Muslim societies in the premodern period.

> Its origin is to be found in the collection of *hadiths*. In order to verify a *hadith*, it was necessary to know who had transmitted it, and from whom he had himself learned it; it was important to be sure that the transmission had been continuous, but also that those who transmitted it were honest and reliable. Gradually the collection of biographies was extended from the narrators of *hadiths* to other groups—legal scholars, doctors, Sufi masters, and so on . . . *as if to show that the history of the Muslim community was essentially that of the unbroken transmission of truth and high Islamic culture* (1991, 165–166; emphasis added).

This great accumulation of intellectual pedigrees is both a schematic reproduction and a lineal history of knowledge, authenticity, and power. The authors who produced *tarajim* gave careful, literate expression to what Roy Mottahedeh has called the dominant Islamic Middle Eastern model of institutionalization: "vertical links tying men together over the generations" (1985, 148).

Given the immense prestige this model still holds in the region, it should come as no surprise that Jordan's nationalist debate—itself a grand exercise in institutionalization—is suffused by genealogical conceptions of community. In the mouths of Hashemites, nationalist rhetoric is devoted to the creation of fealty to King Husayn, a ruler whose political legitimacy rests not on popular sovereignty but on the fact that he is a Hashemite and, as every Jordanian knows, a descendant of the Prophet. For Islamists, the weakness and injustice that beset the Jordanian state are a direct result of *disruptions* in the "unbroken transmission of truth and high Islamic culture." For tribalists, the nation is all too easily equated with the descendants of Bedouin who lived east of the Jordan before the modern state was established. And the champions of practical modernism, for their part, must continually justify their agenda by linking it, literally and figuratively, to ancestral figures and authentic (that is, non-Western) virtues. Despite its persistent concern with modernity, the nationalist discourse in Jordan is actually reproducing and subtly transforming a set of very old, strongly held assumptions about the nature of human communities and their proper formation.[1]

This dialectic of stasis and transformation, which dominated the anthropological imagination in the 1980s (see Ortner 1984), is more aptly conceptualized, in a cultural system that defines itself genealogically, as a dialectic of inheritance and transmission. The shift in terminology is im-

---

1. The same themes dominate the ideological landscape of Morocco, another state controlled by a dynasty who claims descent from the Prophet (Munson 1993; Combs-Schilling 1989). The peculiar brand of Libyan nationalism Qaddafi develops in his *Green Book* is organized around similar motifs (Anderson 1983; Davis 1987), as is the revolutionary Islamic polity envisioned by the followers of Imam Khomeini (Mottahedeh 1985). The importance "premodern" ideas are granted by conservative and revolutionary Middle Eastern regimes alike suggests the obvious: national communities in the region are being imagined in terms metropolitan political theory is likely to misconstrue. Albert Hourani's critique of his own classic, *Arabic Thought in the Liberal Age, 1798–1939*, is worth remembering: "perhaps I should have written a book of a different kind. When I wrote it I was mainly concerned to note the breaks with the past: new ways of thought, new worlds or old ones used in a new way. To some extent I may have distorted the thought of the writers I studied . . . the 'modern' element in their thought may have been smaller than I implied, and it would have been possible to write about them in a way which emphasized continuity rather than a break with the past" (1983, viii–ix).

portant. It frees us from a body of highly specific (and generally unpondered) historiographical assumptions, all of them borrowed from a prevailing Western historicism that, by virtue of its modernity, is inimical to genealogical conceptions of the past. For the academic historian of the twentieth century, genealogy is history of an almost plebeian order; it is schematic, essentializing, and, like so many traditions that claim to be accurately transmitted from remote times, it is probably "invented" as well. Is it any wonder that *ethno*historians, who labor in the same intellectual climate, are prone to view genealogies in a similar light: as mythic charters and self-justifying pedigrees, as historical models that, despite appearances, are not really about the past?

The reluctance to treat genealogical thought, especially that rooted in oral culture, as a kind of history capable of producing its own dialectic of stasis and change gives rise to analytical discontinuities that have rendered entire historical traditions suspect. The gaps between spoken tradition and textual evidence, as Donner points out, have left modern scholars of Islamic history vexed by the possibility that their sources are fraudulent.

> The great majority of the information about early Islamic history . . . is derived not from contemporary documents, but from literary compilations that only attained their present form a century or even two centuries or more after the events they purport to describe. . . . As a result, sharp disagreement has persisted among historians of Islam on what and how much material in the extant sources is older, as it has on the question of how old this "older" material actually is and what interests and attitudes it reflects. Finally, it has been asked how—and even whether—scholars can discriminate between "authentic" older material and tendentious, fabricated, or anachronistic accounts of more recent provenance (preface to al-Duri 1983, vii–viii).

Such concerns are rooted in the notions of historical truth Western-trained academics bring to their work. The notions themselves, I should stress, are not flawed because they are cultural—every method is cultural—rather, they prevent a whole range of questions from being asked. A desire to locate authenticity in texts themselves, not in the "chains of transmission" by which we receive texts, has already impeded the study of history making among tribespeople, who are short on original documents and long on claims to accurate historical speech. It is bound to hinder other areas of historical research as well.

The benefits that come from taking genealogical thought seriously are apparent in Messick's (1993) study of orality and the culture of writing in premodern Yemen. As the following passage shows, genealogies are not simply records of begetting and begotten; they also encode varieties of historical knowledge and scholarly authority that cannot be reproduced by writing alone. The preservation of authoritative speech in textual forms, Messick argues, is driven by a cultural paradox that no longer animates historiography in the West. Its lingering significance in tribal Jordan, however, should be obvious to the reader.

> From the recording of revelation to the documentation of property rights, attempts to inscribe original speech, considered authentic and true, resulted in textual versions of diminished authority. The other side of the paradox was that speech events were fleeting and evanescent. Despite the staggering retentional capacities of human memories, the spoken word needed the services of writing to endure. Writing rescued words from perishing, but only at the cost of another death, that of the original meaning conveyed in speech. In its written form, speech was absent, altered, and open to a potentially infinite number of interpretive readings. Although the lack of transparent meaning in written texts was acknowledged, *links of authoritative communication . . . enabled some writings to claim to be true representations of original words* (1992, 252; emphasis added).

The genealogical paradigm that defined authoritative writing and speech in Zaydi Yemen—via the methodology of *isnad*—is now being superimposed (by Jordan's tribal historians) on a modern, nationalist discourse. This imposition happens unselfconsciously, and all but inevitably, since literacy, rehistoricization, and the publication of oral traditions have all developed within the "age of government." They are taking shape against what Benedict Anderson calls "official nationalism": that is, the "willed merger of nation and dynastic empire" (1991, 86). The result is a specifically genealogical Jordan, and a specifically Jordanian genealogy.

This binary construction quickly became the guiding principle of Dr. Ahmad's postelectoral politics. He spent much of 1990 laying the groundwork for a nationalist agenda that, when its consequences are gauged, brings to mind Gramsci's (1971) observation on power and thought: "intellectuals and their discourse, although constrained by the established order, never just reproduce it, but create, even if inadvertently, the seeds of resistance and contestation" (quoted in Eickelman 1992, 644).

The Judhamite Thesis

Once Dr. Ahmad took his seat in Parliament, he quickly got about the business of making a name for himself. He criticized the king's selection of Mudar Badran as prime minister, drawing the public's attention to Mr. Badran's involvement in a sex scandal. He attacked the Institute of Archaeology and Anthropology at Yarmouk University—where he lectured before being elected to the Lower House—for its sponsorship of foreign researchers who were possibly spies. He discovered, via a misdirected fax, that a cabal of Masons had occupied the upper reaches of the Jordanian government, and he gave lectures outlining the conspiracy to packed houses in Amman and Salt. An editorial cartoon of Dr. Ahmad, shown with bullets shooting from his mouth, was taped proudly on the walls and cabinets of dozens of 'Uwaydi homes.

Meanwhile, opposition was building. A delegation of 'Abbadi shaykhs, mostly of the families Ahmad had defeated in the elections, visited King Husayn and assured him, in no uncertain terms, that they disapproved of everything Ahmad said, thought, stood for, or did. Members of Ahl al-Jabal, a northern tribe, were requesting that the government punish Ahmad for allegedly libelous statements he had made about them in one of his books on tribal law. They had been informed, no doubt by a politically interested source, that Ahmad had written disparaging things about their sexual customs and reputed "lack of origins." After threats and wrangling, it was decided that Dr. Ahmad's offending volume would be removed from the libraries of Jordan's institutions of higher learning, with the option of censoring it altogether held open.

In the midst of this hubbub, Ahmad was more exuberant than ever.

"A day without combat," he told me, "is not a day worth living."

When I asked him about the censorship case—which had fellow 'Uwaydis cursing his decision ever to write books—Ahmad smirked and announced that his career as historian of the Jordanian tribes was over, but another career had begun.

"I do not need to write history anymore," he said, his index finger jabbing the air above him. "I have *become* history."

It was harder now to catch Ahmad at home, but whenever I did talk to him, his conversation was filled with political blueprints and new ideologies. The king had recently hinted that political parties might soon be legalized, and Ahmad was one of the hundreds of men who were now in the process of creating their own. Ahmad's group would be called the Umma Party, *umma* being the name applied to the confederation established by the Prophet Muhammad at Medina. The term *umma*, which can be vaguely translated as "community," is a social category at once larger than the nation (as it applies to the Arab and Islamic communities) and, in Dr. Ahmad's current usage, smaller than the nation, since, as a Jordanian party, the Umma would be only one among scores of others. I asked Ahmad whom he had in mind when he used the term.

AHMAD: The true Jordanians. This is a party for the true Jordanians only.

ANDREW: The tribes, you mean?

AHMAD: Not all the tribes. We know from our history that the true Jordanians are from Judham, which is an ancient Arab tribe that lived in Jordan.

ANDREW: 'Abbad is one of them?

AHMAD: Of course, along with the 'Ajarma, the Bani Sakhr, the Bani Hamida . . .

[Ahmad counts off a handful of names. They all belong to Balga tribes. The tribes located in the north and south of Jordan, I have noticed before, are of little interest to him. His national imagination, expansive though it may seem, is always resolutely local.

Another puzzling element: The names Ahmad is now listing belong to tribes that do not, in the normal run of events, think of themselves as kin.]

ANDREW: But those are all separate tribes. They don't have a common ancestor.

AHMAD: They do not have a common *nasab* (descent), but they have the same *'asab* (group feeling) because, in the past, they became members of tribes that belonged to Judham. It is like a tree.

[Ahmad takes my notebook and draws lines connecting the names I have written to a set of intermediary names, which in turn are linked to Judham. I notice a glaring omission.]

ANDREW: What about the 'Adwan?

AHMAD: No. They are not from Judham.

[Ahmad and I proceed to argue about the Jordanianness of the 'Adwan. It makes no sense to me that a tribe that has lived in Jordan longer than Ahmad's own clan can be denied nationality on these grounds. Ahmad points out that the 'Adwan are oppressors with arrogant minds. They would not consider joining a party controlled by a non-'Adwani anyway, so the point is not worth discussing.

I study the list of names. Most of the population of Jordan falls outside it, but that, to Ahmad, is its beauty. It occurs to me that Ahmad is nationalizing an old Bedouin practice: the creation of a new tribe, usually in reaction to an external threat, usually at the prompting of a powerful shaykh who gives the alliance its name. This is how Ahmad's own tribe, 'Abbad, came into existence (see chapter 2). I share these thoughts with Ahmad, and he is flattered by the analogy.]

AHMAD: Yes. I am the new Ibn Khatlan [the shaykh who created 'Abbad]. Didn't he unify 'Abbad from many families? He created one "group feeling" out of many lines of descent. Now I am doing the same for Jordan. I am showing people how they belong to one family. Jordan is our father and the tribes are our mothers.

[Ahmad neglects to mention the many orphans his model creates.]

The most famous of these fatherless children is the king himself, who, along with a sea of Palestinian foundlings, is certainly not of Judhami *nasab* or *'asab*. Thus, the logic of nationalism is creating its modular product—a bounded, sovereign community that seems "to loom out of an immemorial past" (Anderson 1991, 11)—but the product, as Dr. Ahmad makes it, is customized for a local, non-Western market. It resembles Voltaire's country, a "composition of many families," and the "self-love" that holds Ahmad's Jordan together is not generalizable, even in the abstract, to all the persons who inhabit it.

Such are the consequences when radically different images of community, each based on a unique historicity, are forced to occupy the same political space. If popular *linguistic* nationalism compelled Hapsburgs, Romanovs, and other European dynasts to adopt nationalism as official policy in the nineteenth century (see Anderson 1991), the opposite is happening in twentieth-century Jordan. Official nationalism, fostered by the Hashemites on behalf of their subjects, is giving birth to popular *genealogical* nationalism. The Hashemites have made this ideology "good to think" by encouraging— as modern dynasts are apt to do—both national and genealogical images of community.[2]

In nineteenth-century Europe, genealogical attachment was not an idiom in which the masses chose to delimit their communities. Language played that role, and pedigrees, by and large, were gladly left to monarchs and nobles. In Jordan, however, genealogical identities inform the political

2. Communities of this sort are not unusual. Genealogical (or tribal) nationalism can be found, as Gellner (1983, 85–86) notes, among Somalis and Kurds. It is also common among the Arab states of the Persian Gulf, where national identity is based on the ability to produce a genealogical pedigree proving that one belongs to a certain tribe (or that a male ancestor was living within the boundaries of the state before a specified date). The latter model is implicitly endorsed by Balga tribespeople when they argue that "unless a man has lived here for five generations, he is not a true Jordanian." The fact that Jordan did not exist five generations ago is irrelevant to most advocates of this position, whose primary interest is to exclude Palestinians from the national community.

imagination of royals and commoners alike, and Dr. Ahmad's Judhamite thesis, which combines the logics of lineage and place, leaves the Hashemites without a viable link to the nation. Ahmad's party slogan, which strikes me now as evidence in proof of this argument, was God, Country, and People, a variation on the British import—God, King, and Country—which graces monuments and government buildings all over Amman. The missing monarchic article, I thought, would be obvious to everyone. Its replacement by "People" was Dr. Ahmad's bid to harness the appeal of a more securely modern idea: popular sovereignty. Little would the uninitiated observer know that Ahmad's "People" belonged, in essence, to one big tribe.

The history of popular sovereignty in the West—which grew up in reaction to the divine right of kings—was a hazy thing at best for the members of Dr. Ahmad's inner circle of advisers, all 'Uwaydi kinsmen. They knew only that removing the king's name from anything was bound to be read as an act of subversion. They advised strongly against adopting this provocative slogan, but Ahmad, who was daily proving himself a fearless representative of the People, enjoyed the anxiety his outspokenness was causing them.

"Never worry," he said to me in English as members of his executive committee registered their disapproval of the slogan. "I can pull them all together. They resent me for this, but without a strong leader, they cannot act. This is not a slogan against the King. It is a slogan in favor of the People."[3]

The Experimental Scene

As I left to catch the bus, I was met in the driveway by a chaotic spectacle. A crowd from the neighborhood was gathered around a car. A young man at the back of the car, his head in the trunk, was yelling orders to start the engine. The spectators, hovering at a safe distance, made jokes about imminent explosions. Ahmad's younger brother, Dr. 'Abdullah, was overseeing the operation. The young man busily at work in the trunk, he told me, was an 'Abbadi mechanic blessed with natural engineering talent. He was designing a gadget that would allow a car to run on a canister of butane gas, and Dr. 'Abdullah and Dr. Ahmad had decided to underwrite his research.

---

3. Dr. Ahmad's party never got off the ground. In 1991, Ahmad concluded that *al-Umma* had little chance of being legalized, so he abandoned his efforts to organize it. Ahmad still believes that true Jordanians must have deep genealogical roots in the country—and their own political movement—but he no longer excludes non-Judhami tribes from this brotherhood. He specifically asked me to point out that his position on the 'Adwan has changed. "They are true Jordanian Arabs," he told me in 1995, "and I am not against them."

The mechanic stood back from the trunk and called down a blessing on his work: "In the name of God, the compassionate, the merciful."

The car started, but the engine sounded weak. The mechanic turned the nozzle on the canister, releasing more gas into the hookup. The engine revved slightly. A murmur of approval from the onlookers, then more jokes about things blowing up.

"This," Dr. 'Abdullah said, full of admiration, "is the genius of the 'Abbadi mind. Invention. Progress. This is what we want to encourage in Jordan."

The experimental scene captured perfectly the spirit Dr. Ahmad and his family embodied. They brought to their endeavors a confident sense of purpose quite unlike anything I had seen in Jordan. The aura of invention and genius, of forward momentum, of political possibility, was their daily attire. Yet beneath it all lurked the explosive potential of ideas that, like so many of the "ideologies" and "philosophies" Dr. Ahmad had created, were now threatening to escape the structures that contained them.[4]

4. The bubble burst in 1993, when Dr. Ahmad lost his seat in Parliament to 'Abd Musa Nihar, an 'Abbadi shaykh from the old tribal elite. Ahmad's defeat was widely attributed to his inflammatory attacks on powerful men (the king included). Libel accusations against his books also proved an effective weapon against him, as did the meddling of government officials who were irked by his refusal to support King Husayn's rapprochement with Israel. New electoral laws, which allowed citizens in Dr. Ahmad's district to cast only one vote instead of five, took their toll as well, since they reduced the number of votes Ahmad could attract from the clans of other 'Abbadi candidates (see Appendix B). Dr. Ahmad is now a columnist for *Shihan*, one of Jordan's most popular and controversial newspapers. He continues to lecture and publish books. Convinced that his political setback is only temporary, Ahmad is carefully orchestrating his return to government.

Transliterations of ʿAbbadi and ʿAdwani Poems

To sample the richness of Bedouin verse, the reader should consult Clinton Bailey's comprehensive and elegantly translated collection, *Bedouin Poetry from Sinai and the Negev* (1991). The poetry I collected in Jordan was less diverse in subject matter; most of it dealt with the political history of local tribes. Poems of love, legendary heroes, and tribal events in faraway times and places are also popular among Balga Bedouin. The poetry recited at public occasions, for instance, is usually fanciful poetry of this kind; but the entertainment value of the Bani Hilal epic or the romance of Qays and Layla is quite distinct from the pleasure to be found in reciting poetry that commemorates the deeds of one's own ancestors. It was poetry of the latter sort that Balga tribesmen most wanted me to record.

I taped over forty historical poems from ʿAbbadi and ʿAdwani reciters. The people who helped me translate them—mostly young, highly educated Bedouin—often could not understand the antique vocabulary that fills these compositions. The existence of this semantic gap is not surprising: only one of the poems that appears in this book is less than a century old. Each was delivered at a rapid pace, in a loud, declamatory tone, with numerous elisions and slurrings of speech. I was amazed, however, to discover that even the elders who recite these poems cannot always explain what they mean. In the Balga, the old *gaṣāyid* are fast becoming esoteric knowledge, and the translations I offer in the body of the text, despite the best efforts of the tribesmen who helped me construct them, remain frustratingly imprecise.

Because I was unable to capture in English the rhymes and meters that make these poems appealing to Bedouin—and because I hope readers capable of doing so will suggest alternative translations—I have decided to present English transliterations of the Arabic originals. The notation I employ is basically that suggested by the *International Journal of Middle East Studies*, but the reader is warned that Balga Bedouin pronounce *q* as *g*, or even as *j*; they often change *k* to *tch* (which I symbolize as ḳ); they interchange *n*, *l*, and *r* sounds depending on word position; they replace the *aw* diphthong with a long *o*; and so on. Lexical and grammatical oddities add yet another set of challenges. For a helpful linguistic introduction to Bedouin dialects similar to Balgawi, see Ingham's *Bedouin of Northern Arabia: Traditions of the Al-Dhafir* (1986) and "A Note on Transcriptions" in Abu-Lughod's *Veiled Sentiments* (1986, xv–xix).

From Chapter 2

I CLIMBED GAR⁽ NAJDA AT BREAK OF DAY

This poem, the best known of all 'Adwani *gaṣāyid*, was composed by Sha'ayl Abu Mismara, slave-poet of Shaykh Hamud Salih. It dates to the period around 1812, when the 'Adwan, having been soundly defeated in their latest war with the Bani Sakhr, were living as exiles in 'Ajlun, north of the Zarga River. The poem records Abu Mismara's desire to return to his land after beholding it from the summit of Gar' Najda, a mountain that overlooks the Balga. Although the 'Adwan are badly outnumbered—they were, at the time, only sixty men—Abu Mismara encourages his master, Hamud, to "rise up and attack the thousand." Hamud, inspired by Abu Mismara's words, forms an alliance with the Saltiyya, plunders three herds from the Bani Sakhr in one day, and drives them out of the Balga.

In the following transliteration, I combine two popular versions of the poem: one spoken by Haj Tarki Mithgal Jasim al-Ayub al-'Adwan; the other spoken by Haj 'Abd al-Latif al-Shilash al-Kayid al-'Adwan.

1. ṭallayt gar' najda ḍaḥa l-yōm
   marjab 'ala kull marājīb bādī

2. yā dīrtī yā umm aṣ-ṣa'alīk wa l-ḥazūn
   al-fawāri' tātīk bi-kull wādī

3. yā mā ḥala bi-dīrtnā bi-za'g al-bōm
   linn jīt sarāya ṣadāhā yinādī

4. hādhāk imshaggar wa hādhāk al-kōm
   wa hādhīk yājūz sham'at bilādī

5. linn habba sharāgīhā wa bidāthā wasūm
   nātīk yā ghōr an-na'm bi-l-hidādī

6. yā dīrtī bīk al-'adhā dōm
   wa-l-haṭal sayyāl saḥbatū nādī

7. wa linn tafarrag al-khōlan minn 'agab al-lamlūm
   al-kull rāḥ yadawwarin magayḍ wa birādī

8. radd an-niga wald al-khraysha 'an al-lōm
   mustagwiyan nafsū 'ala ghayr jādī
9. gūm irtaḥal yā ḥamūd, gūm iṭa'n bi-l-gōm
   yā 'ayn as-sittīn 'a[la] alfin 'adādī
10. nanzal iḥmānā wa naḳtaf an-nazal bih dōm
    rīḥat 'ashāba makhtaliṭ li-l-rishādī

Translation:

1. I climbed Gar' Najda at break of day,
   A mountain atop all other peaks ascending.
2. O my country, mother of desolation and rugged terrain,
   The streams pour toward you from every wadi.
3. How lovely in my country is the hooting of owls.
   When you arrive at dawn, their echoes are calling.
4. Over there is Imshaggar, and that is Hisban,
   And yonder is Yajuz, the light of my land.
5. When the east wind blows and winter begins,
   We come, O valley of abundance, at an easy pace.
6. O my country, in you there is always good health,
   and the rains fall and gather, flowing in their path.
7. And when our companions divide after gathering,
   each goes in search of a cool summer place.
8. The son of the Khraysha declared war out of shame,
   puffing himself up in a way that was not real.

[The Khraysha are a Bani Sakhr clan who once were allies of Shaykh Hamud. To avoid the stigma of cowardice, they joined the rest of their tribe in declaring war on the 'Adwan. Their act of betrayal enabled the Bani Sakhr to defeat Hamud and drive the 'Adwan out of the Balga.]

9. Rise up, O Hamud! Rise up and stab the foe!
   O leader of the sixty, attack the thousand!
10. We'll settle on our ground and pitch our tents forever
    Amid the smells of pasture and peppergrass commingling

From Chapter 4

Nimr's epitaph, as best we could decipher it, reads as follows:

تَنَقلك المنايا من ديارك

ويبدلك الدهر دارن ابدارك

ودود القبر يرعى في عيونك

وعيون الناس ترعى في ديارك

تغمده الرحمان نمر ابن عدوان

THE DWAYKI-ʿADWANI EXCHANGE

(From the Histories of the Zyud; recited by Haj Tawfiq al-Ruwayiq al-Dwaykat and Haj ʿAbd al-Karim Muhammad al-Sharrab.)

The Zyudi poet says:

1. ad-dwayk farkh al-bāz wintum shanānīr.
   linn rafraf al-jinḥān yarmī ishwātī
2. abū ḥarīz idhaʿar khayl al-manāʿir
   farrag shamalkū yā ʿaṣātī

To which the ʿAdwani poet responds:

yā dwayk minta fayd ḥarb al-ʿadāwīn
anzal ʿala l-ghōr wa azraʿ basātīn
batīkhtak yā dwayk bi-arbaʿ rabāʿī
yā dwayk minta fayd ḥarb al-ʿadāwīn
shabīhak yā dwayk ʿala l-mazābil yaʿaʿī
uṣliḥ yā dwayk wa azraʿ basātīn
batīkhtak yādwayk bi-arbaʿ rabāʿī

A POETIC ASSAULT ON THE ZYUD

(Haj ʿArif's recitation of the *gaṣīda* commemorating the clash on Wadi Shuʿayb.)

1. gāmat aḍ-ḍabṭa tamūj
   wa imkan minnhā as-sarūj

2. minn al-mawāzīr thāyir hōj
    ṭīr al-galb al-khafīf

3. yōm rāk̲bin bi-l-ʿiyāl
    māḍiyyīn bi-l-faʿāl

4. linnhum ijūnak bi-iḥtimāl
    yā abū khanayfis yā shī ḍaʿīf

5. k̲inn ṣārat ʿajja wa rijāja
    tagūl ṭalābāt ḥāja

6. al-mōzir mōḍi as-sirāja
    kiddū ʿalayhum bi-sīf

7. wa artid li-l-shaykh al-kabīr
    yā mājid waysh illay iṣīr?

8. gāl hādhōla shanānīr
    bi-amr yilfū mak̲ātīf

9. khaṭar al-maghfar gawām
    wa khabar al-gāyimagām

10. gabl irūḥū bi-l-ʿidām
    bi-amr gaṭʿ minn ash-sharīf

11. yā shayn hādhōla al-ʿadwān
    shyūkh al-balga minn zamān

12. bi-l-mashakka innak ghalṭān
    wa ghaṭāk imbāriḥ khafīf

13. yatalū mājid abū ḥamūd
    ḥurr li-l-balga ʿāmūd

14. saylū yakhla sadūd
    baḥar mūhū dowālīf

15. wa ʿabd al-ḥamīd wa ʿafāsh
    waḥadhum ʿala l-jamʿ hāsh

16. wa illay yilkid ʿala l-rishāsh
    mājid linn ṭār al-khafīf

17. ʿalī huwa wa manṣūr
    bi-l-majālis ṣagr aṣ-ṣagūr

18. waḥadhum sabʿ jasūr
    minn farūʿ ʿāliyāt

19. wa akhū shaykha yā nōfān
    yilfi yaʿabat ʿabt ḥiṣān

20. nayif li-l-tāli ḍomān
    ṣāliḥ yilzim li-l-khalāfāt

21. wa aḥmad law innū zaghīr
    minn al-ʿiyāl al-masāṭīr

22. wa amḍa minn as-sīf ash-shaṭīr
    minn farū' 'āliyāt

23. muḍfi huwa wiyyā 'abbās
    wa abū 'abdullah khawāṣ

24. lā yanzalū minn al-mitrās
    minn farū' 'āliyāt

25. laḥajat bi-l-kāyid jahūd
    bi-ṣ-ṣawāri wa l-janūd

26. mann ḥaḍar minn-hum sadūd
    waḥadhum [bi-rayy bakhīf?; birayb bakhīf?]

27. akhawāt mahara ghanmiyyīn
    ṣar'ūhum minn al-yamīn

28. fahd li-l-tāli ḍamīn
    barakāt yilzim li-l-khalāfāt

29. al-ḥajj 'aṭa 'ala ṭūl
    gōṭar ka-innū mahbūl

30. wa khāf minn as-sīf al-maslūl
    wa gafa wa 'āf al-maṣārīf

From Chapter 5

YOU WILL COME TO THE SUITE OF IBN KHATLAN

This poem celebrates the hospitality of Kayid Ibn Khatlan, the last paramount shaykh of 'Abbad. It was composed in the 1870s, the decade of Kayid's death. The poet's words are nostalgic and critical of the shaykhs who followed Kayid. I was told several versions of this *gaṣīda*—usually after asking about the great shaykhs of 'Abbad—but the version given below, recited by Haj Mahmud Nisar Nasir al-Jarmi, was the most complete.

1. yā walad shidd lī adh-dhilūl
   wa l-kharj wa abū ḥamāra

2. tījī darbak 'ala l-ghōr
   wa tidhaj layl wa nahāra

3. tījī shijj ibn khatlān
   imshara'āt al-irkāna

4. as-samin 'ala ḥarg al-gāla
   'ala 'ayn al-jadūr al-fawāra

5. al-laham gayim 'a[la] l-ṣaḥūn
   yishbih ar-rijūm abū ṭawāra

6. wa lī yā shyūkh az-zamān

kullikum ma bīkum ṣagāla
7. yā shīkha minn 'agab kāyid
yā rakham khashsh bi-l-wakāra
8. yā ṣītū waṣal darb al-ḥajj
[linn gōṭar l-ibni bi-zāra?]
9. yā ṣītū waṣal bi-istanbūl
yōm ḥashar al-jind bi-dāra
10. yā shyūkh minn 'agab kāyid
majliskum bi-waṣṭ al-'adhāra

WE TOOK FOR THE TWO SHAYKHS, SHAYKHS IN ABUNDANCE

(A *gaṣīda* commemorating the revenge taken on behalf of Sfug ibn 'Adwan; recited by Haj 'Arif Abu l-'Amash.)

1. gāl yā rākbin minn fōg ṣāfī lōnhā
wa tagūl ṭīr 'ala l-marāwiḥ ṣāhia
2. wallah 'anūd ar-rīm jaffilhā al-hawā
aw ṭīr dawarathā shāḥia
3. tilfī 'ala banāya sābi' minn al-'amad
tad'āk ḥiss al-maw gabal aḍ-ḍāḥia
4. ilfī 'alay wa khabbara yā illay jara
wa khalīlak dhahinak li-l-majāwīb ṣāhia
5. gūl lū 'ammak khaṭīb wa gāri bi-l-warag
tafaḍḍil al-maktūb minn akhū zāhia
6. yā ibn fāyiz lā tabāṭī ghaybinā
tar'a al-baṭa khamin 'allay nāsia
7. 'alayk dīn mā tashīl ḥamūlhā
mā kull dīn li-l-ṣwayṭī hāfia
8. yilfīk ibn 'adwān fōg imshammirat al-'aṣab
tagūl najm minn al-zilāzil hāwia
9. wa lā rabū'ū waḥadhum shārabīn kās al-ghaḍab
yā wayl li-mann yaṭlabūn gāṣia
10. tanāṭiḥu 'iyāl al-mala bi-arḍ al-khala
wa ṭāḥu 'iyāl ash-shyūkh minn karāsia
11. khadhaynā 'an ash-shaykhayn shyūkh wa azwad
wa bi-rajiṣ al-gubbān ḥina ar-rāsia
12. mann ḥārib al-'adwān yartha' bi-r-rasn
yal'ab matīn as-sīf bi-l-'alābia

THE FEAST IN THE *GHOR*

(The 'Adwani insult and the 'Abbadi reply.)

The 'Adwani said:
  lahyat 'abbād mithil al-lubbād
  widdhā mizyān yahalīhā

The 'Abbadi answered:
  igfat 'abbād bi-alfayn ijnād
  alfayn iglā'a tabārīhā
  'abbād idrūs yā māli al-mūs
  jildat wajhak narmīhā

CREDIT FOR THE DEED WAS ʿADWAN'S
ON THAT DAY

(A *gaṣīda* commemorating the battle of Um al-Summag; recited by Haj Ahmad Yusif al-Waraykat.)

1. al-bāriha yā dimūʿ ʿaynī sahāra
   awḍifit ʿan tāli al-layl sahār
2. sirnā wa sayyarnā jamūʿin ikthāra
   laylat gamr ʿashrīn hina li-hum jār
3. jamʿ abū rabīʿa darnak wasāra
   jamʿ al-jawāfira li-l-ṭowābīr niththār
4. amm al-fiʿl li-ʿadwān dhāk an-nahāra
   lamā millū al-mughar wa l-hīshān wa l-ibyār
5. firz al-barāṭim dasharin al-hawāra
   al-khill wa l-mafrūḍ ẓillin ʿala l-dār
6. dablān law lā ad-dirʿ ṣād al-kubār
   ṣād al-kubār fōg ʿadāt al-mahār
7. ash-shaykh fandī ghadat bī(h) ṭiyāra
   lamā ghadat bī(h) minn warā al-mafraj mishwār
8. idaʿayitnā yā ibn fāyiz bi-ʿaynak hagāra
   wa hādha juzz illay li-l-makhālīj ghaddār

HEY BOY! MAKE READY MY STEED

(A *gaṣīda* commemorating the battle between Abu 'Arabi and the 'Adwan; recited by Haj Ahmad Yusif al-Waraykat.)

1. yā walad dinnī li-l-dhilūl
   wa ijlis bi-shidād ash-shahīra

2. ilsif kharj al-'agaylī
   khallī ash-shirāshib tabrīla
3. yakhūn garāyibū abū 'arābī
   jāb al-'asākir li-l-dīra
4. jarrad khiyūl li-l-ṣagr
   wa ḥatta dōlat 'ajīla
5. ṣubaḥ farījin li-l-'adwān
   minn gharbī far' al-aṣīla
6. lā yā zagharūṭin bi-'alī
   yā nāthirāt al-jadīla
7. sa'ad yā rā'ī al-ḥarsha
   ḳinn jāb galā'tū tabrīla
8. yā galā'tū minn khayl ad-dōla
   tagūl kathīr aṣ-ṣahīla
9. amman ḥamad wa dōjān
   mithil isbā' al-jazīra
10. yōm kiddū 'ala khayl at-tarkiyya
    khillū at-tark nathīra

I WENT TOWARD THE WASTELAND, MY AMMUNITION IN TOW

(A *gaṣīda* commemorating Nimr's slaying of the leopard; recited by 'Abd al-Karim al-Waraykat.)

1. ṭallayt anā ṣōb al-khala bi-l-kalāyif
   wa akhammin jīl aṣ-ṣayd mā bīhā rība
2. liddayt winnī li-argaṭ al-jild shāyif
   al-mōt jānī wa l-mināya jarība
3. liddayt winnū jamlat aṣ-ṣayd hāyif
   wa illay ya'da bi-ṣayd mā yin'adī ba(h)
4. ya barūdtī illay 'alay al-waṣāyif
   yā hissā' garribit wa law lā ghada iḍrība(h)
   wa taradd 'alay al-barūda tagūl li-nimr:
5. inkānak mar'ūbin minn al-mōt khāyif
   ḥagg an-naẓar wa afrag sibāya sabība(h)
6. wag' al-nimr 'agab mā kān wāgif
   yā 'arḍ kaffū yā jamā'tī 'ajība
7. wa inḥaṭ jilda(h) 'ala mahar al-waṣāyif
   'ala nahār al-kōn tashūf as-sabība

From Chapter 6

MOVE, O PEN, AND WRITE WHAT WE DESIRE

(A *gaṣīda* calling for the reconciliation of Nimr and Hamud; recited by Haj Khalaf al-Fahd al-Nimr.)

1. sirr yā galam wa iktab ʿala mishtahānā
   wanshar ʿala zayn aṭ-ṭalāyiḥ hibr jād

2. silām minnī li-wuld khālī illay ghazānā
   ḥamūd ʿizz bilādinā wa bī(h) naʿtizz

3. wallah minn ʿilmin lifānā
   dawājīn bi-l-galb nārin wa wizzāz

4. minn ibn shiblī ṣāḥbī minn zamāna
   wa anā ṣadīg lū wa bī(h) maʿtazz

5. yā ibn shaʿayl yā galīl al-amāna
   midda ṭawīla wa inta li-l-nār wizzāz

6. thilātha sanīn inhāk yā zabrigāna
   ṭamayt ṭammia mā ṭamma bī(h) ṭammāz

7. ajīk minn hāna wa ajībak hāna
   wa khalayt lak rūḥ ifdāwī wa lā jāz

8. ʿan darbkum yā ḥamūd mā ḥadd nahānā
   illā al-irjāl al-ghammaz wa illay bi-himmāz

9. law saʾalt ʿannī anā bi-ghāyat al-basaṭ hān
   yamnaʿī rijāl ash-shimāl mā ḥadd lihum jāz

10. gaṣdī shaykh illay bāʿkum wa ishtarānā
    ʿawwād illay li-ḥājat al-amr mirkāz

11. yā ḥamūd mā tanfaʿū bilānā
    wa iḥna bilākum mā linā ʿizz

12. yā ḥamūd shaʿayl khāyin minn zamāna
    shaʿayl liʿīn li-ghāyat al-makar ḥawwāz

13. awwal ʿamānā thumm gillat hadānā
    surbat ʿabīd illay ʿala l-shōr taʿtāz

14. wa rāḥat ilḥānā bayn hāna wa māna
    yaṭʿan bīnā rāʿī misalla wa maghrāz

15. thānī ʿamānā thumm gillat hadānā
    shōrī ʿagab wa illay ghalaṭ shōr kirāz

From Chapter 7

A RECOLLECTION OF UM AL-SUMMAG

(Composed by a poet of the Bani Hasan; recited by Haj Khalaf al-Fahd al-Nimr.)

atlab al-ʿaṭa minn rabb al-birāya
rabb al-ʿarsh wa ʿizz al-manāfī
yaʿṭūn bi-l-ʿaṭa ʿiyāl al-graydī
yā illay bi-l-ʿaṭa rōḍin khaṣābī
yaʿṭī bi-l-ʿaṭa shaykh karīm
nūr bilādinā wismū dhīyābī
wa kamm minn sarbatin farrag mashīra
bi-ḍarb as-sīf maʿ ḍarb al-ḥarābī
wa bi-yaddū shimshīrin yimānī
tagaṭṭ ar-rās minn ḥadd al-ʿalābī

The Parliamentary Elections of 1989

The parliamentary elections of 1989 were part of a reform package offered by King Husayn in response to rioting that broke out in April of that year, when the price of gasoline rose more than 50 percent overnight. Along with the promise of elections, the king dismissed his prime minister, Zaid al-Rifaʻi, appointed a new cabinet, and enlarged the Lower House of Parliament, which he had dissolved in 1988, from seventy-four to eighty seats. A national parliamentary election had not been held in Jordan since 1967—although by-elections, intended to replace deceased members of the Lower House, were held in 1984—and most Jordanians took the king's new interest in Parliament as further evidence that the political climate in their country was gradually becoming more democratic.

In the fifth district of Amman, fifty-two candidates vied for five seats. One of the five seats was set aside for Circassian candidates. Voters were allowed to cast votes for five candidates, with seats being awarded to the top five vote-getters. The winners in the fifth district included three members of the Islamic Movement: Himam ʻAbd al-Rahim Saʻid al-ʻAbd (9,842 votes); Muhammad ʻAbd al-Qadir Yusif Abu Faris (8,601 votes); and Dawud Tahaysu Qawjaq, Circassian member of the coalition (8,012 votes). The remaining seats were taken by ʻAta Fadil Mustafa al-Shahwan, a member of the shaykhly lineage of the ʻAjarma tribe (4,845 votes); and, finally, Dr. Ahmad ʻUwaydi al-ʻAbbadi, "ideologist of the new Jordanian national identity" (4,764 votes). On the national level, thirty-two seats went to candidates identified with the Islamic Movement, sixteen went to liberals, modernists, socialists, and others identified with the left; another thirty-two seats went to tribal and clan leaders who, for lack of a better term, are often described in the Jordanian press as "traditionalists," even though their personal politics can fall right or left of center, and their public agendas can be more or less Islamic.

This fuzziness of political labels was inevitable, since "political issues" (as a means of distinguishing one candidate from another) played a very small role in Jordan's 1989 electoral campaigns. The same was true of the 1984 by-elections. Instead of taking up opposite positions on controversial issues, candidates chose to identify themselves with causes and aspirations they thought *all* Jordanians would support. Layne provides some examples from the 1984 campaigns:

> To uphold justice. To work hard in bringing the voice of the people to the authorities. To support the athletic movement and youth. To support women's rights and the Jordanian countryside. To support the Palestinian people. . . . Frequently a single candidate would list a long series of such issues hoping to win support from all sectors of society. . . . It is therefore not surprising that the political stances of the candidates were rarely mentioned as having any bearing on people's choice (Layne 1986, 127–128).

In 1989, Dr. Ahmad upheld this unitarian tradition; he did not address political issues on which two points of view were possible. Indeed, the campaign themes he used in public—in his speeches, on his posters, banners, calling cards, and flyers—were variations on slogans that, he told me, were designed to convey the impression that Dr. Ahmad was a man of truth and action, not a peddler of bombastic rhetoric.

We have no existence except in Islam.
Truthful words and plain-spoken courage are stronger than slogans.
Action before talk.
Your vote belongs to the one who will take up arms to defend you.
Support with your vote what is useful and righteous.
Serving the people is our goal.
Together in the trenches with those who support the Intifada and the Palestinian cause.
Woman is a pearl well-protected.
Sacrifice before profits.

Behind the banners and pithy slogans, Dr. Ahmad's campaign strategy was a sophisticated exercise in 'asabiyya and reformist sentiment, and its success was rooted in "seventeen years of research." The themes Ahmad stressed— e.g., the perfidy, backwardness, and oppressive nature of shaykhs—were intended to attract the support of lineages that had traditionally been without power. This populist tack was well considered, since the weak lineages greatly outnumber the strong. While the shaykhly families insisted on the status quo, Ahmad's strategy built on the social and political changes that have occurred in the "age of government." If there are no shaykhs today, he asked 'Abbadi voters, then why are all the candidates from shaykhly families? Why must we continue to vote for them? What can they do for us now?

The most effective element of Dr. Ahmad's campaign strategy, however, was his decision to use his full tribal name. As Ahmad himself explained,

> I am the only 'Abbadi candidate who calls himself an 'Abbadi. I use the name of my tribe and take pride in it. The shaykhs use only their family name. I say they are ashamed to be called 'Abbadis. On election day the people will want their tribe to be honored. They fear that 'Abbad will be divided and will lose to another tribe, or to the Palestinians. So what will they do? They will rally round the name of 'Abbad. They will vote for me, God willing, as one of the five votes they cast. That is all I ask of them. "Cast one vote for 'Abbad, and the women will trill their tongues for joy on election day!" And they will do it . . . to overcome their fear. I will benefit and take votes from all the clans, while the shaykhs will take only from their own people.

Before the elections, I put little stock in this argument, but subsequent conversations with 'Abbadi voters convinced me that the 'Abbadi gambit had in fact been successful. Its appeal was rooted in historical analogies. In the beginning, the storytellers say, 'Abbad was a fragmented body of warring clans, but the great Shaykh Ibn Khatlan encouraged them "to adore one another" and unite behind the power of a common name: 'Abbad. Of all the 'Abbadi candidates, only Dr. Ahmad—who calls himself "the new Ibn Khatlan"—seized the power of this story and put it to political use.

On 8 November 1989 the votes were cast in roughly the patterns Ahmad had predicted. The Palestinians of the fifth district supported the Islamic Movement; other Balga tribes backed their own candidates; and while 'Abbadis tended to vote for their own shaykhs and clans, many of them "cast one vote for 'Abbad" as well. The following list ranks the 'Abbadi candidates according to the number of votes they received:

1. Ahmad Salih 'Uwaydi al-'Abbadi (Afgaha clan)   4,764
2. Hamud 'Abd al-Rahman Mustafa al-Jibali (Zyud clan)   3,915
3. 'Awda 'Abd al-Nabi Nahar al-Bakhit (Manasir clan)   3,119
4. Fahd 'Abd al-Rahman Salim al-Hisami (Afgaha clan)   2,951
5. Muhammad Nwayran Nahar al-Bakhit (Manasir clan)   2,260
6. Muhammad Dawud al-Talab al-Salih al-Mahayrat (Afgaha clan)   1,807
7. Muhammad Isma'il Krayum al-Nahar (Manasir clan)   1,659
8. Husayn 'Abd al-Hafid Husayn Abu Ghanmi (Zyud clan)   1,419
9. Jumla Mithgal Krayum al-Nahar (Manasir clan)   702
10. Hatim Nuri Fadil al-Manasir (Manasir clan)   642

Bibliography

al-ʿAbbadi, Ahmad ʿUwaydi

    1982   Bedouin Justice in Jordan (The Customary Legal System of the Tribes and its Integration into the Framework of State Polity from 1921 Onwards). A dissertation presented to the faculty of Cambridge University.

    1984   Muqaddima li-dirasat al-ʿashaʾir al-urduniyya (An introduction to the study of the Jordanian tribes). Amman: Daʾirat al-thiqafa wa al-fanun.

    1986   Al-ʿashaʾir al-urduniyya: al-ʾard, al-taʾrikh, al-ʾinsan (Jordanian tribes: land, people, history). Amman: al-Dar al-ʿarabiyya li-l-tawziʿ wa l-nashr.

    1989   Al-munasibat ʿind al-ʿashaʾir al-urduniyya (Ceremonial occasions of the Jordanian tribes). Amman: Dar al-Bashir.

Abu Hassan, Muhammad

    1987   Turath al-badu al-qadaʾi. Amman: Daʾirat al-thiqafa wa l-fanun.

Abu Jaber, Raouf

    1989   Pioneers over Jordan. London: I.B. Tauris.

Abu Khusa, Ahmad

    1989   Al-ʿashaʾir al-urduniyya wa al-falastiniyya wa washaʾij al-qurba bayn-ha (The Jordanian and Palestinian tribes and the ties of kinship among them). Amman: Sharakat al-sharq al-awsat li-l-tibaʿa.

Abu-Lughod, Lila

    1986   Veiled Sentiments. Berkeley: University of California Press.

    1989   Zones of Theory in the Anthropology of the Arab World. Annual Review of Anthropology 18:267–306.

    1993   Writing Women's Worlds. Berkeley: University of California Press.

Anderson, Benedict

    1991   Imagined Communities. Revised edition. New York: Verso.

Anderson, Lisa

    1983   Qadafi's Islam. In Voices of Resurgent Islam, ed. John Esposito, 134–149. New York: Oxford University Press.

Ardener, Edwin

    1989   The Voice of Prophecy and Other Essays. Ed. Malcolm Chapman. New York: Basil Blackwell.

Armbrust, Walter

    1993   Modernism and Mass Culture in Egypt. A dissertation presented to the faculty of the University of Michigan.

Bailey, Clinton

    1991   Bedouin Poetry from Sinai and the Negev: Mirror of a Culture. Oxford: Clarendon Press.

Bakhtin, M.M.

1986   Speech Genres and Other Late Essays. Eds. Caryl Emerson and Michael Holquist, trans. Vern W. McGee. Austin: University of Texas Press.

Bell, Gertrude

1907   The Desert and the Sown. London: William Heinemann.

Benhke, Roy

1980   The Herders of Cyrenaica. Urbana: University of Illinois Press.

Benjamin, Walter

1973   Illuminations. London: Fontana.

Bloch, Maurice

1986   From Blessing to Violence. Cambridge: Cambridge University Press.

Bourdieu, Pierre

1966   The Sentiment of Honor in Kabyle Society. In Honour and Shame: The Values of Mediterranean Society, ed. J.G. Peristiany. London: Weidenfeld and Nicolson.

1977   Outline of a Theory of Practice. Cambridge: Cambridge University Press.

Braudel, Fernand

1980   On History. Chicago: University of Chicago Press.

Brown, Kenneth

1976   People of Sale. Cambridge: Harvard University Press.

Buckingham, John

1825   Travels Among the Arab Tribes. London: Longman, Hurst, Rees, Orme, Brown, and Green.

Burckhardt, John

1822   Travels in Syria and the Holy Land. London: John Murray.

1831   Notes on the Bedouins and Wahabys. London: Colburn and Bentley.

Burton, Richard

1855   Pilgrimage to Al-Medinah and Meccah. London: Tylston and Edwards.

Caton, Stephen

1990   Peaks of Yemen I Summon. Berkeley: University of California Press.

Chatty, Dawn

1986   From Camel to Truck. New York: Vantage Press.

Clifford, James, and George Marcus

1986   Writing Culture. Berkeley: University of California Press.

Comaroff, Jean

1985   Body of Power, Spirit of Resistance. Chicago: University of Chicago Press.

Combs-Schilling, M.E.

1989   Sacred Performances. New York: Columbia University Press.

Conder, Claude Regnier

1878   Tentwork in Palestine. London: Richard Bentley and Son.

1883   Heth and Moab. London: Richard Bentley and Son.

1889   The Survey of Eastern Palestine. London: Committee of the Palestine Exploration Fund.

1891   Palestine. London: George Philip and Son.

Cunnison, Ian
    1951   History on the Luapula. London: Oxford University Press.
Davis, John
    1987   Libyan Politics. Berkeley: University of California Press.
    1989   The Social Relations of the Production of History. *In* History and Ethnicity, ed. E. Tonkin, M. McDonald, and M. Chapman, 104–120. London: Routledge.
Day, Arthur R.
    1986   East Bank/West Bank. New York: The Council on Foreign Relations.
Dickson, H.R.P.
    1949   The Arab of the Desert. London: George Allen and Unwin.
Dirks, Nicholas B.
    1987   The Hollow Crown. Cambridge: Cambridge University Press.
Doughty, C.M.
    1888   Travels in Arabia Deserta. Cambridge: Cambridge University Press.
Dresch, Paul
    1986   The Significance of the Course Events Take in Segmentary Systems. American Ethnologist 13:309–324.
    1989   Tribes, Government, and History in Yemen. Oxford: Clarendon Press.
    1990   Imams and Tribes: The Writing and Acting of History in Upper Yemen. *In* Tribes and State Formation in the Middle East, ed. Philip Khoury and Joseph Kostiner, 252–287. Berkeley: University of California Press.
Duri, Ahmad 'Abd al-'Aziz
    1983   The Rise of Historical Writing among the Arabs. Ed. and trans. Lawrence I. Conrad. Princeton: Princeton University Press.
Eickelman, Dale
    1976   Moroccan Islam. Austin: University of Texas Press.
    1977   Time in a Complex Society. Ethnology 16:39–55.
    1989   The Middle East. Englewood Cliffs: Prentice Hall.
    1992   Mass Higher Education and the Religious Imagination in Contemporary Arab Societies. American Ethnologist 19:643–655.
Evans-Pritchard, E.E.
    1940   The Nuer. London: Oxford University Press.
Faubion, James
    1993   History in Anthropology. Annual Reviews in Anthropology, 1993:35–54.
Favret-Saada, Jeanne
    1980   Deadly Words. Cambridge: Cambridge University Press.
Finn, James
    1847   Correspondence of the British Consulate in Jerusalem. Public Records Office FO 78/705:84.
    1868   Byeways in Palestine. London: James Nisbet.
    1878   Stirring Times, or, Records from Jerusalem Consular Chronicles of 1853 to 1856. London: James Nisbet.
Foucault, Michel
    1978   The History of Sexuality. New York: Vintage Books.

Fox, Richard
  1985   Lions of the Punjab. Berkeley: University of California Press.
  1991   Recapturing Anthropology. Santa Fe: School of American Research.
Freeth, Zahra, and H.V.F. Winstone
  1978   Explorers of Arabia. New York: Holmes and Meier Publishers.
Gellner, Ernest
  1983   Nations and Nationalism. Ithaca: Cornell University Press.
  1990   Tribalism and the State in the Middle East. *In* Tribes and State For-
              mation in the Middle East, ed. Philip Khoury and Joseph Kostiner,
              109–126. Berkeley: University of California Press.
Gilsenan, Michael
  1976   Lying, Honor, and Contradiction. *In* Transaction and Meaning, ed.
              B. Kapferer, 191–219. Philadelphia: Institute for the Study of Hu-
              man Issues.
  1990   Very Like a Camel: The Appearance of an Anthropologist's Middle
              East. *In* Localizing Strategies: Regional Traditions of Ethnographic
              Writing, ed. Richard Fardon, 222–239. Washington, D.C.: Smith-
              sonian Institution Press.
Goody, Jack
  1977   The Domestication of the Savage Mind. New York: Cambridge Uni-
              versity Press.
Gramsci, Antonio
  1971   The Intellectuals. *In* Selections from the Prison Notebooks, ed. and
              trans. Q. Hoare and G.N. Smith, 3–43. New York: International
              Publishers.
Guarmani, Carlo
  1938   Northern Najd. Trans. Lady Capel-Cure. London: Argonaut Press.
Hashemite Kingdom of Jordan
  1990   Mudhakkira fi ta'rikh al-'arab al-hadith (Notes on the modern his-
              tory of the Arabs). Amman: Ministry of Education.
Herzfeld, Michael
  1987   Anthropology Through the Looking Glass. Cambridge: Cambridge
              University Press.
Hourani, Albert
  1991   A History of the Arab Peoples. New York: Warner Books.
  1983   Arabic Thought in the Liberal Age, 1798–1939. Cambridge: Cam-
              bridge University Press.
Humphreys, R. Stephen
  1991   Islamic History. Princeton: Princeton University Press.
Ibn Khaldun
  1967   The Muqaddimah. Trans. Franz Rosenthal, and ed. N.J. Dawood.
              Princeton: Princeton University Press.
Ingham, Bruce
  1986   Bedouin of Northern Arabia: Traditions of the Al-Dhafir. London:
              Keegan Paul.

Khoury, Philip, and Joseph Kostiner
    1990   Tribes and State Formation in the Middle East. Berkeley: University of California Press.

Klein, Frederick Augustus
    1868   Notes on a Missionary Tour in the Trans-Jordanic Country (Jebl Ajloon & the Belka). Records of the Church Missionary Society. CM/O 41/279 and CM/O 41/280.

Lancaster, William
    1981   The Rwala Bedouin Today. Cambridge: Cambridge University Press.

Lavie, Smadar
    1990   The Poetics of Military Occupation. Berkeley: University of California Press.

Layne, Linda
    1986   The Production and Reproduction of Tribal Identity in Jordan. A dissertation presented to the faculty of Princeton University.
    1989   The Dialogics of Tribal Self-representation in Jordan. American Ethnologist 16:24–39.
    1994   Home and Homeland. Princeton: Princeton University Press.

Leach, Edmund
    1990   Aryan Invasions over Four Millennia. *In* Culture Through Time, ed. E. Ohnuki-Tierney, 227–245. Stanford: Stanford University Press.

Lévi-Strauss, Claude
    1966   The Savage Mind. Chicago: University of Chicago Press.

Lewis, Norman
    1987   Nomads and Settlers in Syria and Jordan, 1800–1980. New York: Cambridge University Press.

Lyotard, Jean-François
    1979   The Postmodern Condition. Trans. Geoff Bennington and Brian Massumi. Minneapolis: University of Minnesota Press.

Marx, Emmanuel
    1977   The Tribe as a Unit of Subsistence. American Anthropologist 79:343–363.

Meeker, Michael
    1976   Meaning and Society in the Near East: Examples from the Black Sea Turks and the Levantine Arabs. International Journal of Middle East Studies 7:243–270, 383–422.
    1979   Literature and Violence in North Arabia. London: Cambridge University Press.

Merrill, Selah
    1881   East of the Jordan. London: Richard Bentley.

Messick, Brinkley
    1993   The Calligraphic State. Berkeley: University of California Press.

Mintz, Sidney
    1985   Sweetness and Power. New York: Viking Penguin.

Mottahedeh, Roy
1985   The Mantle of the Prophet. New York: Pantheon Books.
Munson, Henry Jr.
1984   The House of Si Abd Allah. New Haven: Yale University Press.
1993   Religion and Power in Morocco. New Haven: Yale University Press.
Musa, Suleiman
1959   Ta'rikh al-urdun fi al-qurn al-'ashrin, 1900–1959 (The history of
            Jordan in the twentieth century). Amman: Maktabat al-Muhtasib.
no date   Kitab al-rahhala. Amman.
Musil, Alois
1908   Arabia Petraea, vol. 3. Vienna: Kaiserlishe Akademie der Wis-
            senschaften.
1928   Manners and Customs of the Rwala Bedouins. American Geo-
            graphical Society, Oriental Explorations and Studies, 6. New York:
            Charles R. Krane.
Niebuhr, Carsten
1792   Travels in Arabia and other Countries of the East. Robert Heron,
            trans. Edinburgh: R. Morison and Son.
Ohnuki-Tierney, Emiko
1990   Introduction: The Historicization of Anthropology. *In* Culture
            Through Time, ed. E. Ohnuki-Tierney, 1–23. Stanford: Stanford Uni-
            versity Press.
Oliphant, Laurence
1880   The Land of Gilead. London: W. Blackwood and Sons.
Ortner, Sherry
1984   Theory in Anthropology Since the Sixties. Comparative Studies in
            Society and History 26:126–166.
1989   High Religion. Princeton: Princeton University Press.
1990   Patterns of History: Cultural Schemas in the Foundings of Sherpa
            Religious Institutions. *In* Culture through Time, ed. E. Ohnuki-
            Tierney. Stanford: Stanford University Press.
Palmer, E.H.
1872   The Desert of the Exodus. Cambridge: Deighton, Bell.
Parmentier, Richard
1987   The Sacred Remains. Chicago: University of Chicago Press.
Peake, Frederick
1935   Tarikh sharqi al-urdun wa qaba'il-ha (A history of Transjordan and
            its tribes). Jerusalem.
1958   History and Tribes of Jordan. Coral Gables, FL: University of Mi-
            ami Press.
Pederson, Johannes
1984   The Arabic Book. Trans. G. French. Princeton: Princeton University
            Press.
Peters, Emrys
1967   Some Structural Aspects of the Feud Among the Camel-herding
            Bedouin of Cyrenaica. Africa 37:261–282.

1977   Local History in Two Arab Communities. Bulletin of the British So-
            ciety for Middle East Studies 4:71–81.
Pitt-Rivers, Julian
1977   The Fate of Shechem. Cambridge: Cambridge University Press.
Raban, Jonathan
1979   Arabia: A Journey through the Labyrinth. New York: Simon and
            Schuster.
Rabinow, Paul
1977   Reflections on Fieldwork in Morocco. Berkeley: University of Cal-
            ifornia Press.
Rahman, Fazlur
1980   Major Themes of the Qur'an. Chicago: Bibliotheca Islamica.
Reynolds, Dwight
1992   Andalusian Classical Music in Tlemcen, Algeria: Changing Social
            Roles for the Oral Tradition of Medieval Zajal and Muwashshah.
            Paper presented at the 1992 Annual Meeting of the Middle East
            Studies Association.
Rogers, E.J.
1867   Correspondence of the British Consulate in Damascus. Public
            Records Office FO 78/1978.
Rosaldo, Renato
1980   Ilongot Headhunting 1883–1974. Stanford: Stanford University
            Press.
Rosen, Lawrence
1979   Social Identity and Points of Attachment: Approaches to Social Or-
            ganization. *In* Meaning and Order in Moroccan Society. Cambridge:
            Cambridge University Press.
Rushdie, Salman
1991   Imaginary Homelands. New York: Penguin.
Sahlins, Marshall
1981   Historical Metaphors and Mythical Realities. Ann Arbor: Univer-
            sity of Michigan Press.
Said, Edward
1978   Orientalism. New York: Random House.
Sangye Tenzing (sang-rgyias bstan-'dzin)
1971   Shar-pa'i chos-byung sngon med tshangs-pa'i dbu-gu (The un-
            precedented holy sceptre: A religious history of the Sherpa people).
            Junbesi (Nepal).
Satloff, Robert. B.
1986   Troubles on the East Bank. Washington, D.C.: Center for Strategic
            and International Studies.
Seetzen, Ulrich
1854–59   Reisen Durch Syrien, Palästina, Phönicien, die Transjordan Lander,
            Arabia Petraea und Unter-Aegypten. Berlin: G. Reimer.
Sharabi, Hisham
1988   Neopatriarchy. New York: Oxford University Press.

Shwadran, Benjamin
 1959   Jordan, a State of Tension. New York: Council for Middle Eastern Affairs Press.
Siegel, James
 1979   Shadow and Sound. Chicago: University of Chicago Press.
Simmel, Georg
 1971   On Individuality and Social Forms. Ed. Donald N. Levine. Chicago: University of Chicago Press.
Spoer, H.H.
 1923   Five Poems by Nimr Ibn ʿAdwan. Journal of the American Oriental Society 43:177–205.
Swedenburg, Ted
 1990   The Palestinian Peasant as National Signifier. Anthropological Quarterly 62:18–30.
Tonkin, Elizabeth
 1992   Narrating Our Pasts. Cambridge: Cambridge University Press.
Tristram, H. B.
 1865   The Land of Israel. London: Society for Promoting Christian Knowledge.
 1873   The Land of Moab. New York: Harper.
al-ʿUzayzi, Ruks bin Zaʾid
 1984   Maʿlama li-l-turath al-urduni (Encyclopedia of Jordanian folklore). Amman: Daʾirat al-thiqafa wa al-fanun.
 1991   Nimr bin ʿAdwan: shaʿir al-hubb wa l-wafaʾ. Amman: Daʾirat al-thiqafa wa al-fanun.
Volosinov, V.N.
 1973   Marxism and the Philosophy of Language. Ladislav Matejka and I.R. Titunik, eds. Cambridge: Harvard University Press.
White, Hayden
 1987   The Content of the Form. Baltimore: Johns Hopkins University Press.
Whiting, John D.
 1937   Bedouin Life in Bible Lands: The Nomads of the "Houses of Hair" Offer Unstinted Hospitality to an American. National Geographic Magazine 71, no. 1:58–83.
Wilkinson, John
 1987   The Imamate Tradition of Oman. Cambridge: Cambridge University Press.
Wilson, Mary C.
 1987   King Abdullah, Britain and the Making of Jordan. Cambridge: Cambridge University Press.
Wolf, Eric
 1982   Europe and the People without History. Berkeley: University of California Press.

Wood, W.
    1869   Consular Report on a Visit to Salt. Public Records Office. FO 195/927.

Zeller, John
    1866   Nazareth-Journal of the Rev. J. Zeller. Sept. 10, 1866, Badawins. Records of the Church Missionary Society, CM/072/264.

Index

al-ʿUwaydi, Khlayf, 171–72
al-ʿUwaydi, Zayd, 163–69, 173–74, 280
al-ʿUzayzi, Ruks, 146, 175, 256

Voltaire, 311, 326

Wali of Damascus, 129, 207–8
Waraykat, 57–58, 196
al-Waraykat, ʿAbd al-Karim, 196, 202–3, 206–10, 337
al-Waraykat, Dawjan, 197, 200, 204
al-Waraykat, Haj Ahmad Yusif, 196–206, 211, 336

al-Waraykat, Hamad, 197, 200, 204
al-Waraykat, Saʿad al-ʿAzzam, 197, 200, 204, 209, 210
West Bank, 266, 273, 286–88
White, H., 11, 27, 316
Wolf, E., 26
Wood, W., 83, 260–61

Zeller, Rev. J., 74–75
Zilaga, battle of, 193
al-Zuhri, 319
Zyud, 14, 24, 111–38, 145–46, 164–68, 185, 195, 225–26, 240, 277

Text: 10/13 Aldus
Display: Aldus
Map: Bill Nelson
Composition: Integrated Composition Systems
Printing and binding: Edwards Brothers, Inc.